FOR DUMMIES
BESTSELLING BOOK SERIES

Bahamas For Dummies
2nd Edition

W9-BPK-255

Cheat Sheet

Restaurants: Nassau

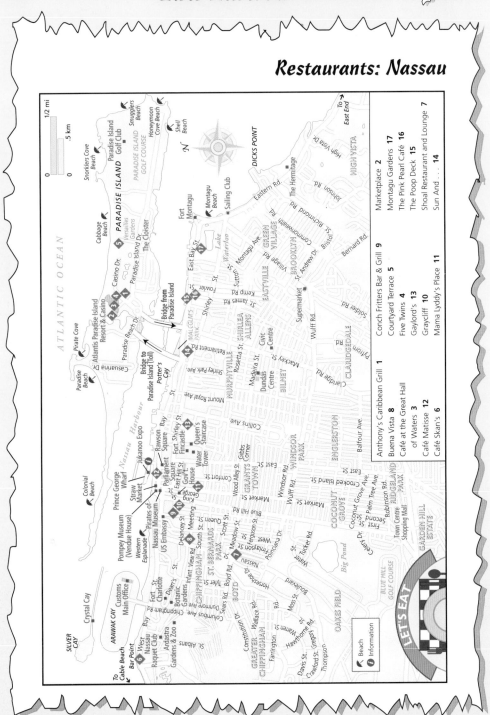

Restaurant	No.
Anthony's Caribbean Grill	1
Buena Vista	8
Café at the Great Hall of Waters	3
Café Matisse	12
Café Skan's	6
Conch Fritters Bar & Grill	9
Courtyard Terrace	5
Five Twins	4
Gaylord's	13
Graycliff	10
Mama Lyddy's Place	11
Marketplace	2
Montagu Gardens	17
The Pink Pearl Café	16
The Poop Deck	15
Shoal Restaurant and Lounge	7
Sun And . . .	14

Bahamas For Dummies®, 2nd Edition

BESTSELLING BOOK SERIES

Restaurants: Freeport/Lucaya

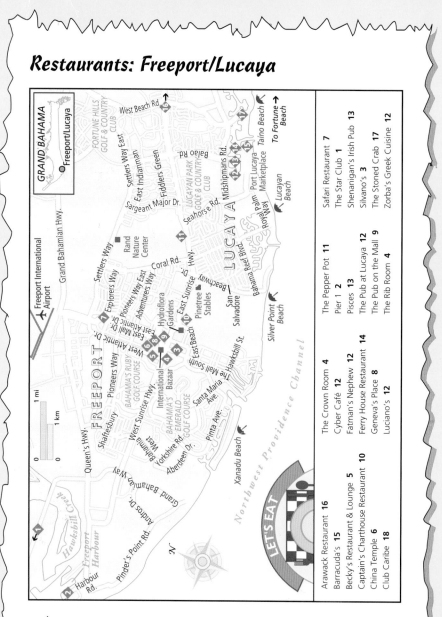

Arawack Restaurant **16**
Barracuda's **15**
Becky's Restaurant & Lounge **5**
Captain's Charthouse Restaurant **10**
China Temple **6**
Club Caribe **18**

The Crown Room **4**
Cyber Café **12**
Fatman's Nephew **12**
Ferry House Restaurant **14**
Geneva's Place **8**
Luciano's **12**

The Pepper Pot **11**
Pier 1 **2**
Pisces **13**
The Pub at Lucaya **12**
The Pub on the Mall **9**
The Rib Room **4**

Safari Restaurant **7**
The Star Club **1**
Shenanigan's Irish Pub **13**
Silvano's **3**
The Stoned Crab **17**
Zorba's Greek Cuisine **12**

For Dummies: Bestselling Book Series for Beginners

Bahamas
FOR
DUMMIES®
2ND EDITION

by Darwin Porter & Danforth Prince

Wiley Publishing, Inc.

Bahamas For Dummies,® 2nd Edition

Published by
Wiley Publishing, Inc.
909 Third Avenue
New York, NY 10022
www.wiley.com

For general information on our other products and services or to obtain technical support, please contact our Customer Care Department within the U.S. at 800-762-2974, outside the U.S. at 317-572-3993, or fax 317-572-4002.

Wiley also publishes its books in a variety of electronic formats. Some content that appears in print may not be available in electronic books.

Library of Congress Cataloging-in-Publication Data: 2002110308

Library of Congress Control Number: 2002110308

ISBN: 0-7645-5442-5

ISSN: 1531-149X

Manufactured in the United States of America

10 9 8 7 6 5 4 3 2 1

2B/RY/RQ/QS/IN

About the Author

Darwin Porter, while still a teenager, began writing about The Bahamas for the *Miami Herald* and has been a frequent visitor ever since. His writing partner is Ohio-born **Danforth Prince,** formerly of the Paris bureau of the *New York Times,* who has co-authored numerous *Frommer's* best-sellers with Darwin, including the *Caribbean, Bermuda, Puerto Rico, Jamaica,* and the *Virgin Islands.* Together, they share their secrets, discoveries, and opinions about The Bahamas with you.

Publisher's Acknowledgments

We're proud of this book; please send us your comments through our Dummies online registration form located at www.dummies.com/register/.

Some of the people who helped bring this book to market include the following:

Editorial

Editors: Kelly Ewing, Project Editor; Amy Lyons, Development Editor

Cartographer: Roberta Stockwell

Editorial Supervisor: Michelle Hacker

Senior Photo Editor: Richard Fox

Cartoons: Rich Tennant, www.the5thwave.com

Production

Project Coordinator: Erin Smith

Layout and Graphics: Melanie DesJardins, LeAndra Johnson, Jacque Schneider

Quality Control: John Bitter, Carl Pierce

Proofreaders: TECHBOOKS

Indexer: TECHBOOKS

Publishing and Editorial for Consumer Dummies

Diane Graves Steele, Vice President and Publisher, Consumer Dummies

Joyce Pepple, Acquisitions Director, Consumer Dummies

Kristin A. Cocks, Product Development Director, Consumer Dummies

Michael Spring, Vice President and Publisher, Travel

Brice Gosnell, Publishing Director, Travel

Suzanne Jannetta, Editorial Director, Travel

Publishing for Technology Dummies

Andy Cummings, Vice President and Publisher, Dummies Technology/General User

Composition Services

Gerry Fahey, Executive Director of Production Services

Debbie Stailey, Director of Composition Services

Contents at a Glance

Introduction *1*

Part I: Getting Started on Your Trip *7*
Chapter 1: Discovering the Best of The Bahamas 9
Chapter 2: Spice of Life 41
Chapter 3: Deciding When to Go 49
Chapter 4: Pillow Talk: Bahamian Accommodations 57
Chapter 5: Planning Ahead for Special Travel Needs 69

Part II: Ironing Out the Details *79*
Chapter 6: Making Your Travel Arrangements 81
Chapter 7: Money Matters 93
Chapter 8: Tying Up Loose Ends 103

Part III: New Providence: Nassau, Cable Beach,
and Paradise Island *115*
Chapter 9: The Lowdown on the New Providence Hotel Scene 117
Chapter 10: Settling In to New Providence 131
Chapter 11: Dining in New Providence 137
Chapter 12: Having Fun On and Off the Beach in New Providence 153

Part IV: Grand Bahama *177*
Chapter 13: The Lowdown on the Grand Bahama Hotel Scene 179
Chapter 14: Settling into Grand Bahama 187
Chapter 15: Dining in Grand Bahama 193
Chapter 16: Having Fun On and Off the Beach in Grand Bahama 207

Part V: The Abacos: Prime Out Islands *225*
Chapter 17: Marsh Harbour (Great Abaco Island) 227
Chapter 18: Elbow Cay 243
Chapter 19: Green Turtle Cay 255
Chapter 20: Treasure Cay 267

Part VI: The Out Islands *277*
Chapter 21: Harbour Island 279
Chapter 22: Eleuthera 293
Chapter 23: Exuma 311
Chapter 24: San Salvador 327

Part VII: The Part of Tens *335*
Chapter 25: Top Ten Myths about The Bahamas 337
Chapter 26: Top Ten Bahamas Moments 341

Worksheets *345*

Index *349*

Maps at a Glance

New Providence and Paradise Islands 13
Grand Bahama Island 16
The Abaco Islands 18
Harbour Island 22
Eleuthera...24
The Exumas 28
San Salvador 29
Nassau and Paradise Island Accommodations 120
Cable Beach Accommodations 123
Nassau and Paradise Island Dining 140
Cable Beach Dining 149
Grand Bahama Accommodations...182
Grand Bahama Restaurants 198
Marsh Harbour Hotels & Restaurants..229
Elbow Cay Hotels & Restaurants 245
Green Turtle Cay..256
Treasure Cay..269
Harbour Island 280
Eleuthera...295
Great Exuma/Little Exuma 313
San Salvador 329

Table of Contents

Introduction 1

    About This Book 2
    Conventions Used in This Book 2
    Foolish Assumptions 3
    How This Book Is Organized 4
        Part I: Getting Started on Your Trip 4
        Part II: Ironing Out the Details 4
        Parts III through VI: The Islands 5
        Part VII: The Part of Tens 5
    Icons Used in This Book 5
    Where to Go from Here 6

Part 1: Getting Started on Your Trip 7

  Chapter 1: Discovering the Best of The Bahamas 9
    Getting the Lay of the Land 9
    Finding the Right Island for You 10
        Knowing New Providence 11
        Getting to know Grand Bahama 15
        Appreciating the Abacos 17
        Hanging out on Harbour Island 21
        Eloping to Eleuthera 23
        Exploring Exuma 26
        Savoring San Salvador 28
    Deciding How Many Islands per Trip 30
    Narrowing Your Island Choices 31

  Chapter 2: Spice of Life 41
    Living on Island Time 41
    Learning the Language 42
    Jumping to Junkanoo or Goombay 42
    Enjoying Island Edibles 43
        Cooking up Bahamian favorites 44
        Eating like a local 46
        Drinking island cocktails 46

  Chapter 3: Deciding When to Go 49
    Forecasting the Weather 49
        Visiting in high season 49
        Checking out the islands in low season 50

Calendar of Events 51

    January 51

    February 52

    March 52

    May 53

    June 53

    July 54

    October 54

    November 54

    December 55

Chapter 4: Pillow Talk: Bahamian Accommodations 57

Deciding What Type of Lodging Suits You 57

    Rooming on the main islands 58

    Choosing the less developed islands 58

Knowing What to Expect at Your Accommodation 59

    Hotels and resorts — your options 60

    The all-inclusive: simplifying your vacation 61

    Villas: vacationing with the comforts of home 62

    Guesthouses: living like a Bahamian 63

What the Hotel Symbols Mean 64

Finding a Room at the Right Price 66

Getting a Great Room 66

Chapter 5: Planning Ahead for Special Travel Needs 69

Traveling with Kids 69

Planning the Perfect Romantic Getaway 71

Saying I Do Bahamian Style 72

    Reviewing the marriage requirements

      for The Bahamas 72

    Working out the wedding cost 73

Traveling Solo 74

Traveling to Gay- and Lesbian-Friendly Destinations 75

Seeking Savings and Specials for Mature Travelers 76

Ensuring Access for Travelers with Disabilities 77

Part II: Ironing Out the Details 79

Chapter 6: Making Your Travel Arrangements 81

Loving or Leaving Your Travel Agent 81

    Finding the best travel agent 82

    Getting the most from your travel agent 83

Picking a Package Tour 84

    Opening your package 84

    Nabbing the best package deal 85

Making Your Own Travel Arrangements 87

    Finding the best airfare 87

    Figuring out who flies where 88

Booking Your Trip Online 90
   Using the best sites 91
   Perusing the best island Web sites 92

Chapter 7: Money Matters 93

Picking Your Poison: Cash, ATMs, Credit Cards,
  or Traveler's Checks 93
   Cashing in 93
   Charging away 94
   Paying with traveler's checks 94
Calculating the Cost of Your Trip 96
   Adding up lodging expenses 96
   Reducing the rack rate 96
   Timing your visit for the best value 97
   Totaling transportation costs 98
   Dealing with dining dollars 98
   Tipping the correct amount 99
   Spending wisely 99
   Considering taxes 100
Keeping a Lid on Your Money 101

Chapter 8: Tying Up Loose Ends 103

Arriving on and Departing from the Islands 103
   Getting a passport 104
   Clearing customs 106
   Taking advantage of duty-free allowances 106
Protecting Your Trip Investment and Your Safety 107
   Covering your losses with travel insurance 107
   Staying healthy and safe 109
Readying to Go 111
   Packing the essentials 111
   Carrying on the basics 113
   Double-checking before you go 114

Part III: New Providence: Nassau, Cable Beach, and Paradise Island 115

Chapter 9: The Lowdown on the New Providence Hotel Scene 117

Finding the Location That's Right for You 117
Checking Out New Providence's Best Accommodations 118

Chapter 10: Settling In to New Providence 131

Arriving in New Providence by Air 131
   Navigating passport control and customs 131
   Getting from the airport to your hotel 132
Cruising to New Providence 132

Getting around New Providence 133
Fast Facts: New Providence 135

Chapter 11: Dining in New Providence 137

Getting a Taste for New Providence 137
   Dining at Nassau's best restaurants 138
   Checking Out Paradise Island's best restaurants 146
   Dining at Cable Beach's best restaurants 148

Chapter 12: Having Fun On and Off the Beach in New Providence 153

Hitting the Beaches 153
Finding Water Fun for Everyone 154
   Dolphin diversions and other ocean adventures 155
   Exploring the Bahamian underwater world 155
   Snorkeling and parasailing 156
On Deck: Riding the Waves without Getting Wet 157
   Taking dinner and sunset cruises 157
   Fishing for fun 158
   Setting sail on charters 158
   Enjoying semi-submarine rides 158
Exploring New Providence on Land 158
   Locating the top attractions 159
   Walking tours 166
   Enjoying New Providence's other activities 166
Getting a Shopper's Guide to New Providence 168
   Antiques 169
   Art 169
   Brass and copper 169
   Cigars 170
   Coins and stamps 170
   Fashion 170
   Handcrafts 171
   Jewelry 171
   Leather 172
   Linens 172
   Maps 172
   Markets 172
   Music 173
   Perfumes and cosmetics 173
   Steel drums 174
Living It Up after the Sun Goes Down:
   New Providence's Nightlife 174
Two Great Day Trips from New Providence 175
   Trip #1: Rose Island respite 175
   Trip #2: Blue Lagoon action 176

Part IV: Grand Bahama 177

Chapter 13: The Lowdown on the Grand Bahama Hotel Scene 179
Finding the Right Location 179
Checking Out Grand Bahama's Best Hotels 180

Chapter 14: Settling into Grand Bahama 187
Arriving in Grand Bahama by Air 187
Navigating passport control and customs 187
Getting from the airport to your hotel 188
Arriving in Grand Bahama by Sea 188
Getting around Grand Bahama 188
Fast Facts: Grand Bahama 190

Chapter 15: Dining in Grand Bahama 193
Grand Bahama's Best Restaurants 194

Chapter 16: Having Fun On and Off the Beach in Grand Bahama 207
Spending Time at the Beaches 207
Finding Water Fun for Everyone 208
Braving the banana boats 208
Sampling jet and water-skiing 208
Checking out kayaking 208
Diving with dolphin or sharks 209
Enjoying parasailing and snorkeling 210
On Deck: Riding the Waves without Getting Wet 211
Keeping Your Feet on Dry Land 211
Seeing Grand Bahama's top attractions 212
Finding other outdoor options 215
Shopping in Grand Bahama 217
International Bazaar 218
Port Lucaya Marketplace 220
Living It Up after the Sun Goes Down: Grand Bahama's Nightlife 221
Two Great Day Trips from Grand Bahama 222
Trip # 1: Kayak and snorkel adventure to Peterson Cay 222
Trip # 2: Kayak challenge to Water Cay 223

Part V: The Abacos: Prime Out Islands 225

Chapter 17: Marsh Harbour (Great Abaco Island) 227
Checking Out Marsh Harbour's Best Accommodations 228
Arriving in Marsh Harbour 231
Getting around Marsh Harbour 232

Dining in Marsh Harbour 233
Fun On and Off the Beach in Marsh Harbour 236
    Hitting the beaches 237
    Finding water fun for everyone 237
    On Deck: Riding the Waves without Getting Wet 238
Exploring Marsh Harbour's Land Attractions 239
Living It Up After the Sun Goes Down 240
Taking a Great Day Trip 241
Fast Facts: Marsh Harbour 242

Chapter 18: Elbow Cay 243

Checking Out Elbow Cay's Best Accommodations 243
Arriving in Elbow Cay 246
Getting around Elbow Cay 247
Dining in Elbow Cay 247
Fun On and Off the Beach in Elbow Cay 251
    Hitting the beaches 251
    Finding water fun for everyone 252
On Deck: Riding the Waves without Getting Wet 252
Exploring Elbow Cay's Land Attractions 253
Living It Up after the Sun Goes Down: Elbow Cay's Nightlife ...253
A Great Day Trip from Elbow Cay 253
Fast Facts: Elbow Cay 254

Chapter 19: Green Turtle Cay 255

Deciding Where You Want to Stay 255
Checking Out Green Turtle Cay's Best Accommodations 257
Arriving in Green Turtle Cay 259
Getting around Green Turtle Cay 260
Dining in Green Turtle Cay 260
Fun on and off the Beach in Green Turtle Cay 263
    Hitting the beaches 263
    Finding water fun for everyone 263
On Deck: Riding the Waves without Getting Wet 264
Keeping Your Feet on Dry Land 264
Living It Up after the Sun Goes Down:
    Green Turtle Cay's Nightlife 265
Taking a Great Day Trip to Swim with the Stingrays 265
Fast Facts: Green Turtle Cay 266

Chapter 20: Treasure Cay 267

Figuring Out Where to Stay 267
Checking Out Treasure Cay's Best Accommodations 268
Arriving in Treasure Cay 270
Getting around Treasure Cay 270
Dining in Treasure Cay 271
Fun On and Off the Beach in Treasure Cay 271
    Hitting the beaches 272
    Finding water fun for everyone 272

Sticking to Dry Land 272
Taking Two Great Day Trips from Treasure Cay 273
    Trip #1: Green Turtle Cay 273
    Trip #2: Elbow Cay and Man-O-War Cay 273
Fast Facts: Treasure Cay 274

Part VI: The Out Islands 277

Chapter 21: Harbour Island 279

Getting the Lowdown on the Harbour Island Hotel Scene 279
Deciding Where to Stay 280
Checking out Harbour Island's Best Accommodations 281
Arriving in Harbour Island 284
Getting around Harbour Island 285
Dining in Harbour Island 285
Fun On and Off the Beach in Harbour Island 288
    Hitting the beach 289
    Finding water fun for everyone 289
    On Deck: Riding the Waves without Getting Wet 289
Exploring Your On-Land Options 290
A Shopper's Guide to Harbour Island 290
Living It Up after the Sun Goes Down 291
Fast Facts: Harbour Island, Eleuthera 291

Chapter 22: Eleuthera 293

Getting the Lowdown on the Eleutheran Hotel Scene 293
Deciding Where to Stay 294
Arriving in Eleuthera 299
Getting around Eleuthera 300
Dining in Eleuthera 301
Having Fun on the Beach 304
Seeing Eleuthera on Dry Land 305
Living It Up After the Sun Goes Down 308
Taking a Great Day Trip 309
Fast Facts: Eleuthera 310

Chapter 23: Exuma 311

The Lowdown on Exuma's Hotel Scene 311
    Finding a location right for you 311
    Checking out the best accommodations 312
Arriving in Exuma 316
Getting around Exuma 316
Dining in Exuma 318
Fun On and Off the Beach in Exuma 320
    Hitting the beaches 321
    Finding water fun for everyone 322
On Deck: Riding the Waves without Getting Wet 323
    Sailing through the day 323
    Fishing for a big one 323

Exploring Exuma's Dry Land Options 324
Fast Facts: Exuma 325

Chapter 24: San Salvador **327**

Getting the Lowdown
on the Hotel Scene 327
Checking Out the Best Accommodations 328
Arriving in San Salvador 330
Getting around San Salvador 330
Dining in San Salvador 330
Having Fun On and Off the Beach 331
Seeing San Salvador on Dry Land 332
Exploring Columbus monuments 332
Lighting the way 333
Living It Up after the Sun Goes Down:
San Salvador's Nightlife 333
Fast Facts: San Salvador 334

Part VII: The Part of Tens **335**

Chapter 25: Top Ten Myths about The Bahamas **337**

The Columbus Landing Was at San Salvador 337
The Bahamas Is One Island 338
The Bahamas Is in the Caribbean 338
The Weather Is Always Hot Enough for the Beach 338
The Islands Are Mountainous 338
Palm Trees Are All Over the Place 339
For Casinos and Hot Nightlife, Pick Any Island 339
All Bahamians Are of African Descent 339
Islanders Resent Tourists 339
Reggae Music Is the Local Sound 340

Chapter 26: Top Ten Bahamas Moments **341**

Walking on the (Wet and) Wild Side 341
Taking a Surrey Ride through Nassau 341
Wandering through Versailles Gardens 342
Making a Date with Dolphins 342
Feeding the Stingrays 342
Digging Your Toes into a Pink Sand Beach 342
Watching the Sun Set on Dunmore Town 343
Visiting a Candy Cane–Striped Lighthouse 343
Living It Up at Miss Emily's 343
Boating in the Abacos 343

Worksheets **345**

Index **349**

General Index **349**

Accommodations Index **363**

Introduction

●●

*L*ying just off the tip of Florida and stretching southeast across 100,000 square miles of the Atlantic Ocean, The Bahamas (with a capital "The") are the American Riviera.

Charting its own course from Britain since 1973, the archipelago is made up of a land mass of 700 islands. The prospect of deciding which island is right for you and your vacation needs isn't as daunting as that figure suggests. Most of the islands — or "islets," in some cases — are not inhabited. Of those that are inhabited, only a few are graced with places to stay.

Don't come looking for mountainous interiors like those found in Jamaica or Puerto Rico. Most of the terrain is flat. Instead of hills, The Bahamas offer seascapes that seemingly stretch on endlessly. For the most part, they're ringed with beaches of white, golden, or, in some rare cases, pink sands. If you're flying over them like a bird, you'll see translucent waters shimmering in the sunlight — pale aquamarine, blue sapphire, or what an aerial photographer called "dancing green."

Entire books have been published on The Bahamas containing little text, just photographs of these swirling water patterns. As more and more of the world's seas such as the Mediterranean grow polluted, the Bahamian waters alone make the island nation worth a trip.

The Bahamas, with justification, are called the South Sea Islands of the Atlantic Ocean. Many of their thousands of miles of perfect coral-sand beaches remain free of footprints.

In the 2nd Edition of *Bahamas For Dummies*, we set out to help discover the islands, focusing on high points but also warning about some low points of every vacation spot. Of course, we hit all the hot spots, the much-trodden Nassau, Paradise Island, and Freeport/Lucaya. But we also take you to the less-visited and harder-to-reach islands, such as the Exumas in the Southern Bahamas, which is perfect for those seeking a true escape for some serious R&R.

About This Book

You can use this book in three ways:

- **As a trip planner.** Whether you think you know where you want to go in The Bahamas or you don't have a clue, this book helps you zero in on the right island (or islands) for you. Expect plenty of insider advice — the kind you'd get from a trusted friend — about where to go or what to avoid. Our tips guide you through all the necessary steps of making your travel arrangements, from finding the cheapest airfare to figuring out a budget and packing like a pro. Chapters are self-contained, so you don't have to read them in order. Just flip to them as you need them.

- **As an island guide.** Pack this book alongside your sunscreen lotion, and it will come in just as handy while you're away. Turn to the appropriate island chapters whenever you need to find the best beaches, a good place to eat, a great snorkeling sail, a challenging golf course, the lowdown on a hot nightspot, or tips on any other diversions.

- **For an overview.** If you want a feel for The Bahamas as a whole, peruse this guide from start to finish to figure out which of the archipelago's pleasurable pursuits are right for you.

 Please be advised that travel information is subject to change at any time — and this is especially true of prices. We therefore suggest that you write or call ahead for confirmation when making your travel plans. The authors, editors, and publisher cannot be held responsible for the experiences of readers while traveling. Your safety is important to us, however, so we encourage you to stay alert and be aware of your surroundings. Keep a close eye on cameras, purses, and wallets, all favorite targets of thieves and pickpockets.

Conventions Used in This Book

Bahamas For Dummies is a reference guide, allowing you to read chapters in any order you want. Instead of providing guidebook "hieroglyphics," we made the book user-friendly by keeping abbreviation and symbols to the minimum.

The following credit card abbreviations are used for establishments that accept them:

- AE: American Express
- DC: Diners Club
- DISC: Discover

✔ MC: MasterCard

✔ V: Visa

We use $ signs — see the price chart table later in this section — so that you can quickly determine whether you want to unpack your luggage at a hotel or dine on the local cuisine. The $ system lists a range of costs so that you can make fast comparisons.

Rates given in hotel recommendations are for two guests spending one night in a standard double room during the high season, which lasts from mid-December to April. In the off-season, tariffs can be lowered anywhere from 20% to 60%.

Most rates listed include room only. In some cases, the price, as stated, includes breakfast. In rare cases of an all-inclusive, such as a few hotels in New Providence, the rates we present will initially seem very high, but it will be noted that one price includes everything: your room, meals, drinks, and all those extras such as tips, taxes, most activities, airport pickups, and returns for your departing flight.

For restaurants, we give the price range for a main course per person.

The following table shows you the system of dollar signs used to show a range of costs for one night in a hotel or the price of a dinner main course at a restaurant.

Cost	Hotel	Restaurant (Main Courses)
$	$100 or less per night	Less than $15
$$	$100–$150	$15–$20
$$$	$150–$225	$20–$25
$$$$	$225–$300	$25–$30
$$$$$	More than $300 per night	$30 and up

Foolish Assumptions

We made some assumptions in preparing this guide.

✔ You may be a first-time visitor to The Bahamas in need of "building blocks" to help you create a trip at a price you can afford.

✔ You may have been to The Bahamas but haven't explored them in a long time, and you want sound advice about what's new and good, and what's changed, since your last trip.

✔ You're a busy person and don't want to read through a lot of background and less-than-urgent information. After all, a vacation shouldn't be homework. You want a book that focuses quickly on the places that will give you the best experience in the islands.

✔ Finally, and most important, we assume that you're seeking value — that you want to get the biggest bang for your buck in The Bahamas. That means you want to be steered clear of pricey tourist traps.

If you fall into any of these categories, *Bahamas For Dummies* is for you.

How This Book Is Organized

This book is divided into seven parts. The chapters within each part cover specific subjects in detail. Skip around as much as you like. You don't have to read this book in any particular order. In fact, think of these pages as an island buffet. You can consume whatever you want — and no one cares whether you eat the guava duff for dessert before you consume the conch chowder.

Part 1: Getting Started on Your Trip

In this part, we compare and contract the most popular islands of The Bahamas so that you can decide which place (or places) suits your tastes. Sure, they all have gorgeous beaches, but that's where the similarity ends. To help you plan a vacation tailored to your preferences, this part guides you through the process of figuring out which resort or hotel is best for you. We explain in detail the various accommodation options awaiting you, from a simple Bahamian inn or guest house to a megaresort.

You get an overview of Bahamian customs, music, festivals, cuisine, and "thirst-busters," while learning the best — and worst — times of the year to travel. You find out about high season when prices go up and low season — for most of the year — when they go down again. Special events may help you decide when to go. Finally, we offer trip-planning tips for newlyweds, about-to-be-newlyweds, families, singles, gays and lesbians, seniors, and persons with disabilities.

Part II: Ironing Out the Details

This part lays out everything you need to know about how to plan and package a worry-free trip and take it on the road. We help you decide whether to use a travel agent, a packager, or the Internet. If you're flying, you discover how to obtain the best fares, or, if you're arriving by cruise ship, we show you how to link up with some of the best deals for your "floating hotel" to The Bahamas. Once you get to where you're going, we tell you how to get around. Because money is foremost in most visitor's vacation plans, we also provide tips about how to stay within a budget. "You also find out everything you need to know about the boring but vital stuff, such as getting a passport, fretting over travel insurance, staying safe, and packing like a pro.

Parts III through VI: The Islands

Here's where the main course is dished out. The chapters in Parts III through VI are the juiciest morsels of the book, because they're packed with all the fun stuff that makes a vacation a vacation. For each island or island group — New Providence, Grand Bahama (Freeport/ Lucaya), the Abacos, the Eleuthera chain (including Harbour Island), the Exumas, Bimini, San Salvador, and some of the less-visited islands for escapists — you get the lowdown on hotels, what to expect when you get there (from landing at the airport to dealing with local taxi drivers), what restaurants to try, and, of course, where to go and what to do, including beaching it.

Each island offers a section called "Fast Facts." For the bigger islands, you find these sections at the end of the "Settling In" chapters. For the smaller islands, you can locate them at the end of the chapter. These quick tips give you handy information you may need, including phone numbers and addresses to use in an emergency, area hospitals and pharmacies, names of local newspapers and magazines, where to find maps, and more.

Part VII: The Part of Tens

As in every *For Dummies* book, this lighthearted part is just for fun. Our ten favorite island experiences are shared with you, along with some common myths about The Bahamas.

The section concludes with some worksheets to make your travel planning easier. Among other things, you can determine your budget and keep a log of your favorite restaurants. You can find these worksheets easily because they're printed on yellow paper.

Icons Used in This Book

Throughout this book, icons highlight useful information. Here's what each symbol means.

The Tip icon alerts you to practical advice and hints to help make your trip run smoothly.

Watch for the Heads Up icon to identify annoying or potentially dangerous situations, such as tourist traps, unsafe neighborhoods, and budgetary rip-offs.

Look to this icon for attractions, hotels, restaurants, and activities that are hospitable to children or people traveling with kids.

Keep an eye out for this icon to help you find money-saving tips and good deals.

If you like "flavor" in your travels and the occasional offbeat experience, this icon has your name tag on it. It marks information that leads you to a typically Bahamian cuisine, places, or experiences that best evoke island living.

When you spot Cupid's symbol, you find information about a hotel, restaurant, locale, or activity that pumps up the volume for loving couples.

Where to Go from Here

There's nothing like a vacation in the islands — when you plan it with the right advice and inside tips, that is. Whether you're a veteran traveler or new to the game, this book helps you put together just the kind of trip you have in mind. So, start turning these pages, and before you know it, you'll feel that warm island breeze on your face!

Part I
Getting Started on Your Trip

The 5th Wave   By Rich Tennant

YEAR 1 - GET RESCUED
YEAR 2 - GET RESCUED !
YEAR 3 - GET RESCUED !! NOW!
          (FOCUS MORE)
YEAR 4 - GET RESCUED
          (SCREAM LOUDER!)
YEAR 5 - BUILD GOLF
          RESORT

"My thinking has changed a little this year."

In this part . . .

We arm you with everything you need to know about the Bahamas before you begin making your travel plans. First, we help you decide exactly where you want to go. After giving you an overview of this sunny archipelago, we introduce the highlights and drawbacks of each island.

We also give you an enjoyable quiz that helps you pinpoint the island or islands that match your preferences. Likewise, we take you through the islands' customs, music, and cuisine, and we help you choose the best times of year to travel. We also offer tips for getting married or honeymooning in the Bahamas, as well as special advice for families, travelers who are single, gay, or physically challenged, and seniors.

Chapter 1

Discovering the Best of The Bahamas

In This Chapter

▶ Getting to know The Bahamas

▶ Picking the right island(s) for you — the fun way

▶ Rating the islands

*W*hen stacked up against any other region of the Caribbean to the south, the Bahamian archipelago, which lies entirely in the Atlantic Ocean, is the No. 1 destination for visitors.

In this chapter, we help you decide which island is best for you by giving you a rundown of the highlights and drawbacks of each of the most popular (and most accessible) islands. If you want casinos and megaresorts, for example, you may want to head for Paradise Beach. But if you seek a remote, tranquil location, with pink sandy beaches and quiet inns, then Harbour Island may be for you. A fun quiz toward the end of this chapter takes you through the process of narrowing your island options.

For details about where to stay, where to dine, and where to play on each of the islands covered in this book, check out Parts III through VI.

Getting the Lay of the Land

Many people think that The Bahamas are in the Caribbean Sea when in fact they're surrounded by the Atlantic Ocean. But at least culturally, The Bahamas are part of the Caribbean.

The island nation of The Bahamas lies on a "submarine platform" that is actually an extension of the U.S. continental shelf. For many millions of years, the land mass of The Bahamas was much larger as most of it was above water until it sank during the Mesozoic period.

The Bahamas is an archipelago of some 700 islands (many mere islets) and some 2,500 coral reefs. These reefs extend for about 800 miles on a northwest/southeast slant. The archipelago lies between the Atlantic Ocean and the Straits of Florida, with channels separating The Bahamas from Cuba and the island of Hispaniola (jointly owned by the Dominican Republic and Haiti).

Only about 20 of the islands are inhabited in this land mass of 4,405 square miles that begin in the north at Little Abaco Island and stretch south to Great Inagua Island, famed for its colonies of flamingos.

Almost nowhere in the world is there such a perfect climate, George Washington called The Bahamas the "isles of perpetual June." They have a warmer climate than their northern latitude would suggest, because they're bathed by equatorial sea currents. What rescues them from torrid hot summer seasons is refreshing tradewinds blowing in from the Atlantic. The effect is kind of like air-conditioning.

The northern locale of these islands means that, during winter months, the weather is sometimes cooler than in the always-warm Caribbean. Yes, we've even seen snowflakes in winter in the North Bahamas, but it's a rare event. (For more details about the best times to travel, turn to Chapter 3.) Without question, most of these islands have beautiful beaches, superb snorkeling, great scuba diving, big-time boating, and fishing, although the latter not as plentiful as it was in Hemingway's heyday because of overfishing. However, each island also boasts its own special look, character, and atmosphere. This variety means that it's easy to tailor a trip to almost any desire or budget.

Finding the Right Island for You

In terms of popularity, the most visited islands are **New Providence,** which includes the resorts of **Nassau, Cable Beach** on its northern shore, and the offshore **Paradise Island. New Providence** is a world of gambling casinos, cruise-ship arrivals, mega-resorts, Las Vegas-like entertainment, and fancy restaurants.

The area's cousin, offering the same diversions but without so much glitter, is the second most visited island: **Grand Bahama Island,** with its vacation "villages" of **Freeport** and **Lucaya.**

New Providence and Grand Bahama are where most of the dry-land sightseeing is concentrated, from forts and museums to aquariums, gardens, and nature preserves. A couple of straw markets plus scores of stores and boutiques duke it out for your attention.

Don't be misled, however, by all that hype in Nassau and Freeport about shopping bargains. It's true you save on tax, but prices on many international goods are list, so you often pay what you would back home. Know the list price before you buy. Otherwise, when you return home, you may discover that your so-called bargain wasn't one at all.

If the thought of taking an elevator to the beach leaves you cold, you may want to pass on the high-rises and impersonal crowds of Nassau, Paradise Island, and Freeport/Lucaya. If so, head to The Bahamas' Out Islands. Bahamian tourist officials promote all the other islands in The Bahamas as "the Family Islands," although we prefer their more raffish and buccaneering name, the "Out Islands," as they are sprinkled over thousands of square miles in the Atlantic east of Florida.

These islands include all islands other than the big three (New Providence, Paradise Island, and Grand Bahama). Most Out Island hotels are small, low-rise accommodations where the staff quickly gets to know you by name.

The Out Islands are the most beautiful part of The Bahamas. Miles of empty, golden sand beaches trim the clear waters. Except for scattered small towns — villages, really — and only a few large-scale beach resorts, nature has been left almost intact. Chickens, donkeys, sheep, and goats wander freely through front yards and on roads. In fact, boats, bicycles, golf carts, and feet are more popular than cars on some islands.

After New Providence and Grand Bahama Island, the most visited of the Out Islands include, in this order, the **Abacos, Eleuthera** (with its major vacation spot of **Harbour Island**), and the **Exumas,** the latter archipelago drawing the boating crowd, especially those who own or rent yachts. Less visited and more alluring to those who seek offbeat locations is **San Salvador,** the latter with a Club Med, the only major resort in the Southern Bahamas.

The Out Islands aren't as easy to get to as Nassau, Paradise Island, or Freeport/Lucaya. In some cases, you have to take a plane (or two), a taxi to a dock, a ferry, and then another taxi to your hotel. The inconvenience of transport is a small price to pay for the tranquility of wandering back into The Bahamas "the way they used to be."

Knowing New Providence

A trio of destinations — Nassau, Cable Beach, and the tony Paradise Island — are the island nation's main vacation areas, outranking its nearest rival, Freeport/Lucaya, in charm, class, and grandeur. These three areas are adjoining, which means that you can stay at one and play at all three.

An architectural delight of Old World charm, Nassau is also The Bahamas' largest cruise-ship port. When ships are in port, the center of the city is congested, with shops, restaurants, and other businesses overflowing. Some cruise-ship passengers head for the beach, while shoppers seek out duty-free items, such as jewelry, cameras, china, crystal, and liquor.

New Providence is a mixture of the ultra-modern and colonial quaint. No longer the haven for pirates and prostitutes, Nassau consists of a historic center that stretches for about a dozen blocks and is four blocks wide. The majority of The Bahamas' roughly 260,000 residents live on New Providence, in and around Nassau, the archipelago's colonial capital. In Nassau, aging forts, small museums, gardens, and a zoo amuse you when you're not bouncing along the waves on banana boats and jet skis, snorkeling and scuba diving, cruising to offshore island playgrounds, or parasailing.

Many government buildings are constructed in a rather grand neocolonial style of architecture, and even smaller buildings have style with wide balconies, louvered windows, and wood construction.

The part of the city that attracts most visitors lies along the waterfront and Bay Street, the "main street" of Nassau, which is a block away from the water. As you proceed inland from Nassau, the buildings become less grand, and the incomes of the families dwindle. Those on the lower scale of the economic ladder live on the fringe of Nassau in claptrap housing.

Emerging in recent years is New Providence's answer to Miami Beach: Cable Beach. Reached by heading west from Nassau along West Bay Street, Cable Beach opens onto a broad strand of golden sands and contains a series of mega-resorts lined up one by one. It also has plenty of casino action and a wide array of watersports facilities for fun on the beach.

Cable Beach's major competition is the even glitzier Paradise Beach, which lies on an island off the shores of Nassau and is reached by bridge. Although technically part of New Providence, Paradise Beach is a world unto itself. It's come a long way since it was called Hog Island.

Paradise Beach boasts the priciest real estate in The Bahamas. Its old world charm is long gone, and today it's home to a colony of high rises, condos, second homes of the wintering wealthy, and gambling casinos. Its centerpiece is the mammoth Atlantis Paradise Island Resort & Casino (see Chapter 9), which is not so much a hotel as a "city" in its own right.

In all three areas of New Providence, golf, tennis, and horseback riding tempt the sports lover. Restaurants and fast-food eateries cater to a range of tastes from the burger-on-the-run crowd to romantic couples enjoying a continental cuisine by candlelight overlooking a lagoon.

New Providence and Paradise Islands

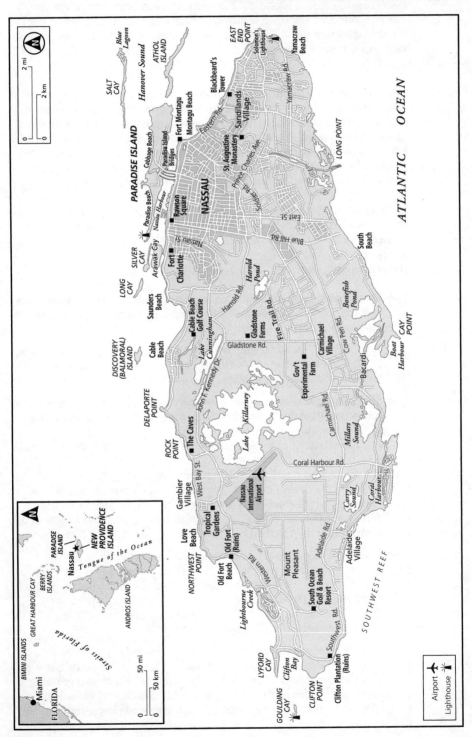

Only a few night clubs in Nassau itself are special. But after dark, Cable Beach and Paradise Island light up with elegant bars, dance floors, casinos, and Las Vegas-style stage shows. Whether you're looking for an old-fashioned guesthouse or a splashy multistory beach resort, you can find it in New Providence.

Drawing everyone from American college students on spring break to honeymooners to middle-aged gamblers, many hotels offer economical air/land package deals. Nassau itself has only a very limited number of hotels and not much in the way of a beach. Most resorts are clustered along Cable Beach on the North Coast and on Paradise Island, which is joined to New Providence by bridge. If you're looking for a moderately priced place to stay, you'll find it on Cable Beach — not on Paradise Island. (For more information on New Providence, see Part III.)

Bottom line: New Providence isn't the place for a cozy retreat. But if you want plenty of diversions and you don't mind crowds, it sizzles more than anywhere else in The Bahamas.

New Providence delivers a punch because it offers

- ✔ **Plenty of sights.** Nassau lures travelers with old forts, impressive colonial buildings, pocket-sized museums, manicured gardens, and a small zoo.

- ✔ **A variety of vacation playgrounds.** Choose among action-packed Cable Beach, historic downtown Nassau, and glitzy Paradise Island — or hang out in all three.

- ✔ **Shops galore.** Here you find The Bahamas' largest selection of duty-free stores and designer boutiques, plus the largest straw market.

But New Providence lies far from paradise. Here's a look at the downside:

- ✔ **No warm and cuddly hotel service.** You won't get the kind of service you might get in an Out Island inn where all the staff knows you by name. With thousands and thousands of visitors arriving in Nassau every day, staffs at restaurants and hotels have grown jaded by tourism.

- ✔ **Crowds and congestion.** If you live in a metropolis and want to escape crowds on your vacation, Nassau is not for you. It's not New York, but it may seem to be when cruise ships pull in at the same time, with passengers overrunning shops at the straw market and in the center of town. Tourists also crowd the golf courses, beaches, and popular restaurants.

- ✔ **A walk on the wild side.** You can find a lot safer places to be at night than downtown Nassau. It has the highest crime rate in all The Bahamas. Our advice is to take a taxi to where you're going after dark in the center of Nassau. Cable Beach and Paradise Island are much safer havens, though you must keep your guard up there, too.

Getting to know Grand Bahama

After New Providence, the second great attraction in The Bahamas is the large island of Grand Bahama, which contains Freeport, the second largest city in The Bahamas. When stacked up against Nassau, Freeport is rather unsophisticated. But its beaches at Lucaya, site of the major tourist development, are top notch, as are its duty-free shopping, its glittering casinos, and its two national parks. When you want to capture some of the spirit of The Bahamas of yesterday, you can escape from all this modernity by heading to the funky little village of West End.

Instead of old island charm, Freeport/Lucaya lures travelers with its array of water sports, its top-notch golf courses, its tennis courts, and its wide choice of international restaurants. The pace of life is slower than on New Providence, and Grand Bahama Island is less congested. As for night life, Freeport/Lucaya is a sleeper, offering little competition to Cable Beach and Paradise. Grand Bahama has some night life, but no one ever accused it of being Las Vegas.

The two main resort areas are Freeport, located inland, and Lucaya, which is along the water (see the Grand Bahama map). Grand Bahama has a much younger and trimmer look than Nassau. Stately palms and pines border broad, landscaped boulevards, modern high-rise hotels, apartment buildings, and condominiums overlook beaches and marinas. Smooth lawns sprouting flowering shrubs surround stucco homes topped with terra-cotta tiles. The flip side of this beauty is that Grand Bahama doesn't offer much history. Too much of its architecture is either kitschy or bland, and local flavor seems rather anemic.

The hotels in Grand Bahama underwent a vast slump at the end of the 20th century, but many of them are bouncing back in reincarnations, having been vastly restored or rebuilt completely. Even so, they are hardly a threat to the glittering array of choices awaiting you on Paradise Beach or Cable Beach.

With all the improvements in hotels, Grand Bahama now offers some winners. Even better news is that hotel rates on the island tend to be moderate. None of the lodgings carry the high price tags that shock you on New Providence.

Grand Bahama has many good restaurants — but not great ones or even world-class ones like some of those found on New Providence. You can still eat well, though, especially if you follow our recommendations.

The night life is not a reason to go to the area. But when compared to night life in the Out Islands, Grand Bahama is practically a Bahamian Atlantic City.

Grand Bahama Island

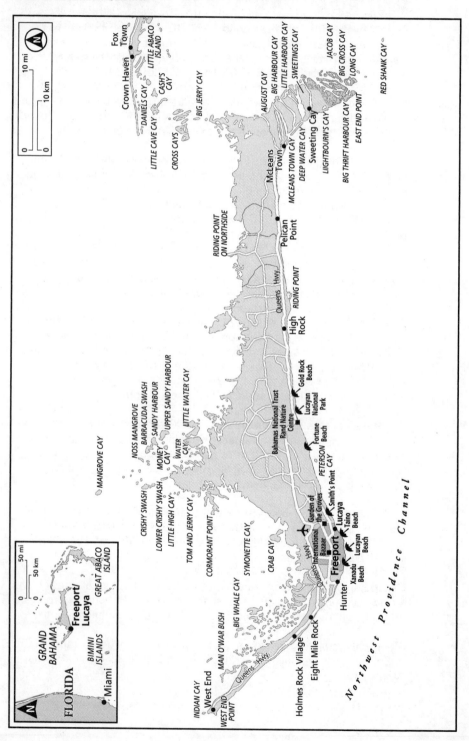

Duty-free shopping remains one of the major attractions of Grand Bahama, especially at the emerging Port Lucaya Marketplace and also at the famous but rather tacky International Bazaar at Freeport.

Grand Bahama is for the active vacationer. Topping most lists are excellent scuba diving, snorkeling trips by kayak to offshore islets, the chance to find out about and pet Flipper's cousins in the Dolphin Experience (see Chapter 16), the island's landscaped gardens and nature reserves, deep-sea fishing, and, of course, the golden sand beaches. (For more information on Grand Bahama, see Part IV.)

Bottom line: Grand Bahama is short on island spice but compensates by its diversity of activities ranging from casino gambling to a widely diversified sports program.

Grand Bahama is a hit with travelers because:

- ✔ **It's a baby.** Developed during the 1960s, the ox-jaw shaped island has been called a "culturally antiseptic mecca for fast-lane vacationers."

- ✔ **International appeal.** Many Americans, Canadians, and Europeans live and work here alongside Bahamians.

- ✔ **Fewer hotels.** The main beach resort area, Lucaya, isn't nearly as crowded with hotels as New Providence's Cable Beach or Paradise Island.

But Grand Bahama has its downside:

- ✔ **Little history.** Unlike Nassau with its buccaneering past, the history of Grand Bahama is rather colorless except when it was a supply depot for the Confederate States.

- ✔ **Less local appeal.** The cultural scene here is much blander than in Nassau or the Out Islands, where you can find lots of flavor and island spice.

- ✔ **A jumping-off point for day trippers.** Unlike New Providence and the Out Islands, Grand Bahama attracts a lot of day-trippers on cheap cruises from Florida, many of whom have never been outside the boundaries of the United States. In general, it's a venue for less sophisticated travelers.

- ✔ **Not many beach hotels.** Not all the best hotels are on the golden sands.

Appreciating the Abacos

With a land mass of 650 square miles, the Abacos form the second largest land mass in this island nation. The boomerang-shaped chain lies at the northernmost tier of The Bahamas, stretching 200 miles from Walker's Cay in the northwest to Cherokee Sound to the southeast.

The Abaco Islands

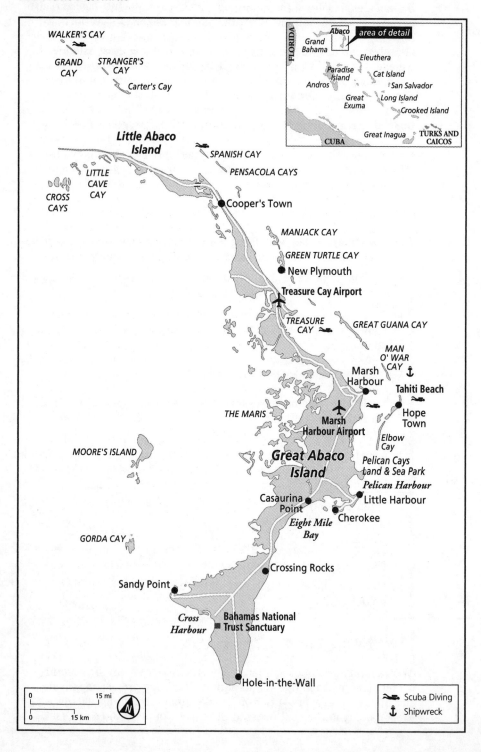

A true water world, the Abacos Islands (see The Abaco Islands map) make a prime target for sailing, scuba diving, snorkeling, fishing, and island hopping. Especially in Elbow Cay and Treasure Cay, the deserted powdery beaches with frothy waves look just like computer-enhanced photographs. Green Turtle Cay boasts one of the fanciest hotels in the Out Islands, but for the most part, lodgings in the Abacos are laid back. Keep in mind that travelers arriving in September and October will find many hotels and restaurants closed for lack of business.

Unlike the relatively flat Grand Bahama Island, the Abacos are among the most beautiful in the nation, lying in the Atlantic. The human-made attractions are appealing as well, including those at Marsh Harbour, the third largest town in The Bahamas. As the boating capital of the northern Bahamas, Marsh Harbour is the gateway to the Abacos.

If you want to tee off, you don't have to go to New Providence or Grand Bahama. One of The Bahamas' best golf courses is in the Out Islands at Treasure Cay. And, if you're into history and colonial architecture, you can enjoy the tidy New England-style seaside villages on Elbow Cay, Green Turtle Cay, and Man-O-War Cay.

Here's a rundown of the Abaco Islands:

- **Marsh Harbour.** Marsh Harbour is the capital of the Abacos. But don't expect congestion, even though it contains the only traffic light in the Out Islands. A legendary port among boaters, especially yachties from Florida, Marsh Harbour lies on Great Abaco Island and is a shipbuilding center. It lacks the New England charm of either New Plymouth or Hope Town and has the feel of a small Florida town.

  Everything is relatively new in Marsh Harbour, most of it dating from the middle of the '80s. Its growth originally fueled by drug money, the town only belatedly discovered tourism. Marinas and a yacht-clogged harbor characterize Marsh Harbour today. To meet the demands of modern tourism in the '90s and at the millennium, some excellent restaurants have opened, as well as hotels, shops, bars, cafes, and boat outfitters. For more information on Marsh Harbour, see Chapter 17.

- **Elbow Cay.** All motor vehicles are banned from the center of Hope Town, the island's Cape Cod-like village. Along the narrow paved streets, you find harborside restaurants and saltbox cottages painted in tropical tones, with pink and yellow bougainvillea dripping over stone or picket fences. Many Americans, Canadians, and Europeans, who first arrived as vacationers decades ago, own some of the biggest and most attractive homes.

  People get around this small island by golf cart, bicycle, and foot. The boat is the primary means of locomotion. Gazing down on a bobbing mass of boats, Hope Town's red-and-white striped lighthouse probably has had more photographs taken of it than any other sight on the island. You can hike or bike to isolated Tahiti Beach, where shelling at low tide is great fun. For more information on Elbow Cay, see Chapter 18.

✔ **Green Turtle Cay.** Eighteenth-century New England-style New Plymouth village is idyllic for strolling. You can find out about the Abacos' seafaring past at the Albert Lowe Museum, housed in an old cottage. Across the street, the Memorial Sculpture Garden honors noteworthy Bahamians.

Boats take people around Green Turtle Cay more than wheels and feet. Coral colonies starting in relatively shallow water make for some of the best snorkeling in The Bahamas, and diving is exceptional. You can spend a day on a deserted beach on an uninhabited island. You can swim with stingrays, and the captain of your boat will spear some lobster and fish and then grill it for you right on the beach.

With rooms decked out with Oriental rugs and Queen Anne chairs, Green Turtle Club & Marina is among the most upscale places to stay in the Out Islands. This tiny cay doesn't have fairways, but if you're a golfer, you can take the ferry and a taxi (or charter a boat) to the championship golf course at Treasure Cay. For more information on Green Turtle Cay, see Chapter 19.

✔ **Treasure Cay.** A little sterile for our taste, Treasure Cay feels too much like a playground designed exclusively for visitors. There wasn't much of a local settlement here before this resort was developed during the 1960s, so you won't find any historic sites or old island communities. If not for the golden crescent beach and the rich blues of the water, you might forget that you're in The Bahamas.

This lack of local color doesn't seem to bother the vacationers who come to fish and play golf on one of the country's best courses. They stay in the attractive hotels, condos, and villas on the marina and beach. Treasure Cay is close to the dock where you catch the ferry to Green Turtle Cay, and you can easily rent a boat to sail off to Elbow Cay, Man-O-War Cay, and other nearby islands. Rooms are hard to come by in June during the Treasure Cay Billfish Championship. For more information on Treasure Cay, turn to Chapter 20.

Bottom line: Nirvana for divers, snorkelers, and anglers, the Abacos offer many opportunities to sail off to different islands, each with its own special allure. Many are uninhabited while on others, human-made attractions run a distant second to natural beauty.

The Abacos are a good choice if you're hoping for:

- ✔ **An underwater wonderland, fish tales, and great greens.** The Abacos have some of the most alluring scuba diving, snorkeling, and fishing around, and, in Treasure Cay, a championship golf course.

- ✔ **Scenic villages.** Historic seaside settlements on Elbow Cay, Green Turtle Cay, and Man-O-War Cay are filled with pretty clapboard cottages surrounded by white-picket fences set off by flamboyant tropical flowers.

- ✔ **Spectacular sailing.** With so many appealing islands clustered together, the Abacos are called "the Sailing Capital of the World."

Locals who love their islands claim that the Abacos are paradise found — and there is no downside. Even so, you may not like

- ✔ **The travel time.** Getting to these islands can take a while. Sometimes you need at least three means of transport — planes, ferries, and taxis — and you can experience long waits and delays.

- ✔ **Potential seasickness.** If you're that rare landlubber who gets seasick when faced with lapping waves, the Abacos may not be for you. Almost everybody in the Abacos uses boats to travel more than they rely on wheels.

- ✔ **Hardly any hotels.** You won't have much of a choice of lodgings, and most are small and low-key.

Hanging out on Harbour Island

Harbour Island is small — barely 2 square miles in size — but it's one of the most beautiful islands in The Bahamas (see Harbour Island map). Its major attraction is a long, broad, pink beach, tinted by pulverized coral and shells. The snorkeling and scuba diving are first rate. You can even reach shipwrecks on a scuba outing. Perched on a bluff overlooking the water are several of the country's prime — and most expensive — inns and small hotels. (Many accommodations and restaurants close here during the fall.) Wander into Dunmore Town, and you stroll past historic churches, eighteenth-century cottages with lacy gingerbread trim, and tropical flowers nuzzling picket fences.

Say "Harbour Island" quickly, and it turns into *Briland,* as it's affectionately known to residents. Briland lures mainly American and Canadian vacationers, and more than a few of them have snapped up prime real estate here. However, the island maintains a distinct Bahamian look and feel. At the harbor's edge, old men shoot the breeze while slapping dominos onto card tables. Chickens and horses wander through front yards. Women trade gossip while selling straw goods and shell jewelry from outdoor stalls. If those wares aren't upscale enough for you, go boutique browsing for Haitian paintings, Balinese silver, and French wine vinegar.

Harbour Island

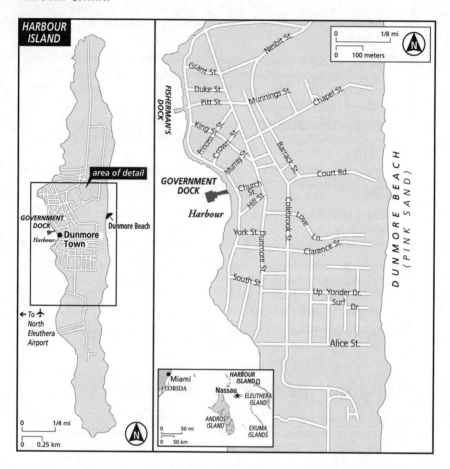

Harbour Island is a place where you can don your drop-dead duds for candlelit cocktails one night and then cool out over *Kaliks* (the local brew) in a smoky pool hall the next. However, hipbones don't usually start slipping until the weekend, when anything from waterside hotel decks to cavelike local bars morph into dance clubs. Mom-and-pop kitchens whip up Bahamian favorites such as cracked conch (pounded, battered, and fried) and peas and rice. Hotels lure diners with gourmet creations. And don't be surprised if your waiter knows you went sailing before you tell him — folks are friendly, and word travels fast. But don't worry: With quiet roads, romantic lookout points, and empty sandy strands, you can find plenty of places to keep your privacy intact. For more information on Harbour Island, see Chapter 21.

Bottom line: With some of The Bahamas' finest small beach hotels, a time-warp waterfront village, and a pink sand beach, you can't go wrong with Harbour Island and if you can afford it.

Harbour Island's highlights include

- ✔ **Pink sand.** The hue of this stunning 3-mile beach is rosy, running the whole length of the island on its eastern side.

- ✔ **Eye candy.** New England meets the tropics here with white picket fences around colonial clapboard houses shaded by palm trees.

- ✔ **Small-town hospitality.** Briland is so petite and friendly that residents may start greeting you by name before you can say "cracked conch."

Before you decide on Harbour Island, however, consider the following:

- ✔ **Cost.** Briland is one of the most expensive islands in The Bahamas.

- ✔ **Travel fatigue.** A trip here from the U.S. requires a plane or two, a taxi, a ferry, and another taxi.

- ✔ **Quiet nights.** What little nightlife there is wakes up mainly on weekends.

Eloping to Eleuthera

Eleuthera is a wisp of an island chain that stretches for a distance of 100 miles from north to south. It lies only 50 miles east of Nassau, but it's a thousand miles removed from that busy scene there.

Even though it's relatively quiet, Eleuthera remains one of the most developed of the Out Islands when stacked up against the Exumas or the southern Bahamas.

However, Eleuthera's heyday is long gone. The chic social set is now but a memory with the closing of such ritzy resorts as the Cotton Club and the Winderemere Club in South Eleuthera. Today, the rich and famous head for Harbour Island because the entire mainland of Eleuthera doesn't really have a state-of-the-art hotel.

At no point is Eleuthera more than 4 miles wide. Despite the island's size, some 10,000 people eke out a living on Eleuthera, which has not always been a friendly place to do that. What Eleuthera offers in great abundance is a galaxy of beaches, an "endless summer," and multihued seas ranging from deep blue to aquamarine.

On Eleuthera, you don't have to bother with historical sites or museums because none exist. What we like to do is drive the Queens Highway for the whole length of the island. We know of no more dramatic drive in all The Bahamas. For the most part, you hug the coastline and are treated to stunning views of sea- or landscapes. The seaside villages you come across have known better days, but it's their decaying gingerbread charm that attracts us in the first place. In Eleuthera, you get the impression that everyone was once here, but now they are gone. You can wander about the most remote places, which you'll have all to yourself.

Eleuthera

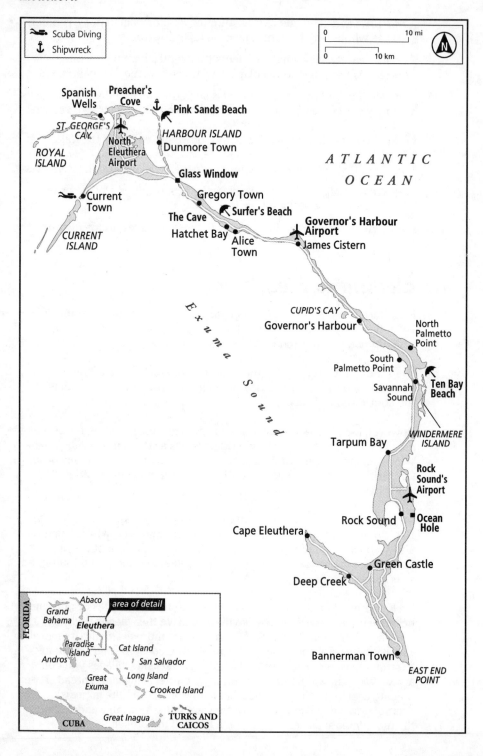

Eleuthera is made up of two main sections, North and South:

- ✔ **North Eleuthera.** Most of the tourist facilities lie in the north part of Eleuthera, which embraces the offshore island of Harbour Island, lying off the east coast. Arrivals for destinations in North Eleuthera or Harbour Island are at the North Eleuthera Airport.

  The road that links all of Eleuthera, Queens Highway, begins in the north at James Bay, taking you south to Lower Bogue, Upper Bogue, Gregory Town, and Alice Town.

  With little facilities, the most isolated of the Eleutheran islands is Spanish Wells, 2 miles west of the North Eleuthera Airport with a population of 800. Settled by the Eleutheran Adventures, Spanish Wells still has a population of white people, most of whom are intermarried with each other and deeply religious.

  The "Bogues," Upper and Lower, are just hamlets to pass through en route south. They face southward into the massive body of water, the Bight of Eleuthera. You first come to Lower Bogue which is 2 miles southwest of the airport. It is not the western-most hamlet, however. That dubious honor goes to a settlement called Current, another white community like Spanish Wells. When you drive 7 miles east of Lower Bogue to The Glass Window, you cross into South Eleuthera.

- ✔ **South Eleuthera:** Five miles south of The Glass Window, Gregory Town comes into view. The center of a prosperous pineapple industry, Gregory Town is one of the most populous settlements on Eleuthera. As you drive from Gregory Town to Governor's Harbour, a distance of 25 miles, you'll be going through one of the most settled parts of Eleuthera, passing the little towns like Alice Town and the oddly named James Cistern. Here, you can stop off at the 2-mile-long sugary sands of Surfer's Beach for a swim.

  If Eleuthera has a capital, it's Governor's Harbour, at the midpoint of the island and the site of Governor's Harbour Airport, which serves Central Eleuthera.

  Queens Highway will take you to Rock Sound, the main center of South Eleuthera and site of the Rock Sound Airport. The highway continues south toward Eleuthera Point, past the funky and bat-tered hamlets of Millars and Bannerman, surrounded by shrub and mangrove.

  Cotton Bay lies off a spur of Queens Highway, 6 miles to the south of Rock Sound. At some future point, the Cotton Bay Club, which closed in 1995, may bounce back. A golf course, designed by Robert Trent Jones, Jr., is still operating here, and many second homes are owned by rich expats from the United States.

The final point for exploration is to drive northwest to Cape Eleuthera, 20 winding miles from the Rock Sound Airport. Cape Eleuthera once was an active development drawing the rich and famous. Now it slumbers with its memories in the Bahamian sun, with big talk of a comeback one day. For more information on Eleuthera, see Chapter 22.

Consider a visit to Eleuthera if you're hoping for:

✔ **Remote seaports and villages from long ago.** Its fashionable heyday long gone, the settlements of Eleuthera exist in a time warp. Far removed from casino wheels and mega-resorts, the little inns of Eleuthera take us back to the '50s.

✔ **Scenery and sights.** Why come here? For the miles and miles of unspoiled beaches, for gingerbread-trimmed houses hung with bougainvillea, for bargains galore, for rolling hills, for lush green forests, for sheltered coves, and for offshore coral reefs.

✔ **Friendly people.** Instead of being locked away in a high-raise hotel, in Eleuthera you get to meet the locals. There are no big towns, only small settlements of welcoming visitors.

For a look at the darker side of Eleuthera, consider

✔ **The absence of any top-rated hotels.** If you want luxury, Eleuthera sends you to Harbour Island. To live on "mainland" Eleuthera, you must settle for "rental units," which are clean but rather basic — definitely not luxurious.

✔ **A traveler, not a tourist.** Visitors who are used to being catered to, such as those who visit Paradise Island, will find that it's pretty much of a do-it-yourself affair on Eleuthera. "Things," as they are called here, aren't very well organized. A lot of personal initiative is needed to make your vacation wheels spin.

✔ **Difficult transportation.** Except for the main highway, roads are often a disaster. Because no major car-rental companies exist, you often have to negotiate with a local for a rental. Expect a beat-up model.

Exploring Exuma

You can see the water's different colors for yourself before you even get to Exuma when you look out of the window as your plane swoops down to land. Strung out like stepping stones, these islands are surrounded by some of The Bahamas most memorable waters (see the Exumas map).

With a cay for every day of the year — and most of them uninhabited — Exuma is prime sailing territory. A bridge joins Great Exuma and Little

Exuma, the two largest islands in the chain. Hotels and island action are concentrated in and around George Town, Exuma's pretty capital on Great Exuma. If you happen to vacation in April, you can catch the wet and dry festivities of the Out Island Regatta (also called the Family Island Regatta). Far up north — and accessible only by chartered boat — the gorgeous Exuma Cays Land and Sea Park covers 177 square miles of islands and marine life. See Chapter 23 for more on Exuma's attractions.

Through your hotel, you can make arrangements for sailing, snorkeling, diving, and fishing. Be forewarned, though, that George Town's few hotels aren't located on the best beaches. For the best sandy stretches, you have to take a ferry to undeveloped Stocking Island, which claims a sole hotel, just across the harbor.

Bottom line: Exuma is a fine choice if sailing, R&R, and absorbing natural beauty is more important to you than manmade sights and late night entertainment.

Exuma has many idyllic qualities, including:

- ✔ **Watercolors.** Bring your camera, or no one at home will believe you when you describe the range of aquatic hues.

- ✔ **Small size.** Petite hotels — a couple on their own islands — and friendly residents quickly make you feel at home.

- ✔ **Parties.** Well, sometimes, at least. On most Saturday nights, everyone heads to Club Peace & Plenty's dance party, and in April, the festivities of the Out Island Regatta bring many a far-flung Bahamian home to Exuma.

But Exuma isn't always convenient because:

- ✔ **The marine park isn't nearby.** You may hear talk of the Exuma Cays Land and Sea Park, but unless you charter a boat (or both a boat and a small plane), you can't get there from George Town, where most vacationers stay.

- ✔ **You may have to take a boat to the beach.** George Town, where most hotels reside, isn't known for its beaches, and not all hotels are on the sand. Better beaches surround Stocking Island, a short ferry ride across the harbor.

- ✔ **April crowds.** During the Out Island Regatta each spring, George Town can get as packed as Cable Beach in February.

The Exumas

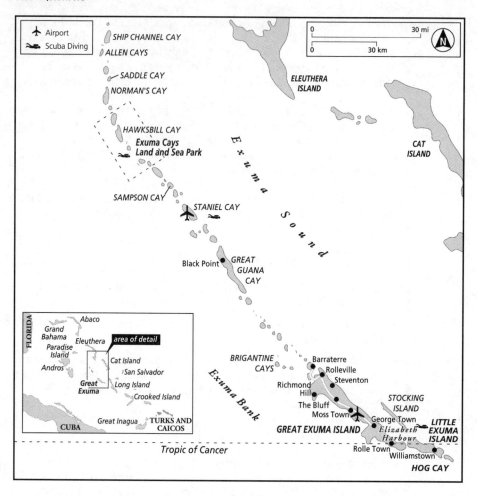

Savoring San Salvador

Lying 200 miles southeast of Nassau, the Bahamian island of San Salvador is often confused with the Central American country of the same name (see the San Salvador map). Some folks say that this scuba-diving mecca was the first place Christopher Columbus stepped ashore in the "New" World (the world that wasn't new at all, of course, to the Indians living there for at least five centuries). However, historians bitterly debate whether the famed explorer ever came here, with some experts believing his first landfall was actually at Samana Cay, another Bahamian island 65 miles to the south. But don't tell that to residents of San Salvador. They point you with pride to all the island's monuments that commemorate the world-changing event.

San Salvador

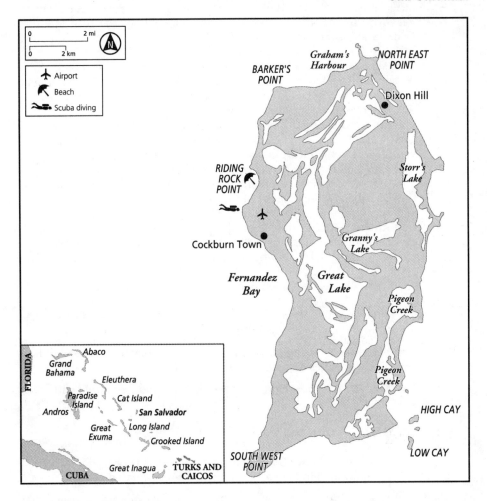

Columbus's momentous visit, if it happened at all, didn't change San Salvador very much. Most of this island is nearly as undeveloped as it was back in the days when Lucayan Indians called it home. The interior is still interlaced with a network of quiet lakes, and the main village, Cockburn Town, couldn't be much drowsier. Each time you see one of the pristine sandy stretches that surround this island, you can hear yourself mutter, "Now *that's* a beach." Climb to the top of Dixon Hill Lighthouse, and you get a sweeping view of the island and its pristine coastline. Bicycling is another good way to see San Salvador.

Today, many visitors are avid divers, who wax poetic about the variety and bright colors of the coral and other marine life. The best diving sites aren't frequented as much as those around New Providence (where Nassau, Cable Beach, and Paradise Island are), because San Salvador has only a couple of hotels. True, one is the sprawling Club

Med but not all the guests here are interested in scuba. Although the other hotel, locally run Riding Rock Inn Resort & Marina, has long been a favorite among serious divers, it's not large enough to cause scuba gridlock at any sites.

The island's two main beach hotels give vacationers a big choice: Do you want a small, unassuming scuba-lover's hangout that's dead-quiet during the day (Riding Rock), or do you want a huge low-rise resort, decorated with an impressive collection of international folk art, that's like a playground for adults (Club Med)? The bar at Riding Rock is the island's social center, and it hosts parties once or twice a week where vacationers hang out with locals. Although something's happening every night at Club Med, you can forget that you're in The Bahamas after dark, because most people here are not locals. For more information on San Salvador, check out Chapter 24.

Bottom line: Since Club Med hit the scene, San Salvador isn't just for divers anymore, but the underwater sights are still the main draw beyond cooling out amid pristine surroundings.

San Salvador may be a good choice if you find the following enticing:

- ✔ **Serene scuba.** More than three dozen unspoiled dive sites are less than 45 minutes from shore.
- ✔ **Fabulous digs.** A great all-inclusive resort, one of the top of Club Med's line, lies along an excellent sandy stretch.
- ✔ **Striking beaches.** Finding shores that are more naturally stunning is hard to do.

But, consider these downsides:

- ✔ **Few hotels.** Your choice of accommodations is basically between an upscale Club Med and a modest diving-oriented resort.
- ✔ **Where's the town?** Cockburn Town is more like a sleepy residential neighborhood.
- ✔ **Little island action.** Don't come here looking for any activities other than what Club Med offers.

Deciding How Many Islands per Trip

One island is certainly enough for most visitors, especially if you stay in Nassau on New Providence or Freeport/Lucaya on Grand Bahama, where you can find sights and activities to keep you busy beyond the waves.

If you need variety to spice up your life, consider an island that makes a good home base for exploring other landfalls by boat, such as an island in the Abacos or the Exumas. From many islands, checking out a second island (or third or fourth) is as easy as hopping in a water taxi, a ferry, or taking a snorkeling cruise.

For example, on a visit to New Providence, based at either Cable Beach or Nassau, all you have to do is cross a bridge to enter another world — Paradise Island. From New Providence, you can also take boats to off-shore cays. If you have the time, you can plan three nights in cosmopolitan New Providence and then spend the rest of your vacation week in, say, Harbour Island in the Eleutheras.

Keep in mind that getting from some islands to others can be tricky, especially when you need to fly. Visiting more than one Out Island by air usually means that you have to return to Nassau between islands because most remote islands don't have air linkage except by expensive charter planes. Therefore, you may spend a whole lot of time sitting around Nassau International Airport, because some flights are once a day (or even once every few days), and delays are common. (See Chapter 6 for more information.)

Narrowing Your Island Choices

The following quiz helps you determine which islands are best suited to your vacation style and interests. You're about to take a quiz, but it's all in fun and you grade yourself.

Step 1: Get to know your "Rate the Islands" scorecard.

Your scorecard at the end of the quiz has a column for each island and a row for each of the categories in our island-rating system. Use this scorecard to compile a rating for each island, based on the special-interest categories that follow.

On a scale of 1 to 4 points, the top vacation destinations are rated in various categories such as dining, night life, price, sights, diving, and more. The lowest rating is 1, the highest 4. When an island isn't listed, it means it flunked completely. For example, golfers don't go to Harbour Island because it has no greens.

Step 2: Score islands based on what interests you.

Rate islands only in categories of interest to you. For example, if you don't play golf, skip that one. Write the scores for each island in the appropriate row under each column in your scorecard. For example, if you're looking for luxury, go across row 1 of your scorecard and put 4 under New Providence, 3 under Harbour Island, 2 under San Salvador, and 1 under Grand Bahama.

Keep racking up points until you review all the categories and give each island a score for every category of interest to you.

1) If you want to be in the lap of luxury . . .

Rating	Island	Why?
4	New Providence	Cable Beach and Paradise Island are graced with the most elegant pockets of posh in The Bahamas, with the Atlantis Paradise Island Resort & Casino being the country's most spectacular hotel.
3	Harbour Island	Some of The Bahamas' most distinctive small hotels overlook the pink sand beach.
2	San Salvador	Home of one of Club Med's snazziest resorts, and the only first-class hotel in the Southern Bahamas.
1	Grand Bahama	The Our Lucaya resort is more affordable than comparable beach resorts on New Providence.

2) If you're watching your wallet but still want to stay on the sand . . .

Rating	Island	Why?
4	Grand Bahama	Beach resorts may not be as plentiful here as they are on New Providence, but they're easier on your pocketbook.
3	New Providence	With a good choice of affordable shoreline hotels, Cable Beach is a better bet than pricier Paradise Island.
2	Elbow Cay	Several small hotels on this tiny cay hug near-empty beaches of golden sand — if you don't mind getting here by plane, taxi, and ferry.
1	Eleuthera	This 100-mile narrow island, or series of islands, has virtually no expensive hotel — at least since the luxury resorts went belly up and a hurricane blew away Club Med. You're housed at a lot of Mom and Pop inns on local beaches.

3) If you want an island (almost) all to yourself . . .

Rating	Island	Why?
4	Exuma	Hotel Higgins Landing on Stocking Island and Latitude Exuma Resort on Rolle Cay are true getaways.
3	Elbow Cay	On this petite island, where there are more boats than cars, you can stay in small, isolated beach hotels that are really intimate inns.
2	Green Turtle Cay	Coco Bay Cottages are tucked away in a quiet corner of this sleepy island on a near-empty beach.
1	Harbour Island	You may not have your own island, but staying at the intimate Landing, an historic seven-room harborfront inn, may make you think the panoramic sunset is for your eyes only.

4) If you want to party the night away . . .

Rating	Island	Why?
4	New Providence	Here you find plenty of dance clubs, bars, and island musical revues, and Las Vegas-styled casinos. Atlantis Paradise Island Resort & Casino alone can keep you entertained for weeks!
3	Grand Bahama	This island doesn't offer as much after-dark action as New Providence, but you can still choose from some good selections, including gambling.
2	Green Turtle Cay	Here you're down to mainly midweek and weekend partying, with dance bands at the hotels.
1	Exuma	Club Peace & Plenty is the place to be on Saturday night if you like to shake it up to a poolside calypso band. Also, you can check out the weekly rake and scrape at Eddie's Edgewater, a local dive.

5) If you like dining really well . . .

Rating	Island	Why?
4	New Providence	This island offers plenty of first-rate restaurants, plus a good selection of local eateries.
3	Harbour Island	The Bahamas' best collection of small beach hotels — plus the historic Landing, a harborside dining spot — offer some of the country's most creative cooking.
2	Green Turtle Cay	Bluff House, New Plymouth Club & Inn, and Green Turtle Club & Marina create a culinary buzz.
1	Grand Bahama	From steak in an elegant dining room to oceanfront seafood, it's all here.

6) If you're looking for the most unspoiled beaches . . .

Rating	Island	Why?
4	**Harbour Island**	The broad beach is 3 miles long, almost deserted, and the sand is actually pink. For once, you can believe all that tourist stuff.
3	**Elbow Cay or Green Turtle Cay**	Many empty sandy stretches encircle uninhabited islands offshore or border populated-but-low-key locales on the cays themselves.
2	**Exuma**	For a drop-dead gorgeous white sand beach, ferry over to Stocking Island from George Town.
1	**San Salvador**	Club Med and Columbus Isle hugs one of The Bahamas' most striking golden strands.

7) If you want to experience island spice . . .

Rating	Island	Why?
4	**New Providence**	Funky Nassau is The Bahamas' political (and cultural) capital, and the place to be during the Christmas/New Year's Junkanoo festival.
3	**Exuma**	You can visit here during the Out Island Regatta each April for a real island vibe. Any time of year is fine because cute, little George Town is never overrun with visitors.
2	**Harbour Island**	Chickens and horses wander in front yards, and residents soon call you by name.
1	**Green Turtle Cay**	This place is home to friendly folks who enjoy showing off their little gem of an island.

8) If you want to tee off . . .

Rating	Island	Why?
4	**Grand Bahama**	The island boasts more golf courses than any other in The Bahamas. The first golf course, The Reef Course, ever to open in The Bahamas made its debut here back in 1969.
3	**Treasure Cay**	The desert-type, windy Dick Wilson course at the Treasure Cay Golf Club is a winner.
2	**New Providence**	This island offers a trio of good courses, plus plenty of hotels and activities, both wet and dry.
1	**Green Turtle Cay**	You can take the ferry and a taxi (or a chartered boat) to the championship Treasure Cay golf course.

9) If you like sightseeing . . .

Rating	Island	Why?
4	**New Providence**	It's the home of Nassau, The Bahamas' stately colonial capital, with historic forts, gardens, museums, and horse-drawn carriages galore.
3	**Green Turtle Cay**	New Plymouth looks like an 18th-century New England seaside village. It lives in a time capsule and its museum evokes the days of the Loyalists who escaped here instead of becoming part of the new American Republic.
2	**Elbow Cay**	Six miles east of Marsh Harbour, Elbow Cay is another Loyalist Cay, settled by blond, blue-eyed people whose descendants are still here. It's like Lilliput, and its 120-foot red-and-white striped lighthouse is the most photographed sight in the Abacos.
1	**Harbour Island**	Harborside Dunmore Town boasts eighteenth-century gingerbread cottages and The Bahamas' oldest Anglican church.

10) If you want the best scuba diving or snorkeling . . .

Rating	Island	Why?
4	**San Salvador**	Scuba divers in the Columbus spirit go exploring here, finding more than a dozen shipwrecks, including the most famous, the Frascate, along with canyons and reefs to the southwest that are spectacular.
3	**Green Turtle Cay**	Its Atlantic shores are lined with excellent reefs teeming with a varied marine life. Loggerhead turtles still crawl ashore to nest. Snorkelers have great visibility in these gin-clear waters.
2	**Harbour Island**	Certified divers ride in underwater scooters, and rushing waters make Current Cut an exhilarating scuba site.
1	**Exuma**	Many excellent reefs are just 20 or 25 minutes away from the George Town area, so long boat rides don't cut into your underwater time.

11) If you want the best sportfishing . . .

Rating	Island	Why?
4	**Treasure Cay**	Anglers snag wahoo, billfish, and other big game all over the Abacos, where the Treasure Cay Billfish Championship is one of The Bahamas' most popular fishing tournaments.
3	**Green Turtle Cay**	The Green Turtle Club & Marina hosts a major fishing tournament each spring.
2	**Exuma**	Just outside George Town, try bonefishing right from the shore. Deep-sea fishing is excellent as well.
1	**Grand Bahama**	Waters off Grand Bahama turn up impressive catches in barracuda, snapper, grouper, yellowtail, wahoo, and kingfish. Some of the best deep-sea fishing charters in The Bahamas are found here.

12) If you want to island hop . . .

Rating	Island	Why?
4	**Elbow Cay**	Frequent ferries connect Marsh Harbour with Elbow Cay and Man-O-War Cay, and you can charter a boat to Treasure Cay for golf or Green Turtle Cay for more quaint beauty.
3	**New Providence**	A bridge links you to Paradise Island, boats cruise to various beach-rimmed uninhabited islets, and planes fly to Grand Bahama and all Out Islands.
2	**Eleuthera**	Eleuthera itself is like a string of little islands, but in the north, you can take the ferry over to remote, isolated Spanish Wells or chic Harbour Island.
1	**Exuma**	Wherever you go in the Exumas, you seem to land on another island in about 15 minutes of boating. It's the sailing capital of The Bahamas.

13) If you're craving peace and quiet . . .

Rating	Island	Why?
4	Exuma	Check out the gorgeous surrounding waters stocked with serene, uninhabited islets.
3	Green Turtle Cay	Historic seaside New Plymouth village enhances Mother Nature's handiwork on this tranquil island.
2	Elbow Cay	The quaintest of all Bahamian villages, this place seems more like a Hollywood set than reality. The population is scarce, and you've got much of the place to yourself except for some feral cats, curly-tailed lizards, and cooing doves.
1	Eleuthera	The celebrities of yesteryear have long departed, leaving this 100-mile long island asleep in the sun. You get not only sun, but sands and not a lot of other people.

14) If you're traveling with children . . .

Rating	Island	Why?
4	New Providence	You can visit an aquarium, zoo, and dolphin encounter program, as well as enjoy children's camps at Atlantis, the Radisson, and elsewhere.
3	Grand Bahama	Our Lucaya's children's program, plus the Dolphin Experience, make a kid's stay enjoyable.
2	Elbow Cay	Here you can find family-friendly villas, but there's not much to do beyond the beach.
1	Exuma	The cottages of Latitude Exuma Resort, the only place to stay on peaceful, undeveloped Rolle Cay, off George Town, are kid friendly.

15) If you want to get there quickly and easily . . .

Rating	Island	Why?
4	**New Providence**	Airlines offer plenty of daily flights (a little more than 3 hours from New York or 50 minutes from Miami).
3	**Grand Bahama**	There aren't as many daily flights, but the trip is a shorter (a 40-minute flight from Miami).
2	**Exuma**	You can catch just one or two flights a day to this island, but travel time from Miami is a comfortable hour and 40 minutes.
1	**San Salvador**	Weekly charters take 3 hours and 15 minutes from New York or an hour and 45 minutes from Miami. Small airlines also connect San Salvador with Florida twice a week and Nassau daily.

Step 3: Tally the scores to determine your final favorite(s)

After you review all the categories and plug scores into your scorecard for all islands in the categories that matter to you, add up each the results.

And the winner is . . . the island with the highest total score. Chances are this island will be the one that most caters to your vacation needs. If a second island scores high, consider dividing your time between the two — that is, if they're close enough or accessible enough. If a third island scores high as well, you have an excuse to plan your next vacation there.

"Rate the Islands" Scorecard

POINTS FOR:	Elbow Cay	Eleuthera	Exuma	Grand Bahama	Green Turtle Cay	Harbour Island	New Providence	San Salvador	Treasure Cay
1) Luxury									
2) Beach Bargains									
3) Solitude									
4) Nightlife									
5) Great Food									
6) Best Beaches									
7) Island Spice									
8) Golf									
9) Sightseeing									
10) Diving/Snorkeling									
11) Fishing									
12) Island-Hopping									
13) Peace & Quiet									
14) Families									
15) Easy Access									
TOTAL SCORE:									

Chapter 2

Spice of Life

● ●

In This Chapter

▶ Discovering the ways of the islands

▶ Enjoying island music

▶ Eating and drinking like a local

● ●

*P*art of the fun of visiting The Bahamas is for a big taste of island life — and that means listening to junkanoo music, eating conch prepared in countless ways, meeting the friendly locals (who'd rather not be called "natives"), proclaiming guava duff your favorite dessert, finding the bar that makes the best Bahama Mamas, and in general, putting yourself on "island time," which is one slow-moving clock.

We deal with some reality here — and not tourist hype. Most of the 3½ million visitors arriving in the islands have little intention of meeting the locals or sampling Bahamian life. Chances are, they'll anchor at their beachfront resort and hardly leave the grounds except for some duty-free shopping. For the traveler — not the tourist — who wants a sample, however small, of island ways, this chapter previews attractions ranging from music to edibles and rum-laced punches to Bahamian talk.

Living on Island Time

The first thing you have to get used to in The Bahamas is that island clocks aren't wound as tightly as in other parts of the world. Life in The Bahamas moves much more slowly than most visitors are used to. Waiters, salespeople, and hotel desk clerks operate at what many outsiders consider too leisurely a pace. Especially in Nassau and Freeport, you may find some poorly trained, less than accommodating tourist industry staff members here and there. But getting annoyed is a waste of energy. Most new arrivals soon learn to go with the flow and get in step with island time where everything takes longer. If you're going to enjoy your vacation, you have to crank your expectations about time — and sometimes service — down a notch.

Learning the Language

Patois is the language of the street, and it has its own cadence and musical rhythm. Sometimes an educated Bahamian dining with you will speak a lilting Queen's English like that taught at Oxford and then suddenly lapse into patois when he hits on an emotional subject.

Accents in The Bahamas resemble those of the Caribbean region, just south of these Atlantic isles. However, a trained ear can easily pick up the difference. Some Bahamians sound as if they were imported from Brooklyn. For example, *woik* is what you do *fuh* a living, and a waiter will *soive* you.

Sometimes the letters *v* and *w* are interchanged. "So you wisitin', ay?" translates into "So you're visiting, are you?" If a Bahamian tells you he's going *spilligatin',* he means that he's planning to "carry on bad." In short, he intends to party and have an all-out good time. If he says he wants to *conversate* (a common Bahamian variation on the word converse) with you for a while, he wants to chat.

Surprisingly, some of the Loyalist villages such as those found in Eleuthera, including Spanish Wells, retain certain pronunciations in use in the England of Shakespeare's day. The glass in which your rum punch is served may be called a goblet. Conversely, some words brought from Africa by the slaves are still in general use — *nyam* meaning to eat or *bobo* for a moron.

Jumping to Junkanoo or Goombay

The Bahamas maintains great pride in its original musical idioms, often comparing their vitality to the more famous musical traditions of Jamaica, Puerto Rico, and Trinidad. Other than the spirituals, which share roots with slave music from colonial North America, by far the most famous musical products are Goombay and its closely linked sibling, Junkanoo.

Goombay music is an art form with melodies and body movements that are always accompanied by the beat of goatskin drums and, when available, the liberal consumption of rum. The most outlandish expressions of Goombay occur the day after Christmas (Boxing Day), especially in Nassau on Bay Street. Dancers outfit themselves in masquerade costumes with bizarre accessories and glittering colors that evoke the plumage of jungle birds. Goombay musicians and dancers are almost always male. See December under "Calendar of Events" in Chapter 3.

Junkanoo music is to The Bahamas what reggae is to Jamaica. In other words, you can't miss hearing the music. All hotels and resorts, and

Tipping tips

You can't forget to tip in The Bahamas because your waiter, taxi driver, baggage carrier, and tour guide will remind you. Many restaurants make it easy (or annoying, if the service wasn't any good) by automatically adding 15 percent to your bill. Taxi drivers usually get 15 percent of the fare and baggage carriers, about $1 per bag. With tour guides, the guideline is a bit looser; many vacationers give a couple of dollars per person for a group tour.

even some restaurants, offer this music as part of the evening's entertainment. Some musical groups even call themselves "Junkanoo." It's a lot safer to hear this music performed by locals in resorts or hotels than it is to wander the back streets of Nassau at night looking for some local club. If you do the latter, you could get mugged — and for no good reason, because the music will probably be just as authentic at the resort.

If you won't be in The Bahamas for Boxing Day, you can still get a taste of **Junkanoo at Café Johnny Canoe** on Cable Beach, where the weekly Friday night parade turns this New Providence restaurant into a party (Chapter 11). If you want a close-up look at the elaborate costumes, stop by the **Junkanoo Expo at Prince George Dock** in Nassau (see Chapter 15).

Enjoying Island Edibles

When it's time to chow down in The Bahamas, settings range from casual family-run restaurants featuring local treats to elegant candlelit dining rooms offering gourmet international fare. The main source of food is the ocean. The steak you order may be juicy, but it didn't come from an island cattle farm. Instead, it was flown in to the restaurant, along with lamb and other meats, as well as most of the fruits and vegetables on your plate.

You find plenty of good food here, and some mediocre eats as well — imported or not. Menus throughout the islands are varied. You may dine on an Indian or Greek appetizer one night, an Italian or Tex-Mex main course another, and a French dessert the next.

Are you traveling with fussy kids? Don't worry. Burgers and fries, pizza, fried chicken, pasta, sandwiches, and other child-friendly "fixin's" are easy to find, especially in Nassau and Freeport/Lucaya, where you see some fast-food chains.

For the tastiest, most authentic (and least expensive) island cuisine, head to the smaller, locally run restaurants, where the home-style cooking revolves around the sea. Even the so-called island dishes at the larger hotels and restaurants have American and continental influences.

In the dining sections of the chapters, we sprinkle in a number of local eateries serving authentic and always affordable Bahamian cuisine. In Nassau, sample island cuisine at **Mama Lyddy's Place**, **The Pink Pearl Café,** or **Shoal Restaurant and Lounge** (see Chapter 11). On Grand Bahama Island, bite down at **Becky's Restaurant & Lounge** or **Fatman's Nephew** (see Chapter 15). Once you reach many of the Out Islands, Bahamian food is all you can order in some of the smaller places, except for a first-class resort here and there, including those found at Harbour Island.

Cooking up Bahamian favorites

The star of the culinary show is conch (pronounced "konk"). On every island, at the edge of the water near boat docks, you see huge mounds of discarded conch shells, the kind with the shiny pink spiral interior, the shells that you put to your ear to hear the waves. Residents claim that conch gives men "strong back." In other words, this tasty mollusk can raise the roof in the boudoir. No wonder the meat is transformed into so many local favorites, including:

- ✔ **Conch chowder:** A rich, spicy soup with vegetables and bits of conch.

- ✔ **Conch fritters:** Golf ball-sized fried appetizers made with chopped conch, herbs, flour, baking powder, and water.

- ✔ **Conch salad:** Minced raw, marinated in lime juice, and mixed with chopped onions and peppers.

- ✔ **Cracked conch:** Pounded until tender, battered, and deep fried like a breaded veal cutlet.

- ✔ **Scorched conch:** Raw meat washed with seawater and lime juice, cut into large pieces and scored with the knife, and then rubbed with hot pepper and topped with sliced fresh tomatoes and onions. (You may catch fishermen on docks preparing this delicacy.)

- ✔ **Steamed conch:** Tenderized by beating or boiling and then cooked with sautéed onions, bell peppers, hot peppers, thyme, tomatoes, and sometimes okra or carrots.

- ✔ **Stewed conch:** Made with a seasoned, flour-thickened gravy.

Fish, another staple, turns up for dinner, lunch, and even breakfast. Grouper, with its mild flavor, and snapper are the usual suspects. *Boil fish* (cooked with salt pork, onions, and green peppers) is a popular morning eye-opener that comes with grits. Many places also often serve delicately sweet johnnycake (a mildly sweet bread) on the side. Also eaten as the day's first meal, stewed fish comes in a rich brown gravy. Steamed fish (which may sound bland, but is far from it), however, isn't eaten before noon and is cooked with a tomato base.

Local lobster is a bit tougher than the Maine variety, but it's prepared in lots of tasty ways: steamed, breaded, sautéed in butter, or topped with grated cheese. To make minced lobster, a Bahamian winner served in the shell, chefs shred the meat and cook it with tomatoes, green peppers, and onions.

A limited number of chickens are raised locally in The Bahamas, mostly on Eleuthera. *Chicken souse* is a popular dish made with chicken, onion, sweet peppers, bay leaves, allspice, and other ingredients, as the cook's imagination dictates. It's simmered in a pot for about an hour, then lime juice is added, and it's simmered a little longer. Pig's feet souse is also a favorite dish.

Goats and sheep are also raised on the Out Islands. On a menu, "mutton" can refer to either meat. It's often curried. Wild boar is caught on some of the islands, and game birds such as ducks and pigeons are hunted. Raccoon stew is also eaten.

Most meats, including pork, veal, and beef, are imported. Even with these meats, however, Bahamian cooks show their ingenuity with interesting variations. For example, at an Out Island inn, we recently enjoyed pork that had been marinated with vinegar, garlic, onion, celery tops, cloves, mustard, and Worcestershire sauce and then baked and served with gravy. Even a simple baked ham is given a Bahamian touch, cooked with fresh pineapple, coconut milk, coconut flakes, mustard, honey, and brown sugar.

Many vegetables are grown in The Bahamas; others are imported. If it's a cucumber, you can be almost certain it's from one of Edison Key's farms in North Abaco. They supply cucumbers to not only their own country, but to about 5% of the stateside market as well. Bahamians also grow their own sweet potatoes, corn, cassava, okra, and peppers (both sweet and hot), among other produce.

Lunch and dinner come with heaping portions of peas and rice, potato salad, coleslaw, or macaroni and cheese and sometimes all these tasty side dishes.

Guava duff is the dessert specialty of The Bahamas, although one cook confided to us, "It takes too long, and we don't like to make it anymore unless there's a special call for it."

The dessert, which resembles a jelly roll, is made with guava pulp that has been run through a food mill or sieve. Nobody seems to agree on the best method of cooking it. One way is to cream sugar and butter and add eggs and spices such as cinnamon and cloves or nutmeg. The flour is made into a stiff dough and mixed with the guava pulp, which is then placed in the top of a double boiler and cooked over boiling water for hours. It can also be boiled or steamed, and threesome cooks insist it should be baked. Guava duff is served with hard sauce (a blend of butter, confectioners' sugar, vanilla, and rum).

Other tasty Bahamian desserts and breads include coconut tarts, coconut jimmie, benne seedcakes, and potato bread.

Eating like a local

Restaurants specializing in island cuisine commonly serve conch, fish (especially grouper), and lobster. Among other favorites, but harder to find outside of people's homes, are crab and rice, okra soup, chicken and dough (dumplings), mutton, wild boar, and *souse*. If you stop by a local restaurant in the morning and see men eating souse or conch salad, chances are they're trying to kill hangovers; locals believe that the hot peppers do the trick. The best places to taste-test some of these treats are

- ✔ Restaurants on Arawak Cay, between Cable Beach and downtown Nassau on New Providence. Sometimes you can make a special request here and then return the next day for your meal.

- ✔ Stands on Potter's Cay, the dock beneath the Paradise Island exit bridge on New Providence (see Chapter 11).

- ✔ Many restaurants in The Bahamas' Out Islands (see Chapters 21 through 24).

- ✔ Kiosks during Bahamian festivals such as Junkanoo (at Christmas and New Year's) and the Family Island Regatta (in George Town, Exuma, in April).

Drinking island cocktails

Vacationers and residents alike satisfy their thirst with beer, much of it imported from the United States, Germany, and the Netherlands.

These imports have a higher alcohol content than the same brands of foreign beer sold in the U.S. The Bahamas' own high-quality brew is called *Kalik,* named for the sound cowbells make in Bahamian Junkanoo music.

If you're not a beer drinker, colorful rum and fruit juice concoctions are the rage. Depending on who makes them, the ingredients and proportions vary; most bartenders won't reveal the secrets of their success. Besides rum punch, the top three tropical island cocktails are

- ✔ **Bahama Mama:** Vat 19, citrus juice (often pineapple), bitters, a dash of nutmeg, crème de cassis, and a hint of grenadine.

- ✔ **Goombay Smash:** Coconut rum, pineapple juice, lemon juice, Triple Sec, Vat 19, and a dash of syrup.

- ✔ **Yellowbird:** Crème de banana liqueur, Vat 19, orange juice, pineapple, apricot brandy, and Galliano.

Of course, colas and other sodas, bottled (and sometimes freshly squeezed) juices, and bottled water are sold on all islands. Although tap water is safe for tooth brushing, most people drink bottled or filtered water.

Chapter 3

Deciding When to Go

● ●

In This Chapter

▶ Getting a handle on the weather

▶ Evaluating the seasons

▶ Planning your trip around special celebrations

● ●

*T*he Bahamas have their high season in winter and their low season in summer, but any time of the year can be a good time for a visit — that is, if the weather holds. Off-season can bring hurricanes, but you'll receive plenty of warnings before these storms arrive.

This chapter highlights not only the weather but the best year-round happenings, ranging from Junkanoo parades to sailing regattas in the Exumas.

Forecasting the Weather

Bahamian weather falls into two main seasons: winter, or *high season,* and summer, or *low season.* Especially in the more northerly Bahamas, high season can also mean surprisingly cool weather. Cool spells, if they descend at all, blow away rather quickly, and you're back on the beach after a day or two. The southerly Bahamian islands, on the other hand, truly live up to their reputation of being "June all year-round."

The Bahamas are in the Atlantic, just north of the warmer Caribbean region. Their location is why winter in the subtropical Bahamas can be spring-like, even though their Caribbean neighbors boast year-round beach weather.

Visiting in high season

High season (or winter) is roughly November through April, which is the cooler, drier, and more expensive time of year to visit. In The Bahamas, temperatures (in degrees Fahrenheit) can reach the high 70s or low 80s, but they can also hover in the low 60s.

If you're not willing to risk a few days that are better suited to golf and tennis than to sand and surf, you may not want to book your vacation during January or February. The mean monthly temperature is 85°F (29°C), with winter generally ranging from the low 70s to the low 80s (in degrees Fahrenheit). Table 3-1 lists the average monthly temperatures, and Table 3-2 gives you the average monthly rainfall in inches.

Spring break occurs during the high season (from late February through mid-April). The weather may not leave you cold, wet, or blown away, but if you're not a 20-something looking to party, you may want to avoid the area. This is the time of year when many hotels, restaurants, and beaches are packed with vacationing American college students who have clearly checked their inhibitions at the airport. During these festive weeks, you can treat yourself to an extra dose of entertainment, including sporting events, beach parties, and musical performances.

Table 3-1				Average Monthly Temperatures							
Jan	Feb	Mar	Apr	May	June	July	Aug	Sep	Oct	Nov	Dec
70°F	70°F	72°F	75°F	77°F	80°F	81°F	82°F	81°F	78°F	74°F	71°F
21°C	21°C	22°C	24°C	25°C	27°C	27°C	28°C	27°C	26°C	23°C	22°C

Table 3-2				Average Monthly Rainfall							
Jan	Feb	Mar	Apr	May	June	July	Aug	Sep	Oct	Nov	Dec
1.9"	1.6"	1.4"	1.9"	4.8"	9.2"	6.1"	6.3"	7.5"	8.3"	2.3"	1.5"
(4.1 cm)	(3.6 cm)	(5 cm)	(12.2 cm)	(23.4 cm)	(5 cm)	(15.5 cm)	(16 cm)	(19.1 cm)	(21.1 cm)	(5.8 cm)	(3.8 cm)

Checking out the islands in low season

Summer, or low season — May through October — is warmer and wetter and therefore the less expensive time to travel. Most rain falls between June and October. However, showers are generally brief, often coming in the late afternoon, and sometimes the sun doesn't bother to stop shining during downpours.

As pleasant as you may find the balmy subtropical summer, it's also hurricane season. Officially, hurricane season lasts from June through November, but these storms are most likely to arrive during late August, September, or October. Although summer or fall travel can save you a few bucks, it can also cancel your trip. You can, of course, insure yourself in case you're forced to cancel your Bahamian vacation because of a hurricane or some other reason (see Chapter 8).

The good news is that hurricanes aren't all that common in The Bahamas. Even if one is slated to hit during your vacation, you usually have enough warning (with the help of satellite forecasts) to rearrange your plans. If you do travel during this time of year, contact your local branch of the National Weather Service — listed under the U.S. Department of Commerce in the telephone directory — to keep abreast of weather patterns.

Although average temperatures in The Bahamas may vary only about 12 degrees Fahrenheit throughout the year (see Table 3-1), days in the high 80s in degrees Fahrenheit are common during the summer, and winter temperatures can sink into the low 60s in degrees Fahrenheit. Especially during winter months, early morning and evening temperatures are often cool enough to require sweaters or jackets, even when you wear beach gear during the day.

Calendar of Events

Here are some special events that you may want to keep in mind when you plan your vacation.

January

New Year's Day Junkanoo Parades (various Bahamian islands) are held throughout The Bahamas, but the most spectacular one is on Bay Street in downtown Nassau on New Providence. The annual Junkanoo Parade begins in the wee hours (around 1 a.m.). People dance down the street to the sound of cowbells, goatskin drums, and whistles. But don't look for familiar faces; they're hidden behind elaborate masks and costumes (ranging from giant conch shells to overgrown silk cotton trees) that have taken months to create. With roots in Africa, this festival (also held on Boxing Day, December 26) is the Bahamian version of Rio de Janeiro's *Carnival* and New Orleans' *Mardi Gras*. A traditional breakfast of *boil fish* and *johnnycake* (see Chapter 2) caps off the parade.

Want to jump up with the Nassau crowd? Visitors are welcome to participate. Contact **X-plorers Junkanoo** to make arrangements at ☎ 242-361-0907 or 242-325-3567; Fax: 242-361-7448; Junkanoo@batelnet.bs; www.batelnet.bs/junkanoo. For more details about the Nassau parade, contact the Ministry of Youth, Sports & Culture, ☎ **242-325-9370**; Fax 242-394-5920.

A Junkanoo Parade also is held on Grand Bahama; call ☎ **242-352-8044** for information.

Some 40 (17- to 28-foot) locally built sailing sloops duke it out for the championship during the **Annual New Year's Day Sailing Regatta**

(Nassau and Paradise Island) organized by The Bahamas Boat Owners Association. For details, contact the Rev. Phillip McPhee, Ministry of Youth, Sports & Culture, ☎ 242-325-9370; Fax: 242-394-5920.

On New Year's Day, with beach party spectators cheering them on, daring (crazy) swimmers plunge into Cable Beach waters, which huge blocks of ice cool, during the **Polar Bear Swim** (Nassau). For details, contact Tom Muir of the Canadian Men's Club, ☎ 242-322-6504.

Test your skill at snagging one of the ocean's fastest fish (wahoo), which can cut through the waves at speeds up to 70 miles per hour. The **Annual Bahamas Wahoo Championships** (Abaco). is held in Marsh Harbour and Treasure Cay. For details, call ☎ 800-32-SPORT or check out the Web site at www.bahamaswahoo.com.

February

More than 500 visiting yachts flock to Exuma for a splashy week of fun and competition during the **Annual Georgetown Cruising Regatta** (Exuma). For details, contact the Exuma Tourist Office at ☎ 242-336-2430; Fax: 242-336-2431.

The **Farmer's Cay Festival**, held February 4, is a rendezvous for yachts-men cruising the Exuma Islands and a homecoming for the people of Farmer's Cay, Exuma. Boat excursions depart Nassau for the festival at 8 p.m. from Potter's Cay on February 3 and return to Nassau at 8 p.m. February 4 from Farmer's Cay Dock. For information, contact Terry Bain in Little Farmer's Cay, Exuma at ☎ 242-355-4006/2093 or the Exuma Tourist Office at ☎ 242-336-2430.

March

The day-long **Annual Garden of the Groves Art Festival** (Grand Bahama) takes place at the flourishing Garden of the Groves. Bring the kids for the local arts and crafts, music, food, and pony rides, as well as a sky-diving exhibition. Call ☎ 242-352-8044.

Hope Town, Elbow Cay, shows off its creativity with a display of water-colors, oils, wood-carvings, and sculpture during its **Annual Art Exhibition** (Abaco). Call Abaco Inn at ☎ 242-366-0133.

The prestigious weeklong **Bacardi Billfish Tournament** attracts the Who's Who of deep-sea fishing March 18 to 23, 2003. Headquarters is the Bimini Big Game Fishing Club & Marina. For more information, call ☎ 800-737-1007 or 242-347-3391.

If you can't get to The Bahamas on Boxing Day (December 26) or New Year's Day, you can still catch Junkanoo festivities at Marsh Harbour during the **Easter Junkanoo Parade** (Abaco). Contact the Abaco Tourist Office, ☎ 242-367-3067.

Men, women, and children are welcome to compete in the popular **Annual Abaco Anglers Fishing Tournament**. Contact the Abaco Tourist Office, ☎ 242-367-3067.

Visitors can join residents on the green during the **Rotary Club of Lucaya Annual Golf Tournament** (Grand Bahama). Call the Grand Bahama Island Tourist Board, ☎ 242-352-8044.

Every single Bahamian living abroad seemingly comes home for the **Family Island Regatta** (Exuma). If you're planning to visit George Town during this weeklong event, book your room months in advance. As the handcrafted sloops, owned and sailed by Bahamians, compete in Elizabeth Harbour, you're busy with nonstop eating, drinking, and socializing. Food stalls, set up along the waterfront, tempt you with fresh pineapple, grilled chicken, peas and rice, and conch in all its incarnations. Special events include a parade, junkanoo bands and police bands, and nightly parties. If you're in Nassau but would like to hop over for the festivities, special excursions are set up to get you here by a motor boat or plane. Contact the Exuma Tourist Office, ☎ 242-336-2430; Fax: 242-336-2431.

May

Taking place in the waters off beautiful Green Turtle Cay, the popular, challenging **Annual Green Turtle Club Billfish Tournament** (Abaco) draws serious anglers, but amateurs are welcome as well. Entertainment and other festivities surround the tournament. Contact the Green Turtle Club & Marina, ☎ 242-365-4271; Fax: 242-365-4272; www.green turtleclub.com/fishtourn.htm.

June

If you feel sorry for the fish, join this tag and release tournament (meaning the fish are caught, quickly tagged, and then thrown back into the ocean) at the Treasure Cay Resort. For details about the **Treasure Cay Billfish Tournament** (Abaco), e-mail info@treasurecay.com, visit the Web site at www.treasurecay.com, or call ☎ 242-365-8535.

July

Regatta Time in Abaco (Abaco) is an eight-day series of five boat races that lures plenty of sailors during The Bahamas' Independence Week. Beach parties, dances, and live music accompany the races. Contact Dave or Kathy Ralph, ☎ **242-367-2677;** Fax: 242-367-3677.

October

Visit the small fishing village of McClean's Town to watch fast-fingered contestants race each other to extract the greatest number of conchs from shells in the shortest amount of time. The **Annual McClean's Town Conch Cracking Contest** (Grand Bahama) takes place on Discovery Day (October 12, also known as Columbus Day), when Columbus first landed in the New World. For details, contact the Grand Bahama Island Tourism Board, ☎ **242-352-8044;** Fax: 242-352-7840.

November

The best celebrations of **Guy Fawkes Day** occur in Nassau. Nighttime parades throughout the streets are held on many of the islands, culminating in the hanging and burning of Guy Fawkes, an effigy of the British malefactor who was involved in the Gunpowder Plot of 1605 in London. It usually takes place around November 5, but check with island tourist offices (☎ **242-328-7810**).

Anglers take up the tough challenge of baiting one of the fastest fishes in the ocean during the **Bimini Big Game Fishing Club All Wahoo Tournament** November 15 to 18. Headquarters is the Bimini Big Game Fishing Club & Marina. For information, contact ☎ **800-737-1007** or 242-347-3391. The three-day **Annual One Bahamas Music & Heritage Festival** is staged at both Nassau and Paradise Island to celebrate national unity November 24 to 26. Highlights include concerts featuring top Bahamian performing artists, as well as "fun walks" on the island and other activities. For more information, contact the **Nassau/Paradise Island Tourist Office** at ☎ **242-326-0633, ext. 4100**).

Traveling on a holiday

Bahamians, like Americans, celebrate familiar holidays, such as New Year's Day, Good Friday, Easter, and Christmas, but you should also prepare for closed businesses, shorter hours, or wild partying on Easter Monday, Whitmonday (seven weeks after Easter), Labour Day (the first Friday in June), Independence Day (July 10), Emancipation Day (the first Monday in August), Discovery Day (October 12), and Boxing Day (December 26).

December

To the tune (and beat) of traditional and Bahamian Christmas music, the renowned Royal Bahamas Police Force Band performs a precision drill during the **Beat Retreat** (Nassau). Contact Sergeant Darville, ☎ **242-322-2020.**

The famed Junkanoo Parade kicks off on **Boxing Day** December 26. (See January events, earlier in this chapter.) This holiday was inherited from Queen Victoria's Day in England when it was a time for the upper-class to give gifts of cash or presents — in boxes, of course — to the lower class, usually servants. These gifts were given in boxes.

Chapter 4

Pillow Talk: Bahamian Accommodations

In This Chapter

▶ Checking out the options

▶ Getting the best room for the cheapest rate

▶ Choosing the best resort or hotel for you

*W*hen you're visiting an archipelago as vast and, in some cases, as difficult to reach as parts of The Bahamas, knowing the pillow you're going to sleep on that night becomes all important. It's not like a visit to London where, if you don't like a particular hotel, you can check out the next morning and take a taxi to one more to your liking.

Throughout the guide, we give you honest and candid descriptions about what to expect from a hotel. Working like a "marriage broker," we hope to match you up with the right mate for your island fantasy. If you land in the wrong place, especially if you've already prepaid, your vacation may spell disaster.

This chapter tells you what you need to know about the types of accommodations awaiting you on each island. In Grand Bahamas and New Providence, you have a choice. In the Out Islands, the lack of accommodations greatly restricts you.

Deciding What Type of Lodging Suits You

Where you want to sleep often determines your choice of island. The type of accommodation you have in mind means that you should consider some islands and write off others. For example, perhaps you're dreaming of napping in your personal hammock at the edge of a secluded beach right in front of your individually decorated bungalow. Your choices are very limited on New Providence and Grand

Bahamas. However, The Bahamas' Out Islands offer lots of small, peaceful, beachfront lodgings.

If your ideal vacation includes a hotel with a wide choice of restaurants, Las Vegas-style extravaganzas, and nightly dancing, steer clear of the Bahamas' Out Islands and head to New Providence, Paradise Island, or Grand Bahama.

Certain hotels allow children under a set age to stay free or at reduced rates in a room with an adult (and many dining rooms offer children's menus with lower prices and smaller portions than the regular fare).

Rooming on the main islands

Rooms in the larger hotels on New Providence, Paradise Island, and Grand Bahama are air-conditioned (some also have ceiling fans) and come with satellite TV and direct-dial telephones. Most have two double beds or one king-size bed in each room, plus a balcony or patio. Many are also equipped with irons and ironing boards, coffeemakers, mini bars or refrigerators, hair dryers, and in-room safes. Some have Internet access, and sometimes CD players. U.S. newspapers — usually from Miami or New York — are generally available. Expect to find daily and nightly activities, along with facilities such as restaurants, shops, hair and nail salons, and (on the premises or nearby) watersports operators. Many hotels also have elevators and rooms that are wheelchair accessible. Likewise, some offer supervised children's programs.

In many cases, you're on your own, without on-premises restaurants or activities desks to provide information, help you set up excursions, call taxis, or assist with other arrangements.

Bahamian landlords offer plenty of villas and condos for rent on the main islands, but first-time visitors may want to skip them because you should be familiar with the island and getting around by car.

The more elegant and expensive villas rentals offer maid service, and in some cases, even your own cook — for an extra fee, of course. At other cheaper rentals, you may have to do your own cleaning and cooking.

Choosing the less developed islands

You won't find high-rise hotels in the Out Islands. A few islands offer posh digs with rooms and facilities as snazzy as those on busier islands — for example, Pink Sands on Harbour Island (see Chapter 21) or Green Turtle Club & Marina on Green Turtle Cay in the Abacos (see Chapter 19). Still, these low-rise lodgings are far less formal than upscale hotels on New Providence, Paradise Island, or Grand Bahama.

Accommodations on the less developed islands may or may not be air-conditioned, but ceiling fans or good cross ventilation do the trick if they're not. Some rooms may have two double beds, while others may have only one. In rare cases, some rooms may offer only twin beds. In the Out Islands, many hotel rooms don't have telephones, and many don't come with televisions or radios. In hotels that do have TVs in the rooms, the channels are centrally controlled (usually at the bar), so don't be surprised if the mystery you're watching suddenly turns into a soccer game just before the murderer's identity is revealed. If any of these things are important to you, ask about them before making your reservation.

In many cases in the Out Islands, you don't have to worry about losing your room key, because you don't get one in the first place. (No one locks their doors.) Forgot your beach reading? You're likely to find a selection of dog-eared paperbacks left by previous vacationers in your room. You can even take one of these books home with you — as long as you leave one of yours behind in its place.

It may surprise you to know that quite a few hotels have *honor bars,* where there's no bartender. Guests simply take or mix their own drinks, write them down, and pay for them when they check out. With this trusting attitude, it's no wonder that staff members at these small, easy-going hotels quickly get to know guests, and they're not shy about sharing tips about their favorite parts of the islands.

Independent-type families with children or groups of friends or relatives traveling together find villas, condos, and hotel rooms with kitchens convenient places to stay on the quieter, less developed islands. On less developed islands, hotels are small enough that managers themselves are usually willing to help you make arrangements for water sports, dining, transportation, and other activities that may or may not be on the premises.

If you or someone in your group is in a wheelchair, ask about the specifics of the landscape and the facilities at hotels on the less developed islands. Some hotels, such as a few on Harbour Island and Green Turtle Cay in the Abacos, have hilly grounds or lots of steps.

Knowing What to Expect at Your Accommodation

The Bahamas offers a wide selection of accommodations, ranging from small private guesthouses to large luxury resorts. Hotels vary in size and facilities, from deluxe (offering room service, sports, swimming pools, entertainment, and so on) to fairly simple Out Island inns.

There is no rigid classification of hotel properties in the islands. The word "deluxe" is often used (or misused) when "first class" may be the more appropriate term. "First class" itself often isn't. For that and other reasons, we present fairly detailed descriptions of the properties so that you'll get an idea of what to expect. However, even in the deluxe and first-class resorts and hotels, don't expect top-rate service and efficiency. "Things," as they are called in the islands, don't seem to work as well here as they do in certain fancy resorts of California, Florida, or Europe.

Travelers to The Bahamas have the following options:

✔ Hotels and resorts

✔ All-inclusive resorts

✔ Out Island Inns

✔ Villas, condos, and timeshares

✔ Guesthouses

✔ Fishing lodges

Hotels and resorts — your options

If you want to live in luxury, your best and sometimes only bets are New Providence with its array of hotels and resorts spread from Cable Beach to Nassau to Paradise Island. The second largest concentration of hotels and resorts is on Grand Bahamas Island, centered mainly at Freeport or Lucaya.

Except for certain pockets of luxury such as Harbour Island off the coast of Eleuthera, resort pickings grow slim as you explore the Out Islands. Hotels are small except Club Med on San Salvador. High rises don't exist. Most of the Out Islands have inns rather than large hotels. Some are very basic, often in dull concrete blocks, but our recommendations have style and a bit of class.

As opposed to renting a private villa, we recommend these mainstream hotels and resort for the following:

✔ Families who want plenty of amusements for their kids and sitters close at hand.

✔ Sports lovers who seek golf or water sports facilities.

✔ Honeymooners or couples who want to focus on each other.

✔ First-time visitors to The Bahamas.

✔ Travelers with disabilities.

Hotels and resorts also have a downside:

- ✔ Island spice doesn't exist in most of these places.

- ✔ Guests tend to be resort bound and don't get to sample an island's offerings or charms.

- ✔ As on a cruise ship, all those extra expenses mount quickly. You may get a shock when it's time to pay up.

The all-inclusive: simplifying your vacation

A hugely popular option in Jamaica, the all-inclusive resort hotel concept finally has a foothold in The Bahamas. At such resorts, everything is included — sometimes even drinks. You get your room and all meals, plus entertainment and many water sports (although some cost extra). Some people find the cost of this all-inclusive holiday cheaper than if they'd paid individually for each item, and some simply appreciate knowing in advance what their final bill will be. The first all-inclusive resort hotel in The Bahamas was **Club Med** (☎ **800-258-2633**) at its property on Paradise Island. This is not a swinging-singles kind of place; it's popular with everybody from honeymooners to families with kids along. There's another Club Med in San Salvador, in the southern Bahamas, which has more of a luxurious hideaway atmosphere.

The biggest all-inclusive of them all, **Sandals** (☎ **800-SANDALS**), came to The Bahamas in 1995 on Cable Beach. This Jamaican company is now walking its sandals across the Caribbean, having established firm beachheads in Ocho Rios, Montego Bay, and Negril. The most famous of the all-inclusives (but not necessarily the best), it caters only to male-female couples, having long ago rescinded its initial policy of "Any two people in love."

Good candidates for all-inclusive resorts are

- ✔ Honeymooners
- ✔ Families
- ✔ Inexperienced travelers
- ✔ The budget-conscious
- ✔ The super-stressed

What's the downside?

- ✔ Because you've paid for everything in advance, you may feel obligated to spend all your time at the resort and not venture out to see what's happening beyond the compound.

✔ In an all inclusive, you could almost be anywhere on any island. You live in a cocoon and miss what makes your island special.

✔ Too exhuberant activity coordinators feel it's their job to keep you occupied day and night. This "organized fun" may not be for you.

Villas: vacationing with the comforts of home

You may want to rent a villa, a good-size apartment in someone's condo or time share or even a small beach cottage (more accurately called a *cabana*).

Private apartments come with or without maid service, so ask up front exactly what to expect. This is more of a no-frills option than the villas and condos. The apartments may not be in buildings with swimming pools, and they may not have a front desk to help you.

Many cottages or cabanas ideally open onto a beach, although others may be clustered around a communal swimming pool. Most of them are fairly simple, containing no more than a plain bedroom plus a small kitchen and bathroom. In the peak winter season, reservations should be made at least five or six months in advance.

VHR Worldwide (☎ 800-633-3284 or 201-767-9393) offers the most comprehensive portfolio of luxury villas, condominiums, resort suites, and apartments for rent not only in The Bahamas, but also in the Caribbean. **Hideaways International** (☎ 888-843-4433 in the U.S., or 603-430-4433; www.hideaways.com) publishes *Hideaways Guide,* a 148-page pictorial directory of home rentals throughout the world, with full descriptions so you know what you're renting. Rentals range from cottages to staffed villas to whole islands. On most rentals, you deal directly with owners. At condos and small resorts, Hideaways offers member discounts. Other services include specialty cruises, yacht charters, airline ticketing, car rentals, and hotel reservations. Annual membership is $129; a four-month trial membership is $49.

Sometimes local tourist offices will also advise you on vacation-home rentals if you write or call them directly

We recommend villas for:

✔ Families.

✔ A group of friends.

✔ Honeymooners or couples craving privacy.

✔ Independent travelers who want to connect with the island.

But staying at a home-away-from-home can also have a downside:

- ✔ You don't get the extensive dining facilities and other amenities of a resort.

- ✔ A villa may not offer daily maid service and other niceties (like a pool or Jacuzzi) that you consider vital to your relaxation.

- ✔ Few are located right on the beach; resorts usually snag the prime real estate.

- ✔ You definitely won't get (or be subjected to, depending on your point of view) the nightly entertainment that almost every Bahamian hotel trumpets.

- ✔ The good news is you're isolated. The bad news is you're isolated, so you'd better really like your traveling companion.

- ✔ Of all the travel options, villas are least likely to live up to their brochure promises.

We recommend condos and timeshares for:

- ✔ Families. You can feed your kids what you want and not have to suffer disapproving looks from the honeymooners at the next table when junior flips his soggy cereal on the floor.

- ✔ A group of friends.

- ✔ Older couples looking for quiet.

- ✔ Long-term vacationers. Cooking your own meals is a great money-saving tactic for an extended stay on an island.

- ✔ Independent travelers who want to connect with the island and its people.

What are some drawbacks of staying at a condo or timeshare?

- ✔ All the comforts of home, plus all the work.

- ✔ Limited amenities.

- ✔ You're trusting your tropical dream to someone else's decorating taste.

- ✔ When dinner time comes, you're the staff as well as the diner.

Guesthouses: living like a Bahamian

The guesthouse is where many Bahamians themselves stay when they're traveling in their own islands. In The Bahamas, however, the term "guesthouse" can mean anything. Sometimes so-called guesthouses are really like simple motels built around swimming pools.

Others are small individual cottages, with their own kitchenettes, constructed around a main building in which you'll often find a bar and restaurant serving local food.

In the Out Islands, the guesthouses are no-frills. Those we've recommended are clean, decent, and safe for families or single women. Many of these guesthouses are very basic. Salt spray on metal or fabric takes a serious toll, and chipped paint is commonplace. Bathrooms can fall into the vintage category, and sometimes the water isn't heated — but when it's 85°F to 92°F outside, you don't need hot water.

On the other hand, some of these places are quite comfortable. A few are almost luxurious; and in addition to giving you the opportunity to live with a local family, they boast swimming pools, private bathrooms in all rooms, and air-conditioning.

We recommend guesthouses for:

- ✔ Older couples who like the bed-and-breakfast concept.
- ✔ Long-term vacationers on tight budgets.
- ✔ The independent traveler who needs a home base.

Here are some of the drawbacks of staying at a guesthouse.

- ✔ You may be far from the beach, without a pool.
- ✔ The digs may not be glamorous.
- ✔ You may not get along with your host.
- ✔ Housekeeping standards vary widely.
- ✔ If a problem occurs, you're stuck dealing one-on-one with the house owner.

What the Hotel Symbols Mean

As you're shopping around for your hotel, you'll see the following terms used:

- ✔ **CP** (Continental Plan), which includes a light breakfast — juice, coffee, pastry or bread, and perhaps a piece of fruit.
- ✔ **BP** (Breakfast Plan), a full traditional American-style breakfast (eggs, bacon, pancakes, French toast, hash browns, and so on).
- ✔ **MAP** (Modified American Plan), breakfast (usually a full one) and dinner.
- ✔ **FAP** (Full American Plan), three meals each day.

✔ **All-inclusive**, which means that you have three all-you-can-eat meals a day, plus soft drinks and alcoholic beverages, which sometimes include premium liquor and excellent wine.

✔ **EP** (European Plan). No meals.

All Bahamian resorts offer a **European Plan** (EP) rate, which means that you pay for the price of a room. That leaves you free to dine around at night at various other resorts or restaurants without restriction. Another plan preferred by many is the **Continental Plan** (CP), which means that you get your room and a continental breakfast of juice, coffee, bread, jam, and so on included in a set price. This plan is preferred by many because most guests don't like to "dine around" at breakfast time.

Another major option is the **Modified American Plan,** which includes breakfast and one main meal of the day, either lunch or dinner. The final choice is the **American Plan** (AP), which includes breakfast, lunch, and dinner. At certain resorts, you'll save money by booking in on either MAP or AP, because discounts are granted. If you dine à la carte for lunch and dinner at various restaurants, your final dining bill will no doubt be much higher than if you stayed on the MAP or AP.

Aside from the savings in cost, meal plans have drawbacks if as part of your holiday you like to eat in various places. You virtually face the same dining room every night, unless the resort you're staying at has many different restaurants on the dining plan. Often they don't. Many resorts have a lot of specialty restaurants, serving — say, Japanese cuisine — but these more expensive restaurants are not included in MAP or AP and charge à la carte prices.

Dining at your hotel at night cuts down on transportation costs. Taxis especially are expensive. Nonetheless, if dining out and having many different culinary experiences is your idea of a vacation, and you're willing to pay the higher price, avoid AP plans or at least make sure that the hotel where you're staying has more than one dining room.

One option is to ask whether your hotel has a dine-around plan. You might still keep costs in check, but you can avoid a culinary rut by taking your meals in some other restaurants if your hotel has such a plan. Such plans are rarer in The Bahamas, which does not specialize in all-inclusive resorts the way that Jamaica or some other islands do.

Before booking a room, check with a good travel agent or investigate on your own what you're likely to save by booking in on a dining plan. Under certain circumstances such as winter, you may not have a choice if MAP is dictated as a requirement for staying there. It pays to investigate, of course.

Finding a Room at the Right Price

Package deals abound, and they're always cheaper than "rack rates." (A rack rate is what an individual pays if he or she literally walks in from the street; these are the rates we've listed in the chapters that follow, though you can almost always do better at the big resort.) So it's sometimes good to go to a reliable travel agent to find out what, if anything, is available in the way of a land-and-air package before booking into a particular accommodation. For more on package deals, see Chapter 6.

The winter season in The Bahamas runs roughly from the middle of December to the middle of April, and hotels charge their highest prices during this peak period. Winter is generally the dry season in the islands, but heavy rainfall can occur regardless of the time of year. During the winter months, make reservations two months in advance if you can. You can't book early enough if you want to travel over Christmas or in February.

The off-season in The Bahamas — roughly from mid-April to mid-December (although this varies from hotel to hotel) — amounts to a sale. In most cases, hotel rates are slashed a startling 20% to 60%. It's a bonanza for cost-conscious travelers, especially for families who can travel in the summer. Be prepared for very strong sun, though, plus a higher chance of rain. Also note that hurricane season runs through the summer and fall.

Getting a Great Room

Somebody has to get the best room at a hotel or a resort, so it may as well be you. Here's how to go about it:

- ✔ Ask detailed questions when booking a room. Don't just ask to be booked into a certain hotel, but specify your likes and dislikes.

- ✔ Call the hotel's local number, its 800 number, or check with a travel agent. Also check its Web site for the best rates.

- ✔ Ask about AARP, AAA, or other discounts.

- ✔ Find out what's included in the rates — a so-called expensive hotel that includes beach chairs, snorkel rentals, or whatever, may cost less than a moderate hotel that charges you every time you breathe.

- ✔ Ask how far your hotel is from the beach.

- ✔ Question whether transfers from the airport are included in the price.

- ✔ Find out what the meal plan option is.

- ✔ Inquire about ceiling fans, air-conditioning, and whether the windows open.

- ✔ Discover whether the room faces the water or the garage in back — if you're not going to spend time a lot of time in your room, the back view makes sense because it's cheaper. Upper-floor rooms with views cost more.

- ✔ Ask for a room, floor, or annex that's been recently renovated.

- ✔ If the kids are along, find out whether they can stay with you for free — and look into a suite, which may cost less than two rooms.

- ✔ Ask about nonsmoking rooms.

- ✔ Avoid rooms overlooking outdoor nighttime entertainment or just over the bar or lounge if you're a light sleeper

- ✔ Find out how much lower the rates are in the off-season.

Ask whether you can get an upgrade or a free night's stay if you stay an extra few days. If you're traveling during the marginal periods between low and high season, you can sometimes delay your travel plans by a week or ten days and get a substantial reduction. For example, a $300 room booked on April 12 may have been lowered to $180 by April 17, as mid-April marks the beginning of the low season in The Bahamas.

Most Bahamian hoteliers wait until the slow season of summer to do major renovations. If you're traveling other than in the winter months, check to see whether your hotel of choice is in the midst of renovations. If it is, request a room away from the work site. Those construction workers are early risers.

Chapter 5

Planning Ahead for Special Travel Needs

. . . .

In This Chapter

▶ Bringing the kids along

▶ Honeymooning or getting hitched on the islands

▶ Traveling if you're single, gay or lesbian, a senior, or physically challenged

. . . .

*O*ne-size fits all doesn't pertain to vacations in The Bahamas. Individual travelers or even those traveling with companions often have special needs.

Some questions immediately come to mind. Where can couples honeymoon or even tie the knot? What discounts or privileges are available for those who, in the words of the French, have reached "the golden age?"

How wheelchair accessible are the islands? Do you have concerns about attitudes toward gays and lesbians? In this chapter, we discuss the challenges — and opportunities — that travelers with special needs may encounter in The Bahamas.

Traveling with Kids

If you want to bring the kids along to The Bahamas, locals will tell you, "It's no problem, Mon." Many families do just that, and for some kids, it will be their first introduction to a foreign country.

Families won't always have it easy, though. Whether your children are toddlers or teens, foreign travel is always a challenge. A traveling "brood" brings added strains on the budget and plays a big part in your choice of a hotel or resort. But in spite of some drawbacks, shared family experiences are most often worth the effort.

Flying with children

If you're traveling with an infant, bring along a car seat to use on the plane. Because many airlines allow children under age two to fly free when sitting on the lap of an adult, you may be tempted not to purchase a seat for your child. However, doing so really isn't safe, because turbulence can easily injure a child. You may wonder why you should bother buying a ticket for your child when empty seats are often available. The problem is that if the plane is full, you're out of luck.

If you're traveling with kids, don't forget gum or lollipops for them to chew or suck during take-off and landing to combat ear pressure pain. And pack a deck of cards or some favorite toys to keep them entertained. You may be used to hearing their mantra of "Are we there yet?," but the whines of bored children can drive other passengers crazy. Flight attendants are quite accommodating if you need to refrigerate baby bottles or if you have other child-related requests.

 To help make matters easier, remember to look for the Kid Friendly icon used throughout this book. This icon calls attention to hotels or resorts, restaurants, or attractions that are especially family friendly.

Kids vacationing at some beach resorts need not settle for just a sandy shore. They're treated to organized programs so comprehensive that they rival summer camp. Some of the larger accommodations offer children's programs year-round.

 Some programs are no more than a bored baby-sitter in a room full of toys or video games. Others have enthusiastic, well-trained staff members who engage children in age-appropriate diversions, from face painting and storytelling to beach Olympics and computer-assisted science projects. Some resorts charge an additional fee for their programs, while others are free to guests. Most resorts usually offer morning and afternoon sessions, and meals and night sessions may also be available. Most programs take children at around age 5 up to about age 12.

 The best kids' programs are at **Atlantis Paradise Island Resort & Casino** (Chapter 9) on Paradise Island, New Providence; **Radisson Cable Beach** (see Chapter 9) on New Providence; and **Our Lucaya** (see Chapter 13) on Grand Bahama.

Here are some questions to ask when you're evaluating a children's program:

- ✔ What is the ratio of caretakers/counselors to children?
- ✔ Are kids divided into groups by age?
- ✔ Exactly what activities will they engage in?

✔ How much time will the kids spend at the pool or beach, and what kind of expert supervision will they have near and in water?

✔ Are meals included?

✔ Will the children leave the drop-off area, and if so, where else will they go?

Remember to specify any food allergies, slather your younger editions with sunscreen, and, of course, make sure that the caretakers know where to find you in case of an emergency.

If you need a baby-sitter for your smallest tots, you can hire one through your hotel. Expect to pay around $10 to $15 an hour, plus $3 for each additional child.

In addition, the following resources may help you plan a family trip:

✔ **Family Travel Network** (www.familytravelnetwork.com) **offers** travel tips and reviews of family-friendly destinations, vacation deals, and thoughtful features such as "What to Do When Your Kids Are Afraid to Travel" and "Kid-Style Camping."

✔ **Travel with Your Children** (www.travelwithyourkids.com) **is** a comprehensive site offering sound advice on just about every topic from how to plan and prepare for your vacation to what to do on the plane.

✔ **The Busy Person's Guide to Travel with Children** (http://wz. com/travel/TravelingWithChildren.html) **offers a** "45-second newsletter" where experts weigh in on the best Web sites and resources for tips for traveling with children.

Planning the Perfect Romantic Getaway

The Bahamas offers so many different types of hotels and resorts that you're certain to find just the right honeymoon retreat to jump-start your new lives together. To zero in on the most romantic choices for hotels, restaurants, activities, and locales, look for the Romance icons throughout this book. Of course, you don't have to be hitched to indulge in these hideaways.

All-inclusive resorts — where one price covers your room, meals, beverages, entertainment, most activities, tips, taxes, and airfare, — are popular among newlyweds. To stay busy day and night, you need never leave these self-contained vacation playgrounds until it's time to go home. Check out Chapter 9 for the descriptions of elegant, couples-only **Sandals Royal Bahamian** and the more moderately priced **Breezes,** both resorts on New Providence. On Grand Bahama, think about **Club Viva Fortuna** (see Chapter 13). On San Salvador, consider **Club Med–Columbus Isle** (see Chapter 24).

If you don't necessarily want all-inclusive but you like a blizzard of action, check into **Atlantis Paradise Island Resort & Casino** (see Chapter 9) off New Providence. You can also find plenty to see and do in and around **Our Lucaya** on Grand Bahama (see Chapter 13).

Some couples prefer quieter, more remote resorts, where the sun, the sand, and each other are the main draws. If you prefer this scenario, the elegant **Ocean Club Golf & Tennis Resort** and the funky, startlingly colorful **Compass Point Beach Resort** are excellent honeymoon haunts on New Providence (see Chapter 9). Small is beautiful at **Green Turtle Club** and **Bluff House** on Green Turtle Cay in the Abacos (see Chapter 19), as well as **Pink Sands** and **Runaway Hill Club** on Harbour Island (see Chapter 21).

Quite a few accommodations, particularly the larger ones, feature honeymoon packages. These packages aren't usually money-savers, but they do include special extras such as a corner room, king-sized bed, champagne, maybe a first-rate meal or two, and transportation in limousines between your hotel and the airport. Each hotel boasts a somewhat different set of perks, so you'll have to ask exactly what your package includes when you make your reservation.

Saying I Do Bahamian Style

The Bahamas are popular honeymoon destinations for just-married spouses, but plenty of couples save the wedding for the island as well. Romantic settings, ranging from the beach at sunset to a harborside gazebo to a poolside patio or an elegant yacht, make tying the knot here tempting. With colorful coral and tropical fish as a backdrop, couples have even signaled "I do" underwater while decked out in scuba gear. Many of the larger hotels (and some of the smaller ones, too) provide a wedding coordinator to help you secure all of your paperwork, find an official to perform the ceremony, and hire photographers — both still and video — and the florist. Coordinators also organize the reception and make any other arrangements you need.

Reviewing the marriage requirements for The Bahamas

You and your intended must both be in The Bahamas for at least 24 hours before you can apply for a marriage license. You can fill out applications Monday to Friday.

For details, contact the office of the **Registrar General** (☎ 242-322-3316 in Nassau or ☎ 242-352-4934 on Grand Bahama). If you're planning to marry in one of the Out Islands, call the **Out Islands Promotion Board** (☎ 800-688-4752).

 If you and your partner are U.S. citizens, you need to get an affidavit to confirm this — and the fact that you're both single — from the American Embassy in Nassau. *Note:* The U.S. Embassy is closed, of course, on both American and Bahamian holidays. You must present proof of identity, such as a passport and, if necessary, proof of divorce. You won't need any blood tests, however. The **Weddings and Honeymoon Unit of The Bahamas Ministry of Tourism** (call ☎ 888/687-8425 or 242-302-2034 for a brochure) can also provide information.

For assistance with planning your nuptials in The Bahamas, call your hotel or the Ministry of Tourism's **People-to-People Program:**

✔ Nassau, New Providence (☎ 242-328-7810)

✔ Freeport/Lucaya, Grand Bahama (☎ 242-352-8044)

✔ Abaco (☎ 242-367-3067)

✔ Andros (☎ 242-368-2286)

✔ Bimini (☎ 242-347-3529)

✔ Eleuthera (☎ 242-332-2142)

✔ Harbour Island (☎ 242-332-2142)

✔ Exuma (☎ 242-336-2430)

✔ San Salvador (☎ 242-356-0435)

Working out the wedding cost

An island wedding in a stunning setting can cost you thousands of dollars less than you may spend at home. Table 5-1 gives you a general idea of how much money you can expect to spend on the ceremony:

Table 5-1	The Cost of a Bahamian Wedding
Marriage license	The Bahamas: $40
Affidavit	$55 and up (U.S. Embassy or Notary Public)
Marriage officer	Weekdays: $150
	Weekends: $175

(continued)

Table 5-1 *(continued)*

Florist	Bouquet: $30 and up
	Boutonniere: $8
Transportation	$85 an hour
Tuxedo rental	$65 and up
Video	$350 and up
Photographer	$300 and up
Music	Steel drum band: $550 an hour
	Organ music in church: $150 an hour
	Violinist: $100 an hour
	Soloist (vocal): $100 an hour
	Violin and flute: $200 an hour
	Violin, flute, and clarinet: $300 an hour

Traveling Solo

You don't need kids or a partner to have a great vacation on these islands, especially in Nassau or Freeport. You do find plenty of couples at the smaller, quieter hotels on these islands, so you don't have nearly as many opportunities to meet other single visitors. However, you can find groups of unattached friends vacationing together. Because hotels in the Out Islands are so much smaller and more intimate than on the busier islands, meeting people is easier.

If you're shy, join a snorkeling sail, a scuba trip, or an excursion to an uninhabited island for a beach picnic. Before you can say Goombay Smash, you'll be chatting with new friends.

On the downside, you do pay more for a hotel room or an air/hotel package if you go it alone than if you travel with a friend because single rates are higher than double rates divided by two. But the good news is that so many affordable hotels are available on New Providence (particularly downtown Nassau, and some on Cable Beach) that you shouldn't have trouble finding a place that suits your wallet.

Club Med–Columbus Isle (see Chapter 24), on San Salvador, attracts plenty of singles. This all-inclusive beach resort offers many diversions designed to get people together. In addition, this place is perfect for two single friends who travel together but like their privacy. (The hotel offers single rooms joined by a shared bathroom.)

If you're a socially minded single, Nassau is a good choice — you can be as busy or as lazy as you want. **Breezes,** a moderately priced all-inclusive resort on Cable Beach (see Chapter 9), is a popular choice because it offers a medley of group activities.

During March and April, droves of U.S. college students on spring break descend on New Providence. So if you've outgrown toga parties and drinking contests, you may want to skip this scene.

For tips on staying safe while vacationing alone, check out Chapter 8.

Traveling to Gay- and Lesbian-Friendly Destinations

If you're gay or lesbian, how comfortable will you feel in The Bahamas? The official word is that everyone is welcome, but the reality is somewhat different, depending on where you go and what you do when you get there. At least one resort (couples-only and all-inclusive Sandals Royal Bahamian on New Providence) unapologetically excludes gay couples altogether.

In The Bahamas, many residents are uncomfortable with PDA (public displays of affection) between same-sex couples. In fact, "Don't ask, don't tell" reigns, because laws remain on the books forbidding homosexual activity. Therefore, if you can't imagine a vacation that doesn't include strolling down the beach hand in hand with your main squeeze, The Bahamas may not be for you. Head for Key West or South Miami Beach, which will welcome you with open arms.

Nevertheless, The Bahamas can be a great vacation choice if you're discreet in public about your sexuality. On the most popular islands (New Providence, Paradise Island, and Grand Bahama), not only can you get lost in the crowds, but you're also more likely to run into other gay vacationers and residents. In fact, one nightclub, **Endangered Species,** on West Street in the Cable Beach Shopping Centre (☎ 242-327-0127) on New Providence, caters to gays. (Open Friday to Sunday 11 p.m. to 4 a.m.) Ask around and folks will direct you to other small hangouts, some of which are open only every other weekend.

Keep in mind that things are changing, so by the time you read these words, you may find a few more island businesses that welcome gays. For specifics, contact **The International Gay & Lesbian Travel Association** (IGLTA), (☎ **800-448-8550** or 954/776-2626; Fax: 954-776-3303; www. iglta.org, which links travelers with appropriate gay-friendly service organizations or tour specialists. With some 1,200 members, IGLTA offers quarterly newsletters, marketing mailings, and a membership directory that's updated quarterly. Membership often includes gay or lesbian businesses but is also open to individuals for an annual fee. Members are informed of gay and gay-friendly hoteliers, tour operators, and airline and cruise-line representatives. Contact the IGLTA for a list of its member agencies, who are listed in IGLTA's information resources.

Seeking Savings and Specials for Mature Travelers

People over a certain age are entitled to some terrific travel bargains. If you're not a member of **AARP,** 601 E St. NW, Washington, D.C. 20049 (☎ **800-424-3410;** www.aarp.org), by all means join. If you're over 50, you get discounts on car rentals and hotels. Just make sure that you travel with your membership card.

The Alliance for Retired Americans, 8403 Colesville Rd, Suite 1200, Silver Springs, MD 20912 (☎ **301-578-8422;**), offers a newsletter six times a year and discounts on hotel and auto rentals; annual dues are $13 per person or couple. *Note*: Members of the former National Council of Senior Citizens receive automatic membership in the Alliance.

In addition, airlines, including American, Continental, US Airways, and TWA, all offer discount programs for senior travelers — ask whenever you book a flight.

The Mature Traveler, a monthly 12-page newsletter on senior citizen travel is another valuable resource. It's available by subscription from *Mature Traveler* for $29.95. Call ☎ **800-460-6676** to receive it.

If you would rather take a cruise, **SAGA International Holidays,** 222 Berkeley St., Boston, MA 02116 (☎ **800-343-0273;** www.sagahollidays. com); offers cruises to The Bahamas for individuals 50 and older.

If you're a traveler in your golden years, you'll enjoy the variety of islands in The Bahamas as much as your younger brethren. However, seniors tend to gravitate toward New Providence and Grand Bahama. On New Providence, for example, the **Nassau Beach Hotel** (see Chapter 9) on Cable Beach receives many repeat guests who've visited for decades, and the **British Colonial Hilton,** in downtown Nassau, gets plenty of older vacationers as well.

Ensuring Access for Travelers with Disabilities

A physical challenge shouldn't stop anybody from traveling, especially because more options and resources are available to help travelers with disabilities than ever before. However, some islands are better bets than others. Many of the larger hotels on New Providence, Paradise Island, and Grand Bahama offer ground-floor guest rooms, wide bathrooms, or elevators that make wheelchair accessibility relatively easy. These islands also have plenty of sidewalks, marina boardwalks, and paved pathways.

On the other hand, most hotels on the smaller islands have hilly grounds, narrow unpaved pathways, or steps leading to guestrooms or dining areas. Several accommodations on Harbour Island, for example, sit at the top of a bluff with long staircases leading down to the beach. Therefore, when you find a hotel that sounds good, call to ask about the specifics of accessibility. If you're in a wheelchair or you have trouble walking but you want to get as close to the sand as possible, look for hotels with accessible beachfront pool patios.

The Out Islands, other than New Providence and Grand Bahama, are more difficult to reach. The planes that service these islands are usually small, and passengers board and disembark on narrow, somewhat rickety staircases. In some instances, you need to change planes once or twice and catch a ferry, as well as take a taxi or two.

If you're a wheelchair-bound traveler heading to New Providence, you can contact **The Bahamas Association for the Physically Disabled** (☎ 242-322-2393) to rent a specially equipped van for airport pickup or to arrange for transportation around the island. You should make reservations as far ahead of your trip as possible. Temporary ramps and other portable aids are also available through this association.

A World of Options, a 658-page book of resources for physically challenged travelers, covers everything from biking trips to scuba outfitters. You can get it from **Mobility International USA,** P.O. Box 10767, Eugene, OR, 97440 (☎ 541-343-1284, voice and TDD; www.miusa.org. For more personal assistance, call the **Moss Resource Net** at **215/456-5995;** www.mossresourcenet.org.

If you're a traveler with mobility challenges, consider joining a tour that caters specifically to you. A good company to contact is **FEDCAP Rehabilitation Services,** 211 W. 14th St., New York, NY 10011. Call ☎ **212/727-4200** or fax 212/721-4374; www.fedcap.org for information about membership and summer tours.

Vision-impaired travelers should contact the **American Foundation for the Blind,** 11 Penn Plaza, Suite 300, New York, NY 10001 (☎ **800-232-5463;** www.afb.org) for information on traveling with Seeing Eye dogs.

Part II
Ironing Out the Details

The 5th Wave   By Rich Tennant

WHILE TRYING TO FIND THE RENTAL RETURN AREA AT MIAMI INTERNATIONAL AIRPORT, FRANK AND MONA DISCOVER THE BAHAMAS.

@RICHTENNANT

In this part . . .

In this part, we share advice on booking your ideal vacation in the Bahamas. Turn to these pages to decide whether to use a travel agent or to handle the arrangements on your own. Likewise, we help you determine the fastest and most economical ways to reach your chosen destination. We also explain how to estimate your trip's price tag and how to stay within your budget.

Finally, we take you step-by-step through all the details that you need to know to ensure a hassle-free vacation, from getting a passport and considering travel or medical insurance to staying safe.

Chapter 6

Making Your Travel Arrangements

· ·

In this Chapter

▶ Finding the right travel specialist

▶ Deciding whether a package tour is right for you

▶ Researching and booking your trip online

▶ Plugging in to the best island Web sites.

· ·

Many people choose to make their own travel arrangements. And why not? Just because you arrange matters yourself doesn't mean that your trip has to be more expensive than if you went to a travel agent. Even if you choose to enlist the aid of a travel agent after you read this chapter, you'll be better prepared to make your travel-related decisions.

In this chapter, you find tips on how to go about planning your own hassle-free vacation. Whether you're the do-it-yourself type or the kind of person who prefers to leave the details to others, reading this chapter can save you time, confusion, and money. You discover the benefits and limitations of package tours, including the fastest ways to comparison shop.

Loving or Leaving Your Travel Agent

In the space of just a few short years, the Internet has transformed many novices into travel specialists. Some folks find it so simple to put together a vacation online that travel agents may as well be extinct. With this book in one hand and a mouse in the other, you can flip, point, and click your way to the sun and sand of your dreams.

However, if any of the following applies to you, tapping the talents of a travel agent may be a better way to plan your trip:

- ✔ You're not as acclimated to the Internet as others.

- ✔ You like discussing your travel options with a human expert.

- ✔ You may need to change your itinerary later.

- ✔ You're considering visiting a few different islands.

- ✔ You have to make several flight connections.

- ✔ You're trying to coordinate a trip for a group of friends or relatives traveling from various parts of the country.

- ✔ You're departing from one city but returning to another.

- ✔ You don't have a lot of time to plan.

Even as helpful as the Web is, you can often get better prices on everything from plane tickets to resorts by going to a travel agent. That means you many want to do research online and check agency rates before making your purchases. Most Web sites are ad driven, and the reviews may be written by the attractions or resorts themselves. As a result, they have little credibility and need to be taken with a grain of salt.

Finding the best travel agent

The best way to find a good travel agent is the same way you find a good plumber or mechanic or doctor — by word of mouth. Any travel agent can come up with a bargain airfare, hotel, or rental car. A good one doesn't let you ruin your vacation by scrimping your way to low airfares — the fares that mean having to change planes four times — and saving money by staying in hotels that have seen far better days. Nor will a good travel agent automatically hook you up with a rental car in Nassau where getting around is cheaper and convenient in taxis, shuttles, public buses, and ferries.

Good travel agents keep abreast of discounts and promotions that make certain flights and hotels especially attractive at particular times. For example, they may get you a room upgrade for the same price or suggest a flight to a Bahamian Out Island on a larger plane from Nassau instead of a smaller plane from Florida. They can even point you toward restaurants that will make you reminisce about that savory conch chowder or velvety smooth guava duff for years.

When you're planning your trip to The Bahamas, you'll find that the most helpful travel agents are those who've been to the places they recommend. Many agents book trips to hotels and even islands that they've seen only in brochures or on Web sites. Fancy photos and glitzy cyber-sites can make a hotel or island with skimpy thrills look like paradise. In many cases, even if the agents have been to the area, they've visited only on *fam trips* (familiarization excursions) sponsored by the larger (richer) hotels in the most popular (most crowded) resort areas. On these trips the agents are only briefly shown the best of what a particular hotel can offer, and they spend no significant time at any one property.

Along with the airlines, the largest resorts have traditionally paid agents commissions for the vacationers they book. Consequently, many agents focus on the most-visited areas and accommodations, ignoring the smaller but intriguing properties that can't afford to pay commissions, such as some of those on less developed Out Islands.

The good news about these commissions is that, instead of your having to dig into your pocket, the airlines and hotels pay your travel agent. Although using some travel agencies doesn't cost you a thing, others now charge customers fees ranging anywhere from $10 to book a seat on a plane to as much as $100 to arrange an entire trip. The money is well worth it, of course, if you're dealing with an experienced, knowledgeable agent who not only saves you money but also helps you design the trip you want. So, choosing your travel agent wisely is crucial.

Remember that guy in accounting who was raving about his Paradise Island vacation last month or your neighbor who showed you those underwater photos of her San Salvador dive trip? Start asking around to see whether any friends or coworkers can recommend travel agents who've served them well while planning their trips.

If no one you know has been to The Bahamas, don't worry; other options exist. **The Bahamas Tourist Office (☎ 800-BAHAMAS** or 212-758-2777) can lead you to a good travel agent in your area.

Technically, The Bahamas aren't in the Caribbean, but that doesn't stop **The Agency Coalition for Caribbean Tourism (☎ 800-931-ACCT;** www.caribtourism.com) from providing you with names and numbers of travel agents near you who specialize in these Atlantic islands. You can also go online to find helpful agents through the **American Society of Travel Agents 703-739-2782** (www.astanet.com), the world's leading association of travel professionals.

Getting the most from your travel agent

Travel agents are most useful when you've done your homework before talking to one. If you decide to use a travel agent, you're already ahead of the game because you picked up this book where accommodation and restaurant choices have been streamlined.

Before you call or meet with a travel agent, select one or two islands, along with some accommodations and attractions that you might like. Jot them down in order of preference. Check prices on the Web to get an idea of current specials or seasonal promotions. (See "Booking Your Trip Online," later in this chapter for more information.) If you narrow your options first, an agent can better help you zero in on the type of trip you want.

Picking a Package Tour

Package tours (also known as *package deals*) are not the same as escorted tours, so we're not referring to a herd of tourists being jostled around to six islands in five days. Most vacationers wouldn't want to visit The Bahamas in such a manner anyway even if such escorted tours existed. Package tours are simply a way of buying your airline ticket and hotel room in one transaction.

Opening your package

A package tour includes your flights, accommodations, land transportation to and from your hotel, taxes, meals (sometimes, but not always), and rental cars if you want), as well as both travel and cancellation insurance. Package tours allow you the convenience of buying everything at the same time so that you save a lot of money in the process.

Your air/hotel package costs you less, and often *much* less, than the hotel and airfare if you book them yourself separately. In some cases, these packages are even cheaper than the hotel alone. If this sounds too good to be true, it isn't. Packages are sold in bulk to tour operators, who resell them to the public. It's like buying your vacation at a membership discount club, except that the tour operator is the person buying the boxes of paper towels and reselling them at a cost that undercuts what you'd pay at your average neighborhood supermarket.

So what's the catch? These economical vacation packages vary as much as paper towels do. Because some packagers buy in bigger bulk than others, they can offer the same hotels for lower prices. Some feature a better class of hotels than others, and some offer flights on scheduled airlines, while others book charters. Also, some packages book only nonstop flights, while others make you change planes.

If you're dreaming of getting away from it all on one of the Bahamas' undeveloped Out Islands, finding good package deals may be hard. Most packagers concentrate on the larger hotels on the more popular islands such as New Providence or Grand Bahama.

Nabbing the best package deal

The best place to start looking for package deals is the travel section of your local Sunday newspaper. Also, check the ads in the back of national travel magazines such as *Travel & Leisure, Caribbean Travel & Life, Islands,* and *Condé Nast Traveler.* **Liberty Travel** (☎ **888-271-1584,** or check your local phone book for a location near you; www.libertytravel.com) is one of the biggest packagers in the country and usually runs a full-page ad in Sunday papers. You may not get much in the way of personalized, first-hand knowledge with the service (so familiarizing yourself with some choices beforehand is particularly important), but you will get a good deal.

Some packagers specialize in types of trips, such as scuba-diving adventures, golf getaways, or casino excursions. Likewise, a few of the larger hotels, such as all-inclusive Club Med on San Salvador, offer money-saving hotel packages that include charter flights. If you already know where you want to stay, call that resort and ask whether it offers land/air packages.

Airlines are another good resource because they package their flights together with accommodations. When you pick an airline, you can choose one on which you accumulate frequent flyer miles and that offers frequent service to your hometown. Although disreputable packagers are uncommon, they do exist. By buying your package through the airline, you can be almost certain that the company will still be in business when your departure date nears.

With so many choices, shopping for the best package deal is a daunting prospect. All those phone calls, all that logging on to the Web. . . . But one company, **TourScan Inc.**(☎ **800-962-2080** or 203-655-8091; www.tourscan.com) cuts through the red tape for you. It researches air/hotel packages offered by different tour operators to the same hotel. Because prices can vary quite a bit even at the same accommodation at the same time of year, this service makes comparison shopping a (tropical) breeze.

Here are some of the packagers that I prefer:

✔ **American Airlines Vacations** (☎ 800-321-2121; www.aavacations.com) can arrange packages to Nassau, Cable Beach, and Paradise Island (New Providence); Freeport/Lucaya (Grand Bahama); and Exuma. These economical deals include discounted airfare, hotel, and, if you like, a rental car, as well as meals (at certain accommodations). Flights from Florida are nonstop. You need to stay for at least three nights, but that is hardly difficult, as even the most hurried traveler to The Bahamas spends that amount of time in the sun and on the sand.

- ✔ **American Express Travel** (☎ 800-941-2639; www.travel impressions.com) books trips to a couple of the smaller Bahamian islands that many packagers ignore: Green Turtle Cay in the Abacos and Harbour Island off the coast of Eleuthera. Of course, it also sets up air/land packages to the most popular resort areas: Nassau, Cable Beach, Paradise Island (New Providence); and Freeport/Lucaya (Grand Bahama). Nonstop charter flights from Newark, New York, and Miami can take you to Nassau or Freeport. A two- or three-night minimum stay is required.

- ✔ **British Airways** (☎ 0845-77-333-77 in the U.K., 800-247-9297 in the U.S.; www.british-airways.com) offers British travelers direct flights from Gatwick Airport outside London to Nassau. Call the airline or visit the Web site for information on package deals.

- ✔ **Caribbean Dive Tours** (☎ 800-404-3483; info@cdtusa.com) makes one-stop shopping especially attractive, because this company arranges scuba- diving trips for individuals or groups that include airfare, hotel, meals (in some cases), and all dives and gear.

- ✔ **Continental Airlines Vacations** (☎ 800-634-5555; www.cool vacations.com) customizes hotel and air packages to Nassau, Cable Beach, and Paradise Island that include transfers to and from the airport. Depending on what hotel you choose, you can throw in breakfast or both breakfast and dinner. No matter where you're starting from, you board a nonjet plane in Florida to get to the islands. Continental's packages require a two-night stay.

- ✔ **Delta Vacations** (☎ 800-872-7786; www.deltavacations.com) coordinates packages from New York or Atlanta to Nassau, Cable Beach, and Paradise Island that include air, hotel, and transfers between your accommodation and the airport. Flights are nonstop from New York or Atlanta.

- ✔ **Grand Bahama Vacations** (☎ 800-545-1300; www.gbvac.com) books charter flights with Laker Airways to Freeport/Lucaya (Grand Bahama) twice a week from Fort Lauderdale, Baltimore, Cleveland, Cincinnati, Hartford, Memphis, Nashville, Raleigh, Richmond, and Pittsburgh, as well as every other Saturday from West Palm Beach. When you reserve your flight, you can also book a bed at one of more than a dozen Grand Bahama hotels.

- ✔ **Maduro Dive Fanta-Seas** (☎ 800-327-6709; www.maduro.com) can set up a complete dive trip with one phone call. Packages for individuals or groups include airfare, hotel, meals (if you want them), and all dives and gear.

- ✔ **US Airways Vacations** (☎ 800-455-0123; www.usairways vacations.com) arranges air/hotel packages, with nonstop service to Nassau from Philadelphia or Charlotte, North Carolina. US Airways requires a two-night minimum stay.

Making Your Own Travel Arrangements

Many people choose to make their own travel arrangements. And why not? Just because you arrange things yourself doesn't mean your trip has to be more expensive than going to a travel agent. In this section, I give you some tips and advice on making your own arrangements. Even if you choose to enlist the help of a travel agent after you read this section, you'll be better prepared to make your travel-related decisions.

Finding the best airfare

Don't fool yourself into thinking that the passenger sitting in an identical seat next to you paid the same fare as you. He or she may have shelled out a whole lot more — or a whole lot less — depending on when, where, and how he or she purchased the seat. While planning a trip, I've often called the same airline three times in a single day and received three different fares for the same dates and destination. What's up with that?

Due to cancellations and ever-changing specials, the number of seats available for a particular flight in a particular fare category can fluctuate wildly from hour to hour, so get a feel for what you're willing to pay. If you come across a fare that looks good, jump on it! Otherwise, you snooze, you lose, because that handsome deal can disappear in a flash.

Consolidators, also known as bucket shops, are a good place to check for the lowest fares. Their prices are much better than the fares you can get yourself, and they're often lower than what your travel agent can get you. How can they do it? They buy the seats in bulk, far in advance. You can see their ads in the small boxes in your Sunday travel section.

However, using a consolidator is sometimes very time consuming. After you finally get past the busy signal, plan on hanging on hold for a good while before you get to an agent — and then he may take your name and number and take his good sweet time getting back to you. (To comparison shop, you have to go through this process a few times.) When you finally get through, some consolidators may not even have the Bahamas flights that you requested at the moment. But, that's the penalty you pay for the great deal you may receive. Some of the most reliable consolidators include **1-800-FLY-4-LESS, 1-800-FLY-CHEAP,** and **1-800-LOW-AIRFARE.**

Another good outfit, **Nassau-Paradise Island Express** (☎ 800-722-4262), specializes in seats to Nassau (New Providence) and Providenciales (the Turks & Caicos) from Newark on Continental and from New York on TWA. Not only are all of these flights nonstop, but you also pay a lot less through this discounter than you would if you booked your flight directly through either airline. Flights are daily to Nassau from Newark or New York and once or twice a week to Providenciales. You can also book your hotel through this company.

Here are some other tried-and-true travel suggestions for keeping more green in your wallet:

- ✔ **Time it right.** You're most likely to find discounted fares to the Bahamas and Turks & Caicos during the summer and fall months (also known as the low season). However, because both countries are popular year-round, specials pop up throughout the year.

- ✔ **Get the advance advantage.** Booking at least 30, 60, or even 90 days in advance can get you cheaper fares, especially if you're willing to buy nonrefundable tickets. With these restricted tickets, you may not get your money back if you need to change your plans. However, you can usually apply the cost of your ticket to another flight — that is, after you pay a penalty (around $75 per ticket).

- ✔ **Choose an off-peak day.** Traveling on a Tuesday, Wednesday, or Thursday can also save you money. Even if you can't travel both ways on these lower-fare days, you can still save if you fly off-peak one way.

- ✔ **Make your reservations right after midnight.** Cinderella knew that things start to shake up 'round midnight. In the middle of the week, just after the clock strikes 12, many airlines download low-priced airfares to their computers, so this is a great time to buy newly discounted seats. Midnight is also the cut-off time for holding reservations, which means that you can snag cheap tickets that were just released because they were reserved but never purchased. Because most travel agents are in dreamland at this hour, you're on your own here, kid (meaning that you can't call an agent to ask questions). (For advice on making reservations on the Web, see "Booking Your Trip Online," later in this chapter.)

Figuring out who flies where

To get you started making your travel arrangements with the fewest hassles, I've broken this section down in two ways: Island by island, so you can tell how easy — or difficult — it is to reach the vacation spot you have in mind, and airline by airline, just in case you have a favorite carrier and/or have some frequent flier miles racked up on one of them.

In this section, I list information only about flights to the Bahamas and Turks & Caicos that are direct (you may touch down once, but you won't have to change planes) and nonstop. Therefore, if you're not starting from one of the cities that I mention, you'll probably have to change planes or even airlines to get to the island of your choice. Keep in mind that, no matter where you start, in order to get to some of the smaller cays, you have to fly to one island, and then take a ferry or switch to a small airline. Planes flying from Florida to the Bahamas and from Nassau (New Providence) to other Bahamian islands often carry fewer than 30 or 40 passengers.

Also, remember that flight schedules always change, so use the information in this section to get a rough idea of what's available. Some routes are seasonal, with fewer flights or no flights at all, at various times of the year. For up-to-the-minute details, call the airlines directly or check their Web sites.

Flying to Nassau, New Providence (for Nassau, Cable Beach, and Paradise Island): American offers about 12 flights each day from Miami to Nassau, as well as less frequent service from Ft. Lauderdale, Orlando, and Tampa. **Bahamasair,** the Bahamas' national carrier, also flies to Nassau from Miami, Ft. Lauderdale, and Orlando. **Continental Airlines** offers daily flights to Nassau from Newark, Miami, Ft. Lauderdale, and West Palm Beach. **Delta** flies daily from New York, Atlanta, Cincinnati, and Orlando. **Air Canada** serves Nassau from Toronto. **TWA** offers daily flights from New York and Miami. **US Airways** flies in from Philadelphia and Charlotte every day.

Flying to Freeport, Grand Bahama (for Freeport & Lucaya): **American** offers about seven flights a day from Miami to Freeport. **Bahamasair** also links Freeport with Miami and Nassau every day. **Continental** serves Freeport daily from Miami, Ft. Lauderdale, and West Palm Beach. **Lynx Air International,** a small airline, travels from Ft. Lauderdale to Freeport a couple times a week. **TWA** offers daily flights from Miami, as well as flights Wednesday through Sunday from New York.

Flying to Marsh Harbour, The Abacos (for Elbow Cay): Air Sunshine, a small commuter airline, offers daily flights from Ft. Lauderdale to Marsh Harbour, where you can catch the ferry to Elbow Cay. **Bahamasair** flies to Marsh Harbour from West Palm Beach or Nassau. **US Airways** flies in daily from Orlando.

Flying to Treasure Cay, The Abacos (for Green Turtle Cay & Treasure Cay): Air Sunshine offers daily service from Ft. Lauderdale to Treasure Cay (to get to Green Turtle Cay, take a ferry from Treasure Cay). **Bahamasair** flies in daily from Nassau. **US Airways** arrives here every day from Orlando.

Getting to Harbor Island: Bahamasair flies daily from Nassau to North Eleuthera, where you catch the ferry to Harbour Island. **US Airways** flies in daily from Miami.

Flying to George Town, Exuma: A couple days a week, **Air Sunshine's** small aircraft head from Ft. Lauderdale to George Town. **Bahamasair** flies to George Town daily from Nassau. **Lynx Air International,** another small airline, makes trips from Ft. Lauderdale a couple times a week.

Flying to San Salvador: Air Sunshine, a small carrier, flies from Ft. Lauderdale to San Salvador once or twice a week. **Bahamasair** flies here daily from Nassau. When you make your hotel reservation (at one of the island's two hotels), ask about charter flights.

Booking Your Trip Online

Booking your flight through an airline's Web site can save you money, and you can sometimes receive bonus frequent flier miles if you purchase your tickets online. Last-minute hot deals are also available from airlines through a free e-mail service called **E-savers.** Each week, the airline sends you a list of discounted flights, usually leaving the upcoming Friday or Saturday, and returning the following Monday or Tuesday. You can sign up at each airline's Web site.

The number of virtual travel agents on the Internet has increased exponentially in recent years. You now have more opportunities than ever to book entire vacations electronically. The bad news is that online travel agencies have more than a few kinks to work out. For example, surfing through Web sites to find just what you want is time consuming. Many limit your options to chain hotels or just a few airlines. Likewise, if you have questions or need to change your travel dates, you may find contacting a human affiliated with the site difficult and or even impossible.

Although travel Web sites are full of last-minute specials and other economical deals, not all online agencies are equipped to share personalized information. You may find a bargain fare online that a human travel agent didn't have the time or energy to dig up. Yet many travel Web sites aren't designed to inform you, for example, that you can save a lot of money if you left a day earlier or a day later than you originally planned.

The good news is that you don't have to book your flight or hotel online to reap the benefits of the Web. You can use it as an endless resource. The Web can be an invaluable tool for checking hotel availability and flight schedules or for comparing the prices of scuba- diving packages, for example. When you want to find the cheapest airfare, why not let the Internet do your legwork for you? After all, searching through millions of pieces of data and returning information in rank order is what computers do best.

Using the best sites

Although some travel Web sites require you to register with them, others don't, but they all provide variations on the same theme: Enter your destination and the dates you want to travel, and the computer looks for the lowest airfares and/or hotel rates. Here are the travel-booking Web sites that are the most useful, warts and all:

✔ **1travel.com** (www.onetravel.com): Look for discount accommodation rates with HotelWiz. After you decide when and where you want to go, the Farebeater service saves you plenty on airline tickets.

✔ **Arthur Frommer's Budget Travel Online** (www.frommers.com): All the detailed travel advice, hotel and restaurant reviews, destination articles, and links to online booking sites help to ensure a smooth ride when planning your trip.

✔ **Away.com** (www.away.com): This site invites you to talk to a travel specialist if you need help planning your trip. After entering your queries, you can either let them know the best time to reach you or you can call them or request that they e-mail you.

✔ **Cheap Tickets** (www.cheaptickets.com): Along with discount airline tickets, at this site you find good prices for hotels, cruises, and rental cars. Sometimes, however, Cheap Tickets may quote you a price that's not available for the dates that you requested. You have to do your homework before you book anything.

✔ **Expedia** (www.expedia.com): This site will e-mail you the best airfare deal once a week, if you so choose. Along with attractive deals on cruise and vacation packages, you can scroll through destination features, late-breaking travel news, and commentary from travel experts.

✔ **LastMinuteTravel** (www.lastminutetravel.com): Visit this Web site if you want to get away in a hurry. You've browsed through but you don't see any trips that suit you at the moment? Simply arrange a free e-mail alert that notifies you as soon as your requested travel option is available.

✔ **Priceline.com** (www.priceline.com): Through this well-known Web site, you can often discover bargains. The catch with Priceline.com is that you have to be a bit adventurous. You can select your destination, the level of hotel you want, and the days that you want to travel. However, you won't know exactly in which accommodation you'll stay, what times your flights leave, or how many airline connections you'll have to make until after your bid is accepted and your credit card charged. After your travel plans are booked, your reservations are nonrefundable.

✔ **Smarter Living** (www.smarterliving.com): Sign up here to receive weekly e-mails alerting you to last-minute bargains on major airlines. Smarter Living informs you about most deals on Tuesday or Wednesday for travel during the upcoming weekend. However, you can book some specials weeks or even months in advance. Through this site, you can also have travel agents fighting over you; enter details of the trip you have in mind — where and when you want to go, how long you want to stay, how much you want to pay and and travel agents compete for your business.

✔ **Travelocity** (www.travelocity.com): This popular site makes finding good deals easier than on some Web sites. If you're not ready to make a final decision, you can hold a reservation for 24 hours in some cases.

✔ **Travelscape.com** (www.travelscape.com): Comparing and booking hotel/air package tours to Nassau and Freeport is especially convenient on this Web site. You can find some good bargains, too. If you already have your hotel, air-only discounts are available as well.

Perusing the best island Web sites

There's nothing quite like seeing full color photos, maps, and videos and reading testimonials from recent vacationers. Destination Web sites give you all that fun, and then some. You can also find plenty of up-to-the-minute information about accommodations, restaurants, sailing, party cruises, scuba diving, snorkeling, golf, and tennis, among other attractions. Check out the sites' Frequently Asked Questions (FAQ) sections or e-mail some queries of your own. In addition, you may come across links to quite a few helpful and related Web sites.

Here are my choices for top destination Web sites for The Bahamas:

✔ **The Bahamas Ministry of Tourism** (www.bahamas.com)

✔ **The Bahamas Out Islands Promotion Board** (www.bahama-out-islands.com)

✔ **Bahamas Tourist Guide** (www.interknowledge.com/bahamas)

✔ **Bahamas Vacation Guide** (www.bahamasvg.com)

✔ **Bahamasnet: The Bahamas Vacation, Hotel, and Travel Guide** (www.bahamasnet.com)

✔ **Virtual Voyages Bahamas Directory** (www.virtualvoyages.com)

Chapter 7

Money Matters

- -

In This Chapter

▶ Choosing between plastic and paper

▶ Planning your budget

▶ Keeping tabs on unexpected expenses

- -

*I*n The Bahamas, U.S. dollars are used interchangeably with the local Bahamian dollar with the same value, so you don't have to worry about exchanging your cash. In this chapter, you plan a budget and find out how to figure out hidden costs. You also see how to cut expenses without scrimping on your fun.

Picking Your Poison: Cash, ATMs, Credit Cards, or Traveler's Checks

Paper or plastic? Your choice is among credit cards, ATM cards, traveler's checks, or cash. All are welcome but some are more convenient (or cheaper) to use than others.

On New Providence (Nassau, Cable Beach, and Paradise Island) or Grand Bahama (Freeport/Lucaya), finding a 24-hour ATM is easy. So you don't need to carry either traveler's checks or a wad of cash. On smaller islands, however, ATMs may be few and far between and or nonexistent.

Cashing in

The Bahamas use American dollars as legal tender and also has its own currency. Pay for something in U.S. dollars, and you may receive change that's a mix of Bahamian and American bills.

Multihued Bahamian cash is as colorful as the country itself, so you may want to tuck a bill or two away as a souvenir.

As you near the end of your trip, ask for your change in American dollars. Otherwise, you'll end up with unwanted Bahamian currency that you need to either spend or exchange at the airport and, if you exchange it there, you lose some to service charges.

Most island ATMs are linked to a national network that most likely includes your bank at home. **Cirrus** (☎ **800-424-7787** or 800-4CIRRUS; www.mastercard.com) and **Plus** (☎ **800-843-7587;** www.visa.com) are the two most popular networks; check the back of your ATM card to see the network to which your bank belongs. The 800 numbers give you specific locations of ATMs where you can withdraw money on vacation.

Withdraw only as much cash as you need to ensure that you don't feel insecure carrying around a huge amount of money.

Note: Many banks impose a fee ranging from $1.50 to $3 every time you use an ATM machine. Your own bank may also charge you an additional fee for using ATMs from other banks.

Charging away

Credit cards are a safe way to carry money, and they provide a convenient record of all your travel expenses.

Even though the Bahamian dollar equals the U.S. dollar, the two are still different currencies. If you use a credit card, when you receive your monthly statement, you'll likely find that a currency conversion charge (usually about 2 percent) was added to your charges.

You can also receive cash advances from your credit card at any bank (though you start paying interest on the advance the moment you receive the cash, and you don't receive frequent flyer miles on an airline credit card). At most banks, you don't need to go to a teller; you can get a cash advance at the ATM if you know your PIN (personal identification number). If you forget your PIN or didn't know that you had one, call the phone number on the back of your credit card and ask the bank to send it to you. Having your PIN sent to you usually takes five to seven business days, though some banks will do it over the phone if you tell them your mother's maiden name or give some other security clearance.

Paying with traveler's checks

Traveler's checks are going the way of typewriters. They date back to B.A. (Before ATMs). In those days, travelers couldn't be sure of finding a place that would cash a personal check for them while on vacation, so they often had to carry large amounts of cash.

Taking monetary precautions

Every credit-card company has an emergency toll-free number to call if your wallet or purse is stolen. The companies may be able to wire you a cash advance from your credit card immediately, and in many places, they can get you an emergency credit card in a day or two. The issuing bank's toll-free number is usually on the back of the credit card. In The Bahamas, call ☎ 800-847-2911. **Visa's** U.S. emergency number is ☎ 800-336-8472. **American Express** cardholders and traveler's check holders can call ☎ 800-233-5432 for all money emergencies. **MasterCard** holders should call ☎ 800-307-7309. Depending on where you are in The Bahamas, these numbers may or may not work. If they don't, your hotel operator can help connect you to the appropriate service.

If you opt to carry traveler's checks, keep a record of the serial numbers so that you can promptly cancel and replace them in the event of loss or theft.

Odds are that if your wallet is gone, you've seen the last of it, and the police aren't likely to recover it for you. However, after you realize that your wallet's gone and you cancel your credit cards, call to inform the police. You may need the police report number for credit card or insurance purposes later.

Because you can replace them if lost or stolen, traveler's checks were a sound alternative to carrying a large amount of cash in your wallet. Actually, traveler's checks still serve this purpose. If you feel that you need the security of traveler's checks and don't mind the hassle of showing identification every time you want to cash a check, you can purchase traveler's checks at almost any bank.

In The Bahamas, some restaurants tack on an additional service charge if you pay with traveler's checks. However, if you're headed to any of the smaller islands, you may not find any ATMs. In that case, traveler's checks are a safer choice than cash. Converting small denominations to cash periodically is best so that you can avoid losing a lot of money in the event of theft.

American Express offers traveler's checks in denominations of $10, $20, $50, $100, $500, and $1,000. You pay a service charge for the checks ranging from 1 to 4 percent, though AAA members can get them without a fee at most AAA offices. You can order American Express Traveler's checks over the phone by calling ☎ 800-221-7282 or visit the Web site at www.americanexpress.com; Amex gold and platinum cardholders who call the toll-free number are exempt from the 1-percent fee.

Visa (☎ 800-227-6811; www.visa.com) and **MasterCard** (☎ 800-223-9920; www.mastercard.com) also issue traveler's checks, which are available at thousands of banks and other locations across the country. Call the toll-free numbers or visit the Web sites to find a location near you. The service charge ranges between 1.5 and 2 percent; checks come in denominations of $20, $50, $100, $500, and $1,000.

Calculating the Cost of Your Trip

In planning a trip to The Bahamas, no one wants to toss a wet beach blanket on the fun. Knowing what you'll pay can lead to a more trouble-free trip. If you run up charges with abandon, your credit card company will love you, but you won't be happy. Taking a few moments to figure out your expenses in advance can ensure a hassle-free vacation later.

You can use the worksheets at the back of this book to jot down anticipated costs so that you can see whether you need to do some nipping and tucking. Better yet, you may even discover that you have more wiggle room than you thought, and you can slip in that oceanfront room or that sunset sail that you really wanted.

To make certain that you're not forgetting any expenses, try taking a mental stroll through your entire trip. Start with the cost of transportation from your home to the airport, your airline tickets, and transfers to your accommodations. Add your daily hotel rate, meals, activities and entertainment, your return to the airport, and finally, your transportation home from the airport. Just to be on the safe side, add another 15 to 20 percent for other costs that may crop up.

Adding up lodging expenses

The biggest chunk of your budget goes toward your accommodations. As you flip through the island chapters, dollar signs ($ to $$$$$) indicate the price category of each hotel. For an explanation of these categories, turn to the Introduction at the beginning of the book. Notice that hotel rates are all over the map, from less than $85 a night for a double room to more than $600. Some rates cover breakfast or breakfast and dinner. The highest charges given are for *all-inclusive* resorts; this means that you can't compare their rates to those of other hotels without taking into account the fact that all meals, beverages, and most activities are included in one price. Also, some rates include taxes and gratuities while others don't.

Reducing the rack rate

The prices of rooms within a single resort can vary as much as hotels. Should you shell out top dollar to stay in an oceanfront suite? That depends on your budget and desires to fall asleep to the sound of the surf or wake up to the sun shimmering on the water. But if you find a garden room steps away from the shore just as attractive and comfortable, you can save the extra cash for something else.

The least you can expect to pay for a double room is about $85 a night (in the low season — summer through fall) or $140 (in high season) at a small hotel — that is, on a rack rate.

A *rack rate* is the maximum that a hotel charges for a room. It's the rate that you get if you walk in off the street and ask for a room for the night. You sometimes see this rate printed on the fire/emergency exit diagrams posted on the back of your hotel door.

Each hotel description quotes rack rates. These rates are a guidepost only, and few people ever pay them. Hotels are always happy to charge rack rates, but savvy travelers know that air/hotel package deals, staying a minimum number of nights, or special seasonal promotions can greatly reduce such rates. Just ask the hotel or your travel agent if they can quote you a better price.

In all but the smallest accommodations, the price of a room depends on how you make your reservation. A travel agent may be able to negotiate a better price with certain hotels than you can get by yourself. (The hotel gives the agent a discount in exchange for steering his or her business toward that hotel.) Making a reservation online through a hotel or airline Web site often allows you to take advantage of special discounts. Reserving a room through the hotel's 800-number may also result in a lower rate than if you call the hotel directly. On the other hand, the central reservations number may not know about discount rates at specific locations. For example, local franchises may offer a special group rate for a wedding or family reunion, but may neglect to tell the central booking line. Your best bet is to call both the local number and the 800-number and see which one gives you a better deal.

Timing your visit for the best value

To save money on accommodations, timing is vital. Room rates drop during the summer and fall. The rates of some hotels go up and down throughout the year. Some rates rise around Christmas, dip right after New Year's, and then go up again until April.

Room rates also change as occupancy rates rise and fall. If a hotel is almost full, it's less likely to extend discount rates; if it's close to empty, it may negotiate. Resorts are most crowded on weekends, and they usually offer discounted rates for midweek stays. Prices are subject to change without notice, so even the rates quoted in this book may be different from the actual rate that you receive when you make your reservation. Mention membership in AAA, AARP, frequent flyer programs, and any other corporate rewards program when you make your reservation. It may save you a few dollars off your room rate.

For more tips on money-saving package deals (also known as package tours), turn to Chapter 6.

Totaling transportation costs

After you pay for airfare (for tips on discounts, turn to Chapter 8), your transportation costs should be low. Taxis, hotel shuttles, and public buses on some islands are readily available. Many vacationers don't rent cars and with good reason. Gas on some islands can cost as much or more than $3.25 per gallon.

Most package deals include transfers between the airport and your hotel. Ferries to Harbour Island, Green Turtle Cay, Elbow Cay, and Man-O-War Cay run $8 to $16 round-trip.

On New Providence (Nassau, Cable Beach, and Paradise Island), you can get to most sights and attractions by foot or by public bus. Cab fares to and from sights can add up fast, but you can always take a taxi tour of several attractions. Half-day tours begin at about $30 for adults. Most main taxi expenses are for transportation to and from restaurants.

Take advantage of the free shuttle buses that some resorts offer, including those on Paradise Island and Cable Beach on New Providence, as well as in George Town, Exuma.

Dealing with dining dollars

Each island chapter in Parts III through VII recommends favorite restaurants. Dollar signs ($ to $$$$$) also give you an idea of whether the restaurant is cheap, expensive, or somewhere in between. See the Introduction for an explanation of these price categories.

The prices quoted are for main courses at dinner, unless stated otherwise. When a restaurant has two dollar signs, for example, it means that most of the dinner courses are in that price range, but some may be more or less expensive. To get a picture of your total expenses, you have to remember to estimate your beverage, appetizer, dessert, and tip as well.

À la carte hotel breakfast buffets can be expensive, but they're often elaborate. With everything from made-to-order omelets and waffles to carved meats, an array of fresh fruit, and a variety of bread and cereal, you often won't need to eat again until dinner.

On the larger islands (New Providence or Grand Bahama), you can sample some top-rate cuisine. But dinner for two at a top-drawer restaurant can easily run more than $100 — before the tip. Costs are high because much of the food is imported. However, quite a few chefs are from Europe, so you're treated to the imaginative creations of some of the continent's best. Some of the best food comes from the marriage of European and island cuisine.

Check out local restaurants outside the hotels and away from resort areas. Not only do you come across savory home-style food, but you save money as well. Look for the Island Spice icon, indicating restaurants (as well as other attractions) with authentic appeal. Many of these local establishments aren't much on decor, and you may sit in metal chairs and dine on plastic tablecloths, but the atmosphere is friendly and the price is usually right.

Staying in a rental with a kitchen or kitchenette can help you cut costs. Even if you don't feel like cooking every meal, you can save plenty by not eating out every breakfast or lunch. Likewise, if your room has only a refrigerator, fill it with drinks, snacks, and fruit from the local grocery store.

Soft drinks can cost $2 or $3 each. Try the local beer, *Kalik,* which is less expensive than imported beers and just as good as many.

Tipping the correct amount

Bring plenty of single dollar bills for tipping. Porters look for $1 per bag. Especially at some of the larger hotels, porters often quickly separate you from your bags and then practically demand a tip for carrying your luggage a few feet. By the time you get to your room, you may be expected to tip two different baggage handlers. To discourage porters from arguing with you when you politely decline their assistance, pack lightly and use luggage with wheels.

Most restaurants automatically add a 15 percent service charge to your check. Ask if you're not sure. Taxi drivers also expect about 15 percent, and ferry captains never refuse a little something extra, either. You can give tour guides a few dollars, depending on the cost and quality of the excursion.

Spending wisely

The cost for activities and attractions can differ greatly from resort to resort and from island to island. All-inclusive resorts often offer a wider variety of activities without the extra charge. The following are some popular activities and what you can expect pay:

✔ **Golfing on the go.** Greens fees run $80 to $100 at most courses for 18 holes, including a shared cart, plus about $25 to $35 for club rentals. If that's not expensive enough for you, try the new course at the **Ocean Club** on Paradise Island, where greens fees run around $225. Some courses offer reduced fees for 9 holes in the afternoon, and rates for both 9 and 18 holes drop during the off-season (roughly May through October). Arrange tee times as far ahead of time as you can.

✔ **Indulging in a water sport.** Even at all-inclusive resorts, you have to pay extra for scuba diving, which starts at $75 for a two-tank dive. To sail off to a reef for snorkeling, expect to spend at least $30. If you want to rent snorkel gear at the beach, you pay about $15. For deep-sea fishing, you'll spend at least $75 per person. For details about boat rentals, windsurfing, water-skiing, and golf (on New Providence, Grand Bahama, and the Abacos), turn to the island-specific chapters.

✔ **Taking a tour.** Save a day for an island tour and especially if you aren't renting a car. Half-day taxi tours start at $30 per adult. On New Providence, ask at your hotel about less expensive group tours. See the individual island chapters in Parts III through VII for information on destination-specific tours.

✔ **Stocking up on souvenirs.** In 1992, the government abolished all import duties on a variety of items, making for duty-free shopping. You save tax on perfumes, crystal, leather goods, watches and clocks, jewelry, fine linens and tablecloths, china, camera equipment, and binoculars and telescopes. If you're in the market for any of these goods, you can pay anywhere from 25 to 50 percent less in The Bahamas than in the U.S. Vacationers can also take home up to two liters of liquor duty-free as long as they are of legal drinking age in their country of citizenship.

✔ **Tasting the nightlife.** When the sun goes down, casinos, bars, and dance floors heat up on New Providence and Grand Bahama. Cover charges for nightclubs run about $5 to $10, plus rather expensive drinks.

Considering taxes

On your hotel bill, you also pay resort taxes and gratuities and sometimes an energy surcharge. Some hotels include these extras in the quoted rates, while others add them on to your bill.

Make sure to clarify any extra charges, because they can easily swell your hotel bill by $20, $30, or even $60 or more per night, depending on the cost of your room.

Total charges vary from hotel to hotel, but you can roughly expect to pay a 12 percent resort tax and about $8 per day, per guest (over age 12) housekeeping gratuity and energy surcharge for use of electricity.

Don't gamble away your last few dollars in cash, because you need extra cash to leave the country. The airports collect a **departure tax** from all passengers over age 12. You pay $15 from New Providence (Nassau) or Out Islands and $18 from Grand Bahama.

Keeping a Lid on Your Money

Before you leave for your vacation, consider costs — hotel taxes, tips, and telephone surcharges, for instance — that can really throw off your budget.

Here are some suggestions on how to keep the cost of a vacation from skyrocketing.

- ✔ **Go in the off-season.** If you can travel at nonpeak times (September through November, for example), hotel prices are often slashed in half.

- ✔ **Travel on off days of the week.** Airfares vary depending on the day of the week. If you can travel on a Tuesday, Wednesday, or Thursday, you may find cheaper flights. If you can, fly on a different day to get a cheaper rate.

- ✔ **Try a package tour.** With one call to a travel agent or packager, you can, for many destinations, book airfare, hotel, ground transportation, and even some sightseeing for a lot less than if you tried to put the trip together yourself. (See Chapter 6 for specific suggestions of package tour companies to contact.)

- ✔ **Carry your own bags.** Travel light and with wheels on your suitcases. Politely but firmly decline porters, no matter how persistently they reach for your luggage.

- ✔ **Reserve a hotel room with a kitchen and do your own cooking.** You can save a lot of money by not eating in restaurants three times a day. Even if you make only breakfast and an occasional bag lunch in the kitchen, your savings add up.

- ✔ **Steer clear of the hotel minibar and room service.** Don't even open that little refrigerator in your room. Likewise, don't order room service. If you do, you have to pay a service charge and tip — for what is often lukewarm food — on top of already-inflated prices. Also, some hotels provide complimentary bottled water, while others charge $5.

- ✔ **Share your room with your kids.** A room with two double beds doesn't cost any more than one with a queen-size bed, and many hotels don't charge you the additional person rate if the additional person is pint-sized and related to you. If you're charged anything, it's at a discounted rate, saving you hundreds over booking a second room.

✔ **Use a pay phone to call home.** Avoid using the phone in your hotel room to call outside the hotel. Charges can be astronomical, even for local calls, which are sometimes at least $1 a pop (instead of 25¢ at a pay phone). When you call long distance, you may think you're saving money by using the toll-free number of your calling card instead of dialing direct. However, most hotels charge you at least $1 to connect you to an outside line for the toll-free call. On top of whatever your calling card bills you, the hotel also charges you just for picking up the phone — whether or not you reach the person you wanted.

✔ **Try expensive restaurants at lunch instead of dinner.** Lunch tabs are usually a fraction of what dinner costs at most top restaurants, and the menu often boasts many of the same specialties.

✔ **Get a room off the beach.** Accommodations within walking distance of the shore can be much cheaper than those right on the beach. Beaches are public, so you don't need to stay in a hotel that's on the sand to spend most of your vacation at the beach.

✔ **Skip the souvenirs.** Your photographs and memories are the best and cheapest mementos. If money is tight, you can do without the T-shirts, woodcarvings, straw hats, shell necklaces, and other trinkets.

✔ **Steer clear of the casinos.** If you can't resist gambling, head to an island without casinos. Only New Providence and Grand Bahama offer casinos.

A fabulous vacation in The Bahamas doesn't have to put you in the poor house. Throughout the book, look for the Bargain Alert icon, which alerts you to money-saving restaurants, hotels, and adventures.

Chapter 8

Tying Up Loose Ends

. . . .

In This Chapter

▶ Getting your entry and departure documents in order

▶ Deciding on insurance

▶ Ensuring a safe vacation

▶ Deciding whether to rent a car

▶ Packing only what you need

. . . .

*B*efore you can start wiggling your toes in the sand, you need to handle a few details. This chapter deals with all the nitty-gritty details of your travel plans, such as insurance and car rentals.

Arriving on and Departing from the Islands

If you're a U.S., Canadian, or British citizen, you don't need a passport to enter The Bahamas, as long as you have two other acceptable forms of identification. If you don't have a passport, you must take the following papers with you:

✔ A certified or original copy of your birth certificate. (It must have a raised seal.)

✔ An official photo identification, such as a valid driver's license.

✔ A return or ongoing airplane ticket.

You may enter with an expired passport, as long as it has expired within the last five years. Whether your passport is current or not, make photocopies of the inside page — the one with your photo — before you leave home. Also copy any other important documents, such as your driver's license, airline tickets, and hotel vouchers. Of course, keep the copies separate from the originals.

Citizens of Ireland, Australia, and New Zealand are required to present a passport.

U.S. citizens under age 17 need only a birth certificate to enter The Bahamas. Minor children from other countries, including Canada, are allowed to travel on their parent's passport.

As you enter the country, you receive an Immigration Card to fill out and sign. Do this paperwork while you're standing in line instead of waiting until it's your turn. Be sure to keep your carbon copy in a safe place, because it's collected when you leave The Bahamas.

Save enough cash for the departure tax that you have to pay at the airport on your way home. The tax is $15 from New Providence or any Out Island, and $18 from Grand Bahama.

Getting a passport

Although not required, a passport is a good document to have, especially because you're traveling to a foreign country. Besides, flipping through the stamps that you get in the back of your passport each time you travel is fun.

U.S. citizens

If you're applying for a passport for the first time, you need to do so in person at one of these locations:

- ✔ A passport office
- ✔ A federal, state, or probate court
- ✔ A post office designated to accept passport applications

At the time you apply, you need to present a certified birth certificate as proof of U.S. citizenship. Taking along your driver's license, state or military ID, and Social Security card is also a good idea. If you've recently married and changed your name, bring a copy of your marriage certificate. In addition, you need two identical 2-x-2 inch photographs; many local photo shops take instant passport photos.

For people over age 15, a passport is good for ten years and costs $60 ($45 plus a $15 handling fee). For people age 15 and younger, passports are valid for only five years and cost $40. If your passport is valid and was issued within the past 12 years and if you're over age 15, you can renew it by mail and skip the $15 handling fee.

Processing usually takes about three weeks, but can take far longer, especially during busy times of year, such as the spring. If you're crunched for time, consider paying an extra $35, plus the express mail service fee, to have your passport sent to you within seven to ten working days. In even more of a hurry? Try **Passport Express** (☎ **800/ 362-8196** or 401/272-4612; www.passportexpress.com), a nationwide service that can get you a new or renewed passport within 24 hours. Getting a new passport with this service costs $150 plus the $95 government fees if you need it in one to six days, or $100 plus the $95 government fees if you need it in seven to ten days. If you're renewing your passport, the government fees drop to $75. For a rushed passport, you must have proof of travel — your tickets.

For more details about getting a passport, call the **National Passport Agency** (☎ **202/647-0518**). To locate a passport office in your area, call the **National Passport Information Center** (☎ **900/225-5674**). The Web page of the **U.S. State Department** (www.travel.state.gov) also offers information on passport services, and you can download an application. In addition, many post offices and travel agencies keep passport applications on hand.

Canadian citizens

Passport information and applications are available from the central **Passport Office** in Ottawa (☎ **800/567-6868;** www.dfait-maeci.gc.ca). Regional passport offices and travel agencies also offer applications. Valid for five years, a passport costs $60. You can include children under age 16 on a parent's passport, but only if they're traveling with that parent. Applications must include two identical passport-sized photographs and proof of Canadian citizenship. Allow five to ten days for processing if you apply in person, or about three weeks if you submit your application by mail.

Residents of the United Kingdom

To pick up an application for a ten-year passport, visit your nearest passport office, major post office, or travel agency. You can also contact the **London Passport Office** at ☎ **020/7271-3000** or search its Web site at www.ukpa.gov.uk. Passports are £28 for adults and £14.80 for children under age 16.

Residents of Ireland

You can apply for a ten-year passport, costing €58 ($51.80), at the **Passport Office,** Setanta Centre, Molesworth St., Dublin 2 (☎ **01-671-1633;** www.irlgov.ie/iveagh). You can also apply at 1A South Mall, Cork (☎ **021-272-525**) or over the counter at most main post offices. Those under age 18 and over age 65 must apply for a €12.70 ($11.35) three-year passport.

Residents of Australia

Apply at your local post office or search the government Web site at `www.passports.gov.au`. Passports for adults are A$136 and for those under age 18 A$68.

Residents of New Zealand

You can pick up a passport application at any travel agency or Link Centre. For more data, contact the **Passport Office,** 47 Boulcott House, Wellington (☎ **0800/225-050;** `www.passports.govt.nz`). Passports for adults are NZ$80 and for those under age 16 NZ$40.

Clearing customs

To clear customs in The Bahamas, you're asked for an oral baggage declaration of the items that you're carrying. (Don't forget to register expensive items such as computers, jewelry, or photography equipment.) However, your luggage is still subject to customs inspection.

The more sloppy and/or unusual you're dressed, the more likely customs officials are to rifle through your bags. This isn't the best time to put those neon-blue highlights in your hair or don ripped black stockings or those jeans with multiple holes.

Each visiting adult is permitted to bring in 200 cigarettes, 50 cigars, or one pound of tobacco, plus one quart of wine or spirits (hard liquor), a laptop computer, cameras, sports equipment, any other personal effects, and any amount of money.

Taking pornography or controlled drugs into the country is illegal. No matter what island vendors tell you, don't try to take any jewelry or other items made from coral or sea turtle shells back to the U.S. Customs officials will confiscate such items at the airport.

Visitors taking off from New Providence (Nassau) or Grand Bahama (Freeport/Lucaya) for most U.S. destinations have the convenience of clearing U.S. Customs and Immigration before leaving The Bahamas. This pre-clearance means that when you reach the U.S., you simply walk off the plane and head home.

Taking advantage of duty-free allowances

Each returning U.S. citizen may take home up to $600 worth of merchandise duty-free, as long as he or she has been away for at least 48 hours and hasn't taken such an exemption within the past 30 days. On the next $1,000 of purchases, you pay a flat rate of 10 percent duty.

Keep receipts for everything of consequence that you buy during your vacation. For more details, contact the **U.S. Customs Service** (☎ **202/354-1000;** www.customs.ustreas.gov).

Protecting Your Trip Investment and Your Safety

You can protect yourself in the event of a cancelled or interrupted trip, a medical emergency, or losing luggage that goes one place while you go to another. Health and safety are the most serious issues when you're on vacation. There are certain precautions and steps that you can take to lower the prospect of turning a memorable vacation into one you'd rather forget.

Covering your losses with travel insurance

Three major types of trip-cancellation insurance exist:

- ✔ Insurance that covers cases where you've pre-pay a cruise or tour that gets cancelled, and you can't get your money back.

- ✔ Insurance that covers you or someone in your family becoming sick or dying, causing cancellation (but beware that you may not be covered for a pre-existing condition).

- ✔ Insurance that covers cancellations due to bad weather, such as a hurricane that makes travel impossible.

Some insurers provide coverage for events such as jury duty; natural disasters close to home, such as floods or fire; and even the loss of a job. A few have added provisions for cancellations because of terrorist activities. Always check the fine print before signing on and don't buy trip-cancellation insurance from the tour operator that may be responsible for the cancellation; buy it only from a reputable travel insurance agency. In addition, don't overbuy insurance coverage. You won't be reimbursed for more than the cost of your trip.

Trip cancellation/interruption insurance is a good idea if you're paying a large portion of your vacation expenses up front, including an air/hotel package deal, an all-inclusive resort, or a cruise. Because young children are prone to accidents or illnesses, consider this coverage.

Your existing health insurance may already cover you if you get sick or are hurt in an accident while on vacation. If you belong to an HMO, your coverage may not be in effect while you're away from home.

Medical evaluation insurance is a good idea, and it's not included in many policies. If you get sick and need to forfeit your nonreturnable ticket and pay for a same-day one-way ticket home, you'll be out big bucks.

On international flights (including U.S. portions of international trips), baggage is limited to approximately $9.07 per pound, up to approximately $635 per checked bag. If you plan to check items more valuable than the standard liability, you may want to purchase "excess valuation" coverage from the airline, which covers up to $5,000.

Be sure to take any valuables or irreplaceable items with you in your carry-on luggage. If you file a lost luggage claim, be prepared to answer detailed questions about the contents of your baggage, and file a claim immediately as most airlines enforce a 21-day deadline.

Before you leave home, compile an inventory of all packed items and a rough estimate of the total value to ensure that you're properly compensated if your luggage is lost. You'll only be reimbursed for what you lost — no more. Once you've filed a complaint, persist in securing your reimbursement; no laws govern the length of time it takes for a carrier to reimburse you. If you arrive at a destination without your bags, ask the airline to forward them to your hotel or to your next destination; they'll usually comply. If your bag is delayed or lost, the airline may reimburse you for reasonable expenses, such as a toothbrush or a set of clothes, but the airline is under no legal obligation to do so.

Lost luggage may also be covered by your homeowner's or renter's policy. Many platinum and gold credit cards cover you as well. If you choose to purchase additional lost-luggage insurance, be sure not to buy more than you need. Buy in advance from the insurer or a trusted agent because prices will be much higher at the airport.

When you don't have travel insurance

If you opt not to purchase any travel insurance and you find that you need to cancel or interrupt your trip, the tour operator's fee (if you bought an air/hotel package) reduces any refund you receive. This fee ($25 per person, for example) may not sound like much, but when you realize that this amount is in addition to any penalties that the hotels and airlines levy, your refund for unused services (if your deal entitles you to any money back at all) shrinks further. To get refunds, you or your travel agent must send written requests to all parties involved, and strict cancellation policies can turn getting a refund into a fruitless quest.

Some credit cards (American Express and certain gold and platinum Visa and MasterCards, for example) offer automatic flight insurance against death or dismemberment in case of an airplane crash. This means that you may not have to purchase coverage for airborne loss of life or limb.

If you feel that you need more insurance than you already have, try one of the companies in the following list, or ask a trusted travel agent for recommendations. But before you sign on that dotted line, make sure that you understand all the restrictions and exclusions. The cost of trip cancellation/interruption insurance should be approximately 6 to 8% of the total value of your vacation. Here are some reputable companies that issue travel insurance:

- ✔ **Access America,** 6600 W. Broad St., Richmond, VA 23230 (☎ **800/284-8300;** www.accessamerica.com)

- ✔ **Travelex,** P.O. Box 641070, Omaha, NE 68164-7070 (☎ **800/228-9792;** www.travelex-insurance.com)

- ✔ **Travel Guard International,** 1145 Clark St., Stevens Point, WI 54481 (☎ **800/826-1300;** www.noelgroup.com)

- ✔ **Travel Insured International, Inc.,** P.O. Box 280568, East Hartford, CT 06128 (☎ **800/243-3174;** www.travelinsured.com)

Staying healthy and safe

Over the counter medications — aspirin, cold remedies, antacids, and so on — are readily available at pharmacies and hotels on New Providence and Grand Bahama, and in many hotels on other islands. For prescription drugs, bring the generic name of your medication, as local pharmacies may only know the generic name if you need a refill. Most hotel shops and pharmacies are not open at night, so travel with any basics you may need, such as medicine for diarrhea or upset stomach, sunburn remedies, anti-itch cream to soothe insect bites, and children's aspirin if you're traveling with little ones. Don't forget any prescription drugs that you're taking, and if you think you may run out, plan ahead to refill your prescription. If you wear contact lenses, pack an extra pair in the event that you lose one. Remember to carry your health insurance card in your wallet.

If you suffer from a chronic illness, talk to your doctor before taking the trip. For conditions such as epilepsy, diabetes, or a heart condition, wear a Medic Alert identification tag, which immediately alerts any doctor to your condition and gives him or her access to your medical records through Medic Alert's 24-hour hot-line. Membership is $35, plus a $20 annual fee. Contact the Medic Alert Foundation, P.O. Box 1009, Turlock, CA 95381-1009 (☎ **800/825-3785;** www.medicalert.org).

Emergencies and medical care

If you get sick, ask a staff member at your hotel to recommend a local doctor — even his or her own doctor if necessary. A local recommendation is probably better than any national consortium of doctors available through a toll-free number. If you can't find a doctor to help you right away, try the emergency room at the local hospital or the local clinic. Many hospital emergency rooms have walk-in-clinics for cases that aren't life-threatening. You may not get immediate attention, but you won't pay the high price of an emergency room visit.

Getting the straight dope on drugs

Some visitors think that on these easy-going semitropical islands, a laid-back attitude exists toward drugs. Quite the contrary. Marijuana, cocaine, and other mood-altering drugs are just as illegal in The Bahamas as they are elsewhere. However, unless you make a point of searching out drug dealers, whatever behind-the-scenes action there is will likely not affect you.

If you choose to indulge, however, don't expect any special treatment because you live elsewhere. Being caught with illegal drugs can send you on a trip to an uncomfortable Bahamian jail. Don't even think about trying to smuggle any drugs back into the U.S.

Addressing other potential hazards

Here are some ways to prevent common vacation disasters:

- ✔ **Drinking the water:** It's safe to drink from the tap, but you may not like the unfamiliar taste. Many hotels supply bottled or filtered water for guests. Before you take a swig from a bottle, though, check whether the hotel gives you the water free. Some resorts charge $5 or more per bottle. Stocking up on bottled water at a nearby drugstore or grocery is always cheaper than buying it at your hotel or taking it from your minibar.

- ✔ **Sunbathing sense:** As all visitors to the islands know, you can get a wicked sunburn even on hazy days if you don't wear sunscreen. Reapply the sunscreen every time you come out of the water even if your sunscreen is waterproof . Reapply the cream periodically throughout the day whether you go into the water or not. If you get your hair cornrowed and you're not used to wearing it that way, put some sunscreen on the delicate skin of your newly exposed scalp. Wide-brimmed hats also come in handy, of course.

- ✔ **Repelling bugs:** Use insect repellent, particularly at dusk, when the mosquitoes and gnats are at their most treacherous.

✔ **Taking a scuba dive:** If scuba is part of your vacation, plan your trip so that you don't fly within 24 hours of diving. Your body needs time to recover from being at a high altitude before it hits the lower depths, and vice versa.

When you're in the water, the stunning shapes and colors of fish, coral, and sea plants may make you want to reach out and touch. Don't. Not only can you destroy delicate marine life by doing so, but you also put yourself in danger. Even innocuous-looking coral can be razor sharp, and a variety aptly known as *fire coral* can burn your skin. Also be warned that shiny jewelry in the water can attract barracudas and sharks.

✔ **Using common sense to keep safe:** Even though you're relaxing on a vacation, keep up your guard. For example, especially in Nassau, don't venture into unknown neighborhoods alone at night. Don't wear flashy jewelry or leave your valuables lying around, even in your locked hotel room. Many of the larger hotels have in-room safes or front desk safety deposit boxes.

Readying to Go

You finally arrive at your hotel. You open your suitcase and realize that you forgot something crucial. If you're visiting more than one island, dragging around overstuffed suitcases is almost as bad, especially when you never use most of what you brought. So how do you find that happy medium between packing too much and bringing too little?

Packing the essentials

The first step to packing essentials is jotting down a list of the things that you may forget: Your glasses if you usually wear contacts, a book to read on the plane, medications, slippers, and so on. Post your list on the inside of your front door so that you're sure to check it right before you leave for the airport. Take everything you think you'll need and then lay it out on the bed. Now get rid of half of it. The more pruning you do now, the more your back and shoulders will thank you later when they're not strained from carrying heavy bags. (And who knows? You may find an outfit or two in an island boutique that you want, so you need to leave some room in that suitcase.) Take enough clothes to have something casual for each day, as well as something dressier to change into for dinner and after-dark fun each night. Pack separates that you can mix and match so that you can wear pieces more than once with a new look.

A few restaurants request that men wear jackets at dinnertime, particularly during the winter season. In restaurant reviews in the island chapters, it's indicated which dining spots request jackets. For the most part, you can dress casually. Although shorts and T-shirts are fine during the day, think long pants and one or two collared shirts for evening wear, especially on New Providence and Grand Bahama. During winter months, The Bahamas cools off significantly in the evening, and air-conditioning keeps most indoor spaces on the chilly side year-round, so bring a light jacket, shawl, or sweater.

You'll also need sneakers or other comfortable walking shoes. If you intend to use a hotel fitness room, be aware that, for safety reasons, some don't permit the use of exercise equipment without sneakers.

Most hotels have irons and ironing boards available through housekeeping, if not already sitting in guest rooms, so don't bother packing a portable iron or steamer. Feel free to bring your hair dryer, because U.S. appliances are compatible. The current in The Bahamas is 110 volts, 60 cycles AC.

Suitcases with wheels come in handy, and they can keep you from having to tip so many porters. Put your name, address, and phone number both inside your suitcase and on your luggage tag, but flip the paper with your information on it so that it's not visible to the casual observer. You may also want to add a temporary luggage tag with the name of your hotel on it.

When packing, start with the biggest, hardest items (usually shoes, which you should put in plastic bags to keep other things clean) and then fit smaller items in and around them. Stick breakable items in between several layers of clothes or keep them in your carry-on bag. Put things that can leak, like shampoo, suntan lotion, and so on, in plastic bags. Lock your suitcase with a small padlock available at most luggage stores if your bag doesn't already have one.

Film is expensive, so stock up before you travel, particularly if you have special needs. For example, although film for color prints is widely available, black-and-white and slide film is not.

Here are some other items you'll need:

- ✔ Sunglasses
- ✔ A baseball cap, visor, or wide-brimmed sun hat
- ✔ Sunscreen
- ✔ Insect repellent
- ✔ At least two bathing suits (because humidity often means that suits are still damp the next morning)

- ✔ Sturdy water shoes (rocks and coral can wreak havoc on bare soles)
- ✔ Your scuba certification card (C-card), logbook recording your recent dives, and any personal scuba gear, if you're a diver
- ✔ Your driver's license, if you intend to rent a car

Carrying on the basics

After September 11, 2001, the carefree traveler can no longer arrive in the islands with only carry-on bags. Airlines have cracked down on the size and number of carry-ons permitted. On most international flights, each passenger can take only one carry-on (purses don't count), and this luggage must fit in the overhead compartment or under the seat in front of you.

So what should you put in this precious single bag?

- ✔ Prescriptions
- ✔ Glasses or contact lenses, cases, lens cleaning fluid, and so on
- ✔ Books or magazines to enjoy during your flight
- ✔ A personal headphone stereo
- ✔ Your airline tickets, passport, and other vital documents
- ✔ A sweater or light jacket for the cool airplane cabin
- ✔ A snack in case you don't like the airline food
- ✔ Your camera and film
- ✔ A bottle of water (planes are notoriously dehydrating)
- ✔ A bathing suit
- ✔ Beach shoes or sandals
- ✔ Sunscreen
- ✔ A pair of shorts and a T-shirt (or other lightweight change of clothes)
- ✔ A change of underwear
- ✔ A hairbrush or comb
- ✔ A toothbrush

Each child with a ticket is also allowed a carry-on. Older children enjoy taking backpacks filled with their stuff. If you're vacationing with babies in tow, bring plenty of diapers, because they're expensive on the islands.

Double-checking before you go

Here's a reminder of a few last-minute details:

- ✔ Cancel or suspend your newspaper delivery.
- ✔ Arrange to have your mail held or picked up.
- ✔ Send your itinerary to a friend or relative.
- ✔ Write down the numbers of your traveler's checks.
- ✔ Make arrangements to get home from the airport.

Part III

New Providence: Nassau, Cable Beach, and Paradise Island

The 5th Wave   By Rich Tennant

It's a group of local musicians here to play for you. It's the customary greeting for new arrivals here on Jackhammer Island.

In this part . . .

*I*n this part, we help you sift through the wide array of accommodations in Cable Beach, Nassau, and Paradise Island, which make up New Providence. We also guide you through the details of getting to (and around) New Providence, home of the Bahamas' historic capital, and seeing the best sights after you arrive.

When it comes to restaurants, we offer tips on finding the most authentic local cuisine and give you our top picks of everything from fast food to fine food. Sure, you can hit the casinos and duty-free shops, but we also steer you to plenty of other diversions, both in the ocean and on dry land.

Chapter 9

The Lowdown on the New Providence Hotel Scene

. . . .

In This Chapter

▶ Deciding among hotel locations

▶ Evaluating the top hotel choices

. . . .

*N*ew Providence reigns supreme when it comes to the number of resorts and activities, from snorkeling and sailing to rock climbing and "ice skating." You can also find a bed-and-breakfast or a small beach hotel away from the crowds. Most accommodations are high-rises with hundreds of rooms. In fact, one, Atlantis Paradise Island, is actually more like an aquatic theme park than a hotel, weighing in with some 2,349 rooms.

In addition to large hotels and a few small ones, New Providence offers villas, townhouses, and condos. These options have fewer services such as restaurants or staff to help make arrangements for tours and activities. Many are located a distance away from sights and attractions, and you'll have to provide your own transportation. Also keep in mind that while you have all the comforts of home, you also have all the work that goes along with it. However, this type of accommodation is good for families or groups of friends who prefer to do their own cooking and are looking for a private vacation. For long-term vacationers, this is a great money-saving tactic for an extended island stay.

Finding the Location That's Right for You

The capital city of Nassau dominates **New Providence Island.** Most of the beach resorts are found at **Cable Beach,** a 10-minute drive west of Nassau. **Paradise Island,** which is connected by bridge to Nassau, is also packed with beach hotels.

Nassau, where Bahamians live and work, and the resort areas of Cable Beach and Paradise Island have distinct personalities. For many, life on scenic Cable Beach revolves around the casinos, while the draw for others is the long stretch of golden sand. A hotel in downtown Nassau can put you on or across from a beach; it can also place you within walking distance of a slew of restaurants, the straw market, duty-free shops, horse-and-buggy rides, and historic sites. You must pay a toll every time you cross the bridge to Paradise Island, where the Atlantis megaresort has spread like juicy gossip. Developed far more recently than Nassau and home to the newer of the two casinos, Paradise Island is short on historic attractions and long on water fun, designer shops, nightlife, and a first-rate (but expensive) cuisine.

If you want to stay on the beach but not cause serious damage to your wallet, look for choices on Cable Beach and Nassau. On Paradise Island, the best hotels — whether on or off the beach — are more expensive.

The casino in Cable Beach sits between the Nassau Marriott and the Radisson. On Paradise Island, the casino is located at the Atlantis Resort. Shuttle buses take you to these gambling meccas if you choose not to stay at one of the other hotels.

You can easily reach other attractions, such as museums, old forts, and the **Ardastra Gardens & Zoo** (see Chapter 12) from Cable Beach, downtown Nassau, or Paradise Island by taxi, guided tour, public bus, rental car, or foot. Likewise, you can make arrangements through your hotel to sail to one of the beach-rimmed offshore islets that offer aquatic activities, including dolphin and stingray encounters.

Some of these side trips are popular among cruise-ship passengers, so depending on when you go, these uninhabited islands may host large crowds.

Here are our top hotel picks in Nassau, Cable Beach, and Paradise Island, along with some handy maps.

Checking Out New Providence's Best Accommodations

The following rack rates are for two people spending one night in a double room in winter or early spring. These charges are published rates available to anybody who walks in off the street and requests a room. You can get discounted hotel rates in many ways. (See Chapter 4 for more details.) Rates at Breezes and Sandals Royal Bahamian may seem extraordinarily high when compared to our other recommendations. But these two hotels are all-inclusive; their charges include meals, beverages, tips, taxes, transportation to and from the airport, entertainment, and most activities.

If a view is important to you, make sure that it's clarified when reserving a room. The most expensive rooms invariably have ocean views; the less expensive accommodations open onto a pool or a garden. Sometimes another building can obscure views from a room. It pays to ask so that you aren't unpleasantly surprised when checking in.

Most New Providence hotels do not quote a meal plan such as MAP (modified American plan or breakfast and dinner). When they do, the extra cost per person is indicated.

Atlantis Paradise Island Resort & Casino
$$$$$ Paradise Island Beach

The Atlantis a $850-million, 2,349-room resort, sprawls from one shore to the other of Paradise Island. Stay here if you'd like to lodge in a mega-resort mini-city. Slip into the Ocean Club Golf & Tennis Resort nearby if you're seeking more tranquility and exclusivity. Dozens of restaurants, bars, lounges, designer boutiques, and a mammoth casino that's open day and night keep many visitors glued to the premises. The resort's comfortable, pleasantly decorated rooms vary in size, view, and location. Although all have balconies, many of the balconies in the plush Royal Towers (the priciest section) are only wide enough for two pairs of feet. The Beach Tower is the least expensive wing, with Coral Towers in the middle. Bathrooms are spacious, well maintained, and completely modern with tub and shower combination. Room service is available around the clock, and you can stay busy on the tennis, volleyball, and basketball courts, the putting green, in exercise classes, or at the spa. However, the centerpiece of the hotel is its water wonderworld of aquariums, freshwater pools, snorkeling lagoons, waterslides, and a white sand beach.

Take one of the waterslides down the life-size replica of a Mayan temple. A 60-foot, nearly vertical drop zips you along a clear tunnel that slices through a shark tank. The 48-foot high corkscrew slide, however, lets you view the sharks at a more leisurely pace. Other aquatic playgrounds range from a shallow children's pool and beachlike zero-entry pool (instead of having steps, the shallow end slopes gradually from dry land, just like a beach) to a river pool that carries you along in an inner tube, as well as a series of pools linked by waterslides. In other words, you're at Disney. It's activity-packed children's program is not only the best in The Bahamas, but in the Caribbean as well. Twenty restaurants are on site, so the food range, price, and type of cuisine are grander or greater than that in many small towns. You can take the kids to have burgers, or you can dine on some of the most superior cuisine in The Bahamas, prepared by top Bahamian, American, or European chefs. For example, Villa d'Este offers a refined Northern Italian cuisine almost as grand as you'd get in Italy, whereas Mama Loo's or Five Twins feature Asian food that would equal some of the finest places in New York.

Casino Dr. ☎ *800-ATLANTIS or 242-363-3000. Fax: 242-363-3524.* atlantis resort.com. *Rack rates: $325 and $450 for a double room. MAP $55 per person or $30 per child up to 12. AE, MC, V.*

Nassau and Paradise Island Accommodations

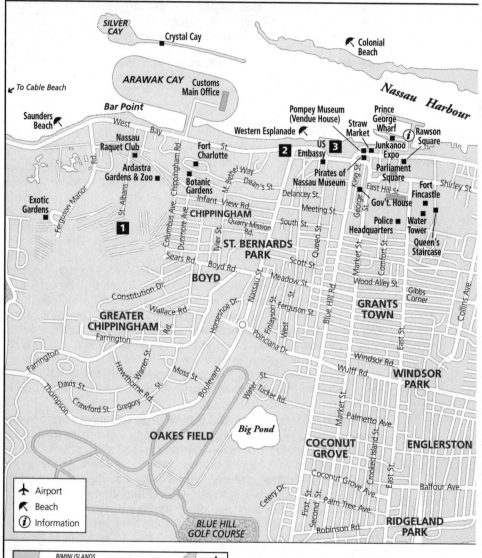

Atlantis Paradise Island Resort & Casino **4**

British Colonial Hilton **3**

Comfort Suites Paradise Island **5**

Dillet's Guest House **1**

Holiday Inn Junkanoo Beach Nassau **2**

Ocean Club Golf & Tennis Resort **7**

Sunrise Beach Club and Villas **6**

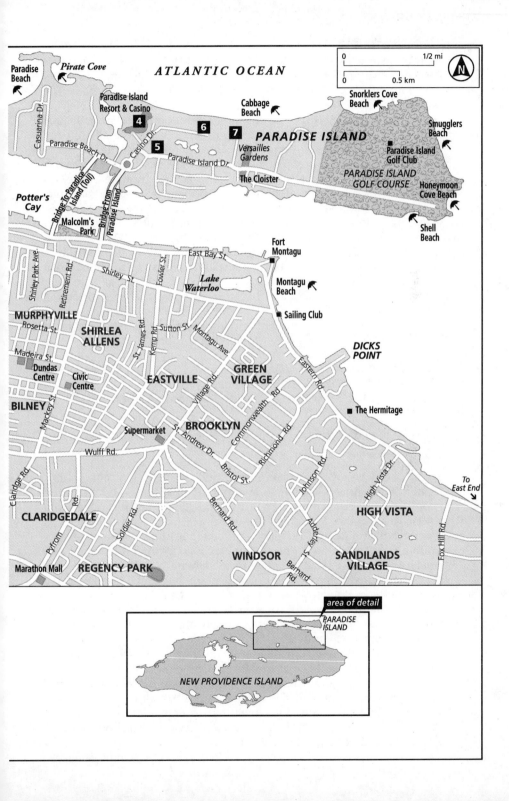

ATLANTIC OCEAN

0   1/2 mi
0   0.5 km
N

Paradise Beach

Pirate Cove

Paradise Island Resort & Casino

Cabbage Beach

Snorklers Cove Beach

Smugglers Beach

4

6

7 PARADISE ISLAND

Casuarina Dr.

Paradise Beach Dr.

Casino Dr.

5

Paradise Island Dr.

Versailles Gardens

Paradise Island Golf Club

PARADISE ISLAND GOLF COURSE

The Cloister

Honeymoon Cove Beach

Potter's Cay

Bridge To Paradise Island (Toll)

Bridge From Paradise Island

Malcolm's Park

Shell Beach

Fort Montagu

East Bay St.

Shirley Park Ave.

Retirement Rd.

Shirley St.

Fowler St.

Lake Waterloo

Montagu Beach

Sailing Club

DICKS POINT

MURPHYVILLE

Rosetta St.

SHIRLEA ALLENS

St. James Rd.

Kemp Rd.

Sutton St.

Montagu Ave.

Eastern Rd.

Madeira St.

Dundas Centre

Civic Centre

EASTVILLE

Village Rd.

GREEN VILLAGE

BILNEY

Mackey St.

Supermarket

BROOKLYN

St. Andrew Dr.

Commonwealth Rd.

Richmond Rd.

The Hermitage

Wulff Rd.

Bristol St.

Johnson Rd.

High Vista Dr.

To East End

Claridge Rd.

CLARIDGEDALE

Pyfrom Rd.

Soldier Rd.

Bernard Rd.

HIGH VISTA

Fox Hill Rd.

Marathon Mall

REGENCY PARK

WINDSOR

Addelay St.

Bernard Rd.

SANDILANDS VILLAGE

area of detail

PARADISE ISLAND

NEW PROVIDENCE ISLAND

Breezes
$$$$$ **Cable Beach**

At the eastern end of the strip of Cable Beach hotels, all-inclusive Breezes, run by SuperClubs, is designed mainly for adult couples and singles, but children are welcome too as long as they're 16 or older. The other major all-inclusive, Sandals (later in this chapter), is more elegant, stylish, and upscale, with better amenities, but that Jamaican chain only accepts male/female couples whereas Breezes is open to all. You can hone your skills on everything from toga and pajama parties to talent shows and comedy cabarets. Island traditions, such as dancers and musicians dressed in whimsical costumes, make lively appearances in *Junkanoo Jamborees* and steel band performances. On site is a large, heated, freshwater swimming pool. You can also find tropical activities, including a good stretch of beach, snorkeling, and scuba lessons. A short walk along the road or the beach takes you to the **Crystal Palace Casino** (see Chapter 12). The refurbished hotel rooms with wooden furniture and Formica tops are comfortable, but never rise beyond the standard of a first-class American motel. Bathrooms are medium in size and are tiled, containing both a shower and bathtub. Although Breezes' price tag sounds expensive at first, it includes all meals, beverages, and most activities. Diners can sample good but unremarkable international cuisine at a food court. The best bet is the Italian dining room.

Just east of the Nassau Beach Hotel, Cable Beach. ☎ *800-GO SUPER or 242-327-5356. Fax: 242-327-5155 or 242-327-1209. Internet:* www.breezes.com. *Rack rates: $430–$540 for a double room, including all meals and most activities. AE, MC, V.*

British Colonial Hilton
$$$ **Nassau**

The grand dame of all Nassau hotels, this landmark seven-floor, 291-room hotel is up and running — and fine tuned at that — by the Hilton people after a series of mishaps. Plush and glamorous, it is once again worthy as a venue for James Bond. Scenes from such 007 flicks as *Thunderball* and *Never Say Never Again* were shot here. There's even a Double O suite filled with Bond memorabilia. Newly refurbished, the rooms open onto a small but good beach situated on the channel separating New Providence from Paradise Beach. The hotel doesn't even try to attract the casino crowd who prefer either the Atlantis or the Nassau Marriott. Business travelers are attracted here, as are visitors interested more in the shopping and sights of Nassau than the roll of the dice. A dignified atmosphere prevails with newly refurbished bedrooms a bit on the small side but many opening on scenic views of the Nassau harbor. Bedrooms are still quite comfortable and capped with rich crown moldings and accessorized with tile or stone-sheathed bathrooms with tub and shower combination. The cuisine at the British Colonial is good standard fare, and chefs don't even try to compete with other top Nassau restaurants such as Buena Vista or Sun And.... The hotel features a medium-sized, unheated freshwater pool.

Cable Beach Accommodations

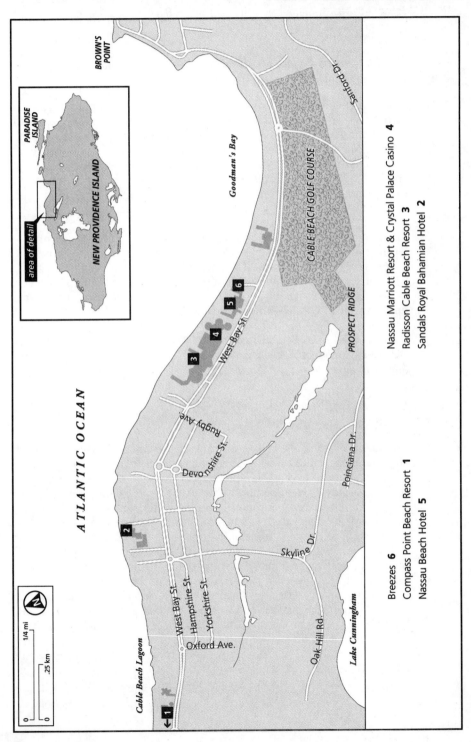

Nassau Marriott Resort & Crystal Palace Casino **4**
Radisson Cable Beach Resort **3**
Sandals Royal Bahamian Hotel **2**

Breezes **6**
Compass Point Beach Resort **1**
Nassau Beach Hotel **5**

1 Bay St. (P.O. Box N-7148). ☎ **800-HILTONS** *in the U.S. or Canada or 242-322-3301. Fax: 242-302-9009. Internet:* www.hilton.com. *Rack rates: $239–$299 for a double room. AE, DC, MC, V.*

Comfort Suites Paradise Island

$$$–$$$$ Paradise Island

Here you're offered modern suites, but don't expect yours to have separate rooms or even a balcony. Instead, you get one motel-like room with sitting and sleeping areas. For families or groups of friends, the rooms offer pullout sofas. However, you can't see the ocean from your bedroom. An open-air restaurant serves only breakfast and lunch. The pool is small and unheated but contains fresh water. Bedrooms are like those in a decent motel. They're comfortable with ample vanities; bathrooms are medium in size and tiled with tub and shower combination.

The real draw of Comfort Suites is that, as a guest, you have full privileges at Atlantis Paradise Island Resort & Casino. This quieter three-story hotel is a good choice if you want access to Atlantis facilities without staying at the overwhelming megaresort. For the most privacy at Comfort Suites, ask for a room that's not along a walkway. Children under age 16 stay free with one or two adults.

Paradise Island Dr., Paradise Island. ☎ **800-517-4000** *or 242-363-3680. Fax: 242-363-2588. Internet:* www.comfortsuites.com/hotel/bs003. *Rack rates: $185–$295 for a double room. AE, MC, V.*

Compass Point Beach Resort

$$$–$$$$$ Gambier

This colorful beach resort is New Providence's most fun place at which to stay. Octagonal cottages with louvered windows are painted in vivid hues of lemon, orange, teal, mauve, and Picasso blue evocative of the Bahamian Junkanoo festival (see Chapter 2). These wooden buildings, some on stilts, some with one or two bedrooms, stud the waterfront and gently sloping hillside. All are decorated with festival motifs such as fish, roosters, and sunbursts. The beach in front of the hotel may be small, but larger Love Beach — popular for snorkeling — is just next door. On site is a small, unheated, freshwater pool. With views of the palm trees and ocean, rocking chairs sit on the decks of Compass Point's 18 units. Inside, the decor is elegantly rustic, with West African batik fabrics and natural wood furniture. Most units aren't air-conditioned, but ceiling fans and cross ventilation keep you cool. The shower-only bathrooms are spacious with the best recorded bathroom music in Nassau. The hotel's owner is music industry mogul Chris Blackwell. All units have refrigerators, and some come with open-air kitchenettes and dining patios. The hotel's oceanfront restaurant offers some of the island's most imaginative cooking.

Adjacent to Love Beach, about a 10-minute drive west of Cable Beach. ☎ **800-688-7678** *or 242-327-4500. Fax: 242-327-3299. Internet:* www.islandoutpost.com. *Rack rates: $245 for a double room. AE, DC, MC, V.*

Dillet's Guest House

$$ Nassau

Located in a residential neighborhood, this bed-and-breakfast is within strolling distance of Saunders Beach, downtown Nassau, and bus stops. Iris Knowles, who runs Dillet's with her daughter, Danielle, was raised in this handsome home, which was built in 1928 by her father. The inn has only seven rooms, decorated with white wicker and pastels. All the guest quarters offer sitting areas, air-conditioning, and ceiling fans. The bathrooms are also attractive but small, each with a shower. Taking up an entire block, the grounds — which include a small unheated freshwater pool — are planted with tropical greenery. You're treated to a Bahamian breakfast including sweet johnnycake and perhaps banana bread or even potato bread flavored with coconut.

Dunmore Ave. and Strachan St. ☎ *242-**325-1133**. Fax: 242-325-7183. Internet:* www.islandeaze.com/dillets. *Rack rates: $125 for a double room, including breakfast. No credit cards.*

Holiday Inn Junkanoo Beach Nassau

$$–$$$ Nassau

If you like spending your cash on things other than your hotel room, this may be the place for you. Just west of downtown Nassau, this hotel is within easy reach of shops, restaurants, and historic sites of Bay Street, the main drag. It's right across the street from the small but adequate Junkanoo Beach. If you're ready to hit a casino, Paradise Island's casino is 2 miles northeast and Cable Beach's casino is 3 miles west. The medium-sized bedrooms have a view of either the beach or of Nassau Harbour, and they come with extras you don't always find in a moderately priced choice, including alarm clocks, two-lines phones, and a working desk. Bathrooms are a bit small but are tiled and equipped with tub and shower

Ice skating in Nassau

You can play ice hockey and ice skate at Breezes. The country's first ice-skating rink is synthetic, of course, but there's nothing artificial about the daily puck fests. Hockey sticks and skates are available if you forget your own. A triple axel at midnight? This 1,600-foot rink is open for skating 24 hours a day.

combination. With diversions such as Nintendo on hand, *kiddie suites* on the ground floor around the swimming pool are good for families. The kiddie suites have a room with a king-size bed, plus a second room (it's small and windowless, however) with bunk beds. The hotel boasts two unheated pools — one small, one large — that contain fresh water. The on-site Bay Street Grille is not reason enough to stay here, although you dine outside in a tropical courtyard overlooking the pool.

Across West Bay St. from the beach, on the edge of downtown. ☎ *800-465-4329 or 242-356-0000. Fax: 242-323-1408. Internet:* www.basshotels.com/holiday-inn. *Rack rates: $149–$179 for a double room. AE, MC, V.*

Nassau Beach Hotel
$$–$$$ Cable Beach

Next door to its sibling, the flashier Nassau Marriott Resort & Crystal Palace Casino, and across the road from the Cable Beach Golf Course, the Nassau Beach Hotel has been going strong since the 1940s. Spruced up during the 1990s, it has weathered competition from the newer, glitzier resorts that reside near it. Claiming a prime slice of the 3,000-foot white sandy beachfront, this hotel is one of the more dignified in the area. But don't let the Georgian-style architecture, gleaming marble and tile lobby, and hushed hues fool you. The Nassau Beach Hotel knows how to party. Check out the nightly Bahamian revue at the popular **King & Knights** club, the loud Friday evening Junkanoo parade at **Café Johnny Canoe** out front, or at one of the hotel's various bars. When hunger hits, you can choose from a wide range of restaurants. The seven on-site restaurants serve a standard international cuisine, all except for the Beef Cellar, which grills the juiciest, most tender, and succulent steaks on Cable Beach. The mid-size accommodations contain summery rattan pieces, comfortable beds, and a marble bathroom with a tub and shower combination.

All rooms come with a balcony or patio, but ask about the view. Although you can see the ocean from most, some units overlook buildings instead. Water sports are extensive, and there are also six tennis courts (four are floodlit for night play), and a fitness center. On site are two pools, one large and the other small; both are freshwater and unheated.

Near the Crystal Palace Casino. ☎ *888-NASSAU-B or 242-327-7711. Fax: 242-327-8829. Internet:* www.nassaubeachhotel.com. *Rack rates: $145–$377 for a double room, $300–$450 for a suite. AE, MC, V.*

Nassau Marriott Resort & Crystal Palace Casino
$$$$ Nassau

Adjacent to the casino that also adjoins the Radisson (which has a better beach), this large, sprawling hotel is an epic extravaganza. Without going outside, you can walk directly from the hotel towers to an array of restaurants, shops, and a fitness center. Most people hang out around the large, heated, freshwater pool with its swirling aqua-slide. If you're traveling with kids, consider the modest children's program and playground. The Marriott doesn't have all the glitz or the size of mega-resort Atlantis, but it is the island's second largest hotel with rainbow-hued towers and wings. It's far flashier than the Radisson for party-loving types. The hotel sells entertainment aggressively but houses you well in its accommodation towers, most of which are far enough away from the noisy public areas for light sleepers. We prefer the Casino Tower and Tower F because they have the grandest seafront vistas. You'll find some of the country's most lavish suites here and can live out your fantasies — for example, you can become Valentino in the Sheik-in-the-desert suite decorated for a sultan. Each comes with a good-sized private bathroom, with tub and shower combination.

Neighboring the Radisson. ☎ *800-222-7466 or 242-327-6200. Fax: 242-327-4346. Internet:* www.marriott.com. *Rack rates: $179–$249 for a double room. MAP $47 per person or $24 ages up to 12 years. AE, DISC, MC, V.*

Ocean Club Golf & Tennis Resort
$$$$$ Paradise Island

Tucked away on the quiet eastern side of Paradise Island, this elegant colonial-style resort is as understated as Atlantis is extravagant (see earlier entry). For class and style, nothing matches it on the island. In a past life, Ocean Club was the private estate of A&P grocery chain heir Huntington Hartford. The resort stretches from the beach to the harbor side of the island. At its core are formal terraced gardens, inspired by Versailles, where stone steps, hand-laid rock ridges, and European bronze and marble statues set off bougainvillea and hibiscus plants. Striking stone arches of a twelfth-century Augustinian cloister that Hartford had shipped from France and reassembled overlook the gardens and the harbor. Guest rooms are spacious, with views of the gardens or the beach and ocean. All units come with patios or balconies; some have king-sized mahogany four-poster beds, cane chairs, tall potted palms, hardwood floors, and sisal rugs, plus luxurious private bathrooms with tub and shower. Each afternoon, champagne and strawberries mysteriously appear in your room. The on-site restaurants offer the finest hotel dining on Paradise Island and also better than the hotel dining rooms in Nassau or Cable Beach. Tennis courts, a large, heated, freshwater pool and a spa are also on the premises. Take the shuttle bus or a short walk to the 18-hole championship golf course. Because Atlantis and Ocean Club share the same owners (Sun International), Ocean Club guests have full access to all the facilities at theme-park Atlantis. A courtesy bus links Ocean Club to Atlantis.

Ocean Club Dr. ☎ *800-321-3000 or 242-363-2501. Fax: 242-363-2424. Internet:* www.oceanclub.com. *Rack rates: $645–$975 for a double room. AE, DC, MC, V.*

Radisson Cable Beach Resort

$$$–$$$$ **Cable Beach**

With a broader beach and a more extensive children's program than the glitzier Nassau Marriott Resort & Crystal Palace Casino, the **Radisson** is a good choice for families. Offering beach olympics, arts and crafts, treasure hunts, storytelling, and other well-supervised activities, the complimentary half- or full-day programs at Camp Junkanoo are open to children between the ages of 4 and 11. Children under age 12 stay free, with one or two adults. Featuring five swimming pools, the Radisson's tropical waterscape also includes rock formations, waterfalls, and whirlpools. All pools are unheated and filled with fresh water; three are large, while the others are small. All with balconies, some 700 guest rooms in two nine-story wings form a U to cup the pools and beautiful sandy shore. Views from lower floors showcase the gardens while higher rooms overlook the ocean. Bedrooms are modernized and comfortable if rather standard, with large windows and a mid-sized bathroom with combination tub and shower. The hotel features a fitness center on the premises, and a golf course is across the road. When you're not working out or teeing off, go snorkeling, scuba diving, sailing, or play some tennis. You can dine at several good restaurants and, at night, listen to live music at the hotel. If you prefer, however, head to the adjoining casino complex for other eats, shops, and entertainment.

Adjacent to the Crystal Palace Casino, Cable Beach. ☎ 800-333-3333 or 242-327-6000. Fax: 242-327-6987. Internet: www.radisson.com. *Rack rates: $220–$350 for a double room. Three meals $99 per person extra or $65 ages 13 to 16, $45 ages 4 to 12. AE, DC, DISC, MC, V.*

Sandals Royal Bahamian Hotel

$$$$$ **Cable Beach**

This Jamaican chain member is a more upscale, all-inclusive hotel than Breezes. With its Romanesque statues, European spa, first-class restaurants, and two large, unheated, freshwater pools surrounded by columns, Sandals Royal Bahamian is an elegant but more expensive alternative. A shuttle ride or a leisurely stroll west of the Crystal Palace Casino, the hotel is removed from the busiest section of Cable Beach. Sandals appeals to newlyweds, and many couples start their honeymoons by having their weddings on the hotel's grounds. With romantic touches such as four-poster beds and luxurious bathrooms, the individual rooms, suites, and villas at Sandals are exclusively for couples. As soon as you enter the lobby that's decked out in marble with chandeliers hanging from fresco-painted ceilings, you feel regal. You can spend a week here and splash in a different pool every single day. You can sail off to the hotel's private island, complete with its own pool and restaurant, or go snorkeling, scuba diving, or waterskiing. The cuisine at more than half a dozen restaurants ranges from homestyle Bahamian and Japanese Teppanyaki to classic French and Northern Italian. Although plentiful and entirely presentable and prepared with first-rate ingredients, the Sandals kitchen never rises to the sublime. After dark, head to the theater for live performances by local bands, dancers, and other entertainers, or spend a quiet evening at the piano bar.

At Sandals, *couples only* means *heterosexual couples only.* Be forewarned: When dealing with this restriction, Sandals doesn't let down its guard. Also, Sandals doesn't allow children.

A short drive or comfortable walk from the Crystal Palace Casino. ☎ *800-SANDALS or 242-327-6400. Fax: 242-327-6961. Internet:* www.sandals.com. *Rack rates: $4,550–$10,290 for 7 days in double room, including all meals, beverages, and activities. Minimum 2-night stay. AE, DISC, MC, V.*

Sunrise Beach Club and Villas
$$$$–$$$$$ **Paradise Island**

This sprawling low-rise hotel, drawing mostly European vacationers, is the kind of place you picture when you think of a tropical getaway. Narrow paths snake through the color-packed grounds, thick with palm trees, hibiscus, crotons, and bougainvillea. This property offers only 35 units for rent, so the atmosphere is far quieter than at such Paradise Island resorts as Atlantis. With varying architectural styles and décor, the one-, two-, and three-bedroom villas and townhouses are set in different areas. Some are tucked into the flourishing gardens, while the more preferable overlook the two pools (one with a cave, waterfall, and children's wading section) or the sand beach. A winding staircase may lead to the bedroom in your unit, or your master bathroom may sport a whirlpool tub. Glass and rattan, chrome, and stained glass highlight some accommodations, while others feature more hardwood. All come with kitchens — some larger, some smaller. Because all the accommodations here have more or less the same comfort level, your selection will depend on your needs. A couple will find comfort in the one-bedroom townhouses, whereas families or groups traveling together prefer the two-bedroom apartments or even the three-bedroom villas, if the brood is large enough. Living up to its name, the resort's **Jungle Bar** makes a scenic spot for a drink, a conch burger (a fried conch sandwich), or other light fare.

Casino Dr. ☎ *888-387-2875 or 242-363-2250. Fax: 242-363-2308. Internet:* www.sunrisebeachvillas.com. *Rack rates: $352–$470 for a one-bedroom villa that sleeps four. AE, MC, V.*

Chapter 10

Settling In to New Providence

● ●

In This Chapter

▶ Knowing what to expect when you get here

▶ Getting around in New Providence

▶ Discovering New Providence from A to Z

● ●

*T*his chapter helps you navigate the ins and outs of arriving in New Providence, collecting your bags, passing through customs, and getting to your hotel. You also discover the best way to explore the island — by car, taxi, *jitney* (public bus or minivan), scooter, pedal bike, ferry, or on foot. Finally, you find tips and contacts for everything from currency exchange, emergencies, and Internet access to pharmacies, photographic supplies, and weather.

Arriving in New Providence by Air

When you fly into New Providence, the fun starts as soon as you hit the hassle-free airport. From collecting your bags and passing through customs to finding the taxi or van that will take you to your hotel, everything runs quickly and smoothly. When you come to the end of a journey, Bahamians say, "Ya reach." You receive a special New Providence welcome as "ya reach" **Nassau International Airport** (☎ 242-377-1759). Spirited live calypso or Bahamian junkanoo music greets you in the arrivals hall. The beat of the music will have your shoulders bouncing and your feet tapping.

Navigating passport control and customs

Start filling out your Immigration Arrival/Departure card as soon as you join one of the lines marked "Visitors." This way, you'll be ready to roll when it's your turn to present the card along with your passport or birth certificate and photo ID, and your return or onward bound airline ticket. Make a note of where you stick your copy of the immigration card, because you need to show it before you leave the country.

Usually getting through customs takes about 15 minutes, depending on how many different pieces of luggage you have. The lines tend to move quickly. Even if you declare you're not bringing in anything illegal, you may be singled out by Customs for a more thorough search.

Before heading to the taxis and hotel vans waiting outside, you can pick up maps and various vacation brochures at the tourist information desk. Likewise, if you need extra money in U.S. dollars, ATMs are on hand.

Getting from the airport to your hotel

Cable Beach, the main resort area on the island of New Providence, is about a 15-minute drive from the airport. **Paradise Island,** joined to New Providence by bridges, is 30 minutes away. If your hotel package includes transportation, you'll be mailed (or your travel agent will give you) a coupon or voucher to use upon arrival. When you find the right bus outside going to your hotel, show the driver the voucher. Buses are labeled and easy to find. Otherwise, you have to take a taxi, which runs about $15 for two passengers to Cable Beach or about $35 to Paradise Island.

To save money, you can share a cab with another couple heading to the same hotel and pay $3 for each additional person — but pretend that you've known each other since kindergarten. If you reveal that you just met at the airport, the driver may try to charge each couple the full rate. Drivers expect and sometimes request a 15 percent tip.

In most cases, you can get around New Providence without a car. If you decide you need wheels, you can pick up your vehicle at the airport if you rented at a major agency. Ideally, reservations should have been made before you left home. For more information, see the section "Getting Around New Providence," later in this chapter.

Cruising to New Providence

Nearly a dozen cruise ships can be in port at one time at Prince George Dock, also known as Prince George Wharf. If you're among the passengers on one of these floating hotels, your ship is as much of an attraction as its destination, meaning that you don't have a whole lot of time for exploring dry land. However, because you disembark near Rawson Square, in the heart of Nassau, you're just a stroll away from the Straw Market and all the shops and restaurants of Bay Street, the main avenue. Read more about these attractions in Chapter 12.

A *jitney* or public bus takes you to the sandy shores of Cable Beach, or to the foot of the Paradise Island bridge, which you can walk across (and pay the 25-cent toll) to **Paradise Beach**, the most popular beach

People-to-People

Pink and white **Government House,** the official residence of the governor-general of The Bahamas, blends colonial British styling with American Colonial. It's not as flamboyant as the changing of the guard at Buckingham Palace but if you're here Saturday morning at 10, you can watch a more modest ceremony, though one still full of pomp and pageantry. Tea parties, usually held the last Friday of each month, give visitors a rare glimpse within this stately old building. To participate in this and other events that give you the chance to mingle one-on-one with Bahamians, contact the **People-to-People Programme.** For details, call the Ministry of Tourism (☎ **800-4-BAHAMAS** or 242-322-7500) *before* you arrive in The Bahamas.

on Paradise Island. Of course, taxis can take you from downtown Nassau across the bridge (for a $2 toll), but the most convenient way for cruise-ship passengers to get to Paradise Island is to take one of the ferries from Prince George Dock for $2 each way.

Getting around New Providence

Two parallel bridges — with traffic flowing in opposite directions — link Nassau and Paradise Island. The older bridge — the *only* bridge for decades before the most spectacular section of the multimillion-dollar Atlantis resort sprouted on Paradise Island in the late 1990s — goes from Paradise Island to Nassau.

The bridge to Paradise Island is about a mile from the center of downtown Nassau. You can walk the whole distance, take a *jitney* to the foot of the bridge and walk across, or take a taxi from Nassau all the way across. Every time you cross the bridge from Nassau to Paradise Island, you must pay a toll. On foot, the toll is 25 cents; by taxi, it's $2, and by car, $1.

Here are more tips about the various modes of transport in New Providence.

   ✔ **Taking a bus.** Some hotels along Cable Beach and on Paradise Island offer guests free bus service within the resort areas. To go elsewhere, you can take taxis or rent a car and brave Nassau traffic. Or, you can get almost anywhere you want to go on New Providence on a jitney. These small buses or large vans travel up and down West Bay Street (the road in front of Cable Beach hotels) to beaches, through downtown Nassau, and to other parts of the island. They run from approximately 6 a.m. to 7 p.m. At 75 cents a ride, they're a convenient, inexpensive way to make your way.

You need exact change in coins; you're welcome to pay with a dollar bill — you just won't get any change. No taxi driver ever has change, or so they say. When you see a jitney coming, flag it down. The buses wait to fill up at depots and are often tightly packed, but with reggae or calypso pumping on the radio, the mood is always festive.

To go east from downtown Nassau toward the Paradise Island bridges, catch a bus at Frederick and Bay Streets, near the Straw Market. These buses don't go over the bridge, so you have to walk or take a cab across. To go west toward Cable Beach, catch a bus near the British Colonial Hilton at Bay Street. If you're traveling from Cable Beach to Paradise Island or vice versa, you must change buses in town.

✔ **Taking a taxi.** Taxis wait outside Cable Beach and Paradise Island hotels, and they're also plentiful in downtown Nassau. Drivers take the same routes so often that many don't bother to use their meters. Therefore, before you hop into a cab, ask your hotel staff the approximate fare to wherever you're going. From Cable Beach to downtown Nassau, you pay about $10 for two passengers. Likewise, the trip from Cable Beach to Paradise Island costs about $15.

For more details, contact The Bahamas Taxicab Union (☎ 242-323-4555 or 242-323-5818).

✔ **Ferrying from island to island.** Ferries run between Prince George Dock, in downtown Nassau, and Paradise Island about every ten minutes. The cost is $2 each way. A ferry is the most scenic way to get from Paradise Island to Nassau and vice versa. Go to the dock and climb aboard the next ferry that's leaving for the brief sail across the harbor.

✔ **Touring town in a horse-drawn carriage.** Riding around in a horse-drawn surrey with a fringe on top is the most romantic way to see Nassau. Your horse may even have a droopy flower stuck in his straw hat. Carriages wait for passengers at Rawson Square, in the heart of Nassau, not far from where the cruise ships dock. Expect to pay about $14 per person for up to three adults for a 45-minute ride.

✔ **Driving around in a car.** If you want to rent a car, you must drive on the left, a holdover of British tradition. If you come from small-town America, drivers in Nassau may appear reckless to you. You can make car rental arrangements at the airport or through your hotel. See chapter 8 for more information.

✔ **Buzzing by on a motor scooter.** Some vacationers love zipping around on the mini-motorcycles or scooters, but the often speedy Nassau traffic makes them far from safe. If you're feeling brave wear a helmet and set out on your adventure, staying on the left side of the road. Ask your hotel for the closest scooter rental outfit. Rates run from about $45 to $50 per day.

> ✔ **Exploring on foot.** Historic downtown Nassau is suitable for walking, but congested between 9 a.m. and 5 p.m. on weekdays. (For details on what you can expect to see, check out chapter 12.)
>
> The city's streets are desolate after dark, so lone strolls at night aren't safe. If you like wandering under the stars, however, Cable Beach and Paradise Island are your best bets.
>
> ✔ **Riding bicycles.** Because traffic is often crazy in and around Nassau, two-wheelers aren't the best way to get from place to place. If you want to bike, you can do so in front of any large hotel complex — Radisson, Cable Beach, or Nassau Beach. (Ask your hotel for information on bike rentals.) A guided tour is your best bet along scenic and shoreline trails. A half-day bicycle tour with **Pedal and Paddle Ecoventures** is $60 (☎ 242-362-2772). (See chapter 12 for more details.)

Fast Facts: New Providence

American Express

If you need help with traveler's checks or other American Express services, visit the office at Playtours on Shirley Street, between Parliament and Charlotte Streets (☎ 242-322-2931).

Babysitting

Most hotels can help you make arrangements to hire an experienced sitter. Expect to pay around $10 to $15 an hour, plus $3 for each additional child.

Banks and ATMs

Major banks throughout Nassau include the Royal Bank of Canada (☎ 242-322-8700), Bank of Nova Scotia (☎ 242-356-1400), and Barclays (☎ 242-356-8000), each with ATMs. However, some accept cards only in the Cirrus network (☎ 800-424-7787 or 800-4CIRRUS) while others take only Plus (☎ 800-843-7587). ATMs at both the Paradise Island and Cable Beach casinos also dispense quick cash.

Credit Cards

Having problems with your plastic? Contact American Express (☎ 800-327-1267),

Citibank Visa/MasterCard (☎ 888-950-5114), Visa (☎ 800-847-2911), or call the toll-free telephone number on the back of your credit card.

Currency Exchange

You don't have to swap your U.S. dollars for Bahamian currency, because American green is accepted everywhere. Because the exchange rate is $1 to $1, there's no confusion.

Directory Assistance

Call ☎ 916.

Emergencies

Ambulance: ☎ 242-322-2221; Bahamas Air Sea Rescue Association (BASRA): ☎ 242-322-3877; Fire: ☎ 911 or 919; Police: ☎ 911 or 919.

Information

Contact the **Ministry of Tourism** (☎ 242-322-7500, near the Straw Market at Bay Street Market Plaza downtown) or ask your hotel for good local maps and other visitor information.

Internet Access

To connect to the Internet, check out **ASAP** (☎ 242-394-6447), a mini business center in the East Bay Shopping Centre, between the Paradise Island bridges. Here you can get online from your own laptop or log on to one of ASAP's computers. Some of the larger hotels also offer guests Internet access for a small fee.

Medical Assistance

Contact government-run **Princess Margaret Hospital** (☎ 242-322-2861) on Shirley Street downtown. Before your trip, check out your health insurance policy to see whether you're covered while you're abroad. If not, you may want to purchase a traveler's insurance plan with emergency medical expense coverage.

Newspapers/Magazines

Both published in the morning, the *Tribune Daily* and the *Nassau Guardian* are the country's two competing daily newspapers. At your hotel and at visitor information stations, you can find various helpful magazines, brochures, and booklets.

Pharmacies

The Prescription Parlor (☎ 242-356-3973) on East Street South is open daily from 7 a.m. to 11 p.m. For about what it costs round-trip to get to the pharmacy by taxi, you can have whatever you need delivered to your hotel. The delivery charge is $6 from about 7 a.m. to 9 p.m., and $25 until 11 p.m. Another reliable pharmacy is Cole Thompson, open 8:30 a.m. to 6:00 p.m. at Bay and Charlotte Streets, ☎ 242-322-2062; or 8:30 a.m. to 9:00 p.m. in the Pilot House building, near the Paradise Island exit bridge, ☎ 242-393-8368.

Photography Supplies

On Bay Street, a block east of Rawson Square, **John Bull** (☎ 242-322-3328) offers a large selection of camera-related supplies. If your video or still camera breaks down in The Bahamas, it's best to wait until you get home to have it fixed.

Police

In an emergency, call ☎ **919**.

Post Office

The main post office is at the juncture of East Hill Street and East Street in Nassau (☎ 242-322-3344).

Safety

Just as you should anywhere in the world, exercise caution and common sense. For example, don't wear flashy jewelry to the beach or turn your back on your camera or handbag. Stay away from desolate or run-down areas — whether residential or commercial — at night. Always packed with visitors, Cable Beach and Paradise Island are safer places for walking and exploring after dark.

Taxis

Taxis wait outside Cable Beach and Paradise Island hotels, and they're also plentiful in Nassau. Before you hop into a cab, ask your hotel staff the approximate fare to wherever you're going. From Cable Beach to downtown Nassau, you pay about $9 for two passengers. Likewise, the trip from Cable Beach to Paradise Island costs about $15. For more details, contact the **Bahamas Taxicab Union** (☎ 242-323-4555 or 242-323-5818).

Time

When you need to synchronize your watches, call ☎ **917**.

Weather

Call ☎ **915** to hear the forecast.

Chapter 11

Dining in New Providence

● ●

In This Chapter

▶ Finding the best food beyond your hotel dining room

▶ Locating restaurants with island ambience

● ●

*F*rom familiar fast-food chains to first-class international dining rooms, New Providence offers vacationers dozens of dining choices. The less expensive places are in and around downtown Nassau, while Paradise Island is home to the widest selection of expensive restaurants.

What you won't find are restaurants devoted to a healthy cuisine, with fresh local ingredients prepared in light (if any) sauces. Don't despair. Although New Providence doesn't offer such restaurants, almost every dining room features dishes whose consumption would win the approval of your heart specialist. So even though you won't find a lot of "healthy choice" restaurants, you can dine well in all the hotel restaurants or first-class establishments.

Getting a Taste for New Providence

Seafood is prepared in creative ways, but beef and lamb are imported. Good restaurants are found in most hotels, but for island spice, you need to venture out to the independently run Bahamian eateries. Some of the best local restaurants are short on decor, but their tasty island food makes up for the lack of frills.

 You can get your just desserts, with each restaurant trying to outdo the next in the sweet surrender department. In years past, the only place you could get good *guava duff* (a warm slice of pastry filled with guava jelly and topped with creamy white sauce) was at the home of a Bahamian. Now, however, many restaurants serve it along with the omnipresent key lime pie. Two of New Providence's oldest and fanciest restaurants — Graycliff and Sun And. . . . — have a fierce competition going as to which one can turn out the best dessert soufflé.

Most restaurants host happy hour (actually two or three hours starting around 5 p.m.), which is a good time to sample whatever tropical rum-based concoction the establishment features. Dining rooms often close between meals, but fast-food joints can satisfy your hunger. A few restaurants in the casino complexes don't allow young children.

See Chapter 2 for details about local specialties and the Introduction for an explanation of price categories used. Our maps also guide you to the restaurants.

Dining at Nassau's best restaurants

Buena Vista
$$$$$ Nassau   CONTINENTAL

Only Graycliff and Sun And . . . (see entry later in this chapter) does cuisine better. For more than half a century, this two-story, 19th-century mansion has been a citadel of fine food enjoyed by candlelight in mellow areas decorated with antique paintings. A pianist entertains softly in winter, recapturing the flavor of the early '40s when the Duke and Duchess of Windsor ran The Bahamas. In fair weather, request a table on the garden terrace and order the bartender's special: a rum punch with coconut milk. Meals are served on the kind of delicate china that your grandmother keeps locked behind glass in a cabinet. The cookery is natural, straightforward, and classic, making the best use of such quality ingredients as tender rack of lamb, roast duckling in a zesty orange sauce, stone crab with mustard sauce (our favorite), and an especially delectable filet mignon in a peppercorn sauce. These dishes are prepared to perfection, if you like heavy sauces, although they hardly tax the imagination of the kitchen staff, who has been doing them for years. Since 1946, the house's special dessert is Mrs. Hauck's orange pancakes with a Grand Marnier sauce.

Delancy and Augusta Sts., behind the Roman Catholic cathedral, a block west of Government House. ☎ *242-322-2811. Reservations recommended. Jackets requested for men. Main courses: $32–$40. AE, MC, V. Open: dinner only Mon–Sat.*

Café Matisse
$$$ Nassau   INTERNATIONAL/NORTHERN ITALIAN

Behind Parliament House, this century-old former private home is a local favorite, attracting both Bahamian government employees and visitors. The joint effort of a Bahamian chef and his Italian-born wife results in a harmonious cuisine that reaches from the islands to the Mediterranean. The Matisse in the name comes from reproductions of paintings by French impressionist Henry Matisse. Pizzas are served, especially the best frutti di mare pie in town; it's topped, of course, with fresh local seafood. But the cuisine of Greg and Gabrielle Curry is far more advanced and challenging than that. You might open your meal with their savory curried shrimp with a fragrant jasmine rice, or the best calamari in Nassau. Our favorite main courses are the grilled seafood, which emerges just right — still juicy, not dried out. Our pasta selection is the cannelloni with lobster sauce. For Bahamian cuisine in Nassau itself, only The Pink Pearl Cafe (see entry later in this chapter) does it better.

If the smell of cigar smoke doesn't thrill you, steer clear of the second-floor veranda, where patrons sipping pre- and post-dinner drinks fill the small tables. Happy hour runs from 5 to 7 p.m., and there's often live jazz a couple nights a week.

Bank Lane at Bay St., near Parliament Square. ☎ *242-356-7012. Reservations suggested for dinner. Main courses: $24–$30. AE, MC, V. Open: lunch and dinner Mon–Sat.*

Café Skan's

$ Downtown Nassau   BAHAMIAN/AMERICAN

Good, filling food easy on the wallet keeps this bustling café packed. Lying across from the straw market, it is more coffee shop than café. The food is just as substantial as that of a regular restaurant, although you can also drop in for lighter fare such as sandwiches and burgers while shopping or strolling about town. Bahamians pile in here early in the morning to devour dishes their mama made for them, including corned beef and grits, chicken souse (chicken parts and vegetables in a seasoned broth), "stew" fish, and broiled grouper with johnnycake, a mildly sweet bread. Of course, you can have "the usual" — a stack of pancakes, fluffy omelets, and French toast. The chefs turn out savory conch fritters or conch chowder, even Bahamian bean soup with dumplings, along with rib-sticking pork chops. Everything is accompanied by generous side dishes such as peas and rice or macaroni and cheese. There is no pretense in the cuisine: It's just good, honest, and straightforward cookery.

Bay St. at Market Plaza, across the street from the straw market. ☎ *242-322-2486. Main courses: $5.95–$15. MC, V. Open: Mon–Sat 8 a.m.–6 p.m., Sun 9 a.m.–4 p.m.*

Conch Fritters Bar & Grill

$–$$ Downtown Nassau   BAHAMIAN/AMERICAN

This casual bar and grill is the best place in the center of Nassau for you to sample conch in many variations, including not only the best conch fritters in town but cracked conch, which is that mollusk's version of breaded veal cutlet. The first local restaurant you notice when coming in from Cable Beach to Nassau, the eatery enjoys a mixed following of locals and visitors. Even if you don't like conch, the chefs turn out many other good-tasting dishes, including some excellent crispy fried chicken or that Florida favorite from the '50s — surf and turf. This is one of the places that offers the famous Bahamian specialty, guava duff, for dessert. The bright decor is enlivened by plants and wood parrots, and live music is presented on most nights.

Nassau and Paradise Island Dining

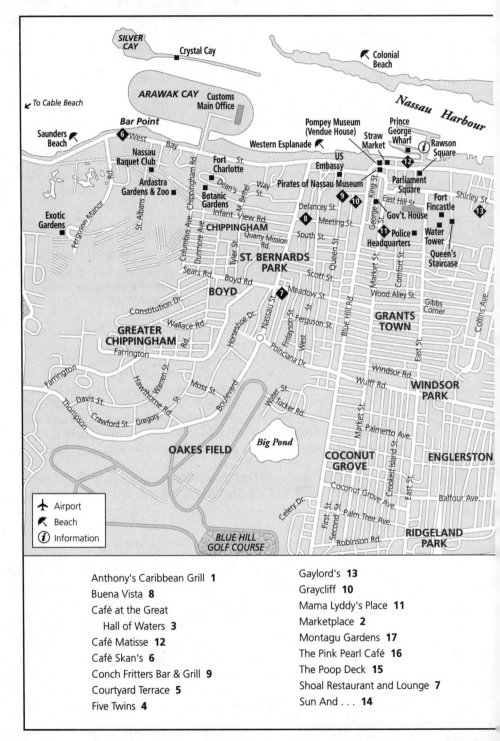

Anthony's Caribbean Grill **1**
Buena Vista **8**
Café at the Great
  Hall of Waters **3**
Café Matisse **12**
Café Skan's **6**
Conch Fritters Bar & Grill **9**
Courtyard Terrace **5**
Five Twins **4**

Gaylord's **13**
Graycliff **10**
Mama Lyddy's Place **11**
Marketplace **2**
Montagu Gardens **17**
The Pink Pearl Café **16**
The Poop Deck **15**
Shoal Restaurant and Lounge **7**
Sun And . . . **14**

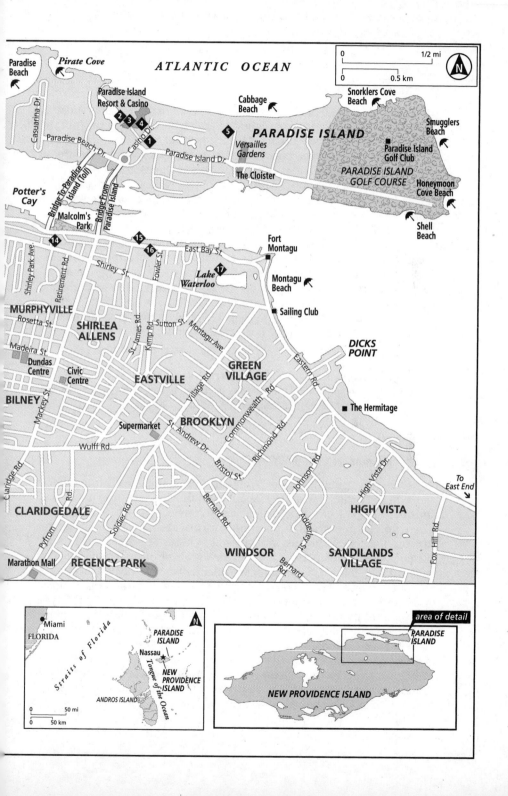

ATLANTIC OCEAN

Paradise Beach

Pirate Cove

Casuarina Dr.

Paradise Island Resort & Casino

Paradise Beach Dr.

Casino Dr.

Cabbage Beach

Snorklers Cove Beach

PARADISE ISLAND

Smugglers Beach

Paradise Island Golf Club

Paradise Island Dr.

Versailles Gardens

PARADISE ISLAND GOLF COURSE

Honeymoon Cove Beach

Potter's Cay

Bridge To Paradise Island (Toll)

Bridge From Paradise Island

The Cloister

Shell Beach

Malcolm's Park

Shirley Park Ave.

Retirement Rd.

Shirley St.

East Bay St.

Fowler St.

Fort Montagu

Lake Waterloo

Montagu Beach

MURPHYVILLE

Rosetta St.

SHIRLEA ALLENS

St. James Rd.

Kemp Rd.

Sutton St.

Montagu Ave.

Village Rd.

Sailing Club

DICKS POINT

Madeira St.

Dundas Centre

Civic Centre

EASTVILLE

GREEN VILLAGE

Eastern Rd.

BILNEY

Mackey St.

BROOKLYN

Commonwealth Rd.

Richmond Rd.

The Hermitage

Supermarket

St. Andrew Dr.

Johnson Rd.

High Vista Dr.

To East End

Claridge Rd.

Wulff Rd.

Bristol St.

Pyfrom Rd.

Soldier Rd.

Bernard Rd.

CLARIDGEDALE

HIGH VISTA

Fox Hill Rd.

Marathon Mall

REGENCY PARK

WINDSOR

Adderley St.

Bernard Rd.

SANDILANDS VILLAGE

Miami

FLORIDA

Straits of Florida

PARADISE ISLAND

Nassau

NEW PROVIDENCE ISLAND

Tongue of the Ocean

ANDROS ISLAND

50 mi

50 km

area of detail

PARADISE ISLAND

NEW PROVIDENCE ISLAND

Marlborough St., opposite the British Colonial Hilton. ☎ *242-323-8801. Main courses: $9.95–$36. AE, MC, V. Open: 7 a.m.–midnight.*

Gaylord's
$$ Nassau   INDIAN

For a change of pace, you can try some spicy northern Indian cuisine, the best in Nassau. In this case, spicy doesn't have to mean bring out the fire hoses. In fact, many dishes aren't hot at all but full of flavor. Silk is draped across ceilings, decorative brass plates and sculpture are on display, and Indian music is piped into this restaurant in a distinctive nineteenth-century building. With plenty of vegetarian choices, the menu ranges from mild, creamy *kormas* (balls of ground meat or vegetables in a thick seasoned sauce) to bold *curries* (stew-like meat, fish, or vegetable dishes flavored with curry), and *tandoori* (marinated meat or fish cooked in a clay oven) main courses. Along with lamb, beef, chicken, and fish, you're likely to find the inevitable conch worked into the selections. Tandoori conch was a first for us, and it's a tasty way to prepare this typically Bahamian mollusk. Vegetable *samosas* (pastry filled with curried vegetables or meat) make good starters. We could make a meal just out of the freshly baked breads alone, especially when they come filled with flavored onions or cheese. For dessert, try the carrot pudding. Take-out meals are also available.

Dowdeswell St., in front of Princess Margaret Hospital. ☎ *242-356-3004. Reservations recommended. Three-course dinners, including wine: $29.95–$49.95. MC, V. Open: DailyMon–Fri for lunch and dinner.*

Graycliff
$$$$$ Nassau   CONTINENTAL

Opposite Government House, Graycliff lies in the most atmospheric mansion in Nassau, far more elegant than Buena Vista. It is a world of antiques, elegant china, and old English silverware. This restaurant, where you should dress in your most formal resort wear, is no longer "the tops" in The Bahamas, a position it held for years. Sun And . . . for example, offers even better food. But for the allure of yesterday, Graycliff still ranks high. It's still charming to order a drink on the balcony bar or ask for a table on the cool terrace, while listening to the soft piano tunes of Coward, Gershwin, and Cole Porter. The cuisine is basically the type that pleased gourmets in decades past before the "revolution" came: perfectly grilled and choice steaks, lobster Graycliff in a white wine medora sauce, plump juicy pheasant in a pineapple sauce, and grouper in a Dijon mustard sauce. Gray continues to attract diners whose big night out involves the consumption of Iranian caviar, fine brandy, a Grand Marnier soufflé, Cuban cigars, as well as a selection from a *carte* of some 175,000 wine bottles.

West Hill St. and Blue Hill Rd., across from Government House. ☎ *242-322-2796. Reservations required. Jackets required for men for dinner. Main courses: $35–$44. AE, MC, V. Open: Mon–Fri for lunch, daily for dinner.*

Mama Lyddy's Place

$ Nassau BAHAMIAN

This cuisine is how your Bahama mama might have cooked for you, assuming you had one. In a nineteenth-century former home in the middle of Nassau, Mama Lyddy's was named in honor of the mother of the folks who run this good, homestyle restaurant. Eat a hearty, good-tasting break- fast, lunch, or an early supper on the front porch or inside amid all the colorful Bahamian art. The food has changed a bit, at least since the land- ing of Columbus, but it is still the same time-tested fare that Bahamians have liked for decades. You can begin your day with boiled or stewed fish, perhaps chicken souse, served with a choice of grits or johnnycake. For lunch or dinner, you may choose pea, okra, or bean soup followed by fried grouper, steamed snapper, minced lobster, or that eternal favorite, baked pork chops. Your choice of two side dishes may include peas and rice, macaroni and cheese, potato salad, coleslaw, and fried *plantain* (a tropi- cal vegetable similar to a banana, but larger and only eaten when cooked). Lemon meringue pie is a popular choice for dessert.

Bring cash or traveler's checks, because Mama Lyddy's doesn't accept plastic. She also doesn't serve alcohol.

Market St. at Cockburn St. ☎ *242-328-6849. Main courses: $8–$15. Credit cards not accepted. Open: Mon–Sat 8 a.m.–6 p.m., until 3 p.m. on Sun and holidays. Lunch and early supper.*

Montagu Gardens

$$ Nassau STEAK/SEAFOOD/PASTA

Overlooking Lake Waterloo, this restaurant at the far eastern end of Bay Street is for those seeking an escape at night from the fray. It offers not only good food, but a quiet table in the courtyard of an old mansion. The succulent steaks and freshly caught seafood are some of the best on the island. The chef is justly proud of his T-bones, filet mignon, and rib eyes, all prepared to order, and he also does spicy baby back ribs and a per- fectly seasoned and cooked rack of lamb. Blackened grouper and well- seasoned dolphinfish are the most praiseworthy. If you've never had Bahamian guava duff before or want to try it again, the chef makes a mean one.

Consider a late dinner here because Club Waterloo, one of Nassau's hottest nightspots (see Chapter 12 for details), is right next door.

East Bay St., next to Club Waterloo. ☎ *242-394-6347. Reservations recommended, particularly on weekends. Main courses: $14.50–$26. AE, MC, V. Open: Mon–Sat for lunch and dinner.*

The Pink Pearl Café

$–$$ Nassau   BAHAMIAN/INTERNATIONAL

This is our favorite of the local eateries devoted to Bahamian dishes, far exceeding the appeal of either Mama Lyddy's Place or Café Skan's. Across Nassau Yacht Haven Marina in a dark pink colonial building with a wrap-around porch, this former private home has been converted into a restaurant and decorated with contemporary art. At night, candles flicker at tables set with crystal. Favorite island dishes are served here with a continental flair. The rich, creamy conch chowder, for example, is not tomato based but like a New England clam chowder. This restaurant is also the best place to order breaded cracked conch, which is crispy on the outside but tender on the inside. Instead of boring peas and rice, it comes with a side of zesty, seasoned mashed potatoes. Two recently sampled main courses won our fickle hearts: filet of snapper and plantain with sautéed spinach and grilled breast of duck with a tangy mango glaze. For dessert, banana lovers order the fritters or the banana-flecked guava bread pudding.

East Bay St., just east of the bridge from Paradise Island to Nassau. ☎ *242-394-6413. Reservations required. Main courses: $17.95–$29.95. AE, MC, V. Open: Mon–Sat for lunch and dinner.*

The Poop Deck

$$–$$$ Nassau   BAHAMIAN/SEAFOOD

Even if this place didn't serve good food, which it does, we'd still hang out here at night. We're drawn to its open-air waterside location with a panoramic view of the marina, which is lit up at night near the bridge over to Paradise Island. In such a setting, only a nautical atmosphere with seafaring artifacts will do. A lot of the food attracts beer-drinking, cigarette-smoking, sports-loving devotees, but it's straightforward and honest and prepared with fresh ingredients. A tasty appetizer is the crab-stuffed mushrooms. A real local dish that we'd recommend is the Bahamian steamed chicken, flavored with tomatoes, onions, and sweet peppers in the Creole style, and accompanied with mango salsa and sweet-potato fish cakes. The cracked lobster, which is batter coated, and sautéed, lures many a diner. If you're dropping in for lunch, burgers and sandwiches are tempting. On our latest rounds, the chef's version of the celebrated guava duff was the best we'd sampled in New Providence.

To sit at one of the best tables, at the edge of the balcony, get here just before noon or 5 p.m. (Don't come alone, though, because single diners aren't seated at these front tables.)

East Bay St. next to Nassau Yacht Haven. ☎ *242-393-8175. Reservations recommended. Main courses: $17–$39. AE, MC, V. Open: Daily for lunch and dinner.*

For more upscale indoor or outdoor beachside dining (with a similar menu, but slightly higher prices), check out the other Poop Deck on West Bay Street.

At Sandyport, 5 minutes west of Cable Beach. ☎ *242-327-3325. Reservations recommended. MC, V. Main courses: $17–$39. Open: Tues–Sun for lunch and dinner.*

Shoal Restaurant and Lounge
$–$$ Nassau   BAHAMIAN

This restaurant is one we return to again and again, although its food is only slightly better than that served at other local favorites such as Conch Fritters, Café Skan's, or Mama Lyddy's. At times, the chefs at all these local dives seem to be using the same recipes handed down from generations. We like to go truly Bahamian here and drop in for breakfast with friends to sample "boil fish," cooked with salt pork, onions, and green peppers. It's always consumed with johnnycake. If you've been eating around Nassau, you already know what johnnycake is by now. Chicken souse is a real morning eye-opener, but it may be for devotees, not for the faint-hearted. We asked our waiter what it's made with. "You wouldn't want to know. Just eat and enjoy," he advised. At night, when we've returned to this no-frills restaurant, we've ordered the crawfish salad or the steamed conch. Of course, steak and lobster are always featured. Dishes come with fried plantain and mounds of peas and rice. Once very scarce on menus, guava duff is now almost a mandatory offering at every restaurant, and a sublime version is offered here as well. The restaurant will provide transportation to and from your hotel. You'll need all the help you can get returning to your hotel if you down at least three of the bartender's lethal Bahama Mamas.

Nassau St., near the College of the Bahamas. ☎ *242-323-4400. Main lunch and dinner courses: $12–$30. AE, MC, V. Open: Dailydaily 7:30 a.m.–midnight.*

Sun And . . .
$$$–$$$$ Nassau   CONTINENTAL

Nassau's finest dining, even better than that at Graycliff or Buena Vista, is served by candlelight on a patio by a rock pool. Near Fort Montagu, Sun And . . . is a classic citadel of refined cuisine and service offered with an overlay of English colonial charm. A fountain-studded Iberian-styled courtyard complete with fountains and a drawbridge sets the romantic aura. The cuisine has constantly improved until it has truly become a world-class restaurant. Exceptional products are prepared with a fine-honed technique. We can't predict what will be on the menu at the time of your visit, but if we awarded toques for grand cuisine, we'd give them to the chef's smoked moulard duck breasts or the duck-stuffed ravioli with porcini mushrooms. Focus on the absolutely sensational boiled lobster or the classic roast spring lamb, almost melt-in-your-mouth tender. Ronny Deryckere's soufflés are incomparable, better than Graycliff. Most diners opt for the Grand Marnier, which is traditional. But our favorite remains the soufflé with rum raisins and Black Label Bicardi.

Lakeview Rd. off Shirley St. ☎ *242-393-1205. Reservations recommended. Jackets requested for men. Main courses: $32–$40. MC, V. Open: Tues–Sun 6:30–9:30 p.m. for dinner only. Closed Aug–Sept*

Checking Out Paradise Island's best restaurants

Anthony's Caribbean Grill
$$ **Paradise Island** **AMERICAN/CARIBBEAN**

Near Atlantis and Comfort Suites, this laid-back tropical spot offers a pleasant alternative to hotel dining rooms. Brightly decorated with Bahamian artwork, Anthony's features an extensive menu that includes familiar but well-prepared dishes that never achieve greatness but are full of flavor, seasoning, and spicing. For a taste of the islands, we go for the peppery jerk chicken on a bed of multicolored pasta, known as "Rasta pasta." Named after the music of The Bahamas, the 20-ounce Junkanoo steak with well-seasoned vegetables is only for the trencherman. The ribs are sizzling in their salsa laced with coconut and mango. But in general, this restaurant is an upscale version of TGI Fridays, serving the usual array of pizzas (some of the pies studded with lobster), burgers, and fried chicken. The bartender is known for his 48-ounce sparklers, with rum, Amaretto, vodka, and fruit punch. "With two of these," the bartender assured us, "we'll carry you out on a stretcher."

Casino Dr., across from Comfort Suites. ☎ *242-363-3152. Main courses: $10.95–$37.95. AE, MC, V. Open: Daily for lunch and dinner.*

Café at the Great Hall Of Waters
$$$$$ **Paradise Island** **INTERNATIONAL**

This restaurant gives you a splashy look at the megaresort and water wonderland of Atlantis, even if you're not a guest of the hotel. Paradise Island has better restaurants, notably Five Twins (later in this chapter) but none this dramatic. You feel like a scuba diver as you look through gigantic picture windows that display the illuminated "ruins" of Atlantis. Everywhere you look, rainbow-hued fish swim past stone archaeological remains, and rows of lobsters parade through the sand. With a ceiling that seems miles away, the Café's multilevel dining areas are located on the lower floor of the Royal Towers. There's a kids' menu, and little ones love taking walks along the aquarium walls between courses. In such a setting, the food becomes almost secondary, although it's quite good.

Lobster is a specialty, but you can also order well-prepared versions of crab legs or grilled salmon. The chefs import top-quality ingredients such as lamb and then do their magic to it. Desserts are uniformly luscious.

Royal Towers, Atlantis Resort. ☎ *242-363-3000. Reservations required. Main courses: $21–$39. AE, MC, V. Open: Daily from 7 a.m.–11 a.m.; noon–2:30 p.m.; and 6 p.m.–10:30 p.m.*

Courtyard Terrace
$$$$$ Paradise Island CONTINENTAL

Within Paradise Island's most exclusive hotel, you dine in a romantic setting. Picture it: your table around a pool with a splashing fountain with candle flames dancing in the trade winds and a four-piece combo playing music on the balcony. You dine amid palms and flowering shrubs, surrounded by colonial-style verandas. The menu is strong on the classics. The chef excels in dishes that have pleased the discerning palate for decades. This cuisine is not experimental. Here you're served freshly grilled grouper or snapper, each perfectly seasoned and prepared and never allowed to dry out. The lobster quiche is light and lively, and the calves' lyonnaise is as good as that served in a typical Left Bank Parisian bistro. The service is smooth, and the wine list carefully chosen, though you don't have a massive selection like that at Graycliff.

Evenings can get a bit chilly, so you may want to bring along some type of evening wrap.

Ocean Club, eastern Paradise Island. ☎ *242-363-2501. Reservations required. Jackets required for men during the winter season. Main courses: $42–$60. AE, MC, V. Open: Daily 7 p.m.–9 p.m.*

Five Twins
$$$$$ Paradise Island ASIAN/SEAFOOD

Save this dining mecca for a special evening. While a singer croons smooth melodies, you can eat by candlelight on fine china, either inside or outside on the terrace overlooking the marina. Attracting high rollers from the nearby casino, this is the best restaurant in this massive gambling and entertainment complex. Revolving around seafood, the Thai-Japanese-Indonesian cuisine is contemporary Pacific Rim with a European flair. Color, texture, artistic presentation, and, of course, flavor play major roles in each dish, whether you choose from freshly caught grouper, snapper, shrimp, or lobster. You might start with nuanced chilled oysters with apple slaw or a pepper-cured salmon with vegetable tempura. The restaurant also features a sushi bar as well as a separate upscale rum and cigar lounge. After dinner, a DJ spins party tunes from a booth suspended above the dance floor. Children under age 12 are not allowed.

Adjacent to the casino, Atlantis Resort. ☎ *242-363-3000. Reservations required. Main courses: $34–$38. AE, DC, MC, V. Open: Daily 6:30 p.m.–2 a.m.*

Marketplace

$$$$ Paradise Island   INTERNATIONAL

Decorated with old vases and terra-cotta tiles, this large buffet-style restaurant is reminiscent of a sprawling market. It serves the finest buffet on Paradise Island. The food is fresh, but it's a mass feeding station. You go here to fill up and for its value, not to find food as good as that at Conch Fritters Bar & Grill or The Pink Pearl Café. Before you start loading your plate, browse past the various cooking stations and do some strategic planning. From fresh fruit to omelets, you can make breakfast as light or as heavy as you want. At lunch and dinner, you can find everything from fresh seafood and made-to-order pastas to freshly carved roast beef and lamb. No intimate affair, this place seats some 400 diners. Sit inside or on the patio overlooking a lagoon.

Royal Towers, Atlantis Resort. ☎ *242-363-3000. Full dinners: $45.98. AE, DC, MC, V. Open: Daily for breakfast, lunch, and dinner.*

Dining at Cable Beach's best restaurants

The Black Angus Grill

$$$$ Cable Beach   STEAK

The casino crowd flocks to this popular restaurant where beef is the star of the show, but poultry and seafood play supporting roles. Because Bahamian cattle farms don't exist, the meat is imported frozen. However, the meat is always juicy, and the chef knows how particular some carnivores are. So, rare means rare, medium-rare means just that, and you won't see any pink if you ask for your meat well-done, whether you order prime rib, filet mignon, or a T-bone steak. If you play both sides of the fence, order the surf and turf — the lobster tail is sweet and plump. Another good choice is the *chicken carbonara* (made with Parmesan cheese, bacon, garlic, and white wine).

On the second level of the casino complex, the Nassau Marriott Resort & Crystal Palace Casino. ☎ *242-327-6200. Main courses: $28–$39.50. AE, MC, V. Open: Mon–Sat for dinner only.*

Café Johnny Canoe

$–$$ Cable Beach   BAHAMIAN/INTERNATIONAL

This brightly decorated spot is so wild and festive you may think at first that it's truly a tourist trap. It's obviously geared to visitors — not locals — but the island cuisine is very authentic and full of regional flavor. At breakfast, the pancakes are light, and the omelets are fluffy. If your palate

Cable Beach Dining

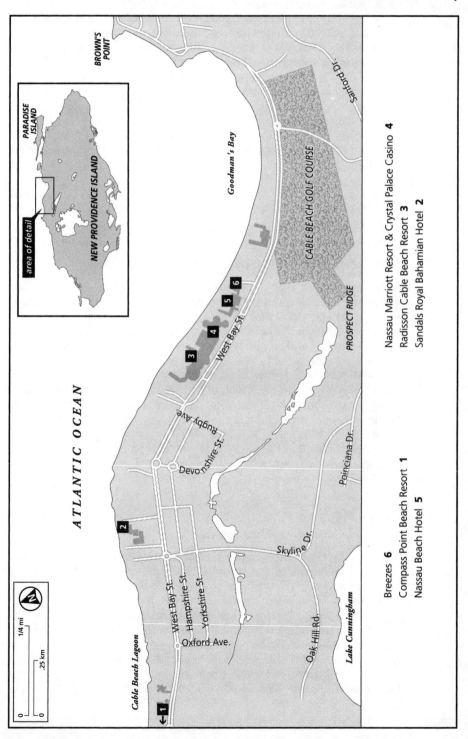

ATLANTIC OCEAN

BROWN'S POINT

PARADISE ISLAND

NEW PROVIDENCE ISLAND

area of detail

Goodman's Bay

CABLE BEACH GOLF COURSE

PROSPECT RIDGE

Sanford Dr.

West Bay St.

Rugby Ave.

Devonshire St.

Poinciana Dr.

Skyline Dr.

Devonshire

West Bay St.

Hampshire St.

Yorkshire St.

Oxford Ave.

Oak Hill Rd.

Cable Beach Lagoon

Lake Cunningham

1/4 mi

.25 km

Nassau Marriott Resort & Crystal Palace Casino **4**
Radisson Cable Beach Resort **3**
Sandals Royal Bahamian Hotel **2**

Breezes **6**
Compass Point Beach Resort **1**
Nassau Beach Hotel **5**

is adventurous and you're here on a Saturday and Sunday, try grand-mother's favorite treats for her family, including tuna and grits, "boil fish," or stewed conch, each dish coming with johnnycakes. For substantial Bahamian fare, you can devour the classic cracked conch with peas and rice or else be regaled with grilled mahi-mahi with macaroni and cheese. If you order fish fingers in America, try the Bahamian version. Here, they're called grouper fingers and are served with creamy cole slaw. The icing on the cake, so to speak, is the guava duff for dessert. Perhaps by now you've become addicted to this unique Bahamian confection. On Friday at 8 p.m., a junkanoo band entertains, as the musicians parade in their colorful costumes, the sound of their island music turning the place into a carnival. Junkanoo music is also presented on three other nights, most often Thursday, Saturday, and Sunday.

West Bay St., in front of the Nassau Beach Hotel. ☎ *242-327-3373. Main courses: $8.95–$23.95. AE, DISC, MC, V. Open: Daily 7:30 a.m.–midnight.*

Compass Point
$$–$$$ Gambier   CALIFORNIAN/INTERNATIONAL

Music mogul Chris Blackwell attracts most visiting celebrities to New Providence to his chic little enclave set along the oceanfront. Informal, low-key, and casually hip, it dazzles with its Junkanoo decorations of every-thing from inlaid conch shells to flamboyant island colors. The cuisine has more modern flair and imagination than any other on New Providence. The chef pairs together seemingly odd combinations of flavors such as conch sushi with mango. However, most of these marriages of flavors come off beautifully. We are especially fond of their blackened grouper with a trop-ical sweet and sour salsa. Treat yourself to the spicy jerk chicken salad or else be tempted by the crab cakes with a papaya relish.

On the water in Gambier Village, about 10 minutes west of Cable Beach. ☎ *242-327-4500. Reservations required. Main courses: $19–$45. AE, MC, V. Open: Daily for breakfast, lunch, and dinner.*

Dickie Mo's
$–$$ Cable Beach   STEAK/SEAFOOD

Two blocks west of the Radisson, casual Dickie Mo's offers a pleasant alternative to restaurants at large Cable Beach hotels. You can sit in one of the nautical dining rooms or on the outdoor patio, with its rustling palm trees. A calypso-singing one-man band usually entertains. To whet your appetite, try a "Playgirl" made with rum, banana liqueur, and fruit punch. The seafood platter comes loaded with shrimp, conch, grouper, scallops, and lobster. If you have a lighter appetite, opt for the snapper, which you can order grilled in garlic butter. If you don't mind working a little for your supper, order the succulent stone crabs and start cracking those shells. The emphasis is on seafood here, but the steak, succulent and tender, is also very good. For dessert, sample some guava duff, that rich Bahamian specialty, which has made a miraculous comeback at many local Bahamian restaurants.

Just west of the Radisson Cable Beach hotel. ☎ *242-327-7854. Reservations recommended. Main courses: $10.95–$35.95. AE, MC, V. Open: Daily for dinner only.*

The Island
$–$$ Cable Beach   BAHAMIAN

For Bahamian cookery, you can certainly find other restaurants more authentic than this tourist-packed spot. However, with its lively atmosphere, this colorful hotel restaurant is a convenient choice if you're staying in Cable Beach. Bahama Mamas flow freely at The Island, where the bar is made from yellow, blue, and red barrels. Sit at a table or in a cozy booth. The cooks do a good job with their Bahamian repertoire, celebrating the island's favorite dishes. Grouper Nassau comes panfried and topped with a savory tomato and sweet pepper sauce. The Bimini dolphin (the fish — not the mammal) is seasoned with cracked pepper, and the cracked conch is, well, cracked conch (which means it's pounded until tender and then battered and fried). For dessert, the tropical cheesecake and the key lime pie are sweet treats. If your supper makes you sing, you're in luck, because you can enjoy karaoke after dinner.

In the Radisson Cable Beach hotel. ☎ *242-327-6000. Reservations recommended. Main courses: $17–$23.95. MC, V. Open: dinner only, closed Tues–Thurs. Call ahead for exact opening times.*

Sole Mare
$$$$ Cable Beach   NORTHERN ITALIAN

Overlooking the ocean from the second level of the casino complex, this restaurant serves an admirable Northern Italian cuisine and even pleases some diners who claim "you can't eat good Italian in The Bahamas." With candlelit tables and a guitarist playing soft tunes, Sole Mare is one of the more elegant choices in Cable Beach. One standout is the pasta with lobster and shrimp sautéed in garlic olive oil and white wine. The veal sautéed with endive, capers, and white wine makes another enticing choice, along with the al dente cappellini with a zesty tomato sauce.

On the second level of the casino complex, the Nassau Marriott Resort & Crystal Palace Casino. ☎ *242-327-6200. Jackets preferred for men. Main courses: $21–$39. Open: Dinner only; day of closing varies depending on hotel occupancy.*

Chapter 12

Having Fun On and Off the Beach in New Providence

....

In This Chapter

▶ Catching some rays on New Providence's best beaches

▶ Enjoying the island's water sports

▶ Exploring New Providence's land attractions, shopping, and nightlife

▶ Taking two great day trips

....

As the home of **Nassau** (The Bahamas' history-packed capital), **Cable Beach** (the hotel-lined resort), and **Paradise Island** (the flashy vacation mecca just offshore), New Providence offers more action, both wet and dry, than anywhere else in The Bahamas. Water sports, from scuba diving and snorkeling to jet skiing and parasailing, keep vacationers entertained when they aren't playing golf or tennis, horseback riding, mountain biking, or just strolling the streets of downtown Nassau. The hottest nightlife, the widest selection of duty-free shops and designer boutiques, the best choice of human-made attractions — from botanical gardens to intriguing museums' — are presented in this chapter.

Hitting the Beaches

Easy-on-the-eyes **Cable Beach,** in the center of New Providence's northern coast, draws the most visitors. Calypso music floats to the sand from hotel pool patios where vacationers play musical chairs and see how low they can limbo. Vendors wend their way between sunblock-slathered bodies. Some sell armloads of shell jewelry, T-shirts, beach cover-ups, and fresh coconuts for sipping the sweet "water" straight from the shell. Others offer their hair-braiding services or sign up visitors for water-skiing, jet skiing, and banana boat rides. Kiosks advertise parasailing, scuba-diving and snorkeling trips, and party cruises to offshore islands.

If you're looking for a tranquil stretch of sand, this 4-mile hotel-studded, people-packed strip isn't it. But if you want clear turquoise water and talcum sand — plus convenient access to hotels, shops, restaurants, and a casino — then this is your beach.

To get away from the crowds, head out to **Delaporte Beach,** just west of the busiest section of Cable Beach. About a 10-minute drive west, near Gambier Village, cozy **Love Beach** — ideal for snorkeling — is adjacent to a single snazzy small resort called **Compass Point.** East of Cable Beach, on the way to the center of Nassau, lie **Goodman's Bay,** with a playground, and **Saunders Beach,** just west of Arawak Cay. Both are more popular with residents, especially on weekends, than with visitors, who tend to stick closer to hotels.

Goodman's Bay and Saunders Beach often host local fund-raising cookouts, where vendors sell fish, chicken, conch, peas and rice, and macaroni and cheese, and people swim and socialize to blaring reggae and calypso music. To find out when one of these beach parties is happening, ask the staff at your hotel or pick up a local newspaper.

If your hotel is near downtown Nassau, you may be right across the road from **Western Esplanade,** west of the British Colonial Hilton. Also called "Junkanoo Beach," this narrow strip of sand is convenient to Nassau and has toilets, changing facilities, and a snack bar.

Across the water on Paradise Island, **Paradise Beach** attracts sun worshippers from all over New Providence. The busiest hotels are clustered toward the western end of the island. The least crowded sandy strands lie to the east, including **Cabbage Beach,** running in front of the elegant **Ocean Club** resort. You can reach Paradise Island from downtown Nassau by walking over the bridge, taking a taxi, or boarding a boat by **Prince George Dock.** (See Chapter 10 for more on getting around in New Providence.)

Finding Water Fun for Everyone

Most water action jumps off from **Cable Beach, Paradise Island Beach,** and **Prince George Dock** in downtown Nassau. From snorkeling sails and sunset cruises to scuba-diving excursions and rides in a semi-submarine, New Providence's aquatic diversions showcase The Bahamas' prime asset. For a change of scenery, many folks board tour boats to **Blue Lagoon Island** and **Rose Island,** two popular cays just offshore.

Jet skiing, parasailing, banana boat rides, water-skiing, and windsurfing are available on the beaches in front of Cable Beach and Paradise Island hotels. However, in many cases, independent vendors who have nothing to do with the hotels run these sports, which means that the hotels aren't responsible for any problems that may arise.

Dolphin diversions and other ocean adventures

Are dolphins really smiling? Why is their skin so warm and smooth? Can they understand each other's chatter? Find out, if you want, the answers to these questions, and many more, during a **Dolphin Encounter** on Blue Lagoon Island (☎ **242-363-1003** or 242-363-6790). This popular activity is often booked well in advance.

The **Close Encounter program** ($75) enables you to stand in shallow water and pet the dolphins, while the **Swim with the Dolphins Program** ($145) lets you delve deeper. Both last about 3 hours, including the boat ride to and from Blue Lagoon, part of Salt Cay, about 3 miles northeast of Paradise Island.

Some marine studies have shown that contrary to popular belief, dolphins don't like to be touched by humans. It's up to you and your political correctness to decide, in lieu of these released findings, whether you want to interplay with an animal that may not be enjoying your company all that much.

Several tour operators take visitors to and from Blue Lagoon Island, but you can't book a Dolphin Encounter through all of them.

Even if you're not a scuba diver, you and your kids can still breathe underwater. Try helmet diving with **Hartley's Undersea Walk** (☎ **242-393-8234;** Internet: www.underseawalk.com), at the **Nassau Yacht Haven** on East Bay Street. During this 3½-hour excursion (about $75), you take a 30-minute boat ride out to a reef. After donning a lead and glass helmet, you descend a ladder into 12 to 15 feet of water. Air is pumped into the helmet through a long tube. You can keep your glasses or contact lenses on because your face and hair stay completely dry. Folks have even been known to take their helmet-clad dogs down under. Following the instructions of your guide, you spend about 20 minutes wandering in slow motion around the ocean floor, past crayon-colored sea plants, coral, and fish.

To secure your reservation, arrive 30 minutes before your scheduled departure time.

Exploring the Bahamian underwater world

If you visit any of the Out Islands, you may want to save your underwater time for those lesser known, less visited reefs. The waters around New Providence offer excellent dive sites, but too many scuba divers may be admiring all the tropical fish, huge sponges, and varied coral reefs around the dramatic caves, cliffs, ocean holes, ledges, and wrecks.

Neophytes can take a quickie *resort course,* also known as a beginner's class (about $70). Full-certification courses run anywhere from $495 to $695. Plan to pay about $70 for a two-tank dive, $55 to $65 for a night dive, and $100 to $125 for a shark dive. Most operators sell you a video-tape of your aqua-action for about $50, and they transport you to and from your hotel.

With more than three decades of experience, **Bahama Divers (☎ 800-398-3483** or 242-393-5644), at the Nassau Yacht Haven, by the bottom of the Paradise Island bridge, is Nassau's oldest and most reliable com-pany. Another good operator is **Dive Dive Dive Ltd. (☎ 242-362-1143** or 242-362-1401) in **Coral Harbour** on the southwest coast, where some reefs are shallow enough for both snorkelers and divers.

Snorkeling and parasailing

If you want shallow diving and snorkeling without having to go out on a boat, New Providence Island offers dozens of possibilities. Our favorite spot is Love Beach, near the hotel, Compass Point.

In another part of the island, **Southwest Reef** lures scuba divers with its giant coral heads standing in anywhere from 12 to 25 feet of water, with staghorn corals and elkhorn along with rainbow-hued fish.

In the western part of the island, the nature reserve at offshore **Gouldings Cay** offers some of the best snorkeling on island, and it's never crowded. You can see some of the most majestic elkhorn coral in all of The Baha-mas. Scenes from *Splash* and *Cocoon,* two films still shown on the late show, were shot here.

Parasailing is another exhilarating sport. You're strapped to a para-chute that's tied with a long leash to a boat. As the boat takes off, you float gently into the air as if you're flying. Independent operators along Cable Beach and Paradise Island Beach charge about $40 for 8 to 10 minutes in the sky.

Excursions by boat take you to the best and most dramatic sites for snorkeling, more impressive than what you can do yourself off the coast. **Barefoot Sailing Cruises (☎ 242-393-0820)** is based at **Bayshore Marina,** on East Bay Street near the Paradise Island bridge. Their 41-foot sailboat takes no more than 16 campers; their 56-foot sail-boat holds a maximum of 30, and their 65-foot catamaran accommo-dates only 65. The size and type of boat you sail on depends on the number of people booked on any given day. A half-day snorkel sail to **Atoll Island** or **Spruce Cay** runs $39 per person, including beverages and snacks, while the full-day trip costs $59 with lunch.

Another good choice is **Flying Cloud** (☎ 242-393-1957), based at the ferry terminal on Paradise Island. This 57-foot catamaran takes a maximum of 50 passengers. Snorkeling cruises go to **Rose Island** for a half-day of fun costing $40 with two drinks, or a full day for $55, with lunch and unlimited rum punch. Snorkel gear and lessons, if necessary, are included in the price, along with transportation to and from your accommodation.

Activities desks of many of the larger hotels push the 3-hour snorkeling sail ($20) and dinner cruise ($50) with **Majestic Tours, Ltd.** (☎ 242-322-2606). However, take one of these popular, inexpensive trips and you may feel like you're in the middle of Times Square on New Year's Eve at midnight. These triple-deck boats hold more than 200 passengers.

On Deck: Riding the Waves without Getting Wet

You can experience Bahamian waters and marine life firsthand without snorkeling or scuba diving. Several water excursions are offered.

Taking dinner and sunset cruises

Barefoot Sailing Cruises (☎ 242-393-0820) offers a 2-hour champagne sunset cruise ($39, including cold hors d'oeuvres). You sail through **Nassau Harbour,** under the bridges, into **Montagu Bay,** over by the cruise ships, and maybe along the northern coast of Paradise Island. You can munch cheese and crackers as you sip your bubbly, and you don't need to dress up — many passengers wear shorts. Prices include ground transportation. Depending on the number of vacationers booked, you may cruise on a 41-foot sailboat carrying no more than 16 passengers, a 56-foot sailboat taking a maximum of 30, or a 65-foot catamaran roomy enough for 65.

Flying Cloud (☎ 242-393-1957) carries up to 50 passengers on its 57-foot catamaran. Depending on the time of year that you go, the 2½-hour evening cruise takes in the setting sun ($30, including hot and cold hors d'oeuvres). During the 3-hour dinner cruise ($50), you can chow down on soup, salad, fish, beef, rice, vegetables, and dessert, served with wine. All rates cover transportation to and from your hotel.

Of the two competitors, we find cruises aboard Barefoot more adventurous and fun, especially when the passengers are few. For a real sailing experience, book on a sailboat instead of the larger catamaran. If the catamarans are crowded, you may feel you're riding on a cattle boat, especially with all the eating and drinking. On a sailboat, the atmosphere is more romantic, and the night is yours.

Fishing for fun

Bahamian waters are thick with game fish, and some travelers spend every day of their vacations casting lines. For a half-day charter for two to six anglers, you'll spend anywhere from $400 to $500 or, for a full day, $800 and up. If you want to join a group for a half day (usually in the morning), you spend about $70 per person. Two of New Providence's best companies are the **Born Free Charters** (☎ 242-363-4144) and **Nassau Yacht Haven** (☎ 242-393-8173).

These are Atlantic waters, not the tranquil Caribbean Sea, and the waves can be rough at times, causing seasickness for those not used to it. If you're prone to motion sickness, ask your captain about sea conditions setting out.

Setting sail on charters

For the best sailing charter, perhaps to some of the Out Islands, try Barefoot Sailing Cruises (☎ 242-393-0820) or **Amarok Sailing Charters** (☎ 800-903-6790 or 242-477-4471). Carrying up to 6 passengers, the crewed 41-foot Amarok ketch specializes in weeklong trips to the Exumas, about 5 hours from Nassau (around $1,634 per couple). You can read more about the Exumas in Chapter 23.

Enjoying semi-submarine rides

To see coral reefs, you can take a ride in a "submarine." Contact **Seaworld Explorer** (☎ 242-356-2548) to board its 45-passenger semi-submersible. The trip begins with a 15-minute catamaran ride and narrated tour along Nassau's coastline. Then you spend about an hour in the "sub." The vessel doesn't actually dive, but it does have windows that are some 10 feet below the surface of the ocean, offering close-up views of fish, coral, and a shipwreck. This 90-minute excursion to the **Sea Gardens Marine Park** costs $37 for adults and $19 for children age 3 to 12. For an additional $3 each way, you can arrange transportation between your hotel and the trip's starting point, Bay Street and Elizabeth Avenue in downtown Nassau.

Exploring New Providence on Land

Wandering the historic streets of Nassau is an adventure in itself. Seeing the sights from a horse-drawn carriage makes you feel as if you've been transported into the past. From impressive old forts, small museums, and attractive pink-and-white government buildings to manicured gardens, aquariums, and a zoo, New Providence and Paradise Island can keep you busy.

Or you can take to the links, play tennis, go horseback riding, or join a bike tour. Shopping is big here, with all kinds of stores lining Bay Street in downtown Nassau and plenty of boutiques in hotels. After dark, New Providence and Paradise Island offer more action than anywhere else in The Bahamas. Casinos take your money, while nightclubs entertain with Las Vegas-style shows. Live music pulls you onto dance floors, and you can sample various versions of Bahama Mamas and Goombay Smashes at dozens of bars.

Locating the top attractions

To get around New Providence, you can rent a car or take taxis or else hop aboard the far cheaper *jitneys,* public buses that run in front of Cable Beach hotels and through Nassau. These vans may take a while, but they eventually get you within shouting distance of the attractions in this section. Jitney routes are often roundabout, but you're treated to impromptu tours of neighborhoods you may otherwise miss.

To get to Paradise Island, you can take a taxi across the bridge from Nassau or else walk. After you're there, you can take shuttle buses around the island or hoof it.

The following are the best attractions that New Providence offers.

Ardastra Gardens & Zoo
Nassau

The gardens here are a treat for the eyes, but the animals are the real draw. You see creatures great and small, from iguanas, *hutias* (indigenous rodents), and peacocks to monkeys, lemurs, and various felines. You can even stroke a tame boa constrictor or have your photo snapped with a colorful macaw on your shoulder. The zoo is known for its marching flamingos performances, which are staged three times a day.

The fun begins when the leggy pink birds trot en masse into the arena. Like a drill sergeant, their trainer shouts commands, and the flamingos all stop on a dime, abruptly change direction, or stretch out their wings. Humans from the audience are summoned to join the flock in hilarious poses. After their performance, you can ask them for their autographs as they gather by the lake studded with wild ducks and Australian black swans. From Cable Beach, take bus #10 that travels along West Bay Street, or you can take a brief taxi ride. Allow about 90 minutes for a visit here.

West Bay St. and Chippingham Rd., near Fort Charlotte, about a mile west of downtown Nassau. Open: Daily 9 a.m.–4 p.m. Admission: $12 adults, $6 children.

Atlantis Aquarium
Paradise Island

The world's largest tropical marine exhibits some 50,000 sharks, stingrays, turtles, and other fish and sea creatures collected from around the planet. Plan to spend about 90 minutes here.

If you want to slide down the waterfall on the "Mayan temple" through a clear tube that cuts through a shark tank, you have to book a room at the Atlantis Resort or one of its sibling properties (**Ocean Club** or neighboring **Comfort Suites**). Only guests of these hotels are treated to the waterslides, the elaborate swimming pools, and the many other outdoor aquatic attractions.

Both guests and nonguests, however, can walk through the acrylic underwater tube, looking up to see hammerheads that seem to swim past palm trees through the sky above you. In the dim passageways of "The Dig," colorful fish swarm around streets and statues evocative of Atlantis.

Feedings of the giant green moray eels occur twice a day; before you visit, check the times. At the touch tank, children get a kick out of handling the spiky sea urchins, large conch shells, soft starfish, and surprisingly heavy sea cucumbers. (Only thing is, we can't guarantee how this marine life feels about this heavy petting.)

Royal Towers, Atlantis Resort, Paradise Island. ☎ *800-ATLANTIS or 242-363-3000. Call to arrange a guided tour. Admission: $25 adults and $19 children.*

Atlantis Paradise Island Resort & Casino
Paradise Island

The entertainment complex of this mega-resort has so much to see, although gambling is the main event here. Although most casinos keep the outdoors outdoors, the unusual design of this huge casino allows sunshine to stream in through skylights. The surrounding rooms and broad corridors are filled with designer boutiques, watering holes, restaurants from casual to glitzy — all on the expensive side — and plenty of gaping vacationers.

Casino Dr., Paradise Island, just across the bridge. Admission: Free.

Fort Charlotte
Nassau

If you have the time or desire to see only one fort in New Providence, make it Fort Charlotte. With a commanding view of the harbor, it was built in 1788 by Lord Dunmore, the royal governor, and named for Queen Charlotte, the wife of King George III. Tour guides tell visitors all about the moat, drawbridge, cannons, underground passages, and dungeons, but relate no stories of battles because the fort never saw one. You won't be charged for admission, but your guide expects a tip. You can combine a visit here with a trip to nearby **Ardastra Gardens & Zoo** and **Arawak Cay** (where local chefs whip up Bahamian favorites in small, no-frills restaurants).

West Bay St. and Chippingham Rd., about a mile west of downtown Nassau. ☎ *242-325-9186. Open: Mon–Sat 8:30 a.m.–4 p.m. Admission: Free.*

Fort Fincastle and the Water Tower
Nassau

Like Fort Charlotte, Nassau's other major fort, Fincastle, never saw a battle either. It was a lighthouse until 1816 when it was turned into a signal tower, lying 200 feet above the sea. Its 126-foot tall Water Tower, reached by an elevator to the observation platform, gives you the most panoramic view of New Providence. The fort is named in honor of Lord Dunmore, the royal governor who ordered its construction in 1793. His second title was Viscount Fincastle.

Young men hang out here, insisting that you go on a guided tour, but you can easily see the remains and enjoy the view on your own. These would-be tour guides are hard to shake off, however.

Bennett's Hill, Elizabeth Ave., just south of Shirley St. Open: Mon–Sat 9 a.m.–4 p.m. Admission for Water Tower: 50 cents.

Hairbraider's Centre
Nassau

Whether you want a single beaded plait, cornrows in an intricate design, or many itty-bitty loose braids with colorful rubber bands, this open-air pavilion is the place to go. Depending on what you want, the cost ranges from $2 to more than $100, and styles can take anywhere from minutes to hours to complete. At one time, hairbraiders roamed the shores of Cable Beach and Paradise Island in search of customers. Although you still may find some of these nimble-fingered women hawking their services on the sand, the government set up the Hairbraider's Centre to cut down on beach vendors.

Agree on a price and style before your Bahamian beautician touches your tresses. Put plenty of sunblock on your newly exposed scalp to avoid a wicked sunburn.

Prince George Dock, near Rawson Square, downtown Nassau.

Historic Nassau

Nassau

Set aside a couple of hours for some good old-fashioned Nassau street-walking. You won't even get arrested. As you wander through the capital, you see that the past has been well preserved. The best time for an amble is after 10 a.m. and before 4 p.m., Monday through Saturday. Many stores and museums are closed on Sundays. Streets are congested on Saturday, but that's the day the Changing of the Guard takes place at Government House. Try to find out from the staff at your hotel when the fewest cruise ships are in port, because those passengers really clog the center of town.

A good place to begin is **Rawson Square,** which links **Bay Street**, the main thoroughfare, with **Prince George Wharf,** also known as Prince George Dock, where the cruise ships dock. Horse-drawn carriages — each carrying up to three passengers — wait here to give leisurely tours. You can also see a statue of former shopkeeper Sir Milo Butler, the country's first native Bahamian — and first post-independence — governor. On the northern side of the square, the **Ministry of Tourism Information Booth** doles out helpful maps and brochures. Across the way is **Parliament Square,** with its statue of a young Queen Victoria and its pink, white-trimmed Georgian-style government buildings dating back to the late 1700s and early 1800s.

Nassau Public Library and Museum, at Bank Lane, is an octagonal building, which has been here since around 1797, and was once the Nassau Gaol (in other words, the local slammer). Shelves of books line the small prison cells. History buffs can check out the timeworn prints and colonial documents in the little museum. Stamp collectors head for the **Nassau General Post Office,** at the end of Parliament Street. You can then walk northeast to the foot of **Queen's Staircase.** These 65 steps lead to **Fort Fincastle** and the **Water Tower**, which both offer views of Nassau and the harbor.

To the west, at Duke and George Streets, stands the pink and white **Government House.** Since 1801, this has been the official residence of the governor-general, the Queen's representative. A statue of Christopher Columbus stands midway up the front steps. The stately white columns and wide circular driveway make this mansion the perfect setting for the dignified **Changing of the Guard Ceremony** that takes place outside every other Saturday at 10 a.m. The real crowd-pleaser of this event is the **Royal Bahamas Police Force Band.** The music is at least as colorful as the uniforms: stark-white tunics, navy trousers with bright red stripes, and white pitch helmets with crimson bands.

If you're into antiques, walk north (back toward Bay Street) to restored **Balcony House,** at Market Street and Trinity Place. This eighteenth-century, two-story house with a balcony is Nassau's oldest wooden residential building. Its rooms are decorated with furniture from the early 1800s through the 1940s. Most visitors rave about the handsome mahogany staircase, salvaged from a wrecked ship during the 1800s. You can spend a half-hour here. A donation is expected.

Head over to Bay Street to the **Pompey Museum** at George Street. Allow at least 30 minutes to absorb its exhibits on Bahamian slavery, emancipation, and contemporary art. Then poke around the open-air **Straw Market,** where vendors sell items such as shell jewelry, clothing made from African and Indonesian fabric, and woodcarvings, along with sun hats, baskets, place mats, and bags woven from straw. Walk east, behind the Straw Market, along waterfront **Woodes Rodgers Walk,** lined with mail boats, sponge boats, and vendors hawking fruit, vegetables, fish, and conch. Continue your stroll until you reach the imposing cruise ships docked back at Prince George Wharf.

Junkanoo Expo

Nassau

Unless you're vacationing at Christmas or New Year's, you'll miss the beloved **Junkanoo Festival.** This country's answer to Carnival and Mardi Gras begins with a parade starting in the wee hours of Boxing Day (December 26) and New Year's Day. However, here at this museum housed in an old customs shed, you feel as if you're witnessing the real deal. With a little imagination, you can picture the colorful costumes and whimsical masks on dancers and musicians as they pulse down Bay Street. You can also watch the video of last year's bash. Some of the hand-crafted costumes on display take months to create.

At the entrance to Prince George Dock. ☎ 242-356-2731. Open: Daily 9 a.m.–5:30 p.m. Admission: $2 adults, 50 cents children.

Pirates of Nassau Museum

Nassau

You need half an hour for the self-guided tour through this museum that brings Nassau's buccaneering days to life. During the eighteenth century, pirates ruled the waves around New Providence as they grew rich from the goods pillaged from merchant ships. You can go below deck on a replica of a pirate ship, *Revenge,* where you can view the kitchen area, hammocks, cannons, and animals, such as goats, chickens in crates, and, of course, rats. Battles rage through the special effects of sounds and lights, and the dungeon feels damp and creepy. You can hear pirates planning their next attack and smell the sea air. Kids of all ages enjoy the wax figures and the recreated ship and buildings, including the favorite pirate hangout: the tavern. Exhibits tell the story of Woodes Rodgers, who was shipped off here by the English crown to clean up the pirate pandemonium.

Corner of King and George Sts., a block south of the Straw Market. ☎ 242-356-3759. Open: Mon–Sat 9 a.m.–5 p.m. Admission: $12 adults; $6 children 3-18, free 2 and under.

Amos Ferguson: The painting painter

The Bahamas' best known artist, Amos Ferguson is a painter who used to be a house painter. Born on the Bahamian island of Exuma in 1920, he once ran a small farm and helped with his father's carpentry business. When he later moved to Nassau, he took up house painting. Using house paint instead of oil or acrylic, he started creating striking color-rich "naïve" pictures. Many vacationers got to know his early work through a Nassau Straw Market vendor named Bea, who eventually became his wife.

During the 1980s, Ferguson tumbled onto the international art scene. Still created with house paint, his often whimsical works are now owned by collectors around the world. His thought-provoking themes revolve around Biblical and historical images, nature and folklore, and the masks, costumes, and music of the Bahamian Junkanoo festival. You can see his paintings at the permanent exhibition upstairs at the Pompey Museum on Bay Street in downtown Nassau.

Pompey Museum
Nassau

Plan to spend at least an hour in this intriguing museum in **Vendue House,** named for the man who led a nineteenth-century revolt against slavery in the Exumas. This limestone building has stood here since around 1769. It was the site of New Providence's slave market until 1834, when the practice of selling people was outlawed throughout the British Empire. While viewing the exhibits on human bondage, the abolition movement, and emancipation, you get a clearer picture of the racial, economic, and political forces that have shaped the present day Bahamas. A 30-minute video presentation focuses on Bahamian history, heritage, and culture. An upstairs exhibition shows the powerful work of Amos Ferguson, the Bahamian "naïve" (meaning simple and one-dimensional; almost childlike) painter that some call "the father of Bahamian art." (See the sidebar "Amos Ferguson: The painting painter" in this chapter.)

Vendue House, Bay St. at George St. ☎ *242-326-2566 or 242-326-2568. Open: Mon–Fri 10 a.m.–4:30 p.m; every other Sat 10 a.m.–1 p.m. Admission: $1 adults, 50 cents children.*

Potter's Cay
Nassau

In the islands, the local market is an integral part of daily life. Already visited the Straw Market? Fine, but that overcrowded bazaar is for tourists. On the other hand, Potter's Cay, beneath the original Paradise Island bridge, is for Bahamians. This is an ideal spot for watching sloops from the Out Islands bring in huge mounds of glistening fish and conch. Seeing restaurant chefs buying fresh seafood straight off the boats is not unusual.

You can even take notes for your own kitchen while a fisherman prepares conch salad that couldn't be any fresher: He bores a hole into the shell, extracts the unfortunate conch, skins it, dices it, marinates it in lime juice, and seasons it with onions and peppers. Lining the water's edge, stalls sell this zesty salad along with conch fritters, conch chowder, fresh herbs, and pineapples (many from Eleuthera), bananas, papayas, limes, and other just-plucked fruit.

Especially if you're not purchasing anything, vendors here don't appreciate having their photographs taken. Point a camera in their direction, and they make their objection abundantly clear. As colorful as this site can be, abstain from capturing it on film, unless you have a very long lens or wide angle lens — or a 007-style camera hidden in your sunglasses.

Located directly under the bridge that links Nassau and Paradise Island.

Queen's Staircase
Nassau

Leading from old Nassau to the remains of Fort Fincastle at the top, these 65 steps were cut by enslaved men from solid limestone during the 1790s. Later, this 102-foot staircase got its name in honor of the 65-year reign of Queen Victoria.

At the bottom of the stairs, "guides" wait to present the history of the staircase. Their recitations are so well memorized that some of them sound like robotic recordings. At the top, it's an easy walk to Fort Fincastle and the Water Tower (see earlier entry).

Across Shirley St., toward the rise away from the harbor, and near Princess Margaret Hospital, downtown Nassau.

The Retreat
Nassau

You can visit the Botanical Gardens, but the 11 acres of this National Trust property are better kept. The flourishing grounds are filled with some 200 species of rare and exotic palms from around the world, other unusual trees, and delicate native orchids.

The Retreat is the place to see and hear all kinds of feathered friends, such as banana quits, northern mocking birds, black and white warblers, and red-legged tanagers.

You can take a half-hour tour on Tuesday, Wednesday, or Thursday at noon, or visit on your own. The Retreat is about a 20- to 30-minute taxi ride from Cable Beach, depending on traffic. If you don't mind a longer trip, you can also get here from the hotel areas by public bus.

Village Road, across from Queens College, just east of downtown Nassau. ☎ 242-393-1317. Open: Mon–Fri 9 a.m.–5 p.m. Tours: Tues–Thurs at noon (price of admission covers the cost of the tour as well). Admission: $2 for adults, $1 for children.

Versailles Gardens and Cloister
Paradise Island

Europe has been literally transported to The Bahamas. This twelfth-century cloister, originally built by Augustinian monks in southwestern France, was reassembled here stone by stone. Huntington Hartford, the A&P heir, purchased the cloister from the estate of William Randolph Hearst at San Simeon in California. Regrettably, after the newspaper czar originally bought the cloister, it was hastily dismantled in France for shipment to America, but the parts had not been numbered — they all arrived unlabeled on Paradise Island. The reassembly of the complicated monument baffled most conventional methods of construction, until artist and sculptor Jean Castre-Manne set about to reassemble it piece by piece. It took him two years, and what you see today, presumably, bears some similarity to the original. The gardens, which extend over the rise to Nassau Harbour, are filled with tropical flowers and classic statues. Unfortunately, although the monument retains a timeless beauty, recent buildings have encroached on either side, marring Huntington Hartford's original vision.

Adjacent to the Ocean Club resort, Paradise Island. Admission: Free.

Walking tours

Goombay Guided Walking Tours, arranged by the Ministry of Tourism, leave from the Tourist Information Booth on Rawson Square at 10, 11:30 a.m., 1, 2:30, and 3:45 p.m. daily. Tours last for 45 minutes and include descriptions of some of the city's most venerable buildings, with commentaries on Nassau's history, customs, and traditions. The hour-long tours require advance reservations, as schedules may vary. The cost is $5 and $2.50 for children under 12. Call ☎ 242-326-9772 to confirm that tours are on schedule.

Enjoying New Providence's other activities

Most of the action on and around New Providence is linked to the Atlantic. But when you're ready to dry off, you have plenty of choices.

Biking the sights

A half-day bicycle tour with **Pedal and Paddle Ecoventures** (☎ 242-362-2772; about $59) can take you on a 3-mile bike ride along some scenic forest and shoreline trails in the Coral Harbour area, on the southwestern coast of New Providence. You pass along a trail that has mangrove creeks and pine forests as a scenic backdrop and can take time off for a kayak trip to a shallow for snorkeling.

Some of the major hotels on Paradise Beach and Cable Beach rent bikes to their guests. You can bike along Cable Beach or the beachfront at Paradise Island, but Nassau is too traffic congested.

Hitting the links

New Providence courses frequently play host to international tournaments. At the 18-hole **Cable Beach Golf Course** (☎ **242-327-6000**), The Bahamas' oldest, greens fees run $100 with carts included. This course is the most convenient for many vacationers, because it's just across the road from the main Cable Beach hotels. Although it's a half-hour drive from Nassau, 18-hole **South Ocean Golf Club** (☎ **242-362-4391**) is the best course on New Providence and one of the best in the country. The rolling terrain of this challenging course overlooks the ocean. Here, greens fees run $110, including the cart.

Working out at gyms and spas

Many of the large hotels have exercise rooms for guests to use. Some also offer spa facilities, including **Sandals Royal Bahamian** and the **Crystal Palace Casino** complex, both on Cable Beach, and **Atlantis Paradise Island Resort & Casino** and **Ocean Club Golf & Tennis Resort,** both on Paradise Island. If your hotel doesn't have a gym or spa, or if you need more extensive equipment or pampering to keep up your routine, check out **Gold's Gym** (☎ **242-394-4653;** daily equipment rates begin at $8) at the foot of the Paradise Island bridge in Nassau or **Windermere Spa & Salon** (☎ **242-393-0033**) at the **Harbour Bay Shopping Centre** on East Bay Street in Nassau.

Saddling up for horseback rides

Small groups of riders spend 90 minutes riding along wooded and beachside trails through **Happy Trails Stables** (☎ **242-362-1820**). The $85 price tag includes transportation between your hotel and the stables. They're in the Coral Harbour area in southwestern New Providence, about 20 minutes from Cable Beach and 45 minutes from Paradise Island. Reservations are required for one of these guided rides, which go out twice a day.

Courting the game of tennis

Among the hotels with tennis courts — some lit for night play — are the **Radisson, Sandals, Nassau Beach Hotel** on Cable Beach, **Atlantis,** and the **Ocean Club** on Paradise Island. Some allow in-house guests to play for nothing while others charge a small hourly fee. If your hotel doesn't have courts, you can arrange to play elsewhere, generally for anywhere from $10 to $15 an hour, plus about $6 to rent a racquet.

Getting a Shopper's Guide to New Providence

As would be expected, more shops are centered in Nassau than elsewhere in The Bahamas.

You can find a variety of bargains in Nassau — Swiss watches, Japanese cameras, French perfumes, Irish crystal and linens, and British china.

You won't have to pay import duties on 11 categories of luxury goods, including china, crystal, fine linens, jewelry, leather goods, photographic equipment, watches, fragrances, and other merchandise. Antiques, of course, are exempt from import duty worldwide. But even though prices are "duty-free," you can still end up spending more on an item in The Bahamas than you would back in your hometown. It's a tricky situation.

If you're contemplating a major purchase, such as a good Swiss watch or some expensive perfume, do some research in your hometown discount outlets before making a serious purchase in The Bahamas. While the alleged 30% to 50% discount off stateside prices may apply on some purchases, it's not true in most cases. Certain cameras and electronic equipment, we have discovered, are listed in The Bahamas, at, say, 20% or more below the manufacturer's "suggested retail price." That sounds good, except the manufacturer's suggested price may be a lot higher than what you'd pay in your hometown. You aren't getting the discount you think you are. Some shoppers even take along department-store catalogs from the States to determine whether the items they're considering are indeed a bargain.

A lot of price-fixing seems to be going on in Nassau. For example, a bottle of Chanel is likely to sell for pretty much the same price regardless of the store.

Mostly European, American, and Asian imports fill vacationers' shopping bags. Bahamian-made goods are much more scarce. Even at Nassau's **Straw Market,** between Bay Street and Woodes Rodgers Walk, you may be surprised at the number of items made in China, Indonesia, and Kenya. But at this open-air market, you'll also find plenty of locally produced straw goods, along with Bahamian sauces and seasonings, perfumes, woodcarvings, shell jewelry, dolls, and art.

Be prepared for persistent vendors. Someone may slip a necklace around your neck in an attempt to convince you that you can't live without it. In addition to the large Bay Street straw market, you can find similar set-ups across from the Radisson and Marriott hotels on Cable Beach.

Pay the first price you're quoted, and the vendor will look at you as if you have three eyes. Bargaining is a way of life here. Don't be afraid to turn your back on something you really want. Chances are, the previously stubborn vendor will call after you with a suddenly reduced price that's "only for you."

While bargaining is *expected* at straw and produce markets, it isn't welcome at all in most stores. At glitzy boutiques, such as those at Atlantis Paradise Island Resort & Casino, salespeople give you a price and stand firm.

Antiques

Marlborough Antiques (corner of Queen and Marlborough Streets; ☎ 242-328-0502) carries the type of antiques you'd expect to find in a shop in London: antique books, antique maps and engravings, English silver (both sterling and plate), and unusual table settings (fish knives and so on). Among the most appealing objects are the store's collection of antique photographs of the islands. Also displayed are works by Bahamian artists Brent Malone and Maxwell Taylor.

Art

Although many locals come to **Kennedy Gallery** (Parliament St.; ☎ 242-325-7662) for custom framing, the gallery also sells original artwork by well-known Bahamian artists, including limited-edition prints, handcrafts, pottery, and sculpture.

Brass and copper

With two branches on Charlotte Street, the **Brass and Leather Shop** (12 Charlotte St., between Bay and Shirley Streets.; ☎ 242-322-3806) offers English brass, handbags, luggage, briefcases, attachés, and personal accessories. Shop No. 2 has handbags, belts, scarves, ties, and small leather goods from such famous designers as Furla, Bottega Veneta, Pierre Balmain, and others. If you look and select carefully, you can find some good buys here.

Cigars

Many cigar aficionados come to the **Tropique International Smoke Shop** (in Nassau Marriott Resort & Crystal Palace Casino, W. Bay St.; ☎ 242-327-7292) to indulge their passion for Cubans, which are handpicked and imported by Bahamian merchants. The staff at this outlet trained in Havana, so they know their cigars.

Remember, U.S. citizens are prohibited from bringing Cuban cigars back home because of the trade embargo. If you buy them, you're supposed to enjoy them in The Bahamas.

Coins and stamps

At the **Bahamas Post Office Philatelic Bureau** (in the General Post Office, at the top of Parliament St. on E. Hill St.; ☎ 242-322-1112), you'll find beautiful Bahamian stamps slated to become collector's items. One of the most sought-after stamps has a seashell motif.

Coin of the Realm (Charlotte St., just off Bay St.; ☎ 242-322-4497) is a family-run shop located in a lovely building hewn out of solid limestone over 200 years ago. The shop offers not only fine jewelry, but also Bahamian and British postage stamps, mint and used, and rare (and not-so-rare) Bahamian silver and gold coins. It also sells old and modern paper Bahamian currency. Bahama pennies that were minted in 1806 and 1807 are now rare and expensive items.

Fashion

One of Nassau's more formal and elegant clothing stores, **Barry's Limited** (Bay and George Streets; ☎ 242-322-3118) sells garments made from lamb's wool and English cashmere. Elegant sportswear (including Korean-made Guayabera shirts) and suits are sold here. Most of the clothes are for men, but women often stop in for a look at the fancy handmade Irish linen handkerchiefs and the stylish cuff links, studs, and other accessories. The name alone will intrigue, but **Bonneville Bones** (Bay St.; ☎ 242-328-0804) hardly describes what's inside. This is the best men's store we've found in Nassau. You can find everything here, from standard T-shirts and designer jeans to elegant casual clothing, including suits. **Cole's of Nassau** (Parliament St.; ☎ 242-322-8393) offers the most extensive selection of designer fashions in Nassau. Women can buy everything from swimwear and formal gowns to sportswear and hosiery. Cole's also sells gift items, sterling-silver designer and costume jewelry, hats, shoes, bags, scarves, and belts.

Fendi (Charlotte St. at Bay St.; ☎ 242-322-6300) is Nassau's only outlet for the well-crafted Italian-inspired accessories endorsed by this famous leather-goods company. With handbags, luggage, shoes, watches, cologne, wallets, and portfolios to choose from, the selection may well solve some of your gift-giving quandaries.

Mademoiselle, Ltd (Bay St. at Frederick St.; ☎ 242-322-5130) specializes in the kinds of resort wear that looks appropriate at either a tennis club or a cocktail party. It features locally made batik garments by Androsia. Swimwear, sarongs, jeans, and halter tops are the rage here, as are the wonderfully scented soaps and lotions. The store's on-site

"Body Shop" boutique supplies all the paraphernalia you need for herbal massages and beauty treatments.

Handcrafts

Everything inside **Island Tings** (Bay St., between East St. and Elizabeth Ave.; ☎ 242-326-1024) pays homage to Bahamian artisans and their ability to craft worthwhile pieces from humble and sometimes unlikely materials. Expect a minilibrary of books on the archipelago's culture and cuisine, as well as sculptures crafted from driftwood and conch shells, utilitarian jewelry, straw goods such as baskets, natural sea sponges, wall hangings, and Junkanoo masks made from all-natural traditional materials and newfangled versions molded from fiberglass. The collection also includes aloe-based skin lotions and perfumes distilled from local plants and flowers.

Sea Grape Boutique (West Bay Rd. (next to Travelers Restaurant). ☎ 242-327-1308) is the finest gift shop on New Providence, with an inventory of exotic decorative items that you'll probably find fascinating. It includes jewelry crafted from fossilized coral, sometimes with sharks' teeth embedded inside, beadwork from Guatemala, Haitian paintings, silver from India, hairbrushes shaped like parrots, and clothing that's well-suited to the sometimes steamy climate of The Bahamas. A second branch of this outfit, Sea Grape, Too, is located in the Radisson Hotel's Mall, on Cable Beach (☎ 242-327-5113).

Jewelry

The jewelry department at **John Bull** (corner of Bay and Charlotte Streets; ☎ 242-322-4253) offers classic selections from Tiffany & Co.; cultured pearls from Mikimoto; the creations of David Yurman, Stephen Lagos, Carrera y Carrera, and Sea Life by Kanbana; Greek and Roman coin jewelry; and Spanish gold and silver pieces. It's the best name in the business. The store also features a wide selection of watches, cameras, perfumes (including Estée Lauder, Chanel, and Calvin Klein at discount prices — though you should check carefully to make sure that you're getting a bargain), cosmetics, leather goods, and accessories. It's also one of the best places in The Bahamas to buy a Gucci or Cartier watch. The outlet has been the authorized agent for Rolex in The Bahamas for 30 years, and the store itself has been doing business since 1929.

Leather

In addition to the stores mentioned in this section, another good store for leather goods is the **Brass and Leather Shop,** described earlier in this chapter in the "Brass & Copper" section.

Gucci (Saffrey Sq., Bay St., corner of Bank Lane opposite Rawson Square; ☎ 242-325-0561), is the best place to buy leather goods in Nassau. The wide selection includes handbags, wallets, luggage, briefcases, gift items, scarves, ties, casual clothes, evening wear for men and women, umbrellas, shoes, sandals, watches, and perfume, all by Gucci of Italy.

The well-known retail outlet **Leather Masters** (Parliament St.; ☎ 242-322-7597) carries an internationally known collection of leather bags, luggage, and accessories by Ted Lapidus, Lanvin, and Lancel of Paris; Etienne Aigner of Germany; and "i Santi" of Italy. Leather Masters also carries luggage by Piel and Marroquinera of Colombia, leather wallets by Bosca, and pens, cigarette lighters, and watches by Colibri. Silk scarves, neckties, and cigar accessories are also featured.

Linens

The Linen Shop (Ironmongery Bldg., Bay St., near Charlotte St.; ☎ 242-322-4266) is the best outlet for linens in Nassau. It sells beautifully embroidered bed linens, Irish handkerchiefs, hand-embroidered women's blouses, and tablecloths. Look also for the most exquisite children's clothing and christening gowns in town.

Maps

Balmain Antiques (Mason's Bldg., Bay St., near Charlotte St; the shop is on the second floor, three doors east of Charlotte Street; ☎ 242-323-7421) offers a wide and varied assortment of nineteenth-century etchings, engravings, and maps, many of them antique and all reasonably priced. Other outlets have minor displays of these collectibles, but this outlet has the finest. Some items are 400 years old. It's usually best to discuss your interests with Mr. Ramsey, the owner, so that he can direct you to the proper drawers. His specialties include The Bahamas, America during the Civil War, and black history. He also has a collection of military historical items.

Markets

The **Nassau International Bazaar** (from Bay Street down to the waterfront, near the Prince George Wharf) consists of some 30 shops selling international goods in a new arcade. A pleasant place for browsing, the $1.8 million complex sells goods from around the globe. With cobbled alleyways and garreted storefronts, the area looks like a European village.

Prince George Plaza (Bay Street) is popular with cruise-ship passengers. Many fine shops, such as Gucci are found here. When you get tired of shopping, you can dine at the open-air rooftop restaurant that overlooks Bay Street.

The **Straw Market** (Straw Market Plaza on Bay Street) seems to be on every shopper's itinerary. Even those who don't buy anything come here to look around. Bahamian craftspeople weave and pleat straw hats, handbags, dolls, placemats, and other items, including straw shopping bags to hold your purchases. You can buy items ready-made (often from Taiwan) or order special articles, sometimes bearing your initials. You can also have fun bargaining for the lowest price. The Straw Market is open daily from 7 a.m. to 7 p.m.

Music

One of the finest record stores in the Bahamas, **Jam Productions** (Shirley St. in the Island Plaza; ☎ 242-394-1789) specializes in contemporary music from the Caribbean and abroad. The store's most intriguing service is its made-to-order tapes, a feature that allows you to customize a selection of your favorite music from any existing albums for sales.

Perfumes and cosmetics

Nassau has several good perfume outlets which also stock a lot of non-perfume merchandise.

- ✔ **The Beauty Spot:** The largest cosmetic shop in The Bahamas, this outlet sells duty-free cosmetics by Lancôme, Chanel, YSL, Elizabeth Arden, Estée Lauder, Clinique, Prescriptives, and Biotherm, among others. It also operates facial salons. Bay and Frederick Sts.; ☎ 242-322-5930.

- ✔ **Lightbourn's:** A pharmacy 100 years ago, Lightbourn's is a family-owned and -operated business that today carries a wide selection of duty-free fragrances and cosmetics. It's known for the quality of its goods and its service. Bay and George Streets; ☎ 242-322-2095.

- ✔ **The Perfume Bar:** This little gem has exclusive rights to market Boucheron and Sublime in The Bahamas. It also stocks the Clarins line (but not exclusively). Bay St.; ☎ 242-322-3785.

- ✔ **The Perfume Shop:** In the heart of Nassau, within walking distance of the cruise ships, the Perfume Shop offers duty-free savings on world-famous perfumes. Treat yourself to a flacon of Eternity, Giorgio, Poison, Lalique, Shalimar, or Chanel. Those are just a few of the scents for women. For men, the selection includes Drakkar Noir, Polo, and Obsession. Corner of Bay and Frederick Streets; ☎ 242-322-2375.

Steel drums

If you've fallen under the Junkanoo spell and want to take home some steel drums, visit **Pyfroms**. The drums will always be useful if island fever overtakes you after you return home. Bay St.; ☎ 242-322-2603.

Living It Up after the Sun Goes Down: New Providence's Nightlife

Nassau, Cable Beach, and Paradise Island were designed for party time. Bars at the larger hotels and at plenty of restaurants are packed after dark. Vacationers and residents bump hips on the crowded dance floors of local nightclubs. For many visitors, the casinos are the focal point of nightlife — and for some, day life as well.

The newer of New Providence's dynamic duo, the casino complex at **Atlantis Paradise Island Resort** (☎ 242-363-3000) is the largest in The Bahamas or even the Caribbean. Craps tables, baccarat, blackjack, roulette, Caribbean stud poker, and more than 1,000 slot machines give you plenty of excuses to try your luck. Tables may be open only from 10 a.m. to 4 a.m. daily, but the one-arm bandits are ready around the clock, as is **Voyagers Disco** (☎ **242-363-3000;** open: 10 p.m.–1 a.m.), which draws the party crowd.

The **Crystal Palace Casino** (☎ 242-327-7711) lies between the Nassau Marriott and Radisson resorts on Cable Beach. Tables are open from 10 a.m. to 4 a.m. during the week, and 24 hours a day on weekends. Slot machines, of course, are willing to eat your coins anytime day or night.

If you'd like to see a performance that evokes the spirit of the islands, then make a reservation for the **King & Knights Night Club** (☎ 242-327-7711) at the Nassau Beach Hotel showroom on Cable Beach. Performances here revolve around limbo, steel drums, fire dancing, and Bahamian Goombay and Junkanoo music and costumes. Of course, expect this place to be filled with visitors, not locals. The damage is about $25 (including one drink). If you like, you can arrive early to have dinner as well; main courses range from $10 to $30.

If you're craving a real slice of local life, find out what's happening at the **Dundas Center for the Performing Arts** (on Mackey Street, Nassau; ☎ 242-393-3728). These plays and musicals put on by local or foreign performers give you a taste of Nassau's artsy scene.

Conveniently located on West Bay Street, across from Saunders Beach, between Cable Beach and downtown Nassau, the **Zoo Nightclub** (☎ 242-322-7195) is the hottest dance club in town. The $10 cover charge gets you access to five different bars, including a sports bar, a café, and three levels of dance floors. The doors open around 8:30 or 9 p.m., but most patrons, an equal mix of locals and visitors, don't start showing up until between 10:30 and 11:30 p.m. The house rocks until 4 a.m.

Often featuring live bands, **Club Waterloo** (☎ 242-393-7324), on East Bay Street, just east of the Paradise Island exit bridge, is another popular dance spot with a choice of bars. The owner doesn't like reggae, so instead you hear rock 'n' roll, calypso, R & B, and club music. The crowd drawn to this place, the actual makeup of which can shift from night to night, is an eclectic blend of locals, Europeans, and American vacationers, both singles and couples. The place is open from 9 p.m. to 4 a.m., but the crowd is sparse before 10 or 11 p.m. If all that dancing makes you hungry, don't despair. Club Waterloo serves snack-type food.

The official cover charge can climb as high as a whopping $40 at Waterloo, but many people know better: Buy a $5 pass from your cab driver and then pay an additional $5 at the door.

Two Great Day Trips from New Providence

Tour operators take vacationers to the two most popular offshore cays, activity-packed **Blue Lagoon Island** and the more tranquil **Rose Island.** You get to decide whether you want to be in a small, personalized group or part of a huge crowd that descends on one of these peaceful islands.

Trip #1: Rose Island respite

One of the most serene sails to the tranquil Rose Island beach, 8 miles east of downtown Nassau, is with **Barefoot Sailing Cruises** (☎ 242-393-0820). Based at **Bayshore Marina,** on East Bay Street near the Paradise Island bridge, this company uses three different boats: a 41-foot sailboat carrying up to 16 passengers, a 56-foot sailboat taking a maximum of 30, and a 65-foot catamaran large enough for 65. The vessel you end up on depends on the number of people booked. For the full-day trip, a $55 charge covers lunch, snacks, drinks, snorkeling gear, and transportation to and from your hotel.

As you sail past small, scenic cays off the coast of New Providence, you realize that half the fun is in getting to Rose Island. The entire day is a 6-hour event, where you have time for sunning, swimming, and snorkeling in water no deeper than 12 feet. The day begins with coffee and donuts and ends with fruit and cookies, with a barbecue lunch sandwiched in between. Rum punch and soft drinks flow freely.

Trip #2: Blue Lagoon action

About 3 miles northeast of Paradise Island, **Blue Lagoon Island,** also known as Salt Cay, snags vacationers with its seven beaches, seaside hammocks, live bands, army of water toys (from snorkel gear to aqua-bikes and kayaks), a children's play area, and dolphin or stingray encounter programs.

A trip here can be enjoyable, but parts of the island are crowded at times, because cruise ships and several tour operators ferry passengers over for day trips. Most visitors plop right down at the first beach they see. For the quietest corners, walk as far as you can after you disembark.

Nassau Cruises Ltd. (☎ 242-363-1000), based between the bridges on Paradise Island, offers a variety of ways to sample the island. Packages begin at $25 per adult and $15 per child, covering only transportation to and from the island. For $65 per adult and $35 per child, you also get lunch, two drinks (fruit or rum punch), and use of all nonmotorized water sports. Add a snorkeling excursion to Stingray City Marine Park, and you pay $85 per adult and $50 per child. Because several departure and return times are available, you can come and go to Blue Lagoon Island as you please. For details about the Dolphin Encounter Program (run by another outfit), see "Dolphin diversions and other ocean adventures," earlier in this chapter.

Part IV
Grand Bahama

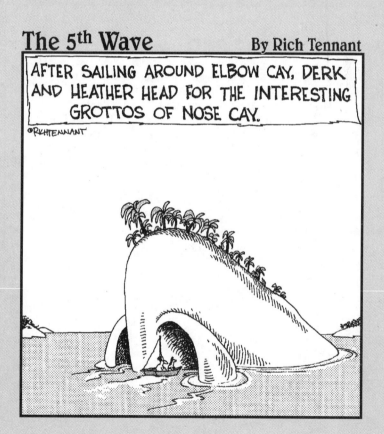

The 5ᵗʰ Wave   By Rich Tennant

AFTER SAILING AROUND ELBOW CAY, DERK AND HEATHER HEAD FOR THE INTERESTING GROTTOS OF NOSE CAY.

In this part . . .

*I*f Grand Bahama, a low-key, yet high-impact island, appeals to you, this part introduces you to the best ways to make the most of your stay. To narrow your search for the right accommodation — one that fits both your style and your budget — check out the descriptions of our favorite hotels. You can also use the advice about arriving and exploring the island to help familiarize yourself with the lay of the land.

Whether you want a meal at the water's edge or in a British-style pub, we give you Grand Bahama's best bets. We also offer plenty of suggestions on how to spend your days and nights, from savoring a beachside nature preserve to rolling the dice.

Chapter 13

The Lowdown on the Grand Bahama Hotel Scene

. . . .

In This Chapter

▶ Deciding among hotel locations

▶ Evaluating the top choices

. . . .

*I*n this chapter, we describe the accommodations that appeal to most first-time visitors. We considered locations, facilities, quality of service, architecture, and proximity to Grand Bahama's best attractions. For more information, see the accommodations map in this chapter.

Finding the Right Location

For some folks, life's a beach. For others, it's a casino. And then some people want both. Deciding between Freeport and Lucaya can be as easy as deciding between dice and saltwater.

In Freeport, the **Casino at Bahamia** is in the **Resorts at Bahamia,** the area's most popular hotel complex, which is about a 15-minute bus ride from the beach. If playing the slots is more important than overlooking the ocean from your bedroom, it's Freeport for you. Even if you lose at the gaming tables, you can save money on accommodations. Freeport hotels in general are less expensive than those in Lucaya.

Beachside Lucaya will give beachless Freeport a run for its money when a brand new casino opens here some time in the future. After digging a little deeper into your pocket for a room, you can treat yourself to both dice *and* sand without missing a beat — or a bet.

Both Freeport and Lucaya have major outdoor shopping complexes complete with pubs and restaurants. Freeport's **International Bazaar,** with its maze of stores, straw goods vendors, and eateries, has been around longer than Lucaya's main shopping and dining center, **Port Lucaya Marketplace.** Not only is Lucaya's younger, but it also sprawls along the water's edge.

Although both Freeport and Lucaya have plenty of good places to leave your money, we prefer Port Lucaya because of its gingerbread-trimmed, wooden buildings and the live music heard most evenings in **Count Basie Square.**

Even if you stay in Freeport, but want to sample Lucaya's attractions, such as its good beaches, buses, minivans, and taxis connect these resort areas. Neither is far from Grand Bahama's golf courses, horse stables, and natural attractions such as **Garden of the Groves, Rand Memorial Nature Centre,** and **Lucayan National Park.**

Checking Out Grand Bahama's Best Hotels

Rack rates are for two people spending one night in a double room during the high season of winter and spring, unless otherwise indicated. Rack rates simply mean published rates, but you can often do better (see Chapter 4 for details). Some rates are much higher than others because they include meals, such as breakfast, both breakfast and dinner, or even three meals a day. Such room rates at all-inclusive resorts cover not only all meals and beverages, but also tips, taxes, transportation to and from the airport, and most activities and entertainment.

Castaways Resort & Suites

$$ Freeport

The 130-room Castaways is a modest and unassuming hotel despite its platinum position adjacent to the International Bazaar and the casino. You stay here because of its location and the low price. It's not on the beach, but a free shuttle can take you to nearby Williams Town Beach or Xanadu Beach. Surrounded by gardens, the four-story hotel has a pagoda roof and an indoor/outdoor garden lobby with a gift shop, a clothing shop, a game room, and tour desks. Rooms are your basic motel style, and the best units are on the ground. Each accommodation comes with a small private bathroom with shower. The Flamingo Restaurant features unremarkable Bahamian and American dishes. There is a large, unheated, freshwater pool area with a wide terrace and a pool bar that offers sandwiches and cool drinks. The Yellow Bird Show Club stays open until 3 a.m. and features limbo dancers and fire-eaters Monday through Saturday.

International Bazaar, Freeport. ☎ *242-352-6682. Fax 242-352-5087. Internet:* www.grand-bahama.com/castaways. *Rack rates: $130–$140 double, $154–$164 suite. Children under 12 stay free in parents' room. AE, MC, V.*

Club Viva Fortuna

$$$$ Fortune Beach, southeast coast

Although families are welcome and the 276-unit Club Viva Fortuna hosts a children's program, most vacationers here are young couples. This European-owned resort has a definite Italian accent. You hear more *ciaos* than hellos. Guests play bocce ball on the beach and dine on Italian and some Bahamian cuisine. Because of its strong continental overlay, the cuisine is better here than at the typical Grand Bahama hotel. Not far from the **Bahamas National Trust Rand Memorial Nature Centre** and **Lucayan National Park,** this beach resort has a one-size-fits-all price tag. You don't need to dig into your pocket for food, drinks, nightly entertainment, or most activities. You have to pay extra for scuba diving, fishing, waterskiing, and horseback riding, but tennis, windsurfing, kayaking, snorkeling, and sailing are among the diversions that come with your room. The gym and sauna are also free to guests who can swim in a large, unheated freshwater pool. Four miles from Lucaya (where the Port Lucaya Marketplace is located) and 6 miles from Freeport (where you can find the Casino at Bahamia and the International Bazaar shopping complex), this 26-acre resort is an attractive getaway. Marble and vaulted wooden ceilings highlight the lobby. Flowers line walkways that wind through the property, which hugs a broad sandy beach. More than half the comfortable rooms have views of the water while the others overlook the gardens. If you want an accommodation in an isolated setting, you won't mind staying here and having to rent a car to explore the rest of the island. Each of the units comes with a small, tiled, and neatly maintained private bathroom with shower.

Doubloon Rd. and Churchill Dr., 4 miles east of Lucaya. ☎ *800-898-9968 or 242-373-4000. Fax: 242-373-5555. Internet:* www.vivaresorts.com. *Rack rates: $178–$324 for a double room, including all meals and most activities. AE, MC, V.*

Our Lucaya

$$$–$$$$ Lucaya

This massive resort is one of the largest in the country and centered between two of the best white sandy beaches in The Bahamas. Our Lucaya is an excellent choice if you're in the market for an expansive beachfront resort with plenty of action — wet and dry, by day and by night. Our Lucaya boasts 1,271 rooms when it's at full capacity. Debuting in April 1999, **Reef Village,** the first of three towers, houses spacious rooms, with and without balconies and ocean views. All are brightly decorated in the bold colors of Junkanoo (the Bahamian festival featuring wild music and dance and even wilder costumes). In 2000, two newer subdivisions of Our Lucaya opened. The smaller and somewhat more private of the two is **Lighthouse Pointe,** a 221-unit, low-rise complex that focuses specifically on adult clientele. It's larger counterpart is the 500-unit **Breakers Cay,** a g rand, ten-story, white-sided tower. Each room comes with a medium-sized private bathroom with tub and shower combination.

Grand Bahama Accommodations

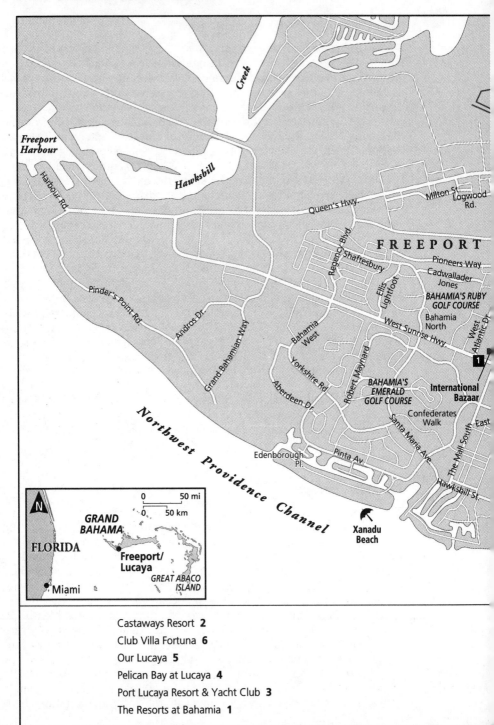

Castaways Resort **2**

Club Villa Fortuna **6**

Our Lucaya **5**

Pelican Bay at Lucaya **4**

Port Lucaya Resort & Yacht Club **3**

The Resorts at Bahamia **1**

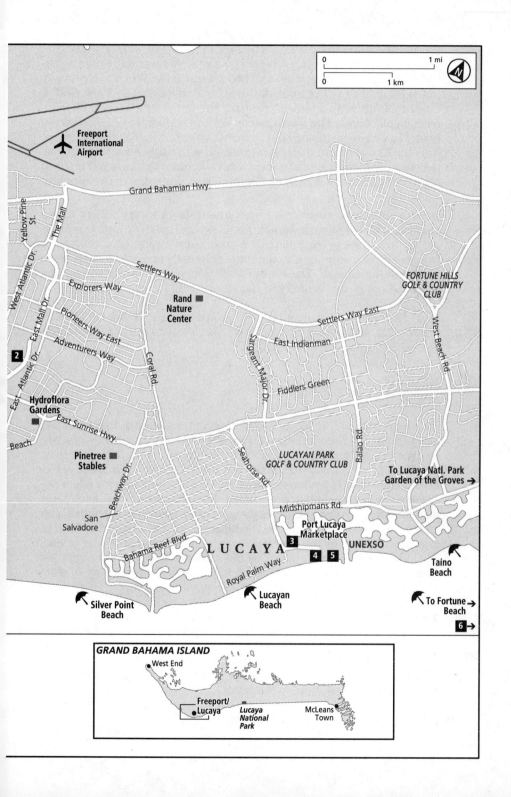

Freeport International Airport

Grand Bahamian Hwy.

Yellow Pine St.

The Mall

West Atlantic Dr.

East Mall Dr.

East Atlantic Dr.

Settlers Way

Explorers Way

Pioneers Way East

Adventurers Way

2

Rand Nature Center

Coral Rd.

Settlers Way East

East Indianman

Sargeant Major Dr.

Fiddlers Green

FORTUNE HILLS GOLF & COUNTRY CLUB

West Beach Rd.

Hydroflora Gardens

East Sunrise Hwy.

Beach

Pinetree Stables

Beachway Dr.

Seahorse Rd.

LUCAYAN PARK GOLF & COUNTRY CLUB

Balao Rd.

To Lucaya Natl. Park Garden of the Groves →

Midshipmans Rd.

San Salvadore

Bahama Reef Blvd.

L U C A Y A

Port Lucaya Marketplace

3

4 **5**

UNEXSO

Royal Palm Way

Lucayan Beach

Taíno Beach

Silver Point Beach

To Fortune → Beach

6 →

0 ___ 1 mi
0 ___ 1 km

GRAND BAHAMA ISLAND

West End

Freeport/ Lucaya

Lucaya National Park

McLeans Town

Head outdoors, and you find a golden sand 7½-acre beach, complete with paraphernalia for scuba diving, snorkeling, jet skiing, banana boat rides, and parasailing, among other activities. In the midst of this oceanfront action is a large free-form swimming pool with its sugar mill tower waterslide, plus another large pool and two smaller ones. When you're ready to tee off, you can check out the 18-holer at the **Lucayan Park Golf & Country Club,** a 45-minute drive from the hotel, or a second championship golf course, **The Reef Course.** With 14 restaurant choices, you're bound to find some dining spot to satisfy your palate. The recipes range from the Caribbean to the Mediterranean, with many American specialties. In a nutshell, the cuisine is viable from place to place and night to night, but overall it's good, standardized fare, not rising to the sublime.

When you need a break, send the kids (infants to age 12) to **Camp Lucaya,** with its own swimming pool, swings, sandpit, and computer games. Activities — from Junkanoo mask painting and beach olympics to kayaking and dolphin encounters — vary daily and are all supervised by a well-trained staff. The after-school program for Bahamian children gives visitors an opportunity to rub elbows with locals.

Royal Palm Way, across from Port Lucaya Marketplace. ☎ *800-LUCAYAN or 242-373-1333. Fax: 242-373-8804. Internet:* www.ourlucaya.com. *Rack rates: $165–$370 for a double room. AE, DC, DISC, MC, V.*

Pelican Bay at Lucaya
$$–$$$ Lucaya

On a peninsula jutting into a series of inland waterways, this hotel has more architectural charm than any other on the island, evoking a Danish seaside village. Next door to UNEXSO, the Underwater Explorers Society, the 69-unit Pelican Bay attracts scuba divers. Lucaya's finest beach is across the road. Townhouse-styled buildings, trimmed with white latticework and gingerbread, are painted different earth tones. Each large unit has a wet bar and bathrobes for use during your stay. Balconies offer vistas of the marina, waterway, whirlpool, or two large, freshwater, unheated pools. For the breeziest stay, request one of the end rooms, which offer cross-ventilation. The older rooms look out on the marina while the newer deluxe units overlook the bay. Bathrooms are of standard size, each with a tiled tub and shower combination.

If you dine at the **Ferry House Restaurant,** which is just a brief stroll away, you can charge the excellent meals to your room. Along the marina, a passageway leads directly to Port Lucaya Marketplace and the water sports vendors. This route isn't the one to take if you've had a few Goombay Smashes or Bahama Mamas. The walkway has no outer wall or rail, so you could fall right in the water.

Royal Palm Way, by Port Lucaya Marketplace and UNEXSO (Underwater Explorers Society), the dive operator. ☎ *800-600-9192 or 242-373-9550. Fax: 242-373-9551. Internet:* www.pelicanbayhotel.com. *Rack rates: $150–$195 for a double room. AE, MC, V.*

Port Lucaya Resort and Yacht Club

$$ Lucaya

With its own 50-slip marina, this 163-room hotel and yacht club attracts boaters and shoppers. Despite being adjacent to Port Lucaya Marketplace, Lucaya's open-air shopping Mecca, the resort is surprisingly tranquil, with a secluded feel. Buildings 1 through 6 are the quietest because they're removed from the music and bustle of the marketplace. Deluxe rooms overlook the marina, and bathrooms with new showers are tidy and well maintained, with adequate shelf space. An Olympic-size unheated, freshwater pool is set off with a whirlpool, and you can sip a drink from the poolside Tiki Bar. Action is easy to come by, as plenty of water sports are at or right near the hotel, and you can reach the beach by walking across the road and through the huge Lucayan resort. If you're traveling with children, consider dropping them off at Our Lucaya's Camp Lucaya. (See the "Our Lucaya" listing, earlier in this chapter, for details.) The **Trade Winds Café,** Port Lucaya Resort's main restaurant, serves standard fare at breakfast and dinner, but far better and more varied dining options are at the nearby marketplace.

Next to Port Lucaya Marketplace. ☎ *800-582-2921 or 242-373-6618. Fax: 242-373-6652. Email: vacation@batelnet.bs. Internet:* www.bahamasnet.com/port/lucayaresort. *Rack rates: $100–$145 for a double room. AE, MC, V.*

The Resorts at Bahamia

$$–$$$ Freeport

Reinventing itself to stay competitive, this mammoth 965-room resort is spending some $42 million on these once-tired 1960s properties, hoping to revive some of their old glitz and glamour. The Resorts at Bahamia are actually two resorts in one: The ten-story Crowne Plaza at Bahamia and the less glamorous three-story Holiday Inn Sunspree at Bahamia. Inland from the sea, the resort doesn't have a natural beach. However, by the time of your arrival, a marine park and a manmade, landlocked beach should be operating. Otherwise, you can take frequent shuttle buses to natural beaches. Flanked by a pair of fine golf courses and catering to the convention crowd, the resort is set on 2,500 acres of tropical grounds. The two "Bahamias" jointly share one of the largest casinos in the country, a serviceable site that's functional but nowhere near as cutting edge as the Atlantis Casino on Paradise Island.

The Holiday Inn at Bahamia attracts families, honeymooners, frugal couples, golfers, and others. The hotel's design is rather like an enormous low-rise wagon wheel, with a Disney-inspired mini-mountain at its core, surrounded by a large, unheated, freshwater pool. The hotel is so spread out that guests often complain that they need ground transport to reach their bedrooms. Nine wings radiate from the pool. Some of the rooms have kitchenettes and are sold as time-share units. Rooms in the 900 wing are the largest and best furnished and are usually the ones that sell first. Accommodations come in several classifications; however, even the standard rooms are well equipped, with dressing areas and full-size bathrooms. Both the resorts also rent a number of suites that are furnished in summery fabrics and beachy but durable furniture.

Crowne Plaza, lying across the Mall from its larger sibling, is smaller, more tranquil, and a bit more posh, containing 22 suites and 352 luxuriously furnished large units. The tower structure adjoins the Casino and the International Bazaar. The somewhat passé and even vaguely campy Arabic motif, the crowning glory of which is the Moorish-style tower (with turrets, arches, and a white dome), continues through the octagon-shaped lobby. Lots of conventioneers and folks on quick getaways from Florida tend to stay here, as do High-Rollers.

With six restaurants and six bars, most palates are catered to with the first-rate (but not great) resort cuisine. The best restaurants are the Crown Room, serving a better-than-usual continental fare at the casino, and the Rib Room for the island's best steaks. The latter evokes the atmosphere of a British hunting lodge.

Neighboring the International Bazaar, the Mall at W. Sunrise Hwy. ☎ 800-545-1300 or 242-350-7000. Fax: 242-350-7002. Internet: www.sunfinder.com. Ask about the resort's daily charter flights from Fort Lauderdale. Rack rates: $149–$189 for a double room. AE, MC,

Chapter 14

Settling into Grand Bahama

● ●

In This Chapter

▶ Knowing what to expect when you get there

▶ Getting around Grand Bahama

▶ Discovering Grand Bahama from A to Z

● ●

*F*or a seamless transition from your world to Grand Bahama's easy-going vibe, this chapter guides you through passport control, baggage claim, and customs. Turn here to find out how much money — and time — you should expect to spend for the taxi ride to your hotel. For your "wheels of choice," we list information on everything from scooters to buses. We also include a rundown on money matters, emergencies, babysitters, and other "fast facts" data.

Arriving in Grand Bahama by Air

Although some people arrive in cruise ships, most visitors swoop down on Grand Bahama in planes. Getting through the airport is generally quite easy.

Navigating passport control and customs

Even at the airport, you're launched into your vacation to the sound of live calypso or reggae music as you enter **Freeport International Airport** (☎ 242-352-6062). With your passport, or birth certificate and photo ID, return airline ticket, and a completed Immigration Arrival/Departure Card, get in the shortest visitors line. Hold on to your copy of the immigration card, because you need to present it before leaving The Bahamas.

The well-marked airport is easy to navigate. You collect your baggage and declare that you haven't brought in any contraband. Customs officials may or may not open your luggage to confirm your claim. You can then pick up maps and helpful brochures at the tourist information desk, get some extra cash in U.S. dollars from an ATM, and head for the exit.

Getting from the airport to your hotel

Downtown **Freeport** is only a five-minute ride from the airport; **Lucaya,** the beach resort area, is a ten-minute drive. Metered taxis greet each flight, ready to whisk vacationers off to hotels. (The cab driver lobby is powerful enough to ban buses at the airport, so you'll have to rely on a taxi.) The cost is about $10 to Freeport and $15 to Lucaya., plus a 15 percent tip. If your vacation package includes transfers, present your voucher to the driver of a clearly marked van. If you want to explore Grand Bahama at your own pace, you can pick up a rental car at the airport. See "Getting around Grand Bahama," later in this chapter.

Arriving in Grand Bahama by Sea

Freeport is a popular port of call for major cruise ships. If you opt for one of these floating resorts, expect limited time ashore. Packed with swimming pools, live bands, stage shows, dance clubs, restaurants, exercise rooms, health spas, culinary demonstrations, and other diversions, these ships are destinations in themselves.

Getting around Grand Bahama

For the most flexibility, you can rent a car, although you don't need one to get around. Whether you board a bus, catch a taxi, rent a car, mount a motor scooter, pedal a bike, or walk, getting to the most interesting parts of this island is relatively easy. Here is a run-down of your choices:

 ✔ **Going by bus.** Grand Bahama's public bus service, run by privately licensed minivans, makes getting around Freeport and Lucaya almost hassle-free. You generally wait five to seven minutes at any given stop. Sometimes vans sit longer because drivers often don't leave until they have a minimum number of passengers. The fare is 75 cents, and exact change is requested, in U.S. or Bahamian coins. If you want to pay with a dollar bill, feel free, but you won't receive any change. When you board, tell the driver your destination.

 ✔ **Taking a taxi.** The majority of taxis are limousines. The government sets fares and requires cabs to have working meters, but many drivers don't turn them on for routine trips, instead quoting you a flat fare. If you're not sure what the approximate cost of a taxi ride should be, ask someone at your hotel desk before leaving. One or two passengers pay $2 for the first quarter mile and 30 cents for each additional quarter mile. For each additional passenger over age 3, you pay a $2 charge, and for each piece of luggage beyond two, the driver collects 50 cents. Taxis wait outside hotels, restaurants, and attractions and cruise the streets where you can flag them down. Two reliable companies to call are Freeport Taxi (☎ 242-352-6666) and G.B. Taxi Union (☎ 242-352-7101).

✔ **Driving around by car.** Unlike Nassau, driving on Grand Bahama, with its long, broad roads, is easy. A car comes in handy if you'd rather not rely on taxis and minivans. Much of the island is undeveloped, so heavy traffic isn't a problem, and you can easily find places to park. Like the British, islanders drive on the left.

Car-rental companies are clustered at Freeport International Airport. Cars begin at $50 a day, jeeps at $70, and vans at $120. Availability varies, so, if you haven't made rental arrangements before you arrive, you may have to call around until you find the size or type of car you want. Here are the best companies:

- Avis ☎ 242-352-7666
- Dollar ☎ 242-352-9325
- Hertz ☎ 242-359-9277

✔ **Zipping around on a motor scooter.** Also known as mopeds or minibikes, these motorized two-wheelers may seem like an ideal way to zip around. But if you're used to driving on the right side of the road back home, a miscalculation while riding a moped on the left here can end up being painful. A wrong turn or a bump in the road may send you flying. If you're willing to risk it, plan on spending about $15 for the first hour, plus $5 for each additional hour or $40 to $55 a day to rent a scooter. You need to have a valid driver's license and leave a credit card or $100 cash as a deposit. Wearing helmets, provided with each rental, is mandatory. You can make arrangements to rent through your hotel or at one of the scooter rental shops you see near gas stations and other spots along the road. If you arrive on Grand Bahama by cruise ship, you can rent motor scooters at Freeport Harbour.

✔ **Pedaling bicycles.** Pancake-flat Grand Bahama, cut with long, wide, straight roads, seems designed for bicycling. As you're whizzing by, driving on the left, the breeze can mask the sun's power, so be sure to slather on plenty of sunblock. Wearing a brimmed hat is also a good idea. Some hotels offer complimentary bikes, while other accommodations, along with roadside bike-rental outfits, let you have one for $15 to $20 a day. See Chapter 16 for more on biking and other activities in Grand Bahama.

✔ **Walking around.** Nearly devoid of hills, Grand Bahama Island is good for long strolls because, outside Freeport and Lucaya, it's largely undeveloped. Flourishing botanical gardens and nature reserves, such as **Lucayan National Park** and **Bahamas National Trust Rand Nature Centre,** are prime locales for hoofing it. For guided nature hikes, contact **Kayak Nature Tours (☎ 242-373-2485).** If human-made wonders are more to your liking, the **International Bazaar** and its surroundings in Freeport and **Port Lucaya Marketplace** and its Lucaya seaside neighborhood are best for a shopper's stroll.

Fast Facts: Grand Bahama

American Express

The **Scotiabank** ATM accepts American Express cards. If you have a problem with your American Express traveler's checks, call ☎ 800-221-7282.

Babysitting

Most hotels can arrange for a babysitter who often is not employed by the hotels. Make arrangements for a sitter as far in advance as possible.

Banks and ATMs

Freeport's banks are open from 9:30 a.m. to 3 p.m. Monday through Thursday and until 5 p.m. on Friday. The international ATMs at Bank of Nova Scotia branches dispense both Bahamian and U.S. currency. This bank also operates two ATMs, which dispense only U.S. dollars, at Crowne Plaza Resort & Casino in Freeport. For 24-hour access to your funds, head to the ATMs at the Royal Bank of Canada, at East Mall and Explorers Way or Boulevard Service Station on Sunrise Highway; these machines offer only Bahamian currency. Bank of Nova Scotia and Royal Bank of Canada ATMs accept MasterCard, Visa, and any credit or bank card linked to the Plus or Cirrus network. The Scotiabank ATM also accepts cards on the Novus network, along with American Express. The island's other major banks are Bank of the Bahamas and Barclays.

Credit Cards

If you have a problem with your credit cards, contact American Express (☎ 800-327-1267), Citibank Visa/MasterCard (☎ 888-950-5114), or Visa (☎ 800-847-2911).

Currency Exchange

U.S. dollars are accepted throughout The Bahamas, so you don't need to bother exchanging your American bills. Whenever you purchase anything, you're likely to receive change in a combination of American and Bahamian currency, which is $1 to $1. It's best to ask for all your change in U.S. dollars before you head home. Otherwise, when you exchange your Bahamian currency at Grand Bahama's airport, you'll lose money on service charges.

Directory Assistance

Call ☎ 916.

Emergencies

Ambulance: ☎ 242-352-2689.

Bahamas Air Sea Rescue Association (BASRA): ☎ 242-352-9246.

Fire Brigade: ☎ 242-352-8888.

National Park Service: ☎ 242-352-5438.

Police: ☎ 919.

Information

Contact the Grand Bahama Island Tourism Board (☎ 242-352-8044 or 242-352-6909). Tourist information desks are found at the airport, the International Bazaar, Port Lucaya Marketplace, and the larger hotels.

Internet Access

Visit the CyberCafe (International Bazaar, downtown Freeport, ☎ 242-351-7283). Open Monday through Saturday 10 a.m. to 6 p.m.

Maps

Maps are easy to come by at the airport, shopping areas, and hotel tourist information desks. You can find good local maps in free visitor booklets, such as *What-to-Do: Freeport/Lucaya, Grand Bahama Island*.

Medical Assistance

Government-run Rand Memorial Hospital (☎ 242-352-6735) is on East Atlantic Drive.

For information about a clinic close to your hotel, call the hospital or ask at your accommodation. Before you leave home, check your health insurance to see whether you're covered while traveling abroad.

Newspapers/Magazines

To keep abreast of island happenings, including fund-raising beach cookouts, plays, and other events, check out *Freeport News,* the local daily. The *Tribune* and the *Guardian,* both published in Nassau, are also widely available here. *What-to-Do* and *Island Scene* are free magazines that are geared to vacationers; they're full of dining and shopping tips, as well as information about Grand Bahama attractions. You can find them at hotels, shops, and tourist offices.

People to People

To participate in this program that enables you to spend some time hanging with a Bahamian family or individuals, call the Grand Bahama Island Tourism Board at ☎ 242-352-8044 or 242-352-8045.

Pharmacies

Try the Sunrise Medical Center (☎ 242-373-3333) on Sunrise Highway in Freeport; or Lucayan Medical East (☎ 242-373-7400) on East Sunrise Highway in Lucaya.

Police

In an emergency, call ☎ 919.

Post Office

For the location closest to you, call ☎ 242-352-9371.

Safety

Freeport and Lucaya are usually safe, as long as you follow the same precautions you would anywhere else in the world: Don't venture into deserted areas alone, especially at night, and be discreet with your money, jewelry, and other valuables. Traveling by the island's privately run minivans is safe.

Shops

Most of Grand Bahama's stores are open Monday through Saturday from 9 or 10 a.m. to 5 or 6 p.m. (or later at Port Lucaya Marketplace). Some pharmacies and shops at Port Lucaya Marketplace, and some stores at the International Bazaar are also open on Sunday, with limited hours. If supermarkets are open on Sunday, they close by 10 a.m.

Taxis

Although all taxis have meters, many drivers don't use them. Rates for two passengers are $2 for the first quarter mile, plus 30 cents for each additional quarter mile; additional passengers over age 3 pay $2. Taxis are easy to come by, but if you'd like to call one, try Freeport Taxi (☎ 242-352-6666) or G.B. Taxi Union (☎ 242-352-7101).

Time

Call ☎ 917.

Weather

For the latest forecast, call ☎ 915.

Chapter 15

Dining in Grand Bahama

● ●

In This Chapter

▶ Finding the best food beyond your hotel dining room

▶ Discovering how to save money on meals

▶ Locating restaurants with island spice

● ●

*M*ost restaurants in Freeport and Lucaya won't give your wallet as much of a workout as those in more expensive Nassau and Paradise Island. You don't have as many dining options either, but from fast food to fine food, the choices of locales and cuisine are plentiful enough. Menus spotlight locally caught seafood and typically Bahamian dishes, but you'll find the usual array of international fare. Nearly all food stuff, especially meats, fruits, and vegetables, are imported.

Have a casual lunch at a waterside café followed by an elegant candlelit dinner at a hotel. Or try an unassuming, family-run spot specializing in Bahamian favorites. Islanders head to the rustic restaurants and bars in the **West End** for the freshest — and cheapest — snapper, jack fish, grouper, conch, and other local seafood. Sunday night is party night in the West End. The trip is a 25-mile drive from Freeport by taxi or rental car. (For details about Bahamian specialties, turn to Chapter 2.)

Grand Bahama chefs aim for international appeal, turning out the usual array of food to please everybody — pasta, barbecued ribs, and burgers, even quesadillas, souvlaki, or Wiener schnitzels. In recent years, sushi appears on more and more menus. Early bird specials and festive happy hours with discounted drinks lure patrons to various spots. Some Freeport and Lucaya restaurants are open for dinner only. Some close between meals, so even when reservations aren't necessary, you may want to call before going out of your way.

See the Introduction at the beginning of the book for an explanation of the price categories used in this chapter. Check the map in this chapter for the locations of dining options.

Grand Bahama's Best Restaurants

Arawak Restaurant
$$ Lucaya FRENCH/BAHAMIAN

A 5-minute drive from Port Lucaya, this clubhouse restaurant offers diners expansive golf course views through walls of windows. After dark, an illuminated waterfall comes to life outside. Everyone is in a festive mood during the 5 to 7 p.m. Friday happy hour. Make a dinner reservation for a Friday or Saturday night, and you're treated to the live music of a pianist or local band. The lobster tails are very good here, and you may find yourself reminiscing about the broiled grouper with basil-roasted potato purée, the pan-seared red snapper with Dijon mustard sauce, and the tender and well-flavored chateaubriand. The steak and lobster and the rack of lamb, even though imported, are full of flavor and well prepared. This is a good place to sample a Bahama Mama.

At Our Lucaya Lucayan Golf Course, Bishop Lane. ☎ *242-373-1066. Reservations recommended. Jackets requested for men. Main courses: $17–$31. AE, DISC, MC, V. Open: Daily for lunch and dinner, Sun brunch 11:30 a.m.–3 p.m.*

Barracuda's
$$ Lucaya INTERNATIONAL

With high ceilings and big windows, this space is the size of an airplane hanger, and it's done up with playful art and a whimsical, hip decor that would be at home in Miami's South Beach. The kitchen turns out light international dishes that are loaded with flavor. Examples include grilled grouper tuna and white-bean salad; stone crab claws; leek tart with mozzarella and apples; chicken breast with fresh ginger; and all manner of steaks, seafood, and pastas. If you want to drink your dessert, consider a China Beach, a chocolate-laced affair that's made with crème de cacao, Kahlúa, and Carolans Irish cream.

In the Reef Village Hotel at the Lucayan Beach & Golf Resort, Royal Palm Way, Lucaya. ☎ *242-373-1333. Main courses: $9.50–$22. AE, DC, MC, V. Open: Daily for breakfast from 7 a.m.–10:30 a.m. and for dinner from 5:30–9:30 p.m.*

Becky's Restaurant & Lounge
$–$$ Freeport BAHAMIAN

Becky's culinary creations make you think you've stumbled into a Bahamian home. No matter what time of day you get to this friendly dining spot, you can order fluffy pancakes, scrambled eggs, or breakfast favorites, such as stewed fish or *boil fish* (fish cooked with salt pork, onions, and green peppers) with grits. For lunch or dinner, the steamed snapper, pan-fried grouper, or cracked conch are island favorites prepared with zest. The lobster, shrimp, steak, ribs, and chicken are more standard fare. We prefer the local specialties instead of the regular

American style food. The bartender makes a Becky's Special, a lips-to-hips concoction of coconut rum and vanilla ice cream with a splash of brandy. During happy hour, complimentary conch fritters come with the two-for-one mixed drinks. About a 5-minute drive from the International Bazaar, Becky's is just across from Hydroflora Garden.

E. Sunrise Hwy. at E. Beach Dr. ☎ *242-352-5247. Main courses: $7.95–$23.95. AE, MC, V. Open: Daily 7 a.m.–11 p.m.*

Captain's Charthouse
$$ Lucaya   INTERNATIONAL

Come here for the type of food your parents enjoyed when they were dating. Seafood, especially lobster, is the star of this restaurant that serves dinner only. However, the chef also does a good job with prime rib, pork chops, chicken, and other comfort food that seems plucked from the 1950s. It's easy to fill up on the delicious freshly baked bread or the salad bar before your main course arrives.

Captain's Charthouse is located away from the tourist fray, but you can arrange complimentary transportation to and from your hotel.

E. Sunrise Hwy. and Beach Dr. ☎ *242-373-3900. Reservations recommended. Main courses: $16.95–$31. AE, DISC, MC, V. Open: 5 p.m.–9:30 p.m. (last seating).*

China Temple
$ International Bazaar   CHINESE

This is a Chinese joint — not a lot more — that also does takeout. Over the years, it's proved to be the dining bargain of the bazaar. The menu is familiar and standard: chop suey, chow mein, and sweet-and-sour. It's certainly not gourmet Asian fare, but it's cheap, and it might hit the spot when you're craving something different.

International Bazaar. ☎ *242-352-5610. Main courses: Dinner $6.50–$17.25; lunch $6.50–$8.25. AE, DISC, MC, V. Open: Mon–Sat from 11 a.m.–10 p.m.*

Club Caribe
$ Just east of Taino Beach   AMERICAN/BAHAMIAN

This casual, laid-back eatery lies 7 miles east of the International Bazaar beside a beach swept by the trade winds. A funky, offbeat charmer, it's a good place to escape from the tourist hordes, especially on cruise-ship arrival days. You can spend the day on the beach here, with its offshore reef. Just bring some snorkel gear to get up close and personal with all the rainbow-hued fish swarming the offshore reef. In between dips, sample the cracked conch or the savory blackened mahi-mahi, served inside or on the deck. Sandwiches, barbecued ribs, and salads are on the lunch menu. Rent a lounge chair, lie back, and sip a tall rum cocktail, such as a raspberry-coconut Ocean Breeze or a Mango Mama. The Friday night fish fry from 6 to 9 p.m. is big fun.

Near Taino Beach, Club Caribe is off the beaten path, but you don't need to bother with a rental car or taxi. Make your reservation in the morning — or better yet, the day before — and you can arrange complimentary round-trip transportation from your hotel. The ride is about 15 minutes from the International Bazaar area and about 7 minutes from accommodations near Port Lucaya Marketplace.

Churchill Beach, Mather Town, just east of Taino Beach. ☎ *242-373-6866. Reservations required. Main courses: $4.50–$12.95. AE, DISC, MC, V. Open: Tues–Sun 11 a.m.–6 p.m.*

The Crown Room

$$$ Freeport   CONTINENTAL

You're never far from the blackjack table if you dine at this formal restaurant with its marble, polished brass, glistening mirrors, and crystal chandeliers. Light jazz music is played in the background as you peruse the menu, which offerings evoke an elegant country club in the States. The Crown Room tries to be regal, and the high prices are somewhat justified because of all the expensive imported ingredients. The hot and cold appetizers are the best items on the menu, ranging from pâté to smoked salmon to snow crab claws. Watch your waiter toss in all the fresh ingredients for a Caesar salad at your table or carve your herb-infused rack of lamb for two. The scallop, shrimp, lobster, and fish dishes are satisfying, craftily executed, but never memorable.

The Casino, the Resorts at Bahamia, the Mall at W. Sunrise Hwy. ☎ *242-352-7811. Reservations required. Jackets requested for men. Main courses: $21.95–$42.95. AE, MC, V. Open: Wed–Sat for dinner only.*

Cyber Café

$ Lucaya and Freeport   AMERICAN

This café is light on food, but heavy on Internet access for those who can't do without a cyber-fix, even when on vacation. You pay $4 to sit down at a computer, plus 40 cents per minute of usage. Services include scanning, copying, printing, and faxing. Coffee, soft drinks, beer, and mixed drinks are on the menu, along with a variety of snacks.

International Bazaar, downtown Freeport, ☎ *242-351-7283. Another branch is in Port Lucaya Marketplace (*☎ *242-374-3839). Open: Daily 9 a.m.–10 p.m.*

Fatman's Nephew

$–$$ Lucaya   BAHAMIAN

The next generation carries on the culinary tradition of the late Fatman, a chef whose Grand Bahama restaurant once had countless loyalists. At this newer location overlooking Port Lucaya Marketplace Marina, the focus is on seafood. You can sample various grilled or spicy Cajun-style fish or try local favorites, such as cracked conch, which is breaded like a veal cutlet. On most days, you encounter at least eight kinds of game fish, including both wahoo and kingfish. Other island dishes are featured, too, including curried chicken along with daily specials as well as burgers and steaks. Sometimes a real authentic dish appears on the menu, such as Bahamian-style shark soup made from the flesh of hammerheads. Not every dish wins an award, but the place is an enduring favorite. The casual atmosphere is idyllic for having drinks and appetizers on the breezy terrace above the water.

Port Lucaya Marketplace. ☎ *242-373-8520. Main courses: $11–$32. MC, V. Open: Daily for lunch and dinner, except Tues when only dinner is served.*

Ferry House Restaurant
$–$$ Lucaya   INTERNATIONAL

A short stroll from Port Lucaya Marketplace, the Ferry House sits in a tranquil spot away from the crush of shops and hotels. The huge windows of this dockside restaurant are always flung open, offering views of pleasure boats and ferries. At night, the lights of the marina sparkle in the water. The menu changes frequently, depending on what fresh fish and other ingredients are available. The bread is baked on the premises. For breakfast, the Danish pastries are a treat. Lunch could be an open-faced Danish sandwich, piled with smoked salmon, herring, or roast beef. You may also find filling salads and vegetable, beef, or chicken quesadillas. Icelandic lamb may be served at dinnertime, along with duck à l'orange, butterflied or coconut- or orange-flavored shrimp. In addition to local fish (snapper, grouper, and dolphin), the chef may prepare imported trout or tuna, even sushi.

Bell Channel, near the Pelican Bay hotel and Port Lucaya Marketplace. ☎ *242-373-1595. Reservations recommended. Main courses: $19–$29. AE, MC, V. Open: Daily 7 a.m.–11:30 p.m. (closed Mon for dinner).*

Geneva's Place
$ Freeport   BAHAMIAN

Ask a native Bahamian where to go for the best local food, and chances are you end up at this unassuming dining spot in downtown Freeport. Run by an amiable family, Geneva's serves up hefty portions of the kind of home cooking you'd get from your own mother — if she were Bahamian. Tender conch comes cracked, stewed, or in a savory chowder. Order your grouper steamed, broiled, or pan-fried and your thick pork chops steamed or fried. Peas and rice is the best side dish.

Kipling Lane, the Mall at W. Sunrise Hwy. ☎ *242-352-5085. Main courses: $9–$25.90. No credit cards. Open: Daily 7 a.m.–11 p.m.*

Grand Bahama Restaurants

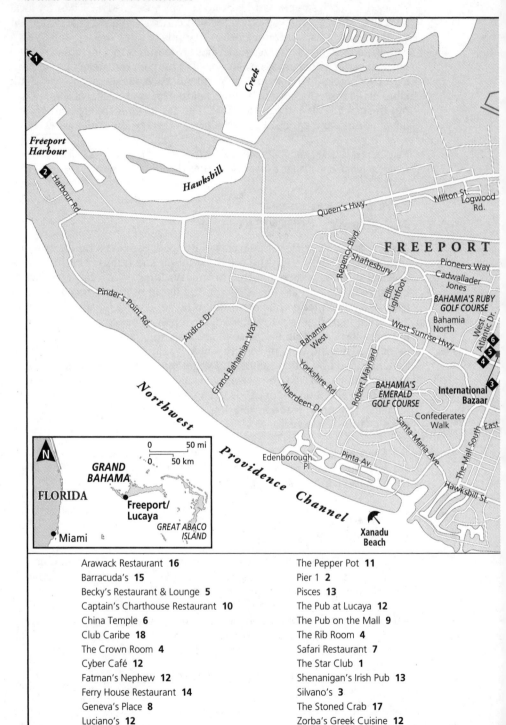

Arawack Restaurant 16	The Pepper Pot 11
Barracuda's 15	Pier 1 2
Becky's Restaurant & Lounge 5	Pisces 13
Captain's Charthouse Restaurant 10	The Pub at Lucaya 12
China Temple 6	The Pub on the Mall 9
Club Caribe 18	The Rib Room 4
The Crown Room 4	Safari Restaurant 7
Cyber Café 12	The Star Club 1
Fatman's Nephew 12	Shenanigan's Irish Pub 13
Ferry House Restaurant 14	Silvano's 3
Geneva's Place 8	The Stoned Crab 17
Luciano's 12	Zorba's Greek Cuisine 12

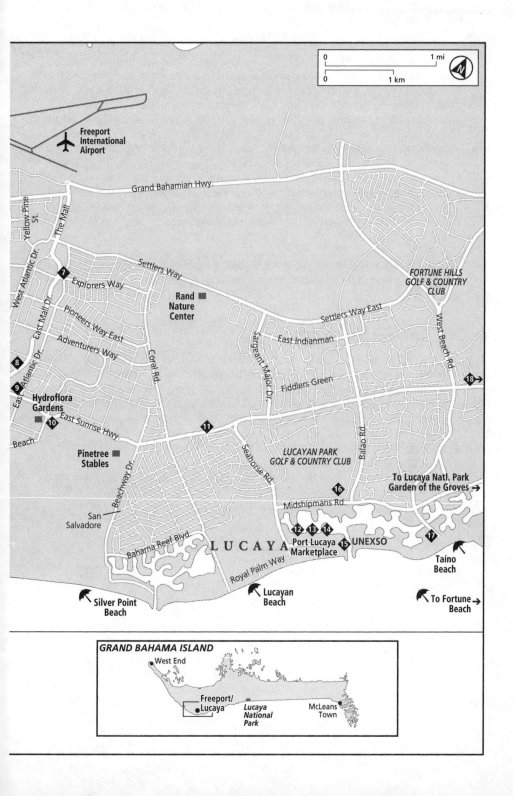

0   1 mi
0   1 km

Freeport
International
Airport

Grand Bahamian Hwy.

Yellow Pine St.

The Mall

West Atlantic Dr.

East Mall Dr.

East Atlantic Dr.

Settlers Way

7 Explorers Way

Pioneers Way East

Adventurers Way

8

9

Hydroflora
Gardens

10 East Sunrise Hwy.

Beach

Coral Rd.

Rand
Nature
Center

Sargeant Major Dr.

Settlers Way East

East Indianman

Fiddlers Green

FORTUNE HILLS
GOLF & COUNTRY
CLUB

West Beach Rd.

18

Pinetree
Stables

11

Seahorse Rd.

LUCAYAN PARK
GOLF & COUNTRY CLUB

Balao Rd.

To Lucaya Natl. Park
Garden of the Groves

Beachway Dr.

San
Salvadore

Bahama Reef Blvd.

16

Midshipmans Rd.

L U C A Y A

Bahama Reef Blvd.

12 **13** **14**
Port Lucaya **15** UNEXSO
Marketplace

17

Taíno
Beach

Royal Palm Way

Silver Point
Beach

Lucayan
Beach

To Fortune
Beach

GRAND BAHAMA ISLAND

West End

Freeport/
Lucaya

Lucaya
National
Park

McLeans
Town

Luciano's

$$$–$$$$ Lucaya   CONTINENTAL

The setting of this elegant restaurant, overlooking the Port Lucaya marina, has a certain continental charm. Whet your appetite with a seafood crêpe, garlic-infused escargot, or chilled melon with port. Both the house salad — with avocados, hearts of palm, baby shrimp, corn, and tomatoes — and the Caesar salad are freshly prepared. Inspired by classical European recipes with some local flair thrown in, the seafood and meat courses are uniformly excellent. You can try the Bahamian grouper filet with toasted almonds and lemon butter. Flambéed with cognac, the scampi is another palate pleaser. The duckling breast comes in a green peppercorn sauce, and the rack of lamb (served for two) is carved tableside. Dessert brings a velvet-smooth crème brûlée, pears over vanilla ice cream topped with raspberry sauce, and more crêpes, among other treats.

Port Lucaya Marketplace. ☎ *242-373-9100. Reservations recommended. Main courses: $16.95–$31.95. AE, DISC, MC, V. Open: Daily for dinner only.*

The Pepper Pot

$ Freeport   BAHAMIAN

This restaurant may be the only place on Grand Bahama that specializes in Bahamian take-out food. You'll find it after about a 5-minute drive east of the International Bazaar, in a tiny shopping mall. You can order take-out portions of the best guava duff on the island, as well as a savory conch chowder, the standard fish and pork chops, chicken souse (an acquired taste), cracked conch, sandwiches and hamburgers, and an array of daily specials. The owner is Ethiopian-born Wolansa Fountain.

E. Sunrise Hwy. (at Coral Rd.). ☎ *242-373-7655. Breakfast $3–$5; main courses: $4–$7.50; vegetarian plates $5.50. No credit cards. Open: Daily 24 hours.*

Pier 1

$$$ Freeport Harbour   BAHAMIAN/SEAFOOD

For some dramatic sunset watching, reserve an indoor or outdoor table at this seafood restaurant perched on stilts above Freeport Harbour. Kids love "walking the plank" to get inside Pier 1. Fish-filled aquariums and other nautical touches decorate the comfortable dining areas. The evening feedings at the shark pool are a special attraction. In fact, baby shark, prepared in a variety of ways, is a house specialty. You can try it blackened, curried and served with bananas, pan-fried, or in spicy fritters. Spicy food is also a specialty at Pier 1: The house salad dressing can clear out those sinuses, and the Bahamian conch salad is fiery as well. If you have a tender palate, go for the fried calamari, Bahamian cracked conch, stone crab claws, or coconut shrimp. If dry land is more your style, order the 12-ounce sirloin or a chicken or pasta dish.

Note that because Pier 1 is not far from the cruise-ship dock, it is often packed with passengers from the ships.

Near the cruise ship dock, Freeport Harbour. ☎ *242-352-6674. Reservations required for dinner. Main courses: $18.95–$40. AE, MC, V. Open: Mon–Sat, 11 a.m.– 11 p.m., Sun 5:30–11 p.m.*

Pisces
$–$$ Port Lucaya Marketplace   BAHAMIAN/INTERNATIONAL

This restaurant is our favorite among the many in the Port Lucaya Marketplace, and we're seconded by a healthy mix of locals and yacht owners who pack the place every weekend. Decorated with Tiffany-style lamps and captain's chairs, it boasts the most charming wait staff on Grand Bahama Island. Lunches are relatively simple affairs, with fish and chips, sandwiches, and salads. Pizzas are available anytime and come in 21 different types, including a version with conch, lobster, shrimp, and chicken. Dinners are more elaborate and better tasting, with a choice of curries (including a version with conch); lobster in cream, wine, and herb sauce; all kinds of fish and shellfish; and several kinds of succulent pasta dishes.

Port Lucaya Marketplace. ☎ *242-373-5192. Reservations recommended. dinner Main courses: dinner $15.95–$27; pizzas $15–$25; lunch $8.95–$11.95. AE, MC, V. Open: Mon–Sat from 11–2 a.m.*

The Pub at Port Lucaya
$–$$ Lucaya   ENGLISH/BAHAMIAN

By day, you can dine on typical English pub grub. Along with fish and chips, you can find dependable chicken and asparagus pie, shepherd's pie, and steak-and-ale pie. Fat burgers add an American twist to the menu. At dinner, Bahamian dishes, such as grilled fish or cracked conch served with a heaping mound of peas and rice, rule the night. Dine inside or al fresco, overlooking the water. Although you shouldn't feel any discomfort here, opt for a Painkiller, a rum-filled cocktail that can leave you smashed.

Port Lucaya Marketplace. ☎ *242-373-8450. Main courses: $6.95–$10.95. AE, MC, V. Open: Daily 11–1 a.m.*

The Pub on the Mall

No matter what you're in the mood for, chances are you can find it at one of the four watering holes under one roof at the Pub on the Mall. Inexpensive pub fare, from fish and chips to T-bone steak and lamb, draws diners to **Prince of Wales Lounge** (☎ 242-352-2700; open noon to 2 a.m. Monday through Saturday, Sunday 5 p.m. to midnight). Arrive between 5 and 7 p.m., and you can feast on salad, one of two main courses, dessert, and coffee, all for only about $8. Thirsty? Try a potent Pub Special: coconut rum, tequila, cherry brandy, pineapple juice, orange juice, grenadine, and bitters served in a pint mug. Sit on the balcony at **Islander's Roost** (☎ 242-352-5110; reservations recommended; open Monday through Saturday, 5:30 p.m. to midnight). The steak, prime rib, and fish here are nothing special, but the frozen daiquiris are sumptuous, and the tropical decor puts you in a vacation mood. For Italian food, consider dinner at **Silvano's** (☎ 242-352-5111).

A 96-inch satellite TV broadcasting American and European sports dominates the **Red Dog Sports Bar** (☎ 242-352-2700; open daily noon to midnight). If you need energy for all that rootin', hootin', and hollerin', order pub grubby chicken and fries, fish and chips, or other light fare, washed down with a brew or two.

The Pub on the Mall is located at the Mall and Ranfurly Circus, opposite the International Bazaar. (Main courses are $12.75 to $29; AE, MC, V.)

The Rib Room

$$$–$$$$ Freeport   STEAK/SEAFOOD

Serious meat-eaters gravitate to this restaurant — decked out in dark leather, wood, and brick — which resembles a British hunting lodge. Plates come loaded with juicy slabs of steak and prime rib, with sides of potatoes and Yorkshire pudding. If you don't want beef, you can choose among fruits of the sea, such as shrimp, Bahamian lobster, and grouper, or opt for chicken. However, the folks in the kitchen clearly cater to carnivores.

Holiday Inn Sunspree at Bahamia, the Mall at W. Sunrise Hwy. ☎ *242-352-6721. Reservations recommended. Jackets required for men. Main courses: $19.95–$33.95. AE, DC, MC, V. Open: Thurs-Sun for dinner only.*

Safari Restaurant

$–$$ Freeport   INTERNATIONAL

The dinner menu at Safari is full of straightforward staples like New York strip steaks, pork chops, hot roast beef, broiled or grilled snapper, broiled chicken, or seafood platters. At breakfast or lunch are informal:

you place your order at a kiosk-style snack bar and carry simple paper plates to an outdoor table near the pool. But at dinner, more formal and good-tasting meals are served in a large, conventional, sit-down restaurant, which has a bar and a stage for live music. After 10:30 p.m. every Wednesday, Friday, Saturday, and Sunday, the place becomes a disco (with a $12 cover charge that includes the first drink). Locals often stop by for dinner and nightclubbing.

E. Mall Dr. ☎ *242-352-2805. American breakfast $4.95; lunch main courses: $3.75–$9.75; dinner main courses: $9.75–$22.95. AE. Open: Daily 7:30–11 a.m., noon–4 p.m., and 5:30–11:30 p.m.*

Silvano's
$–$$ Freeport ITALIAN

The only authentic Italian dining spot in Freeport, this 80-seat reastaurant with its Mediterranean décor serves a fine but not exceptional cuisine. The standard repertoire from Mama Mia's kitchen is presented here with quality ingredients, most often shipped in from the United States. Service is polite and helpful. The grilled veal steak is our favorite, although the homemade pastas are equally alluring. They're served with a wide variety of freshly made sauces. The chef also works his magic with fresh shrimp. Other traditional Italian dishes round out the menu.

Ranfurly Circus. ☎ *242-3525111. Reservations recommended. Main courses: $12–$36. AE, MC, V. Open: daily for lunch from noon–3 p.m. and 5:30–11 p.m.*

The Star Club
$ West End BAHAMIAN

Among the unassuming places to chew and sip in the West End, The Star Club is the one with the most character. Opened back in 1946 as Grand Bahama's first hotel, the colonial wooden and concrete two-story building sits on the waterfront. In its heyday, it welcomed such guests as Ernest Hemingway, Sidney Poitier, and Martin Luther King, Jr. Bahamians know that when other night spots close, The Star Club is still a happening place, because it's open nearly 24 hours a day. After partying elsewhere on the island, many locals head here to listen to music (recorded or the occasional live band), play pool, and watch the sunrise. Conch in all its incarnations, fried chicken, burgers, and fish and chips are on the menu, along with peas and rice. The cook will fill you up with a satisfying meal or snack, but you won't be on the phone to the editors of *Gourmet* magazine. When the weather cooperates, you can watch men preparing fresh conch salad out front at a waterside stand. The owner here claims that it's common knowledge that The Star Club's conch salad is the best on the island. We agree. The bartender won't divulge the secret recipe for his club's legendary Bahama Mamas, but they keep folks coming back for more.

West End is about a 45-minute drive from downtown Freeport.

Bayshore Rd. ☎ *242-346-6207. All courses: $10–$16. No credit cards. Open almost around the clock (hours vary, so call ahead).*

Shenannigan's Irish Pub

$–$$$ Port Lucaya Marketplace   CONTINENTAL

Dark and beer-stained from the thousands of pints of Guinness, Harp, and Killian's that have been served and spilled here, this is the premier Boston Irish hangout on Grand Bahama Island. Many visitors come just to drink, sometimes for hours at a time, soaking up the suds, and perhaps remembering to eventually order some food. If you get hungry, there's surf and turf, French-style rack of lamb for two, seafood Newburg, and several preparations of chicken. Don't expect more than comfort food — it's satisfying and affordable unless you order the expensive steak and lobster combo.

Port Lucaya Marketplace. ☎ *242-373-4734. Main courses: $10.95–$39.95. AE, DC, MC, V. Open: Mon–Thurs 10:30 a.m.–midnight, Fri–Sat 10:30 a.m.–2 a.m.*

The Stoned Crab

$$$ Lucaya   SEAFOOD

The most romantic restaurant on island, The Stoned Crab sits beneath a soaring pyramid-shaped roof at the edge of the beach. You can eat inside, but the best seats in the house are on the al fresco patio. The stone crab claws here are some of the sweetest you'll ever taste, and the fish — try the wahoo, yellowfin tuna, or swordfish — is also beautifully prepared. Other good selections are the crab and avocado cocktail and the broiled seafood platter aromatically seasoned with oregano, garlic, and white wine. For those not wishing to eat fish, a number of continental dishes are offered nightly, including chicken parmigiana. If you're not the designated driver, be sure to order a Stoned Crab, a potent rum and fruit juice cocktail, or an Irish coffee. Because the seafood is freshly caught, not everything on the menu is always available.

Taino Beach. ☎ *242-373-1442. Reservations strongly recommended. Main courses: $23–$39. AE, MC, V. Open: Daily 5 p.m.–10:30 p.m.*

Zorba's Greek Cuisine

$–$$ Lucaya   GREEK/BAHAMIAN

First thing in the morning, you'll see locals standing in line for the Bahamian breakfasts served at Zorba's. From chicken souse to corned beef and grits, all the island eye-openers are on the menu. Eggs and fluffy

Greek pastries snag less daring early risers. Lunch may be a fat gyro or a souvlaki kebab. Dinner can begin with a Greek salad and then move on to moussaka, with baklava for a sweet finish. We can't pretend the food here is like a trip to the Greek isles, but it's satisfying in every way and filling. At this casual dining spot, you can eat inside or enjoy your meal al fresco.

Port Lucaya Marketplace. ☎ *242-373-6137. Main courses: $9.95–$23.95. AE, MC, V. Open: Daily 7 a.m–11 p.m.*

Chapter 16

Having Fun On and Off the Beach in Grand Bahama

In This Chapter

▶ Catching some rays on Grand Bahama's best beaches

▶ Enjoying the island's water sports

▶ Exploring Grand Bahama's land attractions, shopping, and nightlife

▶ Taking two great day trips

*F*rom booze cruises and snorkeling excursions to fishing trips and kayak paddles, Grand Bahama keeps water lovers as busy as they want. Scuba divers seek out spectacular marine life. Dolphins and sharks may swim with other fish, but here they also swim with humans. The variety of beaches rimming the island allows devotees to spend their entire vacation horizontal. Landlubbers can enjoy excellent golf, tennis, horseback riding, hiking, biking, shopping, and sightseeing. Compared with Nassau and Paradise Island, Grand Bahama may not be party central after dark, but you can find more than enough nightspots for drinking, dancing, and romancing.

Spending Time at the Beaches

White sandy beaches hug Grand Bahama's southern shores, some 60 miles of strands. Footprints are few and far between on most of these shores. The busiest beaches are in **Lucaya,** the island's water sports mecca, where the resort hotels are clustered. Built inland, Freeport hotels shuttle their guests to nearby sandy shores. **Xanadu,** at a resort near Freeport, is a favorite for the guests of beachless accommodations and cruise-ship passengers. On weekends, residents head to the sands at **William's Town,** east of Xanadu and south of Freeport. Many visitors get their first glimpse of golden **Taino Beach,** just east of Lucaya, when they stop by **The Stoned Crab** restaurant for a meal (see Chapter 15). Parasailing, jet skiing, and banana boat rides at Taino Beach keep vacationers active.

The farther east you go, the less crowded the beaches become. You'll hit **Churchill Beach,** then **Smith's Point,** followed by **Fortune Beach** (where an all-inclusive resort draws many Europeans) and **Barbary Beach.** About a 20-minute drive from the hotels in Lucaya, stunning **Gold Rock Beach** slumbers at **Lucayan National Park.** One part of it lures residents for weekend picnics, while other sections remain secluded.

Finding Water Fun for Everyone

Fun in the water includes everything from snorkeling to scuba diving, from catamaran or kayak riding to swimming with dolphins or sharks.

Most Grand Bahama hotels rent snorkeling gear or make arrangements for snorkeling trips by boat. If facilities are not available on the premises, hotel staff can point you toward companies with kayaks, jet skis, banana boats, and scuba gear. This section takes a look at the best outfits for aqua action.

Braving the banana boats

You can join a row of other riders on one of these long, yellow inflated boats for a bouncy trip. As you snake through the waves getting splashed, hold on tight to the handles. Try **Paradise Watersports** (Xanadu Beach, Freeport; ☎ 242-352-2887; $10). In general, the price applies to both kids and adults.

Sampling jet and water-skiing

Like aquatic motorcycles, jet skis let you zoom across the waves. Some residents and vacationers object to this form of fun, saying it's at odds with Grand Bahama's tranquility and calm waters. However, if you're interested, have it arranged for you at **Paradise Watersports** (Xanadu Beach, Freeport; ☎ 242-352-2887; $30 for 15 minutes or $50 for 30 minutes). Just be sure that you're comfortable operating the jet ski before you head too far away from shore.

If water-skiing is more to your liking, book with **Paradise Watersports** (Xanadu Beach, Freeport; ☎ 242-352-2887; $20 per person for a mile-and-a-half ride).

Checking out kayaking

To explore Grand Bahama's more pristine corners, you can rent Funyaks through Paradise Watersports (Xanadu Beach, Freeport; ☎ 242-352-2887; $8 for 30 minutes or $12 for an hour, plus a $10 deposit). Or, combine a kayak trip with a guided nature walk: Make a reservation with **Kayak Nature Tours** (☎ 242-373-2485; $69 for adults, $30 for children ages 11 to 16, free for kids age 10 and under; Visa and MasterCard are accepted), run by Bahamian-German husband-wife team Ed and Erika Gates. You spend 90 minutes of this 6-hour adventure paddling double kayaks along a tidal creek, through a mangrove forest with branches creating a shady canopy. As fish dart by, you can spot egrets, greenback herons, and other sea birds.

A trek through **Lucayan National Park** introduces you to ancient Lucayan Indian caves, and you're treated to a picnic lunch on **Gold Rock Beach** where you can swim. Kayak Nature Tours provides air-conditioned transportation to and from your hotel, complete with drivers who provide a running narration about Bahamian history, lore, and sights. The ride is about 40 minutes from the International Bazaar and 30 minutes from Port Lucaya Marketplace. Kayak Nature Tours also hosts kayak trips to nearby islands. (See "Two Great Day Trips from Grand Bahama," later in this chapter.)

Diving with dolphin or sharks

Whether you want to stroke, swim with, or dive with dolphins, even if some folks consider this politically incorrect, you can do it through **The Dolphin Experience** (UNEXSO, Port Lucaya Marketplace; ☎ 888-365-3483 or 242-373-1250). For the **Close Encounter** ($59 for adults, free for children age 5 and younger), a ferry takes you from Port Lucaya Marketplace to 9½-acre Sanctuary Bay 2 miles away. Atlantic bottlenose dolphins nuzzle your dangling legs as you sit on a partially submerged dock. Participants stand waist-deep in the water and pet some of these powerful 6- or 7-foot-long creatures. The butter-smooth skin of these amiable mammals feels amazingly soft and warm. While small groups take turns going into the water, an expert tells you all about the origins, behavior, likes, and dislikes of the dolphins. You spend only about 15 minutes body-to-body with Flipper's cousins.

If you want more time up close and personal, opt for the **Swim with the Dolphins** program ($110). When you're underwater, you can hear their clicks and clucks as they converse with each other. You can also enroll in the day-long **Assistant Trainer Program** ($189; participants must be age 16 or older). Through UNEXSO (the Underwater Explorer's Society), you can also arrange an open-water scuba dive with the dolphins ($169; four additional dives required).

No matter which dolphin program you choose, reserve as far in advance as possible.

Grand Bahama's premier dive operator is **UNEXSO Underwater Explorer's Society** (Port Lucaya Marketplace; ☎ 888-365-3483 or 242-373-1244; www.unexso.com). One of the island's oldest and most reliable companies, it pioneered shark diving ($86) in The Bahamas. UNEXSO schools you on proper human-shark interaction and takes all kinds of precautions to ensure safety.

You can have your shark dive videotaped for $20 and up. If you'd rather snap shots yourself, you can rent underwater cameras from UNEXSO for $10 and up.

Both the National Association of Underwater Instructors (NAUI) and the Professional Association of Diving Instructors (PADI) hold certification classes here, with three full days of training for $400. The one-day quickie resort course ($145) includes a shallow reef dive. Dives start at about $45 for a one-tank plunge and $70 for a two-tank dive, with all necessary gear. The more dives you have in your package, the more the per-dive cost decreases. At night, the colors of the ocean are brilliantly intense. A UNEXSO night dive costs $55.

Bahamian-owned **Caribbean Divers** (Bell Channel Inn, opposite Port Lucaya; ☎ 242-373-9111) is another good outfitter. Its certification courses begin at $325, and its resort course runs $80. Prices begin at $45 for a one-tank dive and $80 for a two-tank dive, including equipment. Caribbean Divers also offers shark dives starting around $100 and night dives for $55. Underwater camera rentals are $40. For the optimal experience down under, the company limits groups to a maximum of 18 divers.

If you're staying in Freeport, **Xanadu Undersea Adventures** (Xanadu Beach Resort; ☎ 800-327-8150 or 242-352-3811) is more convenient. Certification courses begin at $375, and resort courses run $79. You can have your dive videotaped for $35 or rent your own underwater camera for $25, plus film. Dives begin at $37 for one tank and $66 for two tanks. Ask about shark dives for $72 and night dives for $52.

Enjoying parasailing and snorkeling

For parasailing, you're strapped into a harness attached to a parachute on one end and a boat on the other. When the boat takes off, away you go, up toward the clouds. The people, ocean, and beach below shrink to toy-size. Of course, if you've indulged in parasailing before, you already know this. Although you're airborne for only about 5 minutes, the thrill lasts much longer in memory. Contact Paradise Watersports (Xanadu Beach, Freeport; ☎ 242-352-2887), or **Reef Tours** (Bayside, Port Lucaya Marketplace; ☎ 242-373-5880); both $30 per person.

Most hotels either host their own snorkeling excursions or can help you make arrangements for trips elsewhere. Paradise Watersports (Xanadu Beach, Freeport; ☎ 242-352-2887) offers a snorkeling adventure on a 48-foot catamaran. These 90-minute sails leave three times a day and cost $30 per person. Another good outfit is Reef Tours (Bayside, Port Lucaya Marketplace; ☎ 242-373-5880), which runs various 1-hour-and-45-minute excursions costing $30.

On Deck: Riding the Waves without Getting Wet

The best floating party is aboard a 72-foot catamaran with a **Bahama Mama Booze Cruise.** For 2 hours, you can drink, dance, and have fun while you take in the beauty of the ocean. Contact **Superior Watersports** (☎ 242-373-7863; Tuesday, Thursday, Saturday). The cost is $35. You can find out more about the cruises that Superior Watersports offers in the "Living It Up after the Sun Goes Down: Grand Bahama's Nightlife" section, later in this chapter.

To charter a boat for deep-sea fishing, plan to spend about $480 and up for a half-day and around $950 for a full day. Through Paradise Watersports (Xanadu Beach, Freeport; ☎ 242-352-2887), anglers can cast off for about $80 per person for four hours, with groups consisting of a minimum of four and a maximum of six people.

By law, each person is limited to catching six wahoo, dolphinfish, or kingfish per day.

Other good sport-fishing operations to try are **Reef Tours** (Bayside, Port Lucaya Marketplace; ☎ 242-373-5880) and **Running Mon Marina** (Kelly Court, Freeport; ☎ 242-352-6834). For renting boats, the most convenient marinas are Running Mon, **Port Lucaya Marina** (Bayside, Port Lucaya Marketplace; ☎ 242-373-9090), and **Xanadu Marina and Beach Resort** (Dundee Bay Dr., Freeport; ☎ 242-352-3811).

To see Grand Bahama's underwater beauty, climb aboard a glass-bottom boat and watch the fish swarm around a diver with dinner. Try Paradise Watersports (Xanadu Beach, Freeport; ☎ 242-352-2887) or Reef Tours (Bayside, Port Lucaya Marketplace; ☎ 242-373-5880); both charge $25 for adults and $15 for children.

Keeping Your Feet on Dry Land

Youthful Freeport and Lucaya keep visitors amused with golf, tennis, horseback riding, gardens, and nature reserves. Even if you're not interested in shopping, the International Bazaar in Freeport and Port Lucaya Marketplace in Lucaya are scenic places to wander.

Seeing Grand Bahama's top attractions

You can visit attractions by taxi, bus, foot, rental car, or on a guided tour. You have the most flexibility if you strike out on your own, of course. But if you'd rather let a Bahamian take you, perhaps to several far-flung attractions, consider a half- or full-day van tour with family-owned **Forbes Charter Co.** (☎ 242-352-9311). Your driver shares interesting tidbits about the island's past and present, and you can ask questions. Half-day tours begin at about $35 for adults and $25 for children.

Bahamas National Trust Rand Nature Centre
Freeport

Nature buffs, especially bird lovers, need at least 2 hours to appreciate this 100-acre reserve run by the Bahamas National Trust (BNT), a non-profit conservation association. Named in honor of philanthropist James H. Rand, this slice of wild Grand Bahama is 3 miles from the International Bazaar and 3½ miles from Port Lucaya Marketplace. One of the highlights is a pond studded with a flock of pink flamingos, The Bahamas' national bird. You can get a close-up look at this pink endangered species, so bring your camera. Other feathered friends you may spot are a red-legged thrush, a banana quit, or a Cuban emerald hummingbird. A pair of binoculars comes in handy, especially for the 2-hour guided bird walk, held the first Saturday of each month starting at 8 a.m. A variety of orchids is among more than 100 different types of plants here. Several species of Bahamian boa constrictors reside in the exhibit room, along with other indigenous and imported creatures. Taxis and buses will take you here.

E. Settler's Way, a quarter mile east of Coral Rd. ☎ *242-352-5438. Admission: $5 adults, free for ages 12 and younger. Open: Mon–Fri 9 a.m.–4 p.m.*

Parrot Jungle's Garden of the Groves
Freeport

This attractive 12-acre oasis has added a pond-full of alligators and a petting zoo with Vietnamese potbellied pigs, Pygmy goats, and a cockatoo. Macaws on perches welcome visitors, and you can spot an iguana, a peacock, ducks, and raccoons. Allow at least 45 minutes to see the animals and to wander across footbridges and along paths past waterfalls, fruit trees, flowers, and lacy ferns. You can spend a few quiet moments in the historic chapel that sits on a rise overlooking the garden. Built with native stone, the chapel is topped by a Spanish tile roof. The garden — 25 minutes from the International Bazaar and 15 minutes from Port Lucaya Marketplace — honors American financier and developer Wallace Groves, who founded Freeport with his wife, Georgette.

On Magellan Dr., off Midshipman Rd., Lucaya. ☎ *242-373-5668 or 242-373-1456. Open: Daily 9 a.m.–4 p.m. Admission: $9.95 adults, $6.95 ages 3 to 10.*

Hydroflora Garden
Freeport

When the garden was first developed in the 1970s, it was a showcase for _hydroponics,_ the water-based method of growing plants without soil. Today, however, only a small demonstration area of this specialized system of getting nutrients to greenery remains. What makes this garden worth a visit is that it flourishes with dozens of specimens of native and other flora.

During the 30-minute guided tour, you can wander along trails through 3 acres and find out about medicinal and Biblical uses of plants. Hummingbirds hover over bushes, and swallowtail and monarch butterflies flutter by as you pass tropical fruit trees bearing coconuts, mangos, sapodillas, avocados, star fruit, and cashew nuts. Maps are distributed to those who'd rather take their own leisurely walks than join a tour. To get here, you can catch a bus from the International Bazaar, less than a mile away, or from Port Lucaya Marketplace, about a 15-minute ride.

E. Beach Dr. and Alcester, off E. Sunrise Hwy., Freeport. ☎ _242-352-6052. Open: Mon-Fri 9 a.m.-5 p.m., Sat 9 a.m.-4 p.m. Note that the garden closes daily between 1 and 2 p.m. Admission: For the 30-minute guided tour, $6 adults, $3 children over age 7, free for younger children. For an unguided visit, $3 adults, $1.50 children over age 7, free for children under 7._

Lucayan National Park
Lucaya

This is a tropical wilderness, where you may want to spend at least a couple of hours exploring as you follow trails and elevated walkways through the thick forest at this preserve. You come to **Gold Rock Creek,** which is fed by a spring from what may be the world's largest underground freshwater cave system. Visitors are permitted to walk into two caves. One is closed to humans, though, during bat-nursing season — late spring to midsummer. Spiral wooden steps take you down to the freshwater pools, where you can see fish darting back and forth. Through UNEXSO (see "Diving with dolphins and sharks," earlier in this chapter), adventurous folks can arrange to go on a cave dive. Bones and pottery shards of the Lucayan Indians, who once collected fresh water here, have been found in the caves.

Across the road from the entrance to the park, a boardwalk trail through a mangrove forest leads down to one of the island's best beaches, Gold Rock Beach. Pack a lunch and eat it at a seaside picnic table or on the dunes and then cool off in the aquamarine waves.

Before heading out to this remote national park, purchase a ticket ($3 per adult; free for children age 12 and under) at The Bahamas National

Trust (BNT) headquarters (East Settler's Way, a quarter-mile east of Coral Road. ☎ **242-352-5438**). Lucayan National Park is a 30-minute drive east of Freeport and 25 minutes east of Port Lucaya Marketplace. You can take a taxi or join a bus tour.

Twenty-six miles from Freeport and 20 miles east of Lucaya. ☎ *242-352-5438. Open: Daily 9 a.m.–4 p.m.*

Perfume Factory
Freeport

The tour of the fragrance laboratory housed in this replica of a nineteenth-century Bahamian mansion takes a mere 5 minutes. You can discover how the company produces perfumes, colognes, and lotions from tropical ingredients. You're then invited to purchase some. But most people find the mix-your-own sessions here the best reason to visit. Be prepared for an olfactory workout. For $30, you can sniff honeysuckle, lavender, gardenia, jasmine, cinnamon, ginger, and an array of other aromas to decide which two or three essential oils to combine into your own signature creation. You can name your concotion and have it bottled and labeled. Choosing your special scent can take anywhere from 15 minutes to a half-hour.

Behind International Bazaar, Freeport. ☎ *242-352-9391. Open: Mon–Fri 9:30 a.m.– 5:30 p.m., Sat noon–4 p.m. Admission: Free.*

Trekking to the "Wild" West End

Rent a car or hire a taxi and head to West End, which is about 45 minutes from downtown Freeport. Fishing boats recline along the one narrow road that parallels the coastline. This tranquil fishing community is the place to go when you're in the mood to have a few drinks or swap a tale or two with locals or when you have a taste for fresh home-style seafood. Small roadside kitchens move snapper, jack fish, and grouper from the ocean to the frying pan in record time. Conch is cut from the shell and turned into salad right before customers' eyes.

Once the capital of Grand Bahama, West End is inhabited by descendants of the people who first settled the island. Freeport and Lucaya may be new compared to Nassau, but other parts of Grand Bahama were developed long before its modern resort areas. West End is the site of the island's annual Junkanoo parades on Independence Day (July 10) and Boxing Day (December 26). On your way to West End, you pass other old seaside settlements — some dilapidated, some in colorful ruins. Many of the tiny houses are painted bright blues, yellows, and greens. You may also come upon a blue hole. When the tide is right, many locals swim in these natural pools where freshwater floats on top of saltwater.

Finding other outdoor options

Beaches are paramount, but you can find much more to island life than making waves. Grand Bahama gives visitors a choice of options for staying active on solid ground.

Biking through Grand Bahama

A guided bike trip is an ideal way to see parts of Grand Bahama that most visitors miss. Starting at **Barbary Beach,** you can pedal a mountain bike along the southern coast parallel to the beach. Stop for a snack, lunch, and a dip. Finally, you reach **Lucayan National Park,** some 12 miles away. Explore the cave where the Indians buried their dead in the days when Grand Bahama was theirs. Crabs here have been known to come up though holes in the ground carrying bits of bowls once used by the Lucayans. **Kayak Nature Tours (☎ 242-373-2485),** the company that sponsors these trips, transports you home to your hotel by van, so you don't have to exhaust yourself in the heat cycling back. The cost is $80 for adults, half-price for hardy children ages 10 to 16. Visa and MasterCard are accepted. Included are all equipment, sustenance, and round-trip transportation to and from your accommodation.

Teeing up for golf

Grand Bahama is home to more golf courses than any other Bahamian island. Open to the public throughout the year, they play host to a variety of international tournaments. No need to worry if you don't feel like lugging your own clubs. You can rent clubs from any Freeport or Lucaya pro shop.

Bahamia's Emerald Golf Course, the Mall South, at the Resorts at Bahamia (☎ 242-350-7000), was the site of The Bahamas National Open some years back, and more recently, in conjunction with the Ruby course), it's the site of the annual January Grand Bahama Pro-Am Tournament. The course has plenty of trees along the fairways, as well as an abundance of water hazards and bunkers. The toughest hole is the ninth, a par 5 with 545 yards from the blue tees to the hole. In winter, greens fees to either of these courses are $95 per day, reduced to $85 in summer.

The championship course **Bahamia's Ruby Golf Course,** Sunrise Hwy., at the Resorts at Bahamia.(☎ 242-350-7000), received a major upgrade in 2001 by Jim Fazio Golf Design, Inc. The Ruby course was lengthened to increase the rating and to enhance play. A fully automated irrigation system was installed. For greens fees, see the Emerald Golf Course. It's a total of 6,750 yards if played from the championship blue tees.

Fortune Hills Golf & Country Club, Richmond Park, Lucaya (☎ 242-373-4500), was originally intended to be an 18-hole course, but the back 9 were never completed. You can replay the front 9 for 18 holes and a total of 6,916 yards from the blue tees. Par is 72. Greens fees are $31 for 9 holes, $43 for 18.

The best-kept and most manicured course on Grand Bahama is the par-72 **Lucayan Park Golf & Country Club,** Lucaya Beach (☎ 242-373-1066). Recently made over, it's quite beautiful and is known for a hanging boulder sculpture at its entrance. Greens are fast, and there are a couple of par 5s more than 500 yards long, totaling 6,824 yards from the blue tees and 6,488 from the whites. Greens fees are $67 for 18 holes, including a mandatory shared golf cart. We'll let you in on a secret: Even if you're not a golfer, sample the food at the club restaurant — everything from lavish champagne brunches to first-rate seafood dishes.

The first golf course to open in The Bahamas since 1969 made its premiere late in 2000. **The Reef Course** at Royal Palm Way, Lucaya (☎ 242-373-2002), was designed by Robert Trent Jones, Jr., who called it "a bit like a Scottish course but a lot warmer." The course requires precise shot-making to avoid its numerous lakes: There is water on 13 of its 18 holes and various types of long grass swaying in the trade winds. The course boasts 6,920 yards of links-style playing grounds. Residents of Our Lucaya, with which the course is associated, pay $100 for 18 holes or $66 for 9 holes. Nonresidents are charged $120 for 18 holes, but the same price, $66, for 9 holes.

Enjoying hiking and birding

The **Heritage Trail** was carved out by early freed slaves as they made their way from one part of the roadless island to the other. This 8-mile trek, parallel to the beach, takes you to flourishing Lucayan National Park, where you can explore old caves once used by the island's Indians for fishing, collecting fresh water, and burying their dead. But the best part of this all-day excursion is the picnic lunch on a dune, shaded by *casuarinas* — those wispy tropical pine trees — overlooking the beach, and, of course, the swim afterward. You won't have to hike the 8 miles back to your starting point because **Kayak Nature Tours** (☎ 242-373-2485) provides transportation in a van. The cost of the tour is $55 per person. This company also takes vacationers on early morning bird-watching tours that include snacks and transportation to and from hotels.

Hoofing it: Horseback riding

Mount a horse for a ride with **Pinetree Stables** (Beachway Dr., ☎ 242-373-3600) along a wooded trail through a mangrove swamp to a golden sand beach, where you can splash in the water. These stables are conveniently located halfway between the International Bazaar and Port

Lucaya Marketplace. The 2-hour rides cost $65 per person. Groups of up to ten people go out with two guides per trip three times a day, Tuesday through Sunday. Make reservations as far in advance as you can, especially in summer.

Taking time for tennis

Most visitors play tennis in Freeport at the nine hard-surface courts at the **Resorts at Bahamia** (☎ 242-352-9661; $10 an hour for guests, $12 for non-guests). Six of these courts are lighted for night play. In Lucaya, four courts are located at **Our Lucaya** resort (☎ 242-373-1333). You can rent racquets and balls and take lessons at any of these hotels.

Shopping in Grand Bahama

If you in the market for watches, leather, crystal, china, perfume, or gemstone and 14-carat gold jewelry, European and American imports can be considerably less expensive here than at home. Of course, list prices prevail, and it's always good to know what these prices are back home so that you can determine whether you're indeed getting a bargain.

Not a whole lot in the stores is actually produced in The Bahamas — that is, beyond some clothing, lotions, fragrances, crafts, and straw goods. Many of the items at the island's straw markets come from elsewhere, such as all those colorful, flowing Indonesian fabrics that are so popular for women's wear. The variety of shops and high-quality goods makes Grand Bahama a good place for shoppers.

Port Lucaya Marketplace is a 6-acre open-air shopping and dining complex that sprawls along the waterfront in Lucaya. Fire-engine red British telephone booths stand near pastel shingle-roofed buildings festooned with bougainvillea. Many restaurants are on second-story balconies overlooking the channel. Sunlight glints off boats bobbing in the water. Some afternoons and most evenings, live music spills from the bandstand in the lacy harbor-side gazebo at **Count Basie Square**.

Boozing, chowing down, and shopping are big business at Port Lucaya. Nearly 100 pubs, restaurants, and boutiques draw both visitors and residents. Apart from the upscale, you can also see a few island original treasures in specialty shops.

Braiding bonanza

Women braiding hair, with and without all those colorful beads, are around every corner at Port Lucaya Marketplace. Remember that pale skin, newly exposed by parting the hair, can get a wicked sunburn.

At the older **International Bazaar,** near the Resorts at Bahamia in Freeport, the shops, eateries, and architecture take visitors around the world. You enter through a towering torii archway, a symbol of welcome in Japan. Designed in the 1960s, the place has a somewhat seedy feel. In many cases, merchandise and food are only loosely related to the countries represented by the architecture of the section where they are sold. Yet, strolling along the maze of slender, meandering walkways is still amusing. Turn a corner and your surroundings suddenly change from Tokyo to the Left Bank of Paris, from Latin America to Africa, from East India to Hong Kong. You may have a hard time comparison-shopping because figuring out how to get back to a place you came from can be tricky. For the most part, prices here are good — in many cases 20 to 40 percent lower than in the United States.

Behind the entrance to the International Bazaar, the **Straw Market** is packed with stalls where vendors call out to passers-by, "It don't cost anything to look!" Baskets, wide-brimmed hats, bags, placemats, and dolls are among the most popular straw goods. Tables are also piled high with T-shirts for men, women, and children, beach towels, shell jewelry, magnets, mugs, and mahogany African-style Bahamian wood carvings. Linking the Bazaar with the Casino at Bahamia, the **International Arcade** houses branches of glitzy stores, such as Parfum de Paris, Columbian Emeralds, and the Leather Shop. Here, you can also find artisans in booths, including glass blowers and jewelry designers.

International Bazaar

Here's a description of the various shops in the bazaar.

Art

Flovin Gallery: This gallery sells original Bahamian and international art, frames, lithographs, posters, and Bahamian-made Christmas ornaments and decorated coral. It also offers handmade Bahamian dolls, coral jewelry, and other gift items. Another branch is at Port Lucaya Marketplace. In the Arcade section of the International Bazaar. ☎ 242-352-7564.

Crystal & China

Island Galleria: This store boasts an awesome collection of crystal.. Fragile, breakable, and beautiful, it includes works of utilitarian art in china and crystal by Waterford, Aynsley, Lenox, Dansk, Belleek, and Swarovski. Anything you buy can be carefully packed and shipped. Another branch is located in the Port Lucaya Marketplace (☎ 242-373-8400). International Bazaar. ☎ 242-352-8194.

Fashion

Bahamas Coin and Stamp Ltd.: This is the major coin dealer on the island. It specializes in Bahamian coin jewelry, ancient Roman coins, and relics from sunken Spanish galleons. It also carries a vast selection of antique U.S. and English coins and paper money. International Bazaar. ☎ 242-352-8989.

Bahamian Souvenir Outlet: This place, just below the Ministry of Tourism, has lots of inexpensive souvenirs and gifts: the usual array of T-shirts, key rings, mugs, and all that stuff. International Bazaar. ☎242-352-2947.

Bahamian Things: This native art gallery sells an array of locally hand-crafted items, including books on The Bahamas, Abaco ceramics, woodwork, and even handmade Christmas decorations. 15B Poplar Crescent, Freeport. ☎ 242-352-9550.

Caribbean Cargo: This is one of the island's best gift shops, specializing in such items as picture frames, candles, and clocks, and clothes. In the Arcade section of the International Bazaar. ☎ 242-352-2929.

Cleo's Boutique: This shop offers evening wear to lingerie, as well as everything in between. A warm and inviting destination, Cleo's prides itself on capturing the Caribbean woman in all of her moods. You can also find a wide array of costume jewelry beginning at $20 a piece. International Bazaar. ☎ 242-351-3340.

Colombian Emeralds International: This is a branch of the world's foremost emerald jeweler, offering a wide array of precious gemstone jewelry and one of the island's best watch collections. Careful shoppers will find significant savings over U.S. prices. The outlet offers certified appraisals and free 90-day insurance. Two branches are located in the Port Lucaya Marketplace (☎ 242-373-8400). South American Section of the International Bazaar. ☎ 242-352-5464.

Far East Traders: Look for Asian linens, hand-embroidered dresses and blouses, silk robes, lace parasols, smoking jackets, and kimonos. A branch is located inside the Island Galleria at the Port Lucaya Marketplace. International Bazaar. ☎ 242-352-9280.

Intercity Music: This is the best music store on the island; you get not only Bahamian music, but soca, reggae, and all the music of the islands as well. CDs, records, and tapes are sold. You can also purchase Bahamian posters and flags, portable radios, Walkmans, and blank audio tapes, along with accessories for camcorders. A branch office is located at the Port Lucaya Marketplace (☎ 242-373-8820). International Bazaar. ☎ 242-352-8820.

The Leather Shop: This is another good outlet, carrying a much more limited Fendi line, but also many other designers including Land and HCL. Additional leather goods include shoes and gift items. Additional locations include the Port Lucaya Marketplace (☎ 242-373-2323) and Regent's Centre (☎ 242-352-2895). International Bazaar. ☎ **242-352-5491.**

Les Parisiennes: This outlet offers a wide range of perfumes, including the latest from Paris, and it also sells Lancôme cosmetics and skin-care products. There's a branch office at the Port Lucaya Marketplace (☎ **242-373-2974**). In the French section of the International Bazaar. ☎ **242-352-5380.**

Paris in The Bahamas: This shop contains the biggest selection of luxury goods under one roof in the International Bazaar. The staff wears couture black dresses like you would expect in Paris, and everywhere there's a sense of French glamour and conspicuous consumption. The store offers both Gucci and Versace leather goods for men and women; crystal from Lalique, Baccarat, Daum, Kosta Boda, and Örrefors; and a huge collection of cosmetics and perfumes. International Bazaar. ☎ **242-352-5380.**

The Perfume Factory Fragrance of The Bahamas: This is the top fragrance producer in The Bahamas. The shop is housed in a model of an 1800s mansion, in which visitors are invited to hear a 5-minute commentary and to see the mixing of fragrant oils. A "mixology" department lets you create your own fragrance from a selection of oils. The shop's well-known products include Island Promises, Goombay, Paradise, and Pink Pearl (which has conch pearls in the bottle). The shop also sells Guanahani, a fragrance created to commemorate the 500th anniversary of Columbus's first landfall in the New World. (Guanahani was the Indian name for the southern Bahamian island of San Salvador, traditionally claimed to be the site of Columbus's landing.) Other perfumes and colognes include Sand, the No. 1 Bahamian-made men's fragrance in the country. At the rear of the International Bazaar. ☎ **242-352-9391.**

Unusual Centre: Where else can you get a wide array of items made of eel skin or goods made from exotic feathers such as peacock? Another branch is located at the **Port Lucaya Marketplace** (☎ 242-352-3994). International Bazaar. ☎ **242-352-3994.**

Port Lucaya Marketplace

Here's a description of the various shops in the bazaar.

Bandolera: The staff can be rather haughty here, but despite its drawbacks, this store carries a collection of chic women's clothing that's many, many cuts above the usual run of T-shirts and tank tops that are the norm within many of its competitors. Port Lucaya Market-place. ☎ 242-373-7691.

Coconits by Androsia: This is the Port Lucaya outlet of the famous batik house of Andros Island. Its designs and colors capture the spirit of The Bahamas. Fabrics are handmade on the island of Andros. The store sells quality, 100%-cotton resort wear, including simple skirts, tops, jackets, and shorts for women, and it also offers a colorful line of children's wear. Port Lucaya Marketplace. ☎ 242-373-8387.

Flovin Gallery II: This branch of the art gallery located in the Port Lucaya Marketplace sells a collection of oil paintings (both Bahamian and international), along with lithographs and posters. In its limited field, it's the best in the business. It also features a number of gift items, such as handmade Bahamian dolls, decorated corals, and Christmas ornaments. Port Lucaya Marketplace. ☎ 242-373-8388.

Jeweler's Warehouse: This is a place for bargain hunters looking for good buys on discounted, closeout 14-karat gold, and gemstone jewelry. Discounts range up to 50%, but the quality of many of these items remains high. Guarantees and certified appraisals are possible. Port Lucaya Marketplace. ☎ 242-373-8400.

Harley-Davidson of Freeport: This is one of only two registered and licensed Harley outlets in The Bahamas. You can special-order a motorcycle if you feel flush with funds from a casino, but it's more likely that you'll content yourself with T-shirts, leather vests, belts, caps, sunglasses, and gift items. Port Lucaya Marketplace. ☎ 242-373-8269.

UNEXSO Dive Shop: This is the premier dive shop of The Bahamas. It sells everything related to the water — swimsuits, wet suits, underwater cameras, and video equipment, shades, hats, souvenirs, state-of-the-art diver's equipment, and computers. Port Lucaya Marketplace. ☎ 242-373-1250.

Living It Up after the Sun Goes Down: Grand Bahama's Nightlife

Freeport's **Casino at Bahamia,** under a dramatic Moorish-style dome, is the primary attraction after dark — and, for many, during the day as well. Periodic stage shows pack the house with performances by feathered dancers, magicians, singers, comedians, and other entertainers (quite a few of whom are often internationally known headliners).

For an evening with more island appeal, try the **Yellowbird Showroom** (Castaways Resort, ☎ 242-352-6682). Fire eaters, calypso singers, and limbo dancers put on a festive show, Monday, Wednesday, and Friday nights, 9 to 11 p.m. ($20 per person, including one drink). About a 45-minute drive from Freeport, **West End** is a local after-hours target, particularly the **Star Club** (☎ 242-346-6207), which usually stays open until dawn. Where Grand Bahama's local nightclubs leave off, hotel and restaurant bars and lounges pick up the slack, with crowded dance floors and much elbow-bending.

In the Port Lucaya Marketplace's waterfront **Count Basie Square,** live music pumps from the gazebo almost every night, starting around 10 p.m. You can hear calypso played on steel drums, a reggae band, a Junkanoo troupe, or a gospel group. Some say that the idea for the marketplace itself originated with the Count, the legendary American jazz pianist and bandleader who spent his last years on Grand Bahama. Most of Port Lucaya's stores are closed after dark, but the marketplace still throbs with activity under the stars. The bars and restaurants surrounding the square are serious hangout spots for both residents and visitors.

After many vacationers see the waters surrounding Grand Bahama, they can't get enough, even after dark. To be wined, dined, and entertained at sea, make a reservation for a moonlit dinner cruise with **Superior Watersports** (☎ 242-373-7863; Monday, Wednesday, and Friday; Cost: $59 adults, $40 children). You can feast on steak and lobster on a fun-filled 72-foot catamaran.

Two Great Day Trips from Grand Bahama

Whether you're a novice or an experienced kayaker, one of the following excursions will introduce you to another side of The Bahamas.

Trip # 1: Kayak and snorkel adventure to Peterson Cay

You can go from Grand Bahama, one of the country's largest islands, to one of its smallest. Nearby uninhabited Peterson Cay (pronounced "key") is an itty-bitty national park on a reef. After you reach this pristine slip of land edged by a luscious beach, Freeport and Lucaya seem like Las Vegas. To reach the cay, you travel in a kayak. After you arrive at the starting point, about a 25-minute drive from Freeport, you paddle for about 30 minutes each way to the cay. For about 90 minutes, you have a chance to snorkel around the island, where the fish and marine life are colorful. Call **Kayak Nature Tours** (☎ 242-373-2485; cost: $69; Visa and MasterCard are accepted). Snorkel groups are kept to a maximum of ten people each, even when more participants are in the total group of kayakers. The company provides all the necessary gear, and your driver entertains you with a running narration about Grand Bahama as you're transported to and from your hotel.

Trip # 2: Kayak challenge to Water Cay

This day-long adventure is for the experienced kayaker. You paddle through the ocean for about 2½ hours to reach Water Cay. Some 50 years ago, more than 400 people called this tiny island home. They earned a living growing sisal for making rope. As that industry dried up, residents slowly migrated to Freeport. Today, the cay's population has shrunk to barely a baker's dozen. The petite clapboard houses are painted bright blues and greens and pastel yellows and pinks. When the kayakers on this excursion arrive, the women of the settlement greet them with a home-cooked meal. The menu may be chicken, grouper, macaroni and cheese, peas and rice, and coleslaw, followed by coconut pie made from fresh coconuts. You dine in a shady spot by the water's edge. Contact Kayak Nature Tours (☎ **242-373-2485;** Cost: $110; Visa and MasterCard are accepted). The price includes all equipment and transportation to and from your hotel.

Part V
The Abacos: Prime Out Islands

In this part . . .

This section explores the archipelago of Bahamian Islands known as The Abacos, lying north of New Providence. You discover the differences that make the most popular of these serene landfalls special, whether you're considering an inn at a marina in Marsh Harbour, a small beach hotel on Elbow Cay, an upscale yacht club on Green Turtle Cay, or a modern resort on Treasure Cay. In this part, you find plenty of suggestions for having fun in the sun and sampling everything from conch fritters to lobster. Most importantly, you find out the best ways to travel among these small, friendly cays by air, land, and sea.

Chapter 17

Marsh Harbour
(Great Abaco Island)

. . . .

In This Chapter

▶ Finding Marsh Harbour's best accommodations and restaurants

▶ Getting around Marsh Harbour

▶ Exploring the area's best beaches, water sports, and land attractions

. . . .

After Nassau and Freeport, Marsh Harbour, capital of the Abacos, is the largest town in The Bahamas. Its shoreline provides one of the finest anchorages in the Out Islands, which makes it "The Boating Capital of The Bahamas."

As the center of Abaconian commerce, it's also the best refueling stop in the Out Islands, with the largest range of facilities, including not only marinas, but shopping centers, banks, and pharmacies as well. Even though Marsh Harbour is now large enough to boast a Pizza Hut, it's still small enough to walk around. Traffic is hardly a problem. It has only one traffic light.

The town lacks the quaint New England charm of either New Plymouth (see Chapter 20) or the allure of Hope Town (see Chapter 18).

Marsh Harbour is also the major transportation hub of the Abacos, with its airport functioning as the main arrival point for most visitors — at least those who didn't sail in on a boat.

Checking Out Marsh Harbour's Best Accommodations

Abaco Beach Resort & Boat Harbour
$$–$$$ Marsh Harbour

This 82-room beachfront resort — the biggest and best in Marsh Harbour — is a good choice, especially if you're serious about diving or fishing. Extending over a sprawling acreage at the edge of town and fronting a small beach, it's a business with several different faces: the hotel, with handsomely furnished rooms that overlook the Sea of Abaco; the well-managed restaurant and bar; the Boat Harbour Marina, which has slips for 180 boats and full docking facilities; and a full-fledged dive shop. The beach here is small and gravel studded, not reason enough to check in. It's also private, reserved only for residents of the hotel. Each accommodation comes with a small tiled bathroom with shower. The bedrooms are better equipped than those at its rival, Conch Inn Resort (see next entry). Here, they're air-conditioned and contain TV but also such extras as a minibar, hairdryer, and safe, the latter amenities not offered at the other resorts. Angler's Restaurant is one of Marsh Harbour's best (see separate recommendation later in this chapter). A swim-up bar and beachfront bar serve light snacks and grog. On site are two popular bars and two tennis courts, along with a fitness center, sauna, and massage service. Boat rentals can also be arranged for you here at the marina.

The Sea of Abaco. ☎ *800-468-4799* or *242-367-2158. Fax: 242-367-4154. Internet:* www.abacobeachresort.net/. *Rack rates: $195–$275 double, $375 one-bedroom suite, $550 cottage for up to 4. All meals $45 per person extra. AE, DISC, MC, V.*

Conch Inn Resort & Marina
$$ Marsh Harbour

Slightly down the scale from the Abaco Beach Resort & Boat Harbour (see preceding entry), this little nine-room inn lies at the southeastern edge of the harbor. This casual, one-story hotel is leased on a long-term basis by one of the world's largest yacht-chartering companies, The Moorings. A number of sandy beaches are within driving distance. Its motel-style, mid-sized bedrooms are also small, each with two double beds. (Rollaways are available for extra occupants.) Bathrooms are neatly kept with shower-tub combinations. All units overlook the yachts bobbing in the nearby marina. On the premises are an open-air, freshwater swimming pool, fringed with palm trees, and a nearby branch of the Dive Abaco scuba facility. The on-site restaurant and bar (Bistro Mezzamare), under independent management, is recommended later in this chapter.

E. Bay St. ☎ *242-367-4000. Fax: 242-367-4004. Internet:* www.conchinn.com. *Rack rates: $120 double. Extra person $20. MC, V.*

Marsh Harbour Hotels & Restaurants

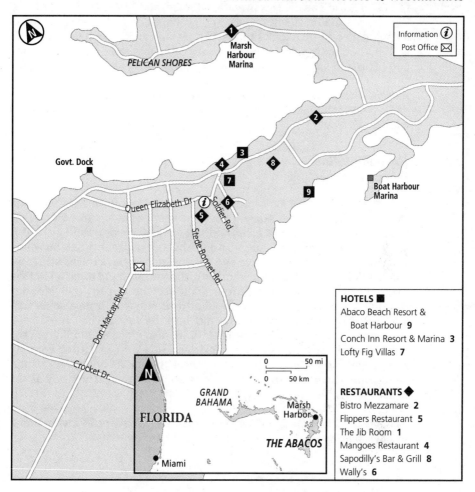

PELICAN SHORES

1 Marsh Harbour Marina

Information ⓘ
Post Office ✉

2

3

Govt. Dock

4

8

7

Boat Harbour Marina

9

Queen Elizabeth Dr ⓘ Soldier Rd.

6

5

Stede Bonnet Rd.

✉

Don Mackay Blvd.

Crocket Dr.

N

0   50 mi
0   50 km

GRAND BAHAMA

FLORIDA

Marsh Harbor

THE ABACOS

Miami

HOTELS ■
Abaco Beach Resort &
 Boat Harbour **9**
Conch Inn Resort & Marina **3**
Lofty Fig Villas **7**

RESTAURANTS ◆
Bistro Mezzamare **2**
Flippers Restaurant **5**
The Jib Room **1**
Mangoes Restaurant **4**
Sapodilly's Bar & Grill **8**
Wally's **6**

Dolphin Beach Resort
$$–$$$ Great Guana Cay

Even better than any of the hostelries of Marsh Harbour, we prefer to escape to the offshore Great Guana Cay and this ten-room charmer. For more details on this cay, refer to "A Great Day Trip from Marsh Harbour," later in this chapter. Set directly astride one of the best beaches in The Bahamas, a 15-minute walk north of Guana Cay's largest settlement (Guana Village), with miles of powder-soft sand in front of you, this resort offers informal but very comfortable lodgings. Four of the units are in the main house and have queen-size beds and ceiling fans, small refrigerators, and microwaves; three of them have private screened-in decks with teakwood furniture. The oceanfront cottages also have queen-size beds, ceiling fans, air-conditioning, and full-size kitchenettes with stoves. Cottages can accommodate between two and four guests, depending on their size. The showers are placed outside but secluded and screened off by island flora. The place is private, intimate, and laid-back. A restaurant, The Landing, is on the premises, and it offers a "conch crawl," which is a Bahamian take on a lobster tank. Nippers, a beachfront bar and grill, is within a 5-minute walk. On site is a salt-water, mid-sized swimming pool, and bikes and kayaks are available to guests, along with snorkeling gear.

Outside Guana Village. ☎ *800-222-2646 or 242-365-5137. Internet:* www. dolphinbeachresort.com. *Rack rates: $120–$155 double, $170–$240 cottage. AE, MC, V.*

Lofty Fig Villas
$$ Marsh Harbour

This family-owned six-unit bungalow colony across from the Conch Inn overlooks the harbor. It doesn't have the services of a resort like Abaco Beach, but it's good for families and self-sufficient types. Built in 1970, it stands in a tropical landscape with a freshwater pool and a gazebo where you can barbecue. Rooms have one queen-size bed and a queen-size hide-a-bed sofa, a fully tiled bathroom with shower, a dining area, a kitchen, and a private screened-in porch. Maid service is provided Monday through Saturday. The hotel is about a 10-minute walk from a supermarket and shops, and restaurants and bars lie just across the street. Marinas, a dive shop, and boat rentals are also close at hand. From the Lofty Fig, you have to walk, bike, or drive a mile east to a point near the Marsh Harbour ferryboat docks for access to a sandy beach and a snorkeling site. (Many visitors opt to go to Guana Cay for their day at the beach, via ferryboat.)

East Bay St. ☎ *and fax 242-367-2681. Rack rates: $135 daily or $877 weekly for 2. Extra person $25. MC, V.*

Nettie's Different of Abaco
$$$ Casuarina Point

Set within the hamlet of Casuarina Point, 18 miles south of Marsh Harbour, this 20-room family-managed bonefishing club is surrounded by a wide deck and a garden. This ecologically conscious place was built at the edge of a saltwater marsh favored by a variety of birds, wild hogs, and iguana; it's a good choice for bird-watchers and superb for bonefishing enthusiasts. It's not luxurious, and it won't be to everyone's liking, but it's a peaceful place near good snorkeling and virgin beaches. The hotel is closely associated with several bonefishing guides in the neighborhood, any of whom can arrange full-day fishing excursions for around $350 per couple. (Not all equipment is included in this fee. Be sure that you understand the arrangements thoroughly before you commit yourself.) Each of the small to mid-sized bedrooms has a screened-in porch, a ceiling fan, a small bathroom with shower, and simple furnishings, but only eight are air-conditioned. During your stay, you'll be in the midst of a closely knit, isolated community that's firmly committed to preserving the local environment and heritage. Nettie has created a living museum that takes you back through 100 years of the island's history. There's a bar and restaurant where the staff will recite a selection of simple Bahamian fare to you before you sit down for your meal. Nonguests are welcome to drop in for two-course meals. The food is quite good.

Casuarina Point. ☎ *242-366-2150. Fax: 242-327-8152. Internet:* www.different ofabaco.com *$1,400–$1,536 double for 4 nights, 3 days including bonefishing; $700–$1,095 double for 4 days, 3 days nonfishing. Rates include all meals. AE, MC, V.*

Sunset Point Resort
$$ Marsh Harbour

One of the newest resorts in the Abacos is this 8-room complex over-looking Bustick Bay, a 10-minute drive south of the airport. On the coast of Abaco (called by locals for some strange reason "the south side"), the resort attracts those who want to go bonefishing in the "Marls" (local name for Bustick Bay). Bedrooms are freshly decorated and generous in size, and each with view of the water, best seen from one of the private balconies. You have a choice of two queen-size beds or a king-size bed if you're feeling romantic. All units are equipped with a small private bath-room with shower. On site is the Lazy Parrot Restaurant, serving a Bahamian and continental cuisine. Kayaks are available to explore local creeks and shallows, and bonefishing guides can be arranged.

Bustick Bay. ☎ *242-367-5333. Fax: 242-367-5332. Rack rates: $130–$140 double. MC, V.*

Arriving in Marsh Harbour

Regardless of where you're going in the Abacos, Marsh Harbour is the easiest town to reach. Minor airstrips are in the Abacos, including Treasure Cay (see Chapter 20), but Marsh Harbour offers the most convenient flights servicing the Abaco chain. Bahamasair is the major carrier from Nassau, with American Eagle winging in from Miami with two daily flights.

At the airport, you'll find taxis waiting to take you where you want to go, along with toilets, phones, and a little snack bar. No car-rental service is at the airport. The location is a 10-minute drive south of Marsh Harbour.

Getting around Marsh Harbour

In many of the smaller islands of the Abacos, including Treasure Cay and Green Turtle Cay, you can manage without a car. If you plan to stay right in Marsh Harbour and visit one of the offshore islands such as Elbow Cay (reached by ferryboat), you still won't need a car. But if you want to explore "mainland" Great Abaco Island, including points south such as Bahamas National Trust Sanctuary, a car is needed because public transportation virtually doesn't exist unless you use taxis which can be expensive.

✔ **Going on wheels.** You won't need a car to get around the town itself, but if you want to explore the rest of the island on your own, you can rent a car, usually for $70 a day or $350 per week (be prepared for bad roads, though). In Marsh Harbour, call **A&P Rentals** at ☎ 242-367-2655 to see whether any vehicles are available.

✔ **Peddling around. Rental Wheels of Abaco** at Marsh Harbour (☎ 242-367-4643) will rent bikes at $8 a day or $35 a week and also mopeds at $25 to $35 per day or $150 to $185 a week. The best place to go biking is to take the long road heading south from Marsh Harbour, perhaps finding a secluded beach to beat the heat of the day.

✔ **Taking a taxi.** Unmetered taxis, which you often have to share with other passengers, meet all arriving flights. They'll take you to your hotel if it's on the Abaco "mainland"; otherwise, they'll deposit you at a dock where you can hop aboard a water taxi to one of the neighboring offshore islands, such as Green Turtle Cay or Elbow Cay. Most visitors use a combination taxi and water-taxi ride to reach the most popular hotels. From Marsh Harbour Airport to Hope Town on Elbow Cay, the cost is about $12 for the transfer. From the Treasure Cay Airport to Green Turtle Cay, the charge is about $15. Elbow Cay costs about $11 for the transfer. It's also possible to make arrangements for a taxi tour of Great or Little Abaco. These, however, are expensive, and you don't really see that much either. It's better to sightsee on foot in one of the Loyalist settlements, such as New Plymouth. Taxis are independently owned and operated, and there's no central number to call. You can easily find a taxi at the airport. If you need one otherwise, you can ask the staff at your hotel to summon one for you.

✔ **Hoofing it.** Marsh Harbour is a small town, and you can get around it on foot, but you won't really find that much to see. We'd suggest saving your legs for a day trip over to Elbow Cay (see Chapter 18) where you can walk endlessly along its beaches of golden sand.

✔ **Hopping aboard a boat.** Because Marsh Harbour is the boating capital of The Bahamas, a boat, of course, is used by some Bahamians more than a car for getting around. **Albury's Ferry Service** (☎ 242-367-3147) will take you to the most interesting offshore islands, including Elbow Cay and Great Guana Cay, to be explored in the pages ahead.

A taste of the Abacos

In Marsh Harbour, conch salad is sold right on the docks. "It'll make a man out of you," one local vendor tells everybody, even if the person is a woman. If you stick around long enough, you'll see Billy Thompson coming by in his little truck. He's said to make the world's best homemade soursop-and-mango ice cream. If you'd like to go really casual, try **Island Bakery**, Don McKay Boulevard (☎ 242-367-2129), which has the best Bahamian bread and cinnamon rolls on the island, often emerging fresh from the oven. You might even pick up the makings for a picnic.

Dining in Marsh Harbour

Angler's Restaurant
$$ Marsh Harbour   BAHAMIAN/SEAFOOD

At the Boat Harbour, overlooking the Sea of Abaco, this is the main restaurant of the town's major resort. With a nautical theme and Bahamian decor, it showcases the cuisine of Austrian-born chef Dietmar Uiberreiter. Within a few steps of your seat, dock pilings rise from the water, yachts and fishing boats come and go, and the place is open and airy. The menu changes daily, but fresh seafood, which the chef prepares with finesse, is always featured, along with a well-chosen selection of meat and poultry dishes. Begin with spicy lobster bisque, or perhaps a timbale of grilled vegetables or crab Rangoon, served on bean-sprout slaw with a pineapple-coconut sauce. Main dishes often dance with flavor, notably the lobster stir in a mango chili sauce, or the guava-glazed charred lamb chops. The freshly caught red snapper we were recently served had just the right infusion of fresh basil.

In the Abaco Beach Resort & Boat Harbour, Boat Harbour. ☎ 242-367-2158. Reservations recommended for dinner. Main courses: $14.50–$28.50. AE, MC, V. Open: daily 7:30 a.m.–2:30 p.m. for breakfast and lunch, 6–10 p.m. for dinner.

Bistro Mezzamare
$–$$ Marsh Harbour   BAHAMIAN/ITALIAN

Only the Angler's Restaurant (see the entry earlier in this chapter) is more sophisticated and international than this winning choice. Set adjacent to the Conch Inn and the upscale marina facilities of The Moorings, it attracts a lot of yachties and visiting professional athletes. The menu includes shrimp and crabmeat salad, lobster salad, seafood platters, at least four preparations of grouper and snapper, and just about everything a chef could conceivably concoct from a conch. The regulars don't even have to consult the menu; they just ask, "What's good?" on any given night. Many diners gravitate to the succulent pasta dishes, such as penne mirella (with shiitake mushrooms). If you're frittering away a few hours, drop in for a "Horny Conch," a rum-based drink with secret ingredients. The bar, set beneath an octagon gazebo near the piers, is a fine place to meet people.

At the Conch Inn (The Moorings), E. Bay St. ☎ *242-367-4444. Main courses: dinner $16–$21; lunch salads, sandwiches, and platters $7–$13. MC, V. Open: Wed–Mon 8 a.m.–9:30 p.m.*

Flippers Restaurant
$$ Marsh Harbour   BAHAMIAN/AMERICAN

This is a straightforward and uncomplicated diner-style restaurant, without the flair and pizzazz of Sapodilly's, Mangoes, or Wally's. It was established in the town's biggest shopping center in the late 1990s, with a well-scrubbed, no-nonsense decor that includes ceramic-tile floors, plastic-laminate bar tops, and half paneling. Menu items include burgers, sandwiches, and platters of grouper, shrimp, steak, chicken, and lobster.

Memorial Plaza. ☎ *242-367-4657. Reservations not accepted. Lunch main courses $5–$12; dinner main courses $17–$28. AE, MC, V. Open: Mon 8 a.m.–3 p.m.; Tuesday to Saturday 8 a.m.–9:30 p.m., Sun noon–3 p.m.*

The Jib Room
$–$$ Marsh Harbour   BAHAMIAN/AMERICAN

This funky restaurant/bar is a hangout for local residents and boat owners who savor its welcoming spirit. If you want the house-special cocktail, a Bilge Burner, get ready for a head-spinning combination of apricot brandy, rum, coconut juice, and vodka. Sunday night brings Jib's steak barbecue, when as many as 300 steaks are served. The only other dinner option is Wednesday, when grilled baby back ribs may be the featured dish of the day. Other choices include a seafood platter, New York strip steak, and broiled lobster — and yes, you've had it all before in better versions, but dishes are well-prepared. Go for the convivial atmosphere rather than the food.

Marsh Harbour Marina, Pelican Shores. ☎ *242-367-2700. Lunch platters $5–$12 each; fixed-price dinners $18–$22. MC, V. Open: for lunch Thurs–Sat 11:30 a.m.– 2:30 p.m.; for dinner Wed–Sat 7–11 p.m.*

Mangoes Restaurant
$–$$ Marsh Harbour   BAHAMIAN/AMERICAN

Set near the harborfront, in one of the town's most distinctive buildings, Mangoes is the best, and certainly the most popular, restaurant on the island, attracting both yachties and locals. It boasts a cedar-topped bar and a cathedral ceiling that soars above a deck jutting out over the water.

Somehow the chefs seem to try a little harder here, offering a typical menu adding a hint of island spirit. Our faithful friend, grilled grouper, is dressed up a bit with mango and tomatoes, and cracked conch make an appearance as well. Your best bet, as in nearly all Bahamian restaurants, is probably the fresh catch of the day, and Mangoes is no exception. At lunch, you can sample their locally famous "conch burger."

Front St. ☎ *242-367-2366. Reservations recommended. Lunch $10.50–$16.50; main courses $13.50–$27.50. AE, MC, V. Open: daily for breakfast and lunch from 7 a.m.–3 p.m. and for dinner from 6:30 to 9 p.m.*

Mother Merle's Fishnet
$ Dundas Town BAHAMIAN

Many of the meals eaten aboard the yachts and sailing craft in the nearby harbor are prepared here. There's no dining room on the premises, so don't expect a place to sit and linger, although the well-prepared food, if you don't mind hauling it off to another venue, makes the limitations most palatable. The setting is a cement house on the town's main street. Inside, you'll find the gentle but aging matriarch Merle Williams, who is assisted by her able-bodied daughters, Angela and Shirley. As Mother Merle tells it, all Bahamian women are good cooks — a bit of an exaggeration — but you'll believe her words when you taste her family's three different preparations of chicken, all prepared by secret family recipes. Locals swear that Mother Merle makes the best cracked conch in the Abacos, and she's also known for her different preparations of grouper.

Dundas Town. ☎ *242-367-2770. Take-out service only. Main courses: $11–$17. No credit cards. Open: Mon–Sat 6:30 p.m.–10:30 p.m.*

Sapodilly's Bar & Grill
$ Marsh Harbour BAHAMIAN

One of Marsh Harbour's newest restaurants occupies an open-air pavilion across the road from the harborfront, in an area of town known as "the tourist strip." Even if you eventually head into the high-raftered interior dining room, take time out for a drink or two on the covered open-air deck, surrounded by vibrant Junkanoo colors and a crowd of local hipsters, yacht owners, marina workers, and businessmen visiting from other parts of The Bahamas. Lunch might consist of grilled fish sandwiches, burgers, salads, and quiche. Dinners are more elaborate, with 12-ounce New York strip steak, a flavor-filled shrimp kebabs in teriyaki sauce, and zesty curried fillets of grouper. Live music plays every Friday and Saturday from 8 to 11 p.m.

E. Bay St. ☎ *242-367-3498. Reservations recommended. Lunch platters and sandwiches $5–$12; dinner main course $17–$26. AE, MC, V. Open: Tues–Sun for lunch from 11:30 a.m.–3 p.m. and daily for dinner from 6 p.m.–9 p.m.*

The premier yachting event

In July, Marsh Harbour hosts **Regatta Week,** the premier yachting event in the Abacos, attracting sailboats and their crews from around the world. Every year, it's held sometime between Independence Day in the United States and Independence Day in The Bahamas (July 4 and July 10). A great number of the yachties participating in this event stay at the Green Turtle Club (see Chapter 19). For registration forms and more information, write to **Regatta Time in Abaco,** P.O. Box AB20551, Marsh Harbour, Abaco.

Wally's
$$ Marsh Harbour   BAHAMIAN/INTERNATIONAL

This eatery occupies a tidy pink colonial villa on a lawn dotted with hibiscus, across the street from the water. It has an outdoor terrace, a boutique, and an indoor bar and dining area filled with Haitian paintings. The special drink of the house is a Wally's Special, containing four kinds of rum and a medley of fruit juices. The chef prepares the best Bahamian cracked conch at Marsh Harbour, as well as tender filet mignon, lamb chops, tarragon chicken, and an excellent version of smothered grouper. Main dishes come with a generous house salad and vegetables. The place really shines at lunchtime, when things can get very busy as hungry diners devour dolphinfish burgers, several kinds of chicken platters, and some well-stuffed sandwiches. Part of the style here comes courtesy of sisters Barbara and Maureen Smith, who head to Paris every fall and bring their culinary discoveries back to their enterprise in Marsh Harbour.

E. Bay St. ☎ 242-367-2074. Reservations recommended for dinner. Lunch sandwiches and platters $9.50–$12; dinner main courses $19.75–$28.50. AE, DISC, MC, V. Open: Mon–Sat for lunch from 11:30 a.m.–3 p.m., Fri–Sat only for dinner from 6 p.m.–9 p.m., except between Mar–July when it's open Tues–Sat for dinner from 6 p.m.–9 p.m. Closed 6 weeks during Sept–Oct.

Fun On and Off the Beach in Marsh Harbour

Exploring almost deserted beaches and sailing to nearby islands such as Elbow Cay are part of the fun of any visit to Great Abaco Island. Nothing's more fun than getting into your rented car and exploring the sparsely inhabited island. The southerly route is more scenic and contains more interest than the trek north.

Hitting the beaches

If you're planning to stay directly in Marsh Harbour, you won't find picture postcard beaches. However, if you head south along the coast, you'll find any number of secluded sandy beaches, all without facilities.

Another possibility, if you're a true beach buff, is to take one of Albury's ferries (☎ 242-365-6010) either to Elbow Cay (see Chapter 18), or Great Guana Cay. (See "Taking a Great Day Trip," later in this chapter.)

Of the major towns of the Out Islands, Marsh Harbour has one of the least promising and least appealing sets of beaches. You can opt for any of a trio of private beaches, but none are very enticing, and all carry the stigma of not really wanting outsiders. The easiest of these three to circumvent is the one at the Abaco Beach Resort, but it's small, not really fabulous, and, again, private. Buy a drink for a local at the hotel bar, and you're in, but that, at best, is a somewhat uncomfortable arrangement.

To compensate, beachgoers get into their cars and head south of Marsh Harbour. After 15 to 20 minutes of southbound driving, and at points south of Little Harbour, lots of good beaches begin to appear. They include unsupervised sands, usually without facilities of any kind, with names like **Guiness Schoener Bay.** The beaches in the vicinity of the hamlet of **Casuarina Point** benefit from some battered, all-Bahamian restaurants in the vicinity.

Some swimmers heading south from Marsh Harbour make it a point to go eastward from the main highway whenever an offshoot road appears, usually at points near Little Harbour or at points south of Little Harbour. Other times, they simply stop their cars wherever they feel like it.

None of the beaches of Great Abaco Island have facilities or lifeguards. Guard your valuables.

Finding water fun for everyone

Water surrounds Great Abaco Island and is a part of daily life but can also provide the most amusement for visitors, far more than land attractions.

Scuba divers check out the nearby **Pelican Cays Land and Sea Park.** Although you won't find organized excursions, Dive Abaco is the best source of information and may arrange a trip here. You can also drive down to the park by following the road immediately south of Marsh Harbour and then turning east at the sign leading toward the park. Several areas here have small beaches suitable for swimming. The easiest jumping-off point is at Pelican Harbour.

Dive Abaco, Marsh Harbour (☎ 800-247-5338 in the U.S., or 242-367-2787), can provide services as simple as renting snorkel gear or as in-depth as offering full dive trips to tunnels and caverns in the world's third-longest barrier reef. Uncertified novice divers can take all-inclusive resort courses for $140. Two-tank dives, including tanks and weights for certified divers, are $75. Trips depart daily at 9:30 a.m., and afternoon trips are dictated by demand. Ask for owner-operator Keith Rogers.

Sea Horse Boat Rentals, at the Abaco Beach Resort/Boat Harbour Marina (☎ 242-367-2513), also rents snorkel gear. One of the best places to snorkel, with a colorful reef, moray eels, and a plethora of beautiful rainbow-hued fish, is **Mermaid Reef,** which is an offshore reef with worthwhile snorkeling possibilities. It lies on a narrow, scrub-covered peninsula known as **Pelican Shore**), which forms the northernmost edge of Marsh Harbour's harborfront. Clients can drive to a point near the origin of Pelican Shore and then trek across a stretch of scrub and sand for the debut of their swim out to Mermaid Reef. Alternatively, some hardy locals sometimes swim from the center of Marsh Harbour across the harbor, walk across the very narrow sands of Pelican Shore, and then swim once again the short distance to Mermaid Reef.

On Deck: Riding the Waves without Getting Wet

Because the Abacos are the boating capital of The Bahamas, many arrive for only one purpose: to charter a boat and go sailing.

Ask about the depth of the harbor before you rent, or even more importantly, before you attempt to navigate your way in or out of Marsh Harbour, because Hurricane Floyd changed the configuration of the channel. Yachts with deep drafts have reported trouble getting in and out of the port recently.

If you'd like to try bareboating in The Bahamas — seagoing without captain or crew — **Abaco Bahamas Charters,** 505 Beachland Blvd. (☎ 800-626-5690; Fax: 242-366-0151), can set you up; weekly charters of a 44-foot boat begin at $2,500, with a $1,500 deposit required. Only experienced sailors can rent.

The Moorings (☎ 800-535-7289 or 242-367-4000) is one of the leading charter sailboat outfitters in the world. It operates from an eagle's nest perch behind the Conch Inn Resort and Marina, overlooking a labyrinth of piers and wharves — at least 75 berths, with more on the way — where hundreds of upscale watercraft are tied up (many of them are for rent). With one of its vessels, you can enjoy short sails between the islands, stopping at white sandy beaches and snug anchorages.

Yacht rentals generally range from $405 to $1,255 a day, with a skipper costing another $144 per day, and an onboard cook (if you want one) priced at an additional $124 per day.

For the more casual boater, **Sea Horse Boat Rentals,** at the Abaco Beach Resort (☎ **242-367-2513**), offers some of the best rentals. An 18-foot Boston Whaler rents for $150 per day, and you can also book a 22-foot Privateer for $170 per day. Other vessels are also for rent, and all boats are equipped with a Bimini top, coolers, a compass, and a swimming platform, along with life jackets, a paddle, docking lines, and other equipment.

Exploring Marsh Harbour's Land Attractions

In monuments or sightseeing attractions, Nassau doesn't fear competition from little Marsh Harbour, which is regarded by some as a mere refueling stopover. However, Marsh Harbour is the best center for exploring the nature-created attractions of Great Abaco Island, which consists of both Great Abaco and Little Abaco.

A recently completed, fully graded, and tarred main highway now links all the settlements on the "mainland," with such colorfully named hamlets as Fire Road, Mango Hill, Coopers Town, Joe Creek, Red Bays, Snake Cay, Little Harbour, Sandy Point, Cherokee Sound, and our favorite, "Hole in the Wall," lying at the "bottom" of Great Abaco.

Driving south for 25 miles from Marsh Harbour along the Great Abaco Highway, you come first to **Cherokee Sound**, with a population of 150 dwellers, at the end of a peninsula jutting out into Cherokee Sound. Residents are descended from Loyalists who fled mainland U.S. in 1783 and remained faithful to the British Crown.

These people faced an inhospitable land and for two centuries have tried to make a living as best they can. The men dive for lobsters or go out at night "sharking." The jaws of the sharks are sold in Marsh Harbour. They also hunt down tiniki crabs. as well as pigeon and wild boar in the remote pinelands of the Abacos.

From Cherokee, you can head north to Little Harbour, about 30 miles to the south of Marsh Harbour. Here you come to **Pete Johnston's Foundry** (☎ **242-367-2720**). In the Abaco gift and souvenir shops, you'll see a remarkable book, *Artist on His Island,* detailing the true-life adventures of Randolph and Margot Johnson, who lived a Swiss Family Robinson-type adventure with their three sons. Arriving on this southerly point of the Abacos aboard their old Bahamian schooner, the *Langosta,* they lived in one of the natural caves on the island until they eventually erected a thatched dwelling for themselves.

That was in 1951. Now the Johnsons, including son Pete, have achieved international fame as artists and sculptors — though they still live at Little Harbour Island, a cay shaped like a circle, with a white-sand beach running along most of it.

Mr. Johnson, using an old "lost-wax" method, casts his bronze sculptures, many of which are in prestigious galleries today. Mrs. Johnson creates porcelain figurines of island life — birds, fish, boats, and fishers. She also works in glazed metals. They welcome visitors at their studio daily from 10 to 11 a.m. and from 2 to 3 p.m. You can also purchase their art, which comes in a wide price range.

Before leaving, you can stop in for a drink at the laidback **Pete's Pub.** This rustic pub is beloved by yachties throughout the Abacos. The art work is intriguing (you can purchase it), and the beer is cold. The pub was constructed in part by the timbers of the **Langosta.** In the evening, Pete might sing a medley of sea chanties accompanying himself on his guitar.

After leaving Cherokee and Little Harbour, you can return to the Great Abaco Highway, heading south once again to reach the little fishing village of **Casuarina Point** west of Cherokee Sound. Here you'll find a lovely stretch of golden sands and some jade-colored boneflats.

The way south comes to Crossing Rocks, a little fishing village 40 miles to the south of Marsh Harbour, noted for its 2-mile-long beach of golden sand. The hamlet where locals barely eke out a living takes its name from the isthmus where Great Abaco Island narrows to its thinnest point.

After traveling south again, you come to a fork in the road, the southern road going to the Abaco National Park (also called Bahamas National Trust Sanctuary) and the aptly named Hole-in-the-Wall, the end of the line for Great Abaco.

Living It Up After the Sun Goes Down

The most popular gathering spot in town is the **Sand Bar** at the Abaco Beach Resort & Boat Harbour (☎ 242-367-2158), opening onto the Sea of Abaco. The yachting crowd, often from Miami, hangs out here, swapping tall tales of the sea while downing lethal rum punches. Another good hangout is at **Wally's,** E. Bay St. (☎ 242-367-2074), the second most frequented place to hang out. You can enjoy Wally's special punch on an outdoor terrace or inside a cozy bar. On Wednesday and Saturday, live entertainment is often presented. **Sapodilly's Bar & Grill,** E. Bay St. (☎ 242-367-3498), attracts an interesting blend of locals and visitors, some of whom play at its pool table, others preferring to mix and mingle at the bar.

Taking a Great Day Trip

The greatest day trip is to Hope Town on **Elbow Cay** (see Chapter 18). Great Guana, is far lesser known but also an intriguing jaunt by ferry from Marsh Harbour.

Longest of the Abaco cays, Great Guana, on the east side of the chain, stretches 7 miles from tip to tip and lies between Green Turtle Cay and Man-O-War Cay. The beachfront running the length of the cay is spectacular, one of the loveliest in The Bahamas. The reef fishing is superb, and bonefish are plentiful in the shallow bays.

The settlement stretches along the beach at the head of the palm-fringed Kidd's Cove, named after the pirate, and the ruins of an old sisal mill near the western end of the island make for an interesting detour. The island has about 150 residents, most of them descendants of Loyalists who left Virginia and the Carolinas to settle in this remote place, often called the "last spot of land before Africa."

As in similar settlements in New Plymouth and Man-O-War Cay, houses here resemble those of old New England. Over the years, the traditional pursuits of the islanders have been boatbuilding, carpentry, farming, and fishing. It won't take you long to explore the village, because it has only two small stores, a one-room schoolhouse, and an Anglican church — that's about it.

Albury's Ferry Service, Marsh Harbour (☎ 242-365-6010), runs a twice-daily service to Great Guana Cay. A round-trip ticket costs $12 for adults, $6 for children.

Instead of driving around the island, most people get around in small boats. On the cay, boats are available to charter for a half day or a full day (or a month, for that matter). For example, a 23-foot sailboat, fully equipped for living and cruising, is available for charter, and deep-sea fishing trips can be arranged.

If you'd like to stay at this remote location, **Dolphin Beach Resort** is a good hotel. (See "Checking Out Marsh Harbour's Best Accommodations," earlier in this chapter.)

Most visitors arrive just for the day, returning to Marsh Harbour for the night.

For fun on the beach, head for **Nipper's Beach Bar & Grill** (☎ 242-365-5143), a dive where visitors hang out with the locals. Right on the sands, you sit in split-level gazebos and take in the surf, the most stunning seascape in the Abacos, with a snorkeling reef just 12 yards offshore. Burgers and well-stuffed sandwiches satisfy your hunger at lunch. But the best times to go are on a Wednesday, for one of the bonfires and fireworks displays, or on a Sunday afternoon, for a pig roast. One guest is said to have consumed five "Nipper Trippers" — and lived to tell about it. This is the bartender's specialty, a mix of five different rums along with tropical juices.

Fast Facts: Marsh Harbour

Babysitting

Hotel staff can help you find a babysitter.

Bank

The most convenient is Barclays Bank on Don MacKay Boulevard (☎ 242-367-2152).

Credit Cards

For credit card assistance, contact MasterCard (☎ 800-307-7309) or call Visa collect (☎ 800-847-2911).

Directory Assistance

Call ☎ 916.

Emergencies

Call the police ☎ 242-367-2560.

Information

When you need visitor-related information, contact the Abaco Tourist Office (☎ 242-367-3067), at Queen Elizabeth Drive in the commercial heart of town (☎ 242-367-3067). It's open Monday to Friday from 9 a.m. to 5:30 p.m.

Medical Attention

The best medical clinic in the Abacos is at the Government Clinic, Queen Elizabeth

Road (☎ 242-367-2510). Hours are Monday through Friday from 9 a.m. to 5 p.m.

Pharmacies

For medication, go to the Chemist Shop Pharmacy, Don MacKay Boulevard (☎ 242-367-3106). It's open Monday through Saturday from 8:30 a.m. to 5:30 p.m.

Post Office

The Marsh Harbour Post Office is on Don MacKay Boulevard (☎ 242-367-2571).

Safety

More crime occurs in Marsh Harbour than anywhere else in the Abacos, but that doesn't mean it's the venue for gangland slayings evocative of Chicago in the '20s. Remember to take the same precautions that you should take whether you're at home or on vacation. Keep valuables in a safe place and don't go into deserted, unfamiliar areas alone at night.

Taxis

Taxis meet incoming flights at the Marsh Harbour airport. During your stay, staff at your hotel can call one for you whenever you need one.

Chapter 18

Elbow Cay

● ●

In This Chapter

▶ Finding Elbow Cay's best accommodations and restaurants

▶ Getting around Elbow Cay

▶ Exploring beaches, water sports, and land attractions

● ●

*V*isit Elbow Cay and you risk coming back year after year, as so many of the Canadians, Americans, and Europeans who now own vacation homes here have done. The main settlement is Hope Town, a charming Cape Cod-like village with narrow paved streets, saltbox cottages, little clapboard houses with white picket fences around flowering gardens, and a red-and-white striped lighthouse. Elbow Cay has only a few hotels, but many villas and private houses are available to rent. See the map in this chapter for more on the layout of Elbow Cay.

Elbow Cay's long and secluded white-sand shores, some backed by sandy dunes, are serious contenders for The Bahamas' most stunning locales. Accommodations are on or near sandy shores, but because the hotels are small and few in number, beaches remain virtually vacant.

Autumn is quiet in these parts, so some hotels and restaurants close in September and October. Elbow Cay is not a bustling island with big resorts, so you'll find few places that have televisions or even phones in the rooms.

Checking Out Elbow Cay's Best Accommodations

Abaco Inn
$$ White Sound

This sophisticated, 22-unit adult retreat lies 2 miles south of Hope Town and faces a white sandy beach on White Sound. The inn stands at the narrowest point in Elbow Cay. On the east side, the more turbulent surf of the ocean washes in. A large saltwater swimming pool looks down upon the Atlantic. At a distance up the shore is a secluded beach where some buffs sun in the nude, which is technically illegal in The Bahamas. More of a resort than its chief rivals, Hope Town Harbour Lodge and Club Soleil Resort, Abaco Inn offers you a choice of eight luxury villa suites with sunrise and sunset sea views or a series of simply but comfortably furnished guest cottages fronting either the Atlantic or White Sound. In the main house is a stone fireplace in the cozy lounge, with a breeze swept deck fronting the water. Yachties favor the bar or the on-site restaurant, one of the island's finest. Shaded by sea grape and palm trees, hammocks wide enough for two are strung outside cottages. Furnishings are rustic but perfectly comfortable, and you'll find a dog-eared selection of books left by previous travelers. Vans periodically take guests to and from Hope Town. The use of bicycles is complimentary, and many people rent boats.

Two miles south of Hope Town. ☎ *800-468-8799 or 242-366-0133. Fax: 242-366-0113. Internet:* www.abacoinn.com. *Rack rates: $140–$165 for a double room. AE, DISC, MC, V.*

Club Soleil Resort
$$ Hope Town

This colorfully landscaped seven-room hotel, with a popular seafood restaurant, is across the harbor from Hope Town. The accommodations aren't as fine as those at Abaco Inn (see the preceding entry), but they're comfortable and far more tranquil because of the secluded position of this club near the lighthouse on the western edge of Hope Town. The resort is reached by boat — either one rented by you and moored at the hotel's marina or else a hotel boat, which can be sent to bring you over. Once here, you'll find several lovely golden sand beaches, although a mid-sized saltwater pool is on site as well. The accommodations are medium in size and come with shower units, each with a clean-cut, tasteful decor. Bedrooms have grace notes like private balconies opening onto the water, tile floors, and cedar-lined closets for storing your stuff. What you won't find are phones, but you'll get a TV with VCR. Fishing, sailing, diving — all sorts of water sports — even boat rentals, can be arranged by the staff.

Near the lighthouse. ☎ *800-688-4752 or 242-366-0003. Fax: 242-366-0254. Internet:* www.clubsoleil.com. *Rack rates: $130 for a double occupancy, $135 for a triple occupancy, $145 for a quadruple occupancy. AE, MC, V*

Hope Town Harbour Lodge
$$–$$$ Hope Town

This Hope Town landmark sits on a narrow bluff between the harbor with its red-and-white striped lighthouse and the ocean with its white sand beach. Snorkeling is idyllic at the reef just offshore, where spotting turtles and dolphins along with all kinds of crayon-colored fish is the norm.

Elbow Cay Hotels & Restaurants

HOTELS ■

Abaco Inn **6**

Club Soleil Resort **2**

Hope Town Harbor Lodge **1**

Hope Town Hideaways **10**

Sea Spray Resort Villas & Marina **7**

RESTAURANTS ◆

Abaco Inn **6**

Boat House Restaurant **8**

Cap'n Jacks **3**

Club Soleil **2**

Harbour's Edge **4**

Hope Town Harbour Lodge **1**

Munchie's **5**

Rudy's Place **9**

COOK'S COVER

ANNA CAY

EAGLE ROCK   HOPE TOWN

PARROT CAYS

Hope Town Harbour

Footpath

Queen's Hwy

WHITE SOUND

AUNT PAT'S BAY

Garbanzo Beach

Tahiti Beach

Tilloo Cay

0   50 mi
0   50 km

GRAND BAHAMA   ELBOW CAY

FLORIDA

GREAT ABACO ISLAND

Miami

Some of the 19 cheerfully decorated guest rooms have decks overlooking the pool and the ocean. Book one of these units, which are across the road from the main building, if you want a mini-fridge, and, more importantly, if you don't want to climb many stairs. Other rooms are smaller and have views of town and the harbor. A few paces down the road from the main building — historic Butterfly House, one of the oldest surviving homes in Hope Town — has been transformed into a two-bedroom, two-bath, two-deck vacation cottage with a full kitchen. As many as six people can stay here comfortably. You can dine by the saltwater pool, on the terrace high above the harbor, or in the more formal wood-paneled restaurant. Boat rentals and water sports are arranged.

Hope Town, between the harbor and the beach. ☎ 800-316-7844 or 242-366-0095. Fax: 242-366-0286. Internet: www.hopetownlodge.com. *Rack rates: $130–$170 for a double room. MC, V.*

Hope Town Hideaways
$$$ **Hope Town Harbour**

This is like living in your own "second home in The Bahamas. These five gingerbread-trimmed villas lie across the harbor from where the ferry-boats arrive from Marsh Harbour. On 11 acres of grounds, which are reached by boat, this hideaway lives up to its name. The accommodations are part of a larger complex of privately owned homes, surrounded by grounds handsomely landscaped with orange trees, mangoes, and flamboyant bougainvillea. One or two couples — the maximum is six guests — can sleep comfortably in the units, each coming with a large kitchen, dining room, a living area with two single daybeds, and two bedrooms. Furnishings are custom built, and each private bathroom comes with a tub and shower. You're not on the beach but can enjoy a fresh-water pool instead..

Near the lighthouse, on a 12-slip marina. ☎ *242-366-0224. Fax: 242-366-0434. Internet:* www.hopetown.com. *Rack rates: $200–$240 for two people in a two-bedroom, two-bathroom cottage. MC, V*

Sea Spray Resort Villas & Marina
$$–$$$ **White Sound**

These villas lie on 6 acres of landscaped grounds 3½ miles south of Hope Town near the southernmost tip of Elbow Cay. With its jagged limestone coast, the beach at this hotel may not be good for swimming, but surfers have a ball in the rolling waves. Fortunately, a good sandy beach (near Abaco Inn, see the earlier entry) is just a 5-minute walk away, and either an energizing hike or an invigorating bike ride can take you to beautiful, secluded Tahiti Beach. Sea Spray's five oceanside and harborside cottages range from one-bedroom, one-bathroom to two-bedroom, two-bathroom. All have decks, barbecue pits, air-conditioned bedrooms, and ceiling fans. Kitchens are fully equipped, but you don't need to cook because you can find a good restaurant right on the premises. Unlike some homelike accommodations, which have limited housekeeping service, these villas come with daily maid service. Grounds are handsomely landscaped, and the waterfront swimming pool is a relaxing spot. Most guests rent boats here at the 60-slip marina.

About 3 miles south of Hope Town. ☎ *242-366-0065. Fax: 242-366-0383. Internet:* www.seasprayresort.com. *Rack rates: $1,350–$1,950 per week. MC, V.*

Arriving in Elbow Cay

Anyone can board a plane and get off in a vacation spot, but it takes a traveler who's determined not to have an ordinary beach vacation to choose an island like Elbow Cay. Not only do you have to board a plane — or two — but you also have to take a taxi, a ferry, and a shuttle van to get to your hotel — That is, unless you sail in on a boat.

The best way to get to Elbow Cay is to fly into **Marsh Harbour** (see Chapter 17), home of the Abacos' main (but small and easy to navigate) airport. From here, you take a taxi to the dock to catch the ferry to **Hope Town,** about 20 minutes away ($8 each way for adults, $4 for children).

You need to coordinate your flight arrival and departure with the ferry schedule. Ask the staff at your hotel for details or call **Albury's Ferry Service** (☎ **242-365-6010**). If contacted, your hotel staff will meet you at the ferry dock.

Getting around Elbow Cay

Many visitors choose to rent boats to get around the island, explore nearby cays, and go on fishing and snorkeling trips. Even if you're not interested in playing sea captain, you can still move easily around Elbow Cay by considering these options:

- ✔ **Going on wheels.** You can't rent a car on Elbow Cay, but that isn't a problem. Besides, all motor vehicles are banned from Hope Town, the scenic seaside village. If you'd like a golf cart delivered to your hotel, call **Island Cart Rental** (☎ **242-366-0448**); these electric carts go for $40 a day or $240 week. Hotels provide shuttle vans to and from town. Some dining rooms offer pick-up and drop-off service at dinnertime if you call ahead. Bicycles — often free for hotel guests — are available at or near most accommodations.

- ✔ **Hoofing it.** The quiet, narrow streets of Hope Town are reserved for pedestrians, and you can walk to many other parts of tiny Elbow Cay.

- ✔ **Hopping onboard a boat.** Because you have so many secluded islands and empty beaches to explore, boats are to the Abacos what cars are to most of the world. You can either rent your own boat or join a snorkeling, scuba diving, or island-hopping excursion. (See "Finding water fun for everyone," later in this chapter, for details.)

Dining in Elbow Cay

No need to dress up at night on Elbow Cay. **Abaco Inn, Club Soleil,** and **Hope Town Harbour Lodge** are where you find the most upscale dining. Several restaurants provide complimentary transportation to and from your hotel.

Kitchens tend to close between meals. Arrive just a few minutes past 2 p.m., when lunch ends, for example, and you can't get anything but drinks. (Along with some hotels, several restaurants close their doors completely during September and October.) You can find a decent variety of culinary offerings on Elbow Cay, from Bahamian favorites to gourmet international dishes. Most places serve variations of rum punch, and both key lime pie and coconut pie are on every menu.

Turn to Chapter 2 for details about Bahamian specialties and tipping, and the Introduction for an explanation of the price categories used in the following restaurant listings.

Abaco Inn
$$$–$$$$ Outside Hope Town   BAHAMIAN/INTERNATIONAL

This beachside inn offers Elbow Cay's best food served in semi-elegant al fresco settings. The best tables are outside on the bluff overlooking the water. Your breakfast may include a colorful frittata. Lobster salad and pasta dishes are the best choices. Before dinner, guests gather on the deck for drinks. Try a Bahama Breeze (Bacardi Gold, coconut rum, banana rum, apricot brandy, and fruit punch). The evening meal, always changing, could be coconut-crusted grouper or tender New Zealand lamb chops, followed by Abaco Inn's smooth crème brûlée. Musicians occasionally entertain.

Two miles south of Hope Town. ☎ *242-366-0133. Reservations recommended at night. Main courses: $18–$32. DISC, MC, V. Open: Daily for breakfast, lunch, and dinner; call to arrange complimentary transportation to and from the inn.*

Boat House Restaurant
$$–$$$ Sea Spray Resort   BAHAMIAN/INTERNATIONAL

You can dine inside, but why would you want to when you can also sit outside on the deck overlooking the marina? For dinner, the chef's signature Calypso grouper gets top billing: A filet is sautéed in lemon and lime juices with a medley of herbs, then broiled with Nassau Royale, a Bahamian liqueur, and served with freshly toasted almonds and mixed vegetables. Lobster here comes any way you like it. For more variety, try the seafood platter, which includes lobster tail, grouper, and savory conch. On Monday nights, catch the Bahamian barbecue buffet, complete with local specialties, such as cracked conch, grouper fingers, savory barbecued chicken or ribs, johnnycake (a mildly sweet bread, similar to a pancake), peas and rice, and coconut pie, all to the live sounds of Bahamian music.

Call for complimentary transportation to and from Sea Spray Resort.

White Sound, 3–1/2 miles south of Hope Town. ☎ *242-366-0065. Reservations recommended at night. Main courses: $15–$28. MC, V. Open: Mon–Sat for breakfast, lunch, and dinner.*

Club Soleil
$$$ Hope Town Harbour   SEAFOOD

Windows around this breezy wood-paneled dining room at the edge of the harbor make you feel as if you're on a boat. You look out to Hope Town, just across the water. A mini version of town is depicted in the restaurant's driftwood wall sculpture that was created by Vernon Malone (brother of Rudy Malone, owner of this hotel and restaurant). Sunday brunch is the big deal here, with the eggs Benedict getting raves from us. Dinner may be poached salmon or a seafood platter (with shrimp, lobster, and two kinds of local fish), with key lime pie for dessert. All dishes are competently prepared with imported ingredients. The chefs manage very well to turn out a tempting-to-the-palate menu that still doesn't reach the taste levels of the Abaco Inn. For a cocktail, try a Tropical Shock, made from dark, light, and coconut rum with fruit juices.

Make reservations through your hotel or at Vernon's Store in Hope Town. If you don't have your own boat, arrange to be picked up at the post office dock in town and ferried across.

Near the lighthouse at Hope Town Harbour. ☎ *242-366-0003. Reservations recommended for dinner and Sunday brunch. Main courses: $16–$28. MC, V. Open: Daily for breakfast, dinner, and brunch on Sunday.*

Cap'n Jacks
$ Hope Town   BAHAMIAN

Depending on when you come, you may find turtle burgers or crawfish on the menu at this casual al fresco dining spot at the edge of the harbor. Any time of year, the grouper and conch are well prepared and the freshest food on the menu. Landlubbers gravitate toward the more routine fried chicken and burgers. The key lime pie and the chocolate silk pie are justifiably popular dessert choices. Come on Wednesday or Friday for the live local music in the evening between 8 and 11 p.m. Try Cap'n Jacks' version of the omnipresent Goombay Smash.

On the harbor in Hope Town. ☎ *242-366-0247. Main courses: $9.50–$21. MC, V. Open: Mon–Sat 8:30 a.m. until the last patron leaves.*

Harbour's Edge
$$–$$$$ Hope Town   BAHAMIAN

Harbour's Edge is almost always busy, if "busy" is an adjective that can be used on sleepy Elbow Cay. Topped with wooden picnic tables, the deck gives you a front-row seat for the view of the candy-cane lighthouse and the boat-packed harbor. For lunch, the *gullywings* (chicken wings), conch chowder, crawfish salad, and fish sandwiches are all eagerly gobbled up. Competently prepared dinners may be grilled, blackened, or fried grouper, or steamed or grilled Bahamian crawfish. Coconut or key lime pie is usually on the dessert menu. Afternoon happy hours, the

Saturday night DJ, and the island's only pool table make this a lively hangout for a loud, young crowd. Try an Over the Edge, the restaurant's signature drink, made with banana rum and various fruit juices.

Just north of the public dock in Hope Town. ☎ *242-366-0292. Main courses: $15–$23. MC, V. Open: Daily for lunch and dinner (except Tues) 10 a.m. until the last patron leaves; closed Sept–Oct.*

Hope Town Harbour Lodge

$$$–$$$$ **Hope Town   BAHAMIAN/INTERNATIONAL**

Lunch by the pool, overlooking a sandy beach, is a special affair at the Hope Town Harbour Lodge. Popular midday treats are the curried tuna, the curried lobster, and the grouper Rueben. Dinner is served either in the dining room, with its pickled wood paneled walls, or on the terrace above the harbor. Consider the Chinese-style grouper spring rolls served with a mustard-laced chutney or the peppered filet mignon. The menu is hardly inventive but items are prepared well and properly seasoned. Sometimes a fisherman will bring in a big marlin that's grilled to perfection.

Between the beach and the harbor in Hope Town. ☎ *242-366-0095. Reservations recommended at night. Main courses: $15–$35. MC, V. Open: for lunch and dinner.*

Munchie's

$ **Hope Town   BAHAMIAN**

Bahamian-born, European-trained Norris Smith spent years as the acclaimed chef at Hope Town Harbour Lodge before opening this snack stand in 1993. He now whips up the island's best burgers and sandwiches made from turkey, beef, conch, or grouper, along with peas and rice, macaroni and cheese, and other local favorites that have brought him a loyal following among both residents and repeat visitors. Take your food with you to the beach, or relax at one of the umbrella-shaded tables.

On Back St., across from Vernon's Store. ☎ *242-366-0423. Prices range from about $5–$10. Open: Daily 10 a.m.–10 p.m.; closed mid-Sept–mid-Oct.*

Rudy's Place

$$ **Just outside town   BAHAMIAN**

At Rudy's, you feel you've been invited to dine with friends, because this rustic restaurant is in a former private residence. The hearty meals include the island's best conch fritters, soup (maybe potato, lima bean, or broccoli), a fresh salad, freshly baked warm bread such as cinnamon raisin and dessert (try the "chocolate suicide" cake). Your main course could be New York strip steak, lamb chops with mint jelly, or turtle steak (an endangered species) sautéed with mushrooms. the most justifiably popular choice is the crawfish, which is removed from the shell, lightly battered, fried, replaced, and baked with Parmesan cheese. The wine list offers a good selection of French, German, Portuguese, and American vintages.

Don't be surprised if your waiter is a child — the son or daughter of one of the other workers. When you call to make a reservation, you can arrange complimentary transportation to and from your hotel.

Center Line Rd. ☎ 242-366-0062. Reservations required. Complete dinner: $20–$30. MC, V. Open: Daily (except Sun) for dinner; closed Sept–Oct.

Fun On and Off the Beach in Elbow Cay

Exploring empty beaches and sailing to nearby cays are activities central to any Elbow Cay vacation. On dry land, the small harbor-side village known as **Hope Town** is the place to wander.

Hitting the beaches

Near Sea Spray Resort, **Garbanzo Beach** lures many surfers. Isolated **Tahiti Beach,** at the southern end of the island (a little more than a mile from Sea Spray), got its name from its thick wall of palms. At low tide, the shelling can be excellent along this gorgeous curve of sand, and these shallow waters make for good bonefishing, too. Across the cut, you can see uninhabited **Tilloo Cay** and the thrashing waves of the Atlantic in the distance.

Tahiti Beach is about a 10-minute bike ride from Sea Spray and about 20 minutes from **Abaco Inn,** both in the White Sound area. To get here, you may have to walk your bike up and down a few of the small, but rocky, rises.

Along the way, you pass sea grape trees, fluffy long-needled pines, and other varied roadside vegetation. Turn left when you come to the first major left (by the house on the bluff). Turn right when you see two stone pillars. Go downhill and turn left at the end of the road at the wire fences. Take this path to the end. Walk along the dense palm grove to the beach. Because you're heading for the shore, which is public, ignore the "Private. No Trespassing" signs.

With their irresistible deserted beaches, pencil-thin Tilloo Cay and the tiny **Pelican Cays** lie to the south of Elbow Cay. They make excellent targets for a day's sail. The waters around Tilloo Cay, packed with grouper and conch, are particularly good for both fishing and swimming. In the **Pelican Cays Land and Sea Park, Sandy Cay Reef** is one of the most colorful dive sites around. The area is protected, so line fishing, spear fishing, craw fishing, and shelling are all taboo.

Finding water fun for everyone

A trip to The Bahamas wouldn't be right if you didn't take part in at least one oceanic activity during your visit.

Through **Froggies Out Island Adventures** (☎ 242-366-0431), two-tank dives start at $55, plus equipment. Resort courses run $130 and certification courses, $500. Half-day snorkel boat trips start at $40, and you can spend plenty of time — as much as 2 whole hours — in the water. If you'd rather stick closer to shore, most hotels have snorkel gear on hand to rent or lend to guests who don't bring their own.

The waves and breezes at **Garbanzo Beach,** in the **White Sound** area, make it prime hang-ten territory. If you don't bring your own surfboard, the staff at nearby **Sea Spray Resort** (☎ 242-366-0065) can help you get one.

On Deck: Riding the Waves without Getting Wet

The waters off the coast of Elbow Cay are a popular spot for boating and fishing. Head down to the marina if you want to join in the fun.

At the 60-slip **Sea Spray Resort** marina (☎ 242-366-0065), 20-foot powerboats run from $135 a day, $120 per day if you rent for 3 days, and $700 per week. For rentals starting at about $90 a day for a 17-foot Boston Whaler, call **Island Marine** (☎ 242-366-0282) or **Dave's Boat Rentals** (☎ 242-366-0029). Ask about recommendations for local fishing guides.

If you want to forego the 20-minute ferry ride to Elbow Cay after you've arrived at the airport in Marsh Harbour, you can rent a boat and get here on your own and then use the boat for your entire vacation. At **The Moorings** (☎ 800-535-7289 or 242-367-4000), rates start at around $350 a day for a 35-foot monohull boat that can carry a maximum of four people.

Exploring Elbow Cay's Land Attractions

No cars are allowed in the heart of **Hope Town.** Bikers and pedestrians have these narrow paved streets, with names like Loves' Lane, to themselves. What you do find are some harbor-side restaurants and pastel-painted saltbox cottages with purple and orange bougainvillea tumbling over stone and picket fences. Amid the usual island fare at the handful of souvenir shops, you see resort wear made from Androsia, the fabric produced on the Bahamian island of Andros.

Stores in Hope Town are shut tight on Sunday, and the various churches — surprising in number for such a tiny village — are in full swing. You may happen upon the outdoor Catholic service held in waterfront **Jarret Park Playground,** next to the main dock.

To find out why Malone is such a common surname, stop by the **Wyannie Malone Museum** (officially open most days from 10 a.m. to noon, but unofficially open "whenever"). This small collection of island lore is in tribute to the South Carolinian widow and mother of four who founded Hope Town around 1783. Like other parts of the Abacos, including **Green Turtle Cay** and **Man-O-War Cay,** Elbow Cay was settled by European Americans loyal to the British Crown. Unwilling to face the outcome of the American Revolution, they began new lives in The Bahamas.

The most photographed site in the Out Islands is **Hope Town's red-and-white striped lighthouse** at the edge of the harbor. Before the lighthouse was erected in 1838, many of Hope Town's residents made a good living luring ships toward shore to be wrecked on the treacherous reefs and rocks turn the salvaged cargoes into cash. To protect their livelihood, some people tried in vain to destroy this beacon while it was being built. Today, you can climb to the top of the 130-foot tower for panoramic views of the harbor and town. Most weekdays between 10 a.m. and 4 p.m., the lighthouse keeper will be happy to give you a peek. The lighthouse is within walking distance of **Club Soleil** and **Hope Town Hideaways.** If you're staying elsewhere, you can make arrangements through your hotel for a visit.

Living It Up after the Sun Goes Down: Elbow Cay's Nightlife

Particularly on Saturday nights (when there's a DJ), a young party crowd gathers at **Harbour's Edge** (☎ 242-366-0292), a Hope Town bar and restaurant with the island's only pool table. On Monday night, Bahamian barbecues draw many people to **Sea Spray Resort** (☎ 242-366-0065), about 3 miles from Hope Town. The food is as good as the low prices, and you can hear live music. Other evenings, people hang out at the bars of hotels and restaurants — or they turn in early to rest up for yet another day of exploring.

A Great Day Trip from Elbow Cay

Spend a day not only scuba diving or snorkeling but also island hopping, with **Froggies Out Island Adventures** (☎ 242-366-0431). You have easy access in and out of the water from this company's double-deck 35- or 55-foot yachts, which come complete with bathrooms. While you sit on the top deck or in the shade down below, your boat may pass a pod of dolphins. You stop at **Fowl Cay National Park,** filled with caves and 55-foot pillars of coral. If you're snorkeling, you may not be able to swim in and out of the grottoes, but you can see plenty of fish, including frown-faced groupers, and other colorful marine life. You may even spot sharks.

You stop at **Guana Cay,** a pretty island that's even quieter than Elbow Cay, for lunch at a restaurant, and then you head to **Man-O-War Cay** to roam around the handsome old shipbuilding village. (For more details about Man-O-War Cay, see Chapter 19.) Nature walks and beachcombing are part of this excursion. Scuba divers pay $85, adult snorkelers $45, and children $25.

Fast Facts: Elbow Cay

Babysitting

Hotel staff can help you find a babysitter.

Bank

Canadian Imperial Bank (CIBC), in Hope Town, is open on Tuesday mornings.

Credit Cards

For credit card assistance, contact MasterCard (☎ 800-307-7309) or call Visa collect (☎ 800-847-2911).

Directory Assistance

Call ☎ 916.

Emergencies

Call the police ☎ 242-367-2560.

Information

When you need visitor-related information, contact the Abaco Tourist Office (☎242-367-3067).

Medical Attention

You need to head to the medical center in Marsh Harbour, a 20-minute boat ride away. In an emergency, contact the staff of your hotel.

Pharmacies

Some hotels and shops in Hope Town carry over-the-counter medications and toilet articles, but for prescriptions, you need to go to Marsh Harbour on the mainland, 20 minutes away by ferry.

Post Office

At the end of what is known as the post office dock (the main public dock in Hope Town), the post office (☎ 242-366-0098) is open weekdays 9 a.m to 5 p.m. (and closed for lunch, usually between 1:30 and 2:30 p.m.).

Safety

Elbow Cay is a very safe island. Remember to take the same precautions that you should whether you're at home or on vacation: Keep valuables in a safe place and don't go into deserted, unfamiliar areas alone at night.

Taxis

Taxis meet incoming flights at the Marsh Harbour airport, and they greet arriving ferries as well. During your stay, staff at your hotel can call one for you whenever you need one.

Chapter 19

Green Turtle Cay

....

In This Chapter

▶ Finding Green Turtle Cay's best accommodations and restaurants

▶ Getting around Green Turtle Cay

▶ Exploring beaches, water sports, and land attractions

....

Green Turtle Cay is about 3 miles west of **Great Abaco,** the "mainland." (See the map in this chapter for more on the layout of Green Turtle Cay.) You'll most likely land at the **Treasure Cay Airport** before taking the ferry to your hotel on the cay. The beach-rimmed coastline of this 3 ½-mile-long, ½-mile-wide island dips in and out of bays and sounds. Most vacationers get around by boat — usually on a rented craft. If you don't charter your own boat, you can easily join fishing, snorkeling, or diving excursions.

One of the best ways to spend a day is exploring deserted beaches on nearby uninhabited islets. On some trips, your captain may spear a few lobsters, catch some fish, and grill it for you right on shore.

Coral colonies starting in relatively shallow water make for exceptional snorkeling, and diving is good here as well. Especially during the spring and summer, anglers and boaters flock to Green Turtle Cay. The fewest visitors check into hotels in the fall.

Deciding Where You Want to Stay

Green Turtle Cay has only two large places to stay. *Large* here means not even 35 rooms. Although some units are plush, don't count on finding a TV or phone in yours. Like the other Abaco Islands, Green Turtle Cay is for vacationers who want a retreat. If you're expecting a large, amenity-studded resort, you'll be disappointed.

Green Turtle Cay

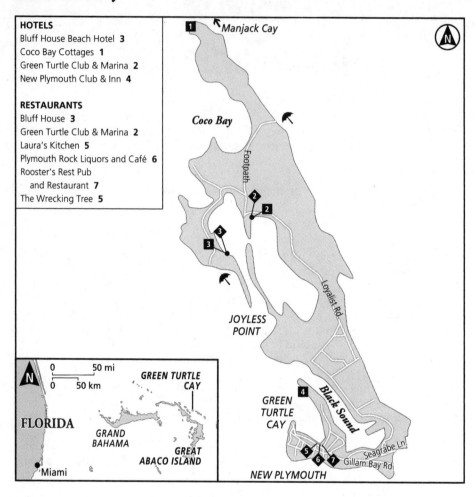

HOTELS
Bluff House Beach Hotel **3**
Coco Bay Cottages **1**
Green Turtle Club & Marina **2**
New Plymouth Club & Inn **4**

RESTAURANTS
Bluff House **3**
Green Turtle Club & Marina **2**
Laura's Kitchen **5**
Plymouth Rock Liquors and Café **6**
Rooster's Rest Pub
   and Restaurant **7**
The Wrecking Tree **5**

The island's two main resorts are on the water in the north. **Bluff House** borders both a quiet sandy bay and a marina, while the **Green Turtle Club,** a short walk from a good beach, sprawls along a marina. If you're vacationing with friends or family, consider renting a beachside cottage. If you seek historic charm , head for the **New Plymouth Inn,** located in the New England-style, eighteenth-century village at the southern end of the island.

Checking Out Green Turtle Cay's Best Accommodations

Bluff House Beach Hotel
$$–$$$ Between White Sound Harbour and Sea of Abaco

With a popular, elegant restaurant, Bluff House sits on the highest spot on the island, which is only 80 feet. The marina hugs one side of the property while a cozy beach borders another. From the main house and pool deck, the view of the water is panoramic. Originally built as a private house during the 1950s, Bluff House grew over the years as the owners added rooms for visiting friends. Today guests stay in 31 units ranging from ordinary hotel rooms to plush three-bedroom villas. The decor is as varied as the accommodations, with hardwood, tiled, or carpeted floors, Oriental rugs and antique floral patterns in some rooms, and airy wicker furniture in others. Spacious, split-level suites with balconies overlook the ocean. Each unit comes with a small tidy bathroom with a shower. Privately owned villas are on the marina as well as near the beach. Swim out to the rocky ledge around the corner, and you can find some good snorkeling. Use of snorkel gear is complimentary to guests, and staff help make arrangements for other water sports. A shuttle bus transports guests to town, in the southern part of the island, three times a week.

Wooden boardwalks and stairs lead up and down throughout the hilly grounds. Don't think about taking high heels to this terrain, and if you have any trouble walking, don't even consider Bluff House.

Northern end of the island between White Sound Harbour and Sea of Abaco. ☎ *800-688-4752 or 242-365-4247. Fax: 242-365-4248. Internet:* www.bluffhouse. com. *Rack rates: $120–$250 for suites, $275–$495 for a villa. AE, MC, V.*

Coco Bay Cottages
$$$ At the Sea of Abaco at the north end

On the north end of Green Turtle Cay, at a point where 500 feet of land separate the Atlantic from the Sea of Abaco, this four-unit cottage complex opens onto a beach on the Atlantic side of the island and another sandy beach on the more tranquil bay. It's ideal for those who'd like to anchor in for a while (literally — lots of folks arrive by private boat, which you can moor here free, or otherwise you come directly by water taxi from the airport dock). It enjoys a 70% repeat clientele. Furnished in a refreshing style of Caribbean furnishings and pastel colors, the ocean-front property occupies five acres, dotted with some 50 tropical fruit trees. Each of the cottages has two bedrooms, a living room, a dining room, and a fully equipped kitchen with microwave, plus a small bathroom with a shower. Rebuilt in 1988 and renovated in 1996, the spacious cottages have improved over the years. Linens and kitchen utensils are provided (you can also stock up on groceries at three shops in New Plymouth), and ceiling fans and trade winds cool the rooms.

In the north near the Sea of Abaco. ☎ *800-752-0166 or 242-365-5464. Fax: 242-365-5465. Internet:* www.cocabaycottages.com. *Rack rates: $185–$250 daily or $1,100–$1,800 weekly. MC, V.*

Green Turtle Club & Marina
$$$ White Sound Harbour

Although the fanciest hotel in the Abacos, the Green Turtle Club is far from stuffy. Witness the lively crowd that gathers in the clubhouse lounge for conversation, backgammon, and predinner cocktails. Yachting flags hang from the ceiling beams, and the walls are papered with business cards and dollar bills scrawled with names. During the coolest time of year, a fire often roars in the hearth in this cozy lounge. With plenty of fishermen and boaters arriving, spring and summer are the most popular — and most expensive — seasons here. Every May, the Green Turtle Club hosts a big fishing tournament. Spread out along the marina and near the pool that is tucked into a gentle rise, the 34 rooms and villas vary in size, view, and décor. In your room, you're likely to find a Queen Anne dresser and four-poster mahogany bed, an Oriental throw rug and vase, an oak floor and wood-trimmed door, a snazzy bathroom with a dressing area, and a patio tiled in terra-cotta. Some of the deluxe rooms even have TVs. Calm **Coco Bay Beach** is only about a five-minute walk from here, and the rougher ocean beach is just ten minutes away. You can arrange a variety of water sports. Once a day, a shuttle bus takes guests into town.

Northern end of the island in White Sound Harbour. ☎ *800-688-4752 or 242-365-4271. Fax: 242-365-4272. Internet:* www.greenturtleclub.com. *Rack rates: $190–$270 for a double room, $325–$455 for a villa. AE, DISC, MC, V.*

New Plymouth Club & Inn
$$ New Plymouth

A true charmer, this nine-room inn is one of the best values in the Abacos. Not only is it a bed-and-breakfast, but it's a bed-and-dinner, too. New Plymouth Club & Inn isn't on the beach; however, it does have a fresh-water swimming pool, and the sandy shores aren't far. You can easily schedule fishing, snorkeling, and scuba-diving trips. Apart from its location right in the center of the pretty town, the best thing about the

New Plymouth Club is the building it occupies: a handsome, two-story home evocative of New England. The ghost of Captain Billy Roberts, once a resident, is said to haunt the place from time to time. Perhaps he can't get enough of the broad verandas, flower beds, and old English-style rooms decorated with antiques and handmade quilts. (Bathrooms have showers instead of tubs.) See whether you can book the room with the canopy bed — that's if some of the inn's many repeat guests haven't snagged it first. The bar, lounge, and popular dining room overlook the gardens and pool patio, where visitors sip cold daiquiris (among other drinks) each afternoon.

Across the road from the Memorial Sculpture Garden. ☎ **242-365-4161.** *Fax: 242-365-4138. Internet:* www.go-abacos.com. *Rack rates: $140 and up, including breakfast for a double room. MC, V. Closed: Sept–Oct.*

Arriving in Green Turtle Cay

Getting to Green Turtle Cay isn't easy. Unless you sail in, you need to take at least one flight, a taxi, and a ferry before you catch a glimpse of your hotel.

Flying into **Treasure Cay,** on the east coast of Great Abaco, is best. The taxi for the short ride from the airport to the ferry dock runs you $8 for two passengers or $7 for one. The 20-minute ferry ride to Green Turtle Cay costs $8 per person each way and drops you off at or near your hotel.

 Treasure Cay is one of three airports in the Abacos, so be sure that you're booked to the right destination. If you fly into Marsh Harbour, you have to take a 45-minute taxi ride for $80 to the Green Turtle Cay ferry dock. Before making your airline reservations, check the ferry schedule with your hotel to be certain that your flight doesn't arrive too late or too early.

A tip on tipping

As your taxi pulls up to the ferry dock on the Treasure Cay side, chances are young boys are waiting to load your bags onto the boat, whether you need help or not. Because there aren't dozens of stores around, these children can't make pocket change bagging groceries — and shoveling snow is out of the question. Be as gracious and as generous as you can.

Getting around Green Turtle Cay

Although you can walk to many parts of Green Turtle Cay, water is the most common mode of transport. Some hotels provide water transport to town or to weekly hotel parties. Many vacationers rent boats (see the section "Finding water fun for everyone," later in this chapter), but if you'd rather not, you still have other choices for getting around. For example,

- ✔ **Going by golf cart.** On Green Turtle Cay, golf carts stand in for rental cars. **D & P Rentals (☎ 242-365-4655)** at the Green Turtle Club marina lets you use one of theirs at $45 for 8 hours or $60 per day.

- ✔ **Hoofing it.** Most of the island is accessible on foot. The virtually car-free streets of New Plymouth, the quiet eighteenth-century seaside village, are prime walking territory.

- ✔ **Pedaling around.** You can bike all over the island, and pedaling is especially scenic in historic New Plymouth. For $10 a day or $50 a week, **Brendal's Dive Center (☎ 242-365-4411)**, at the Green Turtle Club marina, rents cruisers and 10-speeds.

Dining in Green Turtle Cay

The hotel restaurants are the fanciest — and, of course, most expensive — places to dine. They all have just one seating for dinner, so be sure to make reservations. Folks tend to dress for dinner at **Bluff House** and **Green Turtle Club & Marina**. Although this practice may mean shirts with collars for men, neither jackets nor ties are required. In New Plymouth, you can find several casual, local restaurants to try. Lobster season is during August and September.

Turn to Chapter 2 for details about Bahamian specialties and tipping and the Introduction for an explanation of the price categories used in this chapter.

Bluff House

$$ Between White Sound Harbour and Sea of Abaco
BAHAMIAN/CONTINENTAL

At this hilltop hotel restaurant, lunch and breakfast are served on a deck overlooking the harbor. Thursday — with its barbecue buffet and live band — is a big night, and a one-man band usually performs on Tuesday nights. Other evenings are more subdued, with guests sharing boating, fishing, and diving stories over first-rate food at candlelit tables. The house drink is a rum and fruit juice concoction called the Tranquil Turtle. One night you may order the prime rib or lobster, while another evening you can sample the roast lamb wrapped in bacon with honey-rosemary glaze or try the crispy duck breast with a grapefruit and Grand Marnier sauce. Many of the homemade desserts come from local recipes. The chef can handle special requests, such as dishes for vegetarians or diabetics.

In the north between White Sound Harbour and Sea of Abaco. ☎ *242-365-4247. Call by 5 p.m. for dinner reservations. Complete dinner: $33 for adults, $12–$15 for children. AE, MC, V. Open: Daily for breakfast, lunch, and dinner.*

Green Turtle Club & Marina

$$$–$$$$ White Sound Harbour   AMERICAN/BAHAMIAN

Breakfast and lunch are casual here — served on a screened-in patio shadowed by a buttonwood tree. At dinner, in the elegant dining room, women dress up and men wear shirts with collars. Guests gather for drinks — and to swap tales of their days — in the bar before and after the meal. They're escorted to candlelit tables and seated in high-backed Queen Anne chairs. The menu changes daily, but whether you're having New York strip steak, ginger lobster medallions, or broiled grouper in guava sauce, your meal is served on fine china. A well-prepared vegetarian dish is always available. The cuisine is invariably excellent. The Green Turtle Club offers musical entertainment three times a week, with Wednesday being the most popular night.

In the north in White Sound Harbour. ☎ *242-365-4271. Reservations are essential. Main courses: $21–$35. AE, MC, V. Open: Daily for breakfast, lunch, and dinner.*

Laura's Kitchen

$$ New Plymouth   BAHAMIAN

Cozy, family-run Laura's Kitchen may not win awards for its simple decor, but this handsome old cottage is a good place to find Bahamian favorites. The menu includes such good-tasting dishes as cracked conch, tasty grouper, fried shrimp, lobster, fried chicken, and steak. Although vacationers often visit, Laura's has a loyal local following as well.

King Street, near the ferry dock in New Plymouth. ☎ *242-365-4287. Reservations recommended during the winter season; call by 5 p.m. for evening transportation to and from your hotel. Complete dinner: $14–$18. MC, V. Open: for lunch and dinner (closed some Sun); closed Sept–Nov.*

New Plymouth Club & Inn

$$ New Plymouth   BAHAMIAN/CONTINENTAL

Sunday brunch at New Plymouth Club & Inn draws plenty of hungry people. You have serious competition if you want to sit on the screened-in sun porch overlooking the swimming pool and the fragrant oleander, bushy almond leaves, and hibiscus. Before you make your reservation, check the menu board to see what the chef has decided to whip up that day. Surrounded by colonial furnishings, your elegant candlelit evening meal may be grilled lamb chops, veal, grouper almondine, or chicken with an orange glaze. You can fill up on the homemade Bahamian bread, which is slightly sweet and pillow soft.

On the main drag, across from the sculpture garden. ☎ 242-365-4161. Make reservations by 5 p.m. for dinner. Complete dinner: $30. MC, V. Open: Daily for breakfast and dinner.

Plymouth Rock Liquors and Café
$ New Plymouth   BAHAMIAN

Plymouth Rock may be a liquor store, but, with counter and take-out service for breakfast and lunch, it's more than that. For breakfast, you can order eggs or *chicken souse* (a hot and spicy soup-like Bahamian specialty). For lunch, try a conch burger, cracked conch platter, or a more prosaic hamburger. For dessert, many patrons choose the apple turnovers or the hummingbird cake (sweetened with banana and pineapple). Shelves are not only packed with alcohol (the store has 60 types of rum for sale), but you can also browse through a mega-selection of hot sauces, from The Bahamas and elsewhere. When you're through feeding your body, tend to your spirit at the art gallery next door.

Parliament St., next to Barclay's Bank. ☎ 242-365-4234. Lunch: $2.75–$7.50. MC, V. Kitchen open for breakfast and lunch, 9 a.m.–5 p.m.; closed Sun and holidays.

Rooster's Rest Pub and Restaurant
$ Just outside town   BAHAMIAN

Rooster's Rest is best known for the live reggae and calypso music that turns it into Party Central on Friday and Saturday nights. But it's also a good place to sample generous portions of the usual local suspects: fried grouper, cracked conch, peas and rice, and, of course, a Goombay Smash or two.

Gilliam's Bay Rd., across from BATELCO (the Bahamas Telephone Company) and the all-age school. ☎ 242-365-4066. Reservations recommended for dinner. Complete dinner: $10–$18. MC, V. Open: Mon–Sat for lunch and dinner; closed Sun.

The Wrecking Tree
$ New Plymouth   BAHAMIAN

A large, shady cedar tree grows up through the front porch at this popular eatery. Some say that the Wrecking Tree got its name because nineteenth-century wrecking vessels brought their salvage to this spot, but many residents can tell you the true origin: People used to sit under the tree and drink until they got "wrecked." Stop here for pastry, cool drinks, or a Bahamian meal. Start off with zesty conch fritters, and then try the fish, conch, pork chops, ribs, or turtle steak or crawfish.

Bay St. in New Plymouth. ☎ 242-365-4263. Complete dinner: $14–$18. No credit cards accepted. Open for lunch and dinner, 11 a.m.–9 or 10 p.m.

Fun on and off the Beach in Green Turtle Cay

Along with sampling Green Turtle Cay's aquatic diversions, you can visit a museum and wander the streets of New Plymouth, the historic waterfront village.

Hitting the beaches

About a ten-minute walk from **Bluff House** and five minutes from the **Green Turtle Club, Coco Bay** is one of the most beautiful crescents in The Bahamas. Shaded by casuarina pine trees and lapped by lazy waves, this long beach is often empty. The rougher **Ocean Beach,** about a ten-minute stroll from either Bluff House or the Green Turtle Club, is another stunner. Frothy waves thrash the stark white sand, set off by the intense blue of the Atlantic.

You can take a boat trip to one of the nearby uninhabited islands that are ringed with even more pristine beaches. On **Manjack Cay,** for example, the expanse of sugar-white sand seems to go on forever, and the shallow, clear water is a brilliant shade of turquoise.

Finding water fun for everyone

With one of the world's largest barrier reefs, the **Abacos** offers some of The Bahamas' best and least crowded snorkeling and diving sites, with plenty of variety. You can get an eyeful at reefs starting in depths of just 5 feet and ranging to 60 feet and more. Like sheets on a clothesline, sprawling schools of fish billow by coral caverns, huge tube and barrel sponges, and fields of elk and staghorn coral. Sea turtles and large groupers are common sights. In fact, the waters are so clear that you can often see farther than 100 feet.

Scuba divers can poke around the wreck of the *San Jacinto.* At this American steamship that was built in 1847 and sank two decades ago, you can feed the resident bright green moray eel. Plan to spend about $135 for a scuba resort course, $500 for full certification, $55 for a one-tank dive, and $75 for a two-tank dive.

If you like small groups and big fun, try **Brendal's Dive Center** (☎ 800-780-9941 or 242-365-4411) at the **Green Turtle Club Marina.** Whether you're an experienced diver or snorkeler or you're just getting your feet wet, the personal attention makes the difference here. Originally from **Acklins,** a small Bahamian island to the south, Brendal has more than two decades of underwater experience. A special treat for snorkelers is the wild dolphin encounter trip ($75 per person), which includes stops at undisturbed islands. This company also rents kayaks ($25 a day for singles, $35 a day for doubles, or $125 a week for the single, $175 for the double).

On Deck: Riding the Waves without Getting Wet

If you've had enough of sitting on the beach and relaxing, you can explore the ocean. From boat rentals to fishing expeditions, Green Turtle Cay offers an array of things to do.

Based at the Green Turtle Club marina, **Brendal's Dive Center** (☎ 242-365-4411) can rent you a 16-foot sailboat for $60 a day, or you can take a group sunset cruise (complete with rum punch) on a 29-foot sailboat for $60 per person (up to eight passengers). To see the coral without getting wet, Brendal's hosts glass-bottom boat trips for $45 per person.

Contact **Donny's Boat Rentals** (☎ 242-365-4119) in **Black Sound** for speedboats. This company rents Whalers and Makos (types of motor-boats) starting at $75 a day for a 14-footer. Or try **Reef Rentals** (☎ 242-365-4145), directly across from the ferry dock in **New Plymouth.** This fleet includes a sleek motorboat made on **Man-O-War Cay,** the nearby island long known for its excellent boat building. Rentals start at $95 a day for a 19-foot Wellcraft.

Reserving a boat when you make your hotel and airline reservations is a good idea, particularly during the busy spring and summer.

Fishing charters run from $125 to $400 for a half-day and $400 to $600 for a full day. You can make arrangements through your hotel. If you're traveling in May, you could be right on time for the annual **Green Turtle Club Fishing Tournament** (☎ 800-688-4752 or 242-365-4271).

Keeping Your Feet on Dry Land

Walking in New Plymouth is to journey back in time. To get a taste of how Green Turtle Cay and the rest of the Abacos came to be, poke around the **Albert Lowe Museum** (☎ 242-365-4094). Housed in a charming old cottage on Parliament Street in New Plymouth, the museum was founded in 1976 by acclaimed local artist Alton Lowe, who named the place after his father, Albert. Daddy-kins, a direct descendant of one of the European American families who settled the island, was an avid model ship builder. You can see some of his mini-schooners on display, along with paintings by Alton (whose prints are for sale), timeworn photographs, and other historical artifacts, some dating back to the eighteenth century. Admission is about $3 for adults and $2 for students. The museum is usually open Monday through Saturday 9 a.m. to 4 p.m. and closed for lunch between noon and 1 p.m.

Across from New Plymouth Inn on Parliament Street, the **Memorial Sculpture Garden** honors residents of the Abacos, both living and dead. What blooms at this garden are busts of island notables on stone pedestals. Read about some of the American loyalists who came to The Bahamas from New England and the Carolinas. Statues are also dedicated to their descendants and to those people who were enslaved in these islands. You can see everyone from Albert Lowe — whose forebears were among New Plymouth's original European American settlers — to African-Bahamian Jeanne I. Thompson, the second woman to practice law in The Bahamas. This garden is laid out in the pattern of the British flag.

Living It Up after the Sun Goes Down: Green Turtle Cay's Nightlife

On Friday and Saturday nights, a mostly young, mostly local crowd parties to reggae and calypso music at **Rooster's Rest Pub and Restaurant** (☎ 242-365-4066). During the week, the island's calypso-reggae band, the Gully Roosters, plays at the Green Turtle Club one night and at Bluff House another. Hotel and restaurant bars are prime social centers most nights.

Those fruity, rum-based cocktails known as Goombay Smashes are all over Green Turtle Cay. But **Miss Emily's Blue Bee Bar** (☎ 242-365-4181) is said to be the birthplace of this beloved, much-imitated drink. Of course, the original recipe created by the late Miss Emily is a well-kept secret. Everyone from Bahamian prime ministers to international television stars has entered this tiny, unassuming hangout where the walls near the bar are covered with business cards. If you feel guilty about downing too many drinks, just drop some money in the box for St. Peter's Anglican Church. Located on Victoria Street in New Plymouth, Miss Emily's opens around noon and closes "whenever."

Taking a Great Day Trip to Swim with the Stingrays

One of the island's best aquatic adventures is a day sail with **Brendal's Dive Center** (☎ 800-780-9941 or 242-365-4411), at the Green Turtle Club Marina. Whether you're a snorkeler or a scuba diver, the highlight comes when you get to hand-feed some graceful stingrays. Because you're giving them snacks, they won't be interested in nibbling on you. If you don't know how to snorkel or scuba dive, Brendal's is a good place to learn.

On the trip, you stop at a secluded beach on an island so small you can circle it on foot in 20 minutes. After catching your fish or lobster, your captain grills it right on the beach and serves it along with conch salad, homemade bread, and a green salad. The weather, sea conditions, and your preferences determine exactly where else you go. Brendal has managed to strike that rare balance between pure professionalism and laid-back flexibility, so you can design almost any trip you want.

For the most relaxing, intimate scuba or snorkeling excursion, make a special request for the sailboat that carries a minimum of four and a maximum of eight passengers. Otherwise, you'll probably travel in a motorboat that holds up to 24 divers (although rarely that many are on board).

Fast Facts: Green Turtle Cay

Babysitting

Hotel staff can help you find a babysitter.

Banks

On Parliament St. in New Plymouth, Barclay's Bank (☎ 242-365-4144) is open Tuesday through Thursday from 10 a.m. to 1 p.m.

Credit Cards

If you need credit card assistance, contact MasterCard (☎ 800-307-7309) or call Visa collect (☎ 800-847-2911).

Directory Assistance

Call ☎ 916.

Information

For visitor-related information, contact the Abaco Tourist Office (☎ 242-367-3067).

Medical Attention

Contact the government clinic (☎ 242-365-4028), a "you-can't-miss-it" pink and white building in New Plymouth.

Police

Call ☎ 242-365-4450.

Post Office

Open Monday through Friday 9 a.m to 5 p.m., the post office (☎ 242-365-4242) is on the main drag in New Plymouth.

Safety

Green Turtle Cay is a very safe island. However, you still need to take the same precautions that you should take anywhere you go: Keep valuables in a safe place and don't go into deserted, unfamiliar areas alone at night.

Taxis

Taxis meet incoming flights at the Treasure Cay airport, and they greet arriving ferries as well. During your stay, staff at your hotel can call one for you whenever you want.

Chapter 20

Treasure Cay

● ●

In This Chapter

▶ Reviewing Treasure Cay's accommodations and restaurants

▶ Getting around Treasure Cay

▶ Exploring water sports and land attractions

● ●

Attractive condos, villas, a championship golf course, a marina, tennis courts, and a golden sand beach draw visitors to **Treasure Cay,** especially in winter.

This resort looks and feels like the planned vacation community it is — a bit sterile for our tastes. Don't be surprised if your stay makes you forget you're in The Bahamas. Not much existed in the area before Treasure Cay was born in the 1960s, so you won't find any historic sites or long-standing communities full of local color.

The good news is that you can sail to nearby islands (**Green Turtle Cay, Man-O-War Cay,** and **Elbow Cay**) to visit three of The Bahamas' oldest and most charming villages.

Figuring Out Where to Stay

You have a choice of two settings, either at a 150-slip marina, one of the best boat hangouts in the islands, or on a 3½ mile beach of stark white sand and calm, clear water. *National Geographic* dubbed it one of the ten best strands in the world. That's a bit of an exaggeration, but when faced with a beach like this, why quibble? The two hotels also offer a variety of accommodations from standard hotel rooms and suites to apartments and villas.

Rooms can be scarce in June when the place is packed with anglers angling for fame in one of the country's most popular fishing tournaments: the **Treasure Cay Billfish Championship.**

When an island isn't an island

Cay is pronounced "key" in The Bahamas and means "a little island." So how come Treasure Cay, on the east coast of **Great Abaco** (an island near Grand Bahama, in the northern Bahamas) is part of the mainland? It used to be a separate chunk of land, known as Lovel's Island, at least as far back as the 1780s. Eventually, landfill erased the sliver of Carleton Creek that ran between Treasure Cay and Great Abaco.

Most vacationers rent golf carts or bikes to get to local restaurants and to explore their surroundings. The marina and golf course are close to both hotels. At the shopping center near the marina, you can find the bank, post office, grocery store, and car rental and sports shops, along with two souvenir stores.

Checking Out Treasure Cay's Best Accommodations

Banyan Beach Club
$$$ Treasure Cay Beach

Right on the beach that is widely known as one of the world's top ten because of its gentle curve, white sand, and turquoise water, Banyan Beach Club offers 21 spacious condos that are ideal for families. Some of these one- and two-bedroom units have an additional sleeping area: a loft, which is reached by a spiral or ladder-style staircase, with two twin beds. Queen-sized beds are in downstairs rooms. Patios or balconies have expansive views. The one-bedroom units face the swimming pool, while the larger apartments, with two or three bathrooms, overlook the beach. All units come with kitchens complete with a dishwasher, microwave, blender, coffee maker, and other conveniences, such as a small bathroom with shower. The upstairs apartments in both shingle-roof buildings have high-angled ceilings. Guests get acquainted at the Monday night cocktail parties or over hamburgers and hot dogs at the beach bar and grill. Treasure Cay's golf course is within strolling distance, but most people get there on the golf carts they rent to cruise the resort. At Treasure Cay's marina, less than a mile away, water sports are easily arranged.

Half a mile south of Treasure Cay Hotel Resort & Marina. ☎ *888-625-3060 or 242-365-8111. Fax: 242-365-8112. Internet:* www.banyanbeach.com. *Rack rates: $175–$200 for a double room. MC, V. Closed Sept–Oct.*

Treasure Cay

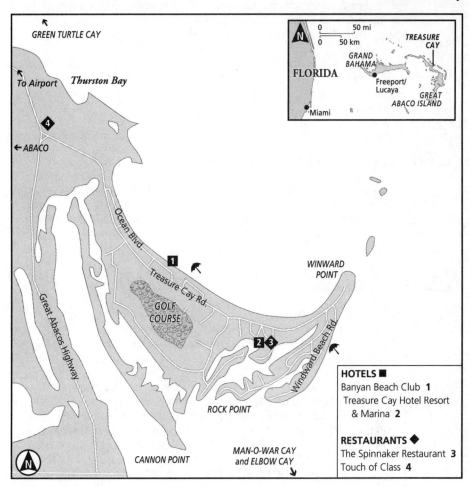

Thurston Bay

To Airport

← ABACO

Ocean Blvd

Treasure Cay Rd.

GOLF COURSE

Great Abacos Highway

WINWARD POINT

Windward Beach Rd

ROCK POINT

CANNON POINT

MAN-O-WAR CAY and ELBOW CAY

0 50 mi
0 50 km

N

FLORIDA

GRAND BAHAMA

Freeport/ Lucaya

Miami

TREASURE CAY

GREAT ABACO ISLAND

HOTELS ■
Banyan Beach Club **1**
Treasure Cay Hotel Resort & Marina **2**

RESTAURANTS ◆
The Spinnaker Restaurant **3**
Touch of Class **4**

Treasure Cay Hotel Resort & Marina
$$$-$$$$ On the marina

This resort offers two distinct experiences: You can stay in a hotel room downstairs or in a suite upstairs at the marina, or you can savor tranquility in a beach villa on stilts. Each of the homelike villas comes with two bedrooms, two full bathrooms, a kitchen, living room, dining room, and deck — but no phone to ensure peace and quiet. Sleeping from four to six people, with a maximum of four adults in the largest units, these villas overlook both the elaborate pool lagoon and the ivory shore so pretty you'd think it was a computer-generated photo. The long beach is usually rather quiet, but sailboats and yachts fill the marina. At the marina, hotel rooms, which do contain phones, have views of the pleasure craft or the gardens. The 18-hole course designed by renowned golf-course architect Dick Wilson is part of the resort, along with the **Spinnaker Restaurant,** which serves American and Bahamian dishes at the marina, and the beach bar. Tennis courts are lit for night play, and you can rent windsurfers and other water-sports equipment.

Treasure Cay Marina. ☎ *800/327-1584 or 242-365-8535. Fax: 242-365-8362. (Fort Lauderdale office). Internet:* www.treasurecay.com. *Rack rates: $180–$250 for double rooms, $395 for villas. In winter, there is a three-night minimum stay in the villas. AE, MC, V.*

Arriving in Treasure Cay

Treasure Cay is the site of one of the three airports in the **Abacos,** the group of islands just west of Grand Bahama in the northern Bahamas. Taxis meet arriving flights, and they charge about $14 for one or two people for the 10- to 15-minute ride to the Treasure Cay resorts.

Getting around Treasure Cay

Renting a car isn't necessary. To get where you're going, you can walk, bike, take a golf cart or a taxi. Some restaurants outside the resort will even send a shuttle to pick you up from your hotel. Here's a closer look at transportation options:

✔ **Taking a taxi.** For details about taxi fares, call the **Treasure Cay Airport Taxi Stand** (☎ **242-365-8661**). Except for moving between the airport or ferry dock and your hotel, you won't need a cab. The bank, grocery store, shops, and post office are all within the village-like Treasure Cay resort. For that special occasion when you need airport pickups or a trip to dinner in style, call **Elegante Limo Service** (☎ **242-365-8248** or 242-365-8053; $115 an hour for up to ten passengers); this company also rents golf carts.

✔ **Going by car.** The only real reason to rent a car ($75 a day at the Treasure Cay resort, ☎ **242-365-8535**) is for the 35-minute drive to **Marsh Harbour** to catch the ferries to **Elbow Cay** and **Man-O-War Cay,** two offshore islands. A more scenic way to get to these islands is to rent or charter a boat from Treasure Cay. (See the section "Finding water fun for everyone," later in this chapter.)

✔ **Wheeling around on a bicycle or golf cart.** Through **Wendell's Bicycle Rentals** (☎ **242-365-8687**), across from the bank in the Treasure Cay shopping center, you can rent beach cruisers (single-gear bikes with wide wheels) or mountain bikes (wide-wheeled bikes with multiple gears) for $7 a day or $42 a week. Four-seater electric golf carts go for $40 a day or $245 a week through Wendell's or **Claridge Golf Carts** (☎ **242-365-8248** or 242-365-8053), just outside town.

Dining in Treasure Cay

Many vacationers stay in accommodations with kitchens or kitchenettes. However, if you know you're never going to feel like putting fire to a pan, consider purchasing the Treasure Cay Hotel's meal plan ($60 per person for three meals a day or $50 for breakfast and dinner at **The Spinnaker**) or dine at nearby local restaurants, some of which provide transportation.

The Spinnaker Restaurant

$$$ Treasure Cay Marina   AMERICAN/BAHAMIAN

Serving good, reliable seafood, steak, pasta, and Bahamian specialties, this resort restaurant at the **Treasure Cay Marina** has a prime waterside spot. For lunch, the cracked conch makes a good choice. At night, the portions of meat and potatoes or fresh fish (prepared in a variety of ways, from steamed to blackened) are generous. Guests of the **Banyan Beach Club,** about a half-mile away, usually arrive by golf cart.

On the water in Treasure Cay Marina. ☎ 242-365-8469. Reservations suggested for dinner. Main courses: $21.95–$30. AE, MC, V. Open: Daily for breakfast, lunch, snacks, and dinner.

Touch of Class

$$-$$$ North of Treasure Cay resort   BAHAMIAN

Call ahead, and this popular local eatery can send a courtesy van to pick you up at your hotel. Touch of Class is the spot when you're ready to try some real Bahamian food, such as turtle steak with mushrooms and onions; fried, freshly caught grouper filet with a sauce of tomatoes, sweet peppers, and onions; or tender cracked conch — all served with a mound of peas and rice. If you can't decide, try the seafood plate, which offers a sampling of grouper, lobster, conch, and turtle. Both the key lime pie and the banana cream pie are luscious desserts.

On Queen's Hwy., a 10-minute drive from Treasure Cay resort. ☎ 242-365-8195. MC, V. Open nightly for dinner only 6:30–9 p.m.

Fun On and Off the Beach in Treasure Cay

Highlighted by the Treasure Cay Billfish Championship each spring, watersports in Treasure Cay mean big fun. Golfers don't have to head to Nassau or Freeport for a great game. Treasure Cay may be far less developed than the more popular islands, but its golf course is a big draw, as are its tennis courts

Hitting the beaches

If you desire a beach with some of the softest, whitest sand you can imagine and water in some of the most amazing shades of blue and green, then **Treasure Cay Beach** is it. What's especially alluring about this beach is that — unlike eye-catching strands on busier, more built-up islands — this shore is never crowded.

Finding water fun for everyone

Treasure Cay's excellent boating, fishing, scuba diving, and snorkeling make it tempting to spend most of your time in the water.

Treasure Cay makes a good starting point for exploring the Abacos by sea. At **Rich's Boat Rentals** (☎ 242-365-8582), 21-, 24-, and 27-footers start at around $130 a day. A guided charter starts at about $250 for a half-day or $400 for a full day. With 20- to 25-foot fully equipped boats, **J.I.C. Boat Rentals** (☎ 242-365-8465) is another good outfit. (See the section "Taking Two Great Day Trips from Treasure Cay," later in this chapter, for more information.)

Treasure Cay's surrounding waters offer some of the country's best fishing, including deep-sea, sea bottom, and drift fishing. Charters start at $275 for a half-day and $375 for a full day. Make arrangements through your hotel, Rich's Boat Rentals (☎ 242-365-8582), or J.I.C. Boat Rentals (☎ 242-365-8465).

Certified divers can hook up with **C&C Dive** (☎ 242-365-8506). A shorter one-tank dive goes for $55 and a longer two-tank dive for $80. Rich's Boat Rentals (☎ 242-365-8582) can book you on a snorkel sail ($35 per person with a six-person minimum) or on a beach snorkel trip after which the freshly caught grouper and lobster are grilled right on the beach costing $65 per person.

Sticking to Dry Land

If you prefer to stick to dry land, check out the following options.

The **Treasure Cay Golf Club** (☎ 242-365-8045) offers one of the best courses in The Bahamas. The course is a 72-par 18-holer. Greens fees run $75 for 18 holes or $45 for 9.

Reserving tee times is necessary from October to June.

Treasure Cay Hotel Resort & Marina (☎ 242-365-8535) offers six tennis courts — three clay surfaces ($16 an hour) and three hard surfaces ($14 an hour). They're lit for night play.

Taking Two Great Day Trips from Treasure Cay

You can get some local flavor and a blast from the past if you sail off to one, two, or three of the Abacos' nearby historic villages.

Trip #1: Green Turtle Cay

A brief ferry ride takes you across the water to **Green Turtle Cay,** one of the prettiest islands in The Bahamas. The hamlet of **New Plymouth** may make you think you landed in Cape Cod, mainly because it shares a similar architectural heritage with that New England summer haunt. White picket fences enclose the front yards of the small clapboard houses. In this subtropical village, these buildings are trimmed in pastel pinks, blues, and greens and are shaded by bushy palm trees. Once the most prosperous settlement in the Abacos, New Plymouth was founded by British loyalists who fled the U.S. after the American Revolution. Stroll around the quiet streets, sip a Goombay Smash, stop for a meal, and visit the art and maritime museum.

The ferry from Treasure Cay to Green Turtle Cay runs several times a day. To get to the ferry dock from the Treasure Cay Resort, you have to take a 15-minute taxi ride to the departure dock. This trip costs $15 for one or two passengers. Before long, the ferry will pull up to New Plymouth (about $12 round trip for adults, $6 for children). For more details about hotels, restaurants, sights, and activities on Green Turtle Cay, check out Chapter 19.

Trip #2: Elbow Cay and Man-O-War Cay

Elbow Cay and **Man-O-War Cay,** two nearby islands, make wonderful boating targets. The red-and-white striped lighthouse in Elbow Cay's **Hope Town's** boat-studded harbor is the most photographed man-made attraction in the Out Islands. Sandy dunes back some of the broad, quiet beaches on this long slim island. Saltbox houses with picket fences make this another contender for a Cape Cod fishing village look-alike. Take a load off at one of the harborside bars and restaurants.

In The Bahamas, you can expect to find at least one small bar for every small church, but not on Man-O-War. You'll see cozy houses of worship, but you won't find any bars or liquor stores at all. Folks on this uncrowded island take their religion very seriously. Don't risk offending anyone by publicly sipping any beer or other alcohol you may have brought along or by walking around in your bathing suit or other skimpy attire.

As you wander through Man-O-War Cay's trim streets lined with brightly painted cottages, you notice something different right away: Unlike most of The Bahamas (where the majority of residents are of African ancestry), nearly everyone here is a direct descendant of one European American couple who settled the island in the 1820s.

Man-O-War Cay's boat-building history is celebrated at the waterfront **Sail Shop,** which offers colorful bags handmade from the canvas once used for all those sails.

To strike out on your own or for a guided charter, contact **Rich's Boat Rentals** (☎ **242-365-8582**) or **J.I.C. Boat Rentals** (☎ **242-365-8465**). It should take you about an hour on the water to get from Treasure Cay to Man-O-War Cay (45 minutes on a good day) and about 10 minutes more to Elbow Cay.

For a different kind of scenic adventure, you can also rent a car in Treasure Cay ($75 a day), drive 35 minutes to Marsh Harbour, and then take the 20-minute ferry ride (through **Albury's Ferry Service** ☎ **242-367-3147**) to Elbow Cay or Man-O-War Cay. To either island, the fare is $8 each way or $12 same-day roundtrip for adults; and $4 one-way or $6 same-day roundtrip for children. However, your time will be limited by the ferry schedule, so you'll probably make it to only one of the two islands. (For information about Elbow Cay's hotels, restaurants, and sightseeing opportunities, see Chapter 18.)

Fast Facts: Treasure Cay

Babysitting

Hotel staff can help you find a babysitter.

Banks

The Royal Bank of Canada, in the Treasure Cay shopping center near the hotel, is open Tuesday through Thursday from 9:30 a.m. to 2:30 p.m.

Credit Cards

If you need credit card assistance, contact MasterCard (☎ 800-307-7309) or call Visa collect (☎ 800-847-2911).

Directory Assistance

Call (☎ 916).

Information

For visitor-related information, contact the **Abaco Tourist Office** (☎ 242-367-3067).

Medical Care

If health problems arise, contact the Corbett **Medical Center** (☎ 242-365-8288), behind the Treasure Cay administration building, near the marina.

Police

In an emergency, call ☎ 242-365-8048.

Post Office

In the Treasure Cay shopping center near the marina, the post office (☎ 242-365-8230) is open Monday through Friday from 9 a.m. to 5 p.m.

Safety

Although Treasure Cay is a safe resort, don't forget to take the same precautions that you should whether you're at home or on vacation: Keep valuables in a safe place and don't go into deserted, unfamiliar areas alone at night.

Taxis

Taxis meet incoming flights at the airport. During your stay, staff at your hotel can call one for you whenever the need arises.

Part VI
The Out Islands

In this part . . .

We help you get acquainted with four of the Bahamas' most appealing Out Islands. This section reviews one of the most intriguing of all Bahamian islands — actually a series of islands — called Eleuthera. A slender wisp of an island, 50 miles east of Nassau, Eleuthera is visited mainly for its offshore Harbour Island. Harbour Island is known for its attractive eighteenth-century harborside houses and its small hotels overlooking a pink sand beach. (Yes, pink.) Although Exuma is sailing heaven, avid scuba divers also can't get enough of San Salvador.

In this part, you find all the data needed for a great trip, including recommendations of accommodations to tips on how to get there, how to get around, what to see and do once there, and where to find the best food and the liveliest nightlife.

Chapter 21

Harbour Island

. . . .

In This Chapter

▶ Reviewing Harbour Island's best accommodations and restaurants

▶ Getting around Harbour Island

▶ Exploring the best beaches, water sports, and historic land attractions

. . . .

*I*f you're looking for a small, sophisticated hotel on a never-crowded sandy shore, head for **Harbour Island**. This 3½-mile-long, ½-mile-wide cay off northern **Eleuthera** is home to The Bahamas' coziest collection of distinctive oceanfront accommodations. This 3-mile-long sandy stretch is *pink*. It really is rosy. Mother Nature created this stunning pastel hue over the eons by pulverizing coral and shells. Scoop up a handful of the speckled sand, and you'll see.

Getting the Lowdown on the Harbour Island Hotel Scene

Most of the hotels in Harbour Island are expensive. Some daily rates appear high, however, until you notice that they include breakfast and dinner.

If you stay in a moderately priced or inexpensive hotel, you can still treat yourself to the fancy resorts and restaurants by dining at them now and then, and you always have access to that dreamy pink beach. See the map in this chapter for more on the island's accommodations.

No matter where you stay, you receive as much — or as little — personal attention as you want. Your accommodation may even have an honor bar where you just sign for whatever drinks you fix yourself.

Most hotels and restaurants close during parts of September, October, and November.

Harbour Island

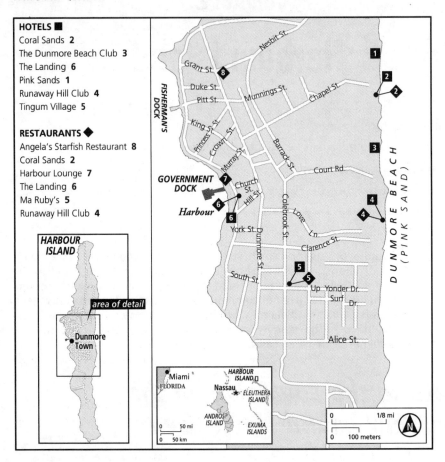

HOTELS ■
Coral Sands **2**
The Dunmore Beach Club **3**
The Landing **6**
Pink Sands **1**
Runaway Hill Club **4**
Tingum Village **5**

RESTAURANTS ◆
Angela's Starfish Restaurant **8**
Coral Sands **2**
Harbour Lounge **7**
The Landing **6**
Ma Ruby's **5**
Runaway Hill Club **4**

Deciding Where to Stay

You can find plenty of elbow room between the hotels along the pink sand beach. Personable hotel managers and other staff members can help you make arrangements for fishing (the bonefishing here is excellent), sailing, snorkeling, and scuba-diving trips.

Because most of the resorts are on a bluff high above the sand, stairs lead from them down to the coast.

Harbour Island (shortened to *Briland* by locals) could stop with the beautiful beach and the great hotels, and it still would be a top-notch vacation choice. But this island also offers the well-preserved 17th-century **Dunmore Town,** the first capital of The Bahamas. Dunmore Town is within walking distance (or biking and golf cart reach) of all accommodations. The western shore offers panoramic sunsets, while the **Pink Beach** along the eastern coast is the only place to be at sunrise.

Sunbathing along the calm, reef-protected Pink Sand Beach on the eastern coast is best before the bluffs throw afternoon shadows across it.

What little after-dark action the island does have "jumps up" on weekends at or close to the hotels. However, most vacationers turn in early, not wanting to miss that sunrise.

Checking out Harbour Island's Best Accommodations

Coral Sands
$$$ On the beach

You can sleep especially well at this sprawling 27-room beach resort where the newest owner, a Connecticut-based bedding company, has replaced all the mattresses with its super-durable, super-comfortable brand. Dating back to the 1960s, Coral Sands has finally exchanged its rather retro look for a totally fresh face. Done in tones of pink and turquoise that bring the sand and water indoors, guest rooms are decorated with wicker furniture and attractive artwork. Some units contain balconies or patios. Some larger, some smaller, some oceanview, some gardenview, some upstairs, some downstairs — the rooms are found in various buildings surrounded by greenery. In the newest of these blocks of buildings, four oceanfront one-bedroom apartments with wraparound decks can be turned into two- or three-bedroom units by adding adjoining rooms. Bathrooms are mid-sized and well kept, mostly with shower and tub combos.

A favorite spot is the spacious **Commander's Beach Bar & Restaurant,** on a deck hanging high over the pink shore. Lunch and light supper are served here. You can have elegant dinners at the other restaurant, **Poseidon,** on a broad veranda at the main building.

Chapel St. ☎ *800-468-2799 or 242-333-2350. Fax: 242-333-2368. Internet:* www.coralsands.com. *Rack rates: $205–$330 for a double room, $450 for a one-bedroom apartment. AE, MC, V.*

The Dunmore Beach Club
$$$$$ On the beach

On a bluff above that pink sand beach, this 12-room inn is the quintessentially elegant hideaway, with 8 acres of well-manicured grounds.

If you'd rather have a root canal than wear a jacket or a cocktail dress to dinner, you shouldn't check in here. Dunmore Beach Club isn't the only Harbour Island hotel where guests dress up at night, but it is a bit on the stuffy side. This hotel was once the hangout of the Duke and Duchess of Windsor and their friends, and a subdued, slightly stiff atmosphere of the private club it once was still lingers.

The grounds are thick with lush vegetation, and the rooms, simply decorated in tranquil colors, are perfectly comfortable. Rooms are in scattered cottages with private patios that have views of the water. Bathrooms have twin sinks and lighted makeup tables. Hot tubs are large enough for romantic trysts, and the stall showers are spacious as well. Wrap yourself in a monogrammed robe. A tennis court is on site, and rates include three top-notch meals a day. A stairway connects the hotel to the beach.

Colebrook St., Eastern coast. ☎ *242-333-2200. Fax: 242-333-2429. Internet:* www.dunmorebeach.com. *Rack rates: $445–$495, including breakfast, lunch, and dinner. Children's discounts are available. MC, V.*

The Landing
$$$–$$$$ **Dunmore Town**

This intimate inn is understated, tasteful, and lovely, giving you a touch of class like Dunmore Beach Club but for less money. Set in buildings that have stood here since the early 1800s, this small inn is located in the heart of historic Dunmore Town. You have to go all the way across Harbour Island to reach the beach — but, this feat is hardly a difficult. The seven guest rooms are decorated plantation-style, with mahogany-stained four-poster beds and hardwood floors. Some rooms have broad verandas and ceiling fans, and most of them look out to the harbor across the road. Bathrooms are large and tiled, containing tubs and showers.

If you're traveling with children, ask for a room with an extra single bed. The Landing's restaurant is reason enough for staying here.

Bay St., across from Government Dock. ☎ *242-333-2707 or 242-333-2740. Fax: 242-333-2650. Internet:* www.harbourislandlanding.com. *Rack rates: $205–$295 for a double room, including breakfast. MC, V.*

Pink Sands
$$$$$ **On the beach**

This 25-room inn is the epitome of Out Island chic, a classier joint than even the Dunmore Beach Club, its chief rival. It's also less snobbish and a lot more hip than Dunmore, as such former guests as Julia Roberts, Robin Williams, Susan Sarandon, Tim Robbins, or Keith Richards may testify. Set on 8 landscaped acres and adjacent to 3 miles of pink sandy beach, it was recreated in 1992 from an inn that went "gone with the wind" in a hurricane. Jamaica-born Chris Blackwell, who brought Bob Marley to world attention, took over Pink Sands and transformed it into the pocket of posh it is today. The airy, spacious bedrooms have either an ocean or a garden view. Smaller units contain art-deco touches straight out of Miami's South Beach; larger, more expensive units have Indonesian (especially Balinese) furnishings and art, as well as huge decks. All rooms have kitchenettes or kitchens, central air-conditioning, pressurized water systems, walk-in closets, satellite TVs, CD players and a CD selection, wet bars, private patios with teak furnishings, and beautifully tiled bathrooms with tubs and showers. The interior design features marble floors with area rugs, oversized Adirondack furnishings, local artwork, and batik fabrics. The rooms have dataports, and fax machines and cellular phones can be supplied if you need them.

Paths curl through the resort's sprawling, plant-filled grounds. You may want to rent a golf cart or bicycle for getting around both Pink Sands and the rest of the island.

When not on the beach, guests head for the swimming pool, the tennis courts (one of the three lit for night play), the exercise room, or the library. You can have breakfast and dinner surrounded by leafy greenery on the main dining terrace. (A full breakfast and the four-course candlelit evening meal are included in the daily rates.) The beachside **Blue Bar** serves lunch and hosts the Saturday night Bahamian barbecues. For a few extra bucks, you can even order room service, an alien concept at most Out Island hotels.

Eastern coast. ☎ *800-688-7678, 242-333-2030, or (in Florida) 305-531-8800. Fax: 242-333-2060. Internet:* www.pinksandsresort.com. *Rack rates: $655–$765 for a 1-bedroom cottage, including breakfast and dinner. AE, MC, V.*

Runaway Hill Club
$$$$ On the beach

Guests who first meet at Runaway Hill often book their next vacation together here the following year. Because this inn has only ten rooms (most with patios or balconies), everyone quickly gets to know each other. Set on a rise high above the swimming pool and pink sand beach down a staircase, the main building was once a private home. With its individually and beautifully decorated rooms, it looks as if it still is. Our favorite place to sleep is the huge downstairs room with ceramic floor tiles in an intricate pink pattern and a spacious bathroom with twin sinks. The newest rooms, in a separate hilltop villa, are more similar in size and decor. No matter where you stay, you find artfully arranged furnishings and well-maintained private bathrooms with either shower or tub and shower combinations. Colorful knickknacks decorate the bar, lounge, and dining room. Guests dress up for the elegant candlelit dinners here, joined by those lucky nonguests who have managed to reserve tables as well. The friendly staff is always on hand to help make arrangements for water sports and other activities.

Colebrook St., Central Harbour Island. ☎ *800-728-9803 or 242-333-2150. Fax: 242-333-2420. Internet:* www.runawayhill.com. *Rack rates: $250–$260 for a double room. AE, MC, V. No children under 18 accepted. Closed Sept–mid-Nov.*

Tingum Village
$ Southern Harbour Island

You won't find anything fancy about Tingum Village, and with just 15 rooms in cottages with large terraces, "village" is certainly a misnomer. However, the hotel's proximity to the island's beach (a 4-minute walk away), its excellent Bahamian restaurant, **Ma Ruby's** (see the section "Dining in Harbour Island," later in this chapter), and the friendliness of the staff all make up for the lack of bells and whistles common at pricier Harbour Island hotels. A local family runs this quiet, low-key establishment. The hotel feels more like the "real" Bahamas than most of the island's more polished, but foreign-owned-and-managed, accommodations. The neat, clean rooms look out to a grassy expanse edged by palms, hibiscus, and other thick vegetation. If you want a hot tub in your room, book one of the two suites. Adjoining the pleasant bar, Ma Ruby's sits on a breezy patio at the edge of the garden.

American Express card users have to pay an additional 6 percent, so you may want to consider bringing other plastic.

Colebrook St. ☎ *242-333-2161. Fax: 242-333-2161. Internet:* www.wheretostay.com. *Rack rates: $85–$125 for a double room. AE, MC, V.*

Arriving in Harbour Island

Harbour Island, a mile and a half off the coast of **Eleuthera,** is one of those special places that requires a bit of work and patience to reach. If you come by air, you need to fly into the small, unassuming **North Eleuthera Airport** (from Miami, Fort Lauderdale, or Nassau). Then you take a 5-minute taxi ride to the dock (about $4 per person) and a 10-minute ferry ride to Harbour Island's Government Dock ($5 per person). Next, unless you're staying at The Landing, which is just across the road, you take a short taxi ride to your hotel ($4 per person).

Another way to get to Harbour Island is to board a speedy 177-passenger catamaran in Nassau. Just contact **Bahamas Fast Ferry** (☎ 242-323-2166). You begin this 2-hour trip at the **Potters Cay Dock,** under the bridge leading from Paradise Island to downtown Nassau. The fare for one of these daily excursions is $100 round-trip or $55 one-way for adults and $60 round-trip or $35 one-way for children ages 2 to 11. This ferry also pulls up to Government Dock, where taxis wait to take you to your hotel.

Getting around Harbour Island

You have three main options of transport: Take a taxi, ride a bike, or walk. Harbour Island is very small — just 3 miles long and one-half mile wide — so you can get where you need to go easily. Here's a closer look at transportation choices.

- **Taking a taxi.** The island is so small that you really need a cab only when arriving and leaving with luggage. Taxis wait for incoming ferries at Government Dock, and the staff at your hotel can call you a taxi when it's time to say *adios,* or if you're going out to dinner. Most people get around comfortably by foot, bicycle, scooter, or golf cart.

- **Wheeling around.** You won't see many cars on Harbour Island's nearly deserted roads. Because getting around is easy, you have no need to rent wheels. If you do feel the need to move faster than your feet can carry you, call **Michael's Cycles** (☎ **242-333-2384**), on Colebrook Street near **Seagrapes** nightclub. You can choose among bicycles ($10 a day), two-seater scooters ($30 a day), four-person golf carts ($50 a day), and Jeeps ($60 a day).

- **Hoofing it.** Dunmore Town (which is great for strolling), restaurants, nightspots, and most other places are within walking distance of hotels on this compact island. The best place for a walk is the 3-mile Pink Sand Beach along the eastern shore.

Dining in Harbour Island

For such a small island, a surprising selection of first-rate dining rooms, most of them at hotels, await you.

Vacationers tend to dress up for dinner, especially at the more expensive resorts during the winter season. Dinner reservations are crucial, and you may need to make yours in the morning. On the other hand, local spots featuring home-style Bahamian cooking are casual affairs. The majority of restaurants are closed between meals. Some restaurants also close completely for various chunks of time between September and November.

See Chapter 2 for details about Bahamian specialties and tipping, and the Introduction for an explanation of the price categories used in the restaurant listings in this chapter.

Angela's Starfish

$ Just outside Dunmore Town   BAHAMIAN

For more than a quarter of a century, this family-run restaurant has been churning out Bahamian dishes that keep folks streaming through the doors. Sit inside, where the casual decor has nautical touches, or on the palm-shaded lawn overlooking the water and mainland Eleuthera. At night, tiny bulbs hidden inside conch shells illuminate the tables. The honey-brown cracked conch is the perfect combination of crispy on the outside and tender on the inside. Fish, chicken, and pork chops, all served with mounds of peas and rice, are also well prepared. Key lime and coconut pie are the featured desserts.

You're welcomed here as long as you heed the sign that requests that patrons refrain from swearing and wearing bare-backed clothing.

At the top of the hill at Dunmore and Grant Sts. ☎ *242-333-2253. Main courses: $10–$25. No credit cards accepted. Open: Daily 11 a.m.–8 p.m.*

Coral Sands

$$–$$$ Northern Harbour Island   BAHAMIAN/INTERNATIONAL

You have a choice of settings at this beach resort, **Commander's Beach Bar & Restaurant** or **Poseidon.** We prefer the more casual beach bar because of its dramatic locale — on a broad, sunny deck hanging high above the rosy sand. This is the perfect spot for a long, tall rum punch. Your lunch or light supper may be soup, lobster salad, or a thick sandwich. Arrive on a Thursday night, and the lively music of a calypso band accompanies your meal. On Saturday evenings, a single musician performs at the more subdued, more elegant restaurant on the veranda of the main building. The menu, which incorporates herbs freshly plucked from the resort's garden, is always changing. Perennial winners are the local conch, grouper, and lobster dishes, prepared with imaginative twists on Bahamian recipes. For dessert, the velvet-smooth chocolate mousse, won our hearts.

Chapel St. ☎ *242-333-2350. Reservations recommended for dinner. Main courses: $12–$30. AE, MC, V. Main restaurant open for dinner Fri–Wed 7–9 p.m.*

Harbour Lounge

$$$–$$$$ Dunmore Town   BAHAMIAN

Arrive early to stake out a spot on the terrace to watch the sun slide into the harbor while you sip a Bahama Mama. Because you're right on **Bay Street,** the main thoroughfare, this restaurant is also the place to see and be seen. Along the water across the street, vendors sell straw goods, fruit, and vegetables. After dinner, a very local crowd gathers at the bar.

Specialties include the blackened grouper, garlic shrimp with pasta, lobster, cracked conch, and key lime pie. The food is some of the most satisfying and authentic on the island, a true "taste of The Bahamas."

Bay St., in Front of Government Dock. ☎ *242-333-2031. Reservations recommended. Main courses: $18–$35. MC, V. Open: Tues–Sun lunch served 12–2:30 p.m., dinner served 6–9:30 p.m., open for drinks all day.*

The Landing
$$$$$ Dunmore Town   INTERNATIONAL

The cozy atmosphere of this intimate restaurant makes it clear that the owners enjoy their hands-on involvement. Dating back to 1800, this handsome building across from the harbor is part of a hotel with a handful of guest rooms. Both dinner and Sunday brunch are special events here. Dine in the bright yellow and white dining room or in the garden. Linens and fine china dress the tables, where you sit in saddle-back chairs. The owners always hire a first-rate chef whose cooking pays tribute to the aristocratic credentials of the place. For your evening meal, you can choose among rock Cornish hen, cappellini with lobster, and Angus beef. The golden-brown, pan-fried grouper with mashed potatoes, eggplant, and green salsa is another bestseller. Dessert offerings may include ice cream, sorbet, and rich, but surprisingly light, chocolate cake, followed by various gourmet coffees.

Bay St., across from Government Dock. ☎ *242-333-2740. Reservations required. Main courses: $18–$38. MC, V. Open: Daily (except Wed) 6 p.m.–10 p.m. for dinner, Sun 9 a.m.–2 p.m. for brunch.*

Ma Ruby's
$ Tingum Village   BAHAMIAN

Matriarch Ma Ruby is known for her cheeseburgers, which were ranked as among the ten best in the world by "Mr. Cheeseburger in Paradise" himself, Jimmy Buffet. But we'd come back on another day and sample her conch burger, which we feel is worthy of an award as well — that and her hearty, flavorful Bahamian meals, such as conch fritters, stewed grouper, and baked chicken. Treat yourself to the peas and rice. For dessert, try the key lime pie or cheesecake. You dine on a courtyard patio by a grassy garden enclosed by palm trees.

Note that you pay a 6 percent surcharge if you use an American Express card.

Colebrook St., Southern Harbour Island. ☎ *242-333-2161. Dinner reservations requested by 6 p.m. Main courses: $8–$20. AE, MC, V. Open: daily for breakfast, lunch, and dinner.*

Pink Sands

$$$$$ **Northern Harbour Island**   **INTERNATIONAL**

The four-course dinner menu is *prix fixe* at this snazzy beach resort that attracts celebrities. You can dine on a garden patio where the candlelit teak tables are tucked discretely into private leafy corners. The gourmet food, mainly European, is sometimes jazzed up with Caribbean and Asian influences. You can begin with leek and potato soup with smoked mahi-mahi or a savory tiger shrimp bisque with cognac. Your main course may be filet of grouper with saffron-scented risotto, grilled beef tenderloin with roasted portobello mushrooms and braised potatoes, or salmon baked in an herb crust and served with tomato-scallion beurre blanc. Mango cream pie is a luscious dessert. A lengthy wine list features excellent choices from France, South Africa, Australia, Chile, and the U.S.

Chapel St., Eastern coast. ☎ *242-333-2030. Reservations required. Four-course dinner: $75. AE, MC, V. Open to nonguests for dinner only.*

Runaway Hill Club

$$$$$ **On the beach**   **CONTINENTAL**

To see the daily *prix fixe* menu, stop by in the morning to read what's on the old brass music stand by the entrance to the inn. Showing up early helps you for two reasons: First, dinner reservations go quickly at Runaway Hill. Second, this wonderfully decorated former home, overlooking the ocean, is gorgeous by daylight. See it, and you just may want to book a room here for your next vacation. At night, the small, elegant dining room glows with candlelight. Without ever rising to spectacular highs, the cuisine is turned out with skill and a certain flair by the chef. Your four-course meal may include lobster bisque followed by seafood pasta with scampi, pork tenderloin, rack of veal, or veal piccata. Dessert could be chocolate pie with walnuts or an imaginative strawberry creation.

The restaurant has just one seating (8 p.m.), following cocktails (7:30 p.m.), so tables are at a premium. Men are asked to wear shirts with collars, and women really play dress-up.

Colebrook St., Central Harbour Island. ☎ *242-333-2150. Early reservations essential. Complete four-course dinner: $60. AE, MC, V. Open: Mon–Sat (for nonguests, dinner only); closed from Sept–mid-Nov. No children.*

Fun On and Off the Beach in Harbour Island

Fishing (especially bonefishing), scuba diving, and snorkeling are the main aquatic diversions. Relaxing on the beach, wandering around historic Dunmore Town, and socializing with residents round out the roster of activities.

Hitting the beach

Three exquisite miles of mostly unpopulated pink sand run along the eastern coast of the island, overlooked by a few small hotels. **Pink Sand Beach** is truly amazing. Take a stroll or plan a picnic and don't forget to watch the sunrise — it's spectacular. Sunbathing along this calm strand is best in the morning.

Finding water fun for everyone

You may not be able to see forever in these waters, but on a clear day, visibility is often as great as 200 feet. This news is especially welcome because this area boasts such a diversity of dive sites.

In **Current Cut,** between Eleuthera and Current Island, experienced scuba divers get to drift dive at exhilarating speeds with the current that rushes through an underwater chasm. Divers are carried between the rock walls for about a half-mile, along with a blizzard of reef fish, stingrays, and even some mako sharks. Another exceptional dive site is the wreck of a 197-foot steel freighter that sank in 1917.

For both scuba and snorkeling trips, the place to go is **Valentines Dive Center** (☎ 242-333-2080), on the harbor side of the island in the heart of Dunmore Town. A scuba resort course costs $85. A 2-tank dive for certified divers runs $65 and a 4-tank trip, $115. Half-day snorkeling sails cost $30 per person.

For an unusual adventure, certified divers can try *reef running,* a ride on an underwater scooter ($115); decked out in your scuba gear, you cover much more marine territory than with regular diving.

On Deck: Riding the Waves without Getting Wet

Harbour Island offers a good choice of water diversions — where you never have to get wet.

You can rent a motor boat through **Michael's Cycles** (☎ 242-333-2384), on Colebrook Street near Seagrapes nightclub. Plan to spend about $70 for a full day on a 13-footer (or $60 for a half-day) and $120 for a full day on a 17-footer ($100 for a half-day). Kayaks here go for $30 a day ($15 for a half-day). For a sunset cruise through the harbor ($30), contact Valentines Dive Center (☎ 242-333-2080) in Dunmore Town.

Make arrangements for fishing guides and charters through your hotel or by contacting Valentines Dive Center (☎ **242-333-2080**). Bonefishing, which is excellent in these waters, runs anywhere from $125 to $350 for a half-day, depending on your guide and the number of other anglers. Deep-sea fishing charters begin at $325 for a half-day.

Exploring Your On-Land Options

On the harbor side of the island, **Dunmore Town** is named for the 18th-century royal governor of The Bahamas who helped develop it and had a summer home here. You could walk around these narrow, virtually car-free lanes in less than 20 minutes. Or you can stroll leisurely to savor the sight of the old gingerbread cottages that line the waterfront. Overhung with orange, purple, and pink bougainvillea, white picket fences enclose these wooden houses painted pastel blue, green, and lilac. Wind chimes tinkle in front of shuttered windows, and coconut palms and wispy casuarina pines shade grassy yards.

Americans and Canadians now own some of these houses, which have whimsical names, such as "Up Yonder" and "Beside the Point," instead of numbers. A few of them are available as vacation rentals. One of the oldest, **Loyalist Cottage,** was built in 1797. It survives from the days when the original settlers, loyal to the British Crown, left the American colonies after the Revolutionary War. The porches along the harbor make for prime sunset watching. Lucky for you, they're not all on private homes. The terrace at Harbour Lounge Bar and Restaurant is an idyllic perch. Just across the road from Loyalist Cottage, you can browse through straw goods, T-shirts, and fruits and vegetables at the vendors' stalls.

On Sundays, residents dressed to kill stand in sociable clusters outside churches before and after services. Two of The Bahamas' first houses of worship are found in Dunmore Town — and are still going strong: **St. John's,** the oldest Anglican church, was established in 1768, and **Wesley Methodist Church,** was built in 1846.

Spend some time wandering the streets — some hilly, some flat — away from the heart of town. You can see roosters doing their jerky march through front yards and horses grazing in small fields. In this locals' area are two unassuming but perfectly good Bahamian restaurants, bars, and nightclubs.

A Shopper's Guide to Harbour Island

Dunmore Town is no Nassau, but you can find several stores in town carrying worth-a-look items, such as local artists' works, Androsia resort wear (made from the colorful batik fabric created on the Bahamian island of Andros), and handcrafts such as music boxes in the shape of Harbour Island cottages and one-of-a-kind toothbrushes.

The standout boutique is **Miss Mae Tea Room and Fine Things** (☎ 242-333-2002), on Dunmore Street. Among the ever-changing, always artful, mostly imported merchandise, you may find Haitian-style paintings, silver jewelry from Bali, local painted boxes, antique chests, gourmet wine vinegar from France, and Italian olive oil.

 A few vendors sell fruit, vegetables, T-shirts, and straw goods (baskets, bags, hats, place mats) along **Bay Street,** at the edge of the harbor. You can hone your bargaining skills at this open-air mini-marketplace.

Living It Up after the Sun Goes Down

During the week, life after dark means hanging out at hotel and restaurant bars. Some resorts serve live music with dinner two evenings a week. The other nightspots see most of their action on weekends. The youngest, liveliest local crowd gravitates toward **Seagrapes** (no phone), a large club at Colebrook and Gibson Streets. On Friday or Saturday, you're likely to catch a live band here, but the dance floor is packed even when the DJ reigns.

The poolroom at the **Vic-Hum Club** (☎ 242-333-2161), on Barrack Street, is another popular haunt. Calypso, American pop, and R & B pumps from the speakers, and classic record album sleeves — no, not CD covers — decorate the walls and ceilings. Ask the owner to show you "the world's largest coconut," which measures some 33 inches around. Pool, satellite TV sports, and periodic live music entertains patrons at hilltop **Gusty's** (☎ 242-333-2165), on Coconut Grove Avenue in the north. Get here early enough and you have the perfect perch for sunset watching.

Fast Facts: Harbour Island, Eleuthera

Banks

You can find **The Royal Bank of Canada** (☎ 242-333-2250) up the hill from the main dock in Dunmore Town.

Information

In the unlikely event that your request stumps the staff at your hotel, try the Harbour Island Tourist Office (☎ 242-333-2621) across from the ferry dock on Bay Street.

Medical Attention

Contact the Harbour Island Medical Clinic (☎ 242-333-2227) or Harbour Pharmacy

Health Care and Prescription Service (☎ 242-333-2514).

Police

In an emergency, call the police (☎ 242-333-2111).

Post Office

For information, call the post office (☎ 242-333-2215).

Chapter 22

Eleuthera

● ●

In This Chapter

▶ Reviewing Eleuthera's best accommodations and restaurants

▶ Getting around Eleuthera

▶ Exploring the island's beaches, watersports, and land attractions

● ●

*T*ourists flock to Harbour Island where they're coddled in comfort. The adventure traveler heads for mainland Eleuthera. Although Harbour Island is flourishing, the great heyday of tourism and chicdom for Eleuthera itself has dwindled since The Bahamas became independent. Many embittered locals blame the late prime minister, Lynden Pindling, for discouraging foreign investment.

At one time, some of the best known names in the world-visited Eleuthera. If celebs come today, it's to visit Harbour Island, not the "mainland." However, Eleuthera's natural attractions, which made it alluring in the first place, are still here to welcome you.

Getting the Lowdown on the Eleutheran Hotel Scene

Because all the luxury properties on Eleuthera have gone belly-up, nearly every place you stay on the mainland is affordable. If you like to spend big bucks, you can always sail over to Harbour Island. Otherwise, you can expect a reasonably priced vacation.

Although we personally like Eleuthera in the late summer and fall when most visitors have departed, not all inns and hotels are likely to be open, especially in late September, October, and November. If business is slow, hoteliers simply close their doors.

With the closing of Club Med, all the hotels remaining on Eleuthera are small. It's impossible to find anything with more than 20 units; three- to four-room rentals are the norm.

Don't come expecting a lot of personal attention. Eleuthera caters to self-sufficient types who can take care of themselves. We've often met the owner when checking into a rental and didn't see him or her until again when it was time to pay the bill.

Deciding Where to Stay

The very dearth of accommodations will make the decision for you. In days of yore, **Rock Sound** with its fabled Windermere Club or Cotton Bay Club was far chicer than today's Harbour Island. Chartered planes carrying CEOs landed several times a day. Rock Sound was called, "Where Who's Who in America goes barefoot in the sand." Those days are now memories. Except for private villas, Rock Sound is devoid of rentals.

As you leave Rock Sound heading north of its airport, you come to **Tarpum Bay** where you'll find only a handful of simple inns. North of here at the settlement of **Palmetto Point** is a cluster of other modest villas. **Governor's Harbour** — or at least its economy — has never recovered from the day a hurricane washed away Club Med. However, a number of offbeat accommodations, such as Duck Inn and Orchid Gardens, are far superior to any place you'll locate south of Governor's Harbour.

As you move north into **Hatchet Bay** and **Gregory Town**, you'll come upon some other modest digs. Although simple, the little Mom and Pop places are clean, comfortable, well-maintained, and affordable. Check them out.

The Adventurer's Resort
$ Spanish Wells

Because the 1999 hurricane demolished all the competition, this hotel has emerged as the most appealing, most solid-looking, and most recommendable spot in Spanish Wells. It occupies a two-story, pale lavender-colored building in a well-tended garden about a quarter mile west of the town center. There's no restaurant or bar on-site, but the staff member will direct you to nearby eateries and to the beach, which lies about a half mile away. The 18-room small bedrooms have simple, durable furniture with tropical upholstery; six of the units are apartments with kitchenettes. All accommodations are equipped with air-conditioning and TV but no phone. Maid service is provided when you rent the regular double room, but not the apartments.

Harbourfront (P.O. Box El 27498). ☎ *242-333-4883.* Fax: *242-333-5073. Internet:* www.bahamasvg.com. *Rack rates: $75 double, $110 1-bedroom apt with kitchenette, $165 2-bedroom apt with kitchenette. AE, MC, V.*

Eleuthera

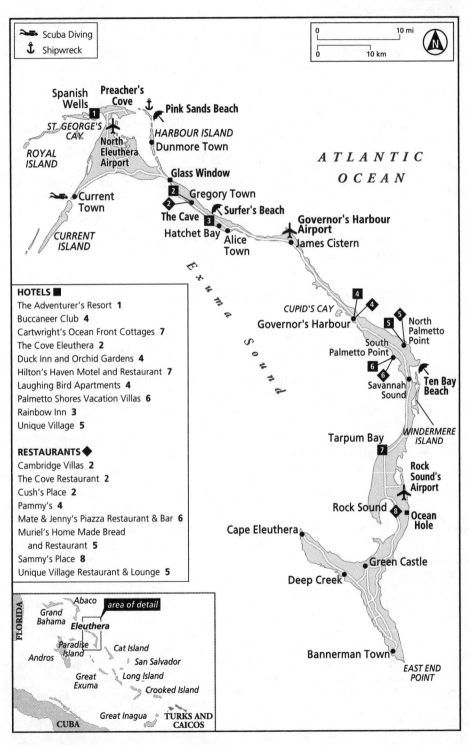

Scuba Diving
⚓ **Shipwreck**

0   10 mi
0   10 km
N

Spanish Wells
Preacher's Cove
⚓ Pink Sands Beach
ST. GEORGE'S CAY
North Eleuthera Airport
HARBOUR ISLAND
Dunmore Town
ROYAL ISLAND
Current Town
Glass Window
Gregory Town
Surfer's Beach
The Cave
Hatchet Bay
Alice Town
James Cistern
CURRENT ISLAND

ATLANTIC OCEAN

Governor's Harbour Airport

E x u m a   S o u n d

CUPID'S CAY
Governor's Harbour
North Palmetto Point
South Palmetto Point
Savannah Sound
Ten Bay Beach
WINDERMERE ISLAND
Tarpum Bay
Rock Sound's Airport
Rock Sound
Ocean Hole
Cape Eleuthera
Green Castle
Deep Creek
Bannerman Town
EAST END POINT

HOTELS ■
The Adventurer's Resort **1**
Buccaneer Club **4**
Cartwright's Ocean Front Cottages **7**
The Cove Eleuthera **2**
Duck Inn and Orchid Gardens **4**
Hilton's Haven Motel and Restaurant **7**
Laughing Bird Apartments **4**
Palmetto Shores Vacation Villas **6**
Rainbow Inn **3**
Unique Village **5**

RESTAURANTS ◆
Cambridge Villas **2**
The Cove Restaurant **2**
Cush's Place **2**
Pammy's **4**
Mate & Jenny's Piazza Restaurant & Bar **6**
Muriel's Home Made Bread and Restaurant **5**
Sammy's Place **8**
Unique Village Restaurant & Lounge **5**

FLORIDA
Abaco
Grand Bahama
area of detail
Eleuthera
Paradise Island
Andros
Cat Island
San Salvador
Great Exuma
Long Island
Crooked Island
Great Inagua
TURKS AND CAICOS
CUBA

Buccaneer Club
$ Governor's Harbour

This three-story, five-room farmhouse, built more than a century ago, offers views over the harbor. Today, it sports yellow-painted plank siding, white trim, and an old-fashioned design. The beach lies within a 10-minute stroll, although a small, saltwater pool is located on site. Bedrooms are comfortable, unpretentious, well-maintained, clean, and outfitted with simple but colorful furniture, plus a small bathroom with a shower-tub combination. Rooms are air-conditioned and contain TV but no phone. Your host and hostess are Michelle and Dwight Johnson, an Indian/Bahamian entrepreneurial team who foster a calm, quiet atmosphere. Lunch and dinner are served daily in an airy, newly built annex with island murals. Good-tasting specialties include Bahamian and American standbys: steaks, burgers, club sandwiches, cracked conch, grilled grouper with lemon butter sauce, and chili.

Haynes Dr. at Buccaneer Dr. ☎ **242-332-2000.** *Fax: 242-332-2888. Rack rates: $94 double. DISC, MC, V.*

Cartwright's Ocean Front Cottages
$ Tarpum Bay

Cartwright's is a cluster of three simple cottages right by the sea, with fishing, snorkeling, and swimming at your door. This is one of the few places where you can sit on your patio and watch the sunset. The small cottages, most recently renovated in 1996, are fully furnished, with utensils, stove, refrigerator, pots and pans, and maid service provided. Each unit comes with a small bathroom containing a shower stall. You'll be within walking distance of local stores and restaurants. Rooms are air-conditioned but contain no phone. Regular hotel services are skimpy, although laundry service is available, as well as babysitting, if arranged in advance.

Bay St., Tarpum Bay, Eleuthera, The Bahamas. ☎ **242-334-4215.** *Email:* cartwrights@hotmail.com. *Rack rates: $90 1-bedroom cottage, $130 2-bedroom cottage, $150 3-bedroom cottage. No credit cards.*

The Cove Eleuthera
$$ Gregory Town

On a private sandy cove 1½ miles northwest of Gregory Town and 3 miles southeast of the Glass Window, this 26-unit resort is set on 28 acres partially planted with pineapples; it consists of a main clubhouse and seven tropical-style buildings, each containing four units, nestled on the oceanside. The resort, a favorite with families, was devastated during the hurricanes of 1999, and a radical rebuilding program was needed. By late 2000, rooms were back in shape. Each one has tile floors and a porch, with no TVs or phones to distract you. All accommodations are equipped with a small bathroom with shower stalls. The restaurant serves three good meals a day, and the lounge and the Pineapple Patio, poolside, are open daily for drinks and informal meals. Kayaks, bicycles, two tennis courts, and a small freshwater pool compete with hammocks for your time. There's fabulous snorkeling right off the sands here, with colorful fish darting in and out of the offshore reefs.

Queen's Hwy. ☎ *800-552-5960 in the U.S. and Canada, or 242-335-5142. Fax: 242-335-5338. Internet: www.thecoveeleuthera.com. Rack rates: $130–$145 double, $149 triple. 1 child under 12 stays free in parents' room. MAP (breakfast and dinner) $33 per person extra. AE, MC, V.*

Duck Inn and Orchid Gardens
$$$ Governor's Harbour

The three accommodations you'll rent here are larger, plusher, more historic, and more charming than what you'd expect in a conventional hotel. All come with kitchenettes, air-conditioning, and TV but no room phone. The complex consists of three clapboard-sided houses, each built between 80 and 175 years ago, and each almost adjacent to another, midway up a hillside overlooking the sea. Nassau-born John (J.J.) Duckworth and his Michigan-born wife, Katie, along with their son John Lucas, are your hosts. Much of their time is spent nurturing a sprawling collection of beautiful orchids being cultivated for export to Europe and the United States. The collection of orchids, some 4,000 strong, is one of the largest in North America.

Queen's Hwy. ☎ *242-332-2608. Internet: www.theduckinn.com. Rack rates: $110 studio for 2, $220 4-bedroom cottage for up to 8. MC, V.*

Hilton's Haven Motel and Restaurant
$ Tarpum Bay

Across the road from the beach and a short drive from the Rock Sound airport, this Bahamian two-story, 11-room structure with covered verandas is modest and completely unpretentious, with decent prices. Comfortably furnished apartments, each with a private sun patio and bathroom with shower stalls, come with either air-conditioning or ceiling fans, but no phones. What makes this place special is Mary Hilton herself, everybody's "Bahama Mama." In fact, as a professional nurse, she has delivered some 2,000 of Eleuthera's finest citizens. She started Hilton's Haven to provide retirement income for herself. "Hilton is my God-given name," she says. "I never met Conrad." The main tavern-style dining room, with a library in the corner, provides well-cooked food daily; the emphasis is on freshly caught fish. You can order grouper cutlets with peas 'n' rice, steamed conch, and the occasional lobster.

Tarpum Bay. ☎ *242-334-4231. Fax: 242-331-4020. Email: hilhaven@batelnet. bs. Rack rates: $80 double, $125 apt for 4. MAP (breakfast and dinner) $11 per person extra. No credit cards.*

Laughing Bird Apartments
$ Governor's Harbour

These four simple apartments lie near the edge of town on a beach in the center of Eleuthera and are a good bet if you want to settle in for a week or so. Efficiencies come with a living/dining/sleeping area, with a separate kitchen and a separate bathroom with shower stall. Apartments front the beach on an acre of landscaped property. The units are bright, clean, and airy and have air-conditioning and containing TV but no phone. The staff offers bike rentals, tables and chairs for outdoor eating, and a garden bar-becue and can also make arrangements for waterskiing, surfing, fishing, sailing, tennis, golf, and snorkeling.

Haynes Ave. and Birdie St. (P.O. Box EL25076), Governor's Harbour. ☎ **800-688-4752** *in the U.S., or 242-332-2012. Fax: 242-332-2358. Internet:* www.vrbo.com. *Rack rates: $95–$105 double, $115–$120 triple, $125–$130 quad. DISC, MC, V.*

Palmetto Shores Vacation Villas
$$ Palmetto Point

This is a good choice if you want your own apartment and value inde-pendence and privacy over hotel services. Asa Bethel rents 12 villas suit-able for two to four guests. Units are built in a plain Bahamian-style, with living rooms, kitchens, small bathrooms with shower-tub combinations, and wraparound balconies that open directly onto your own private beach. Furnishings are simple but reasonably comfortable, VCRs are included, and the villas lie within walking distance of local shops and tennis courts. Bedrooms are air-conditioned and contain TVs plus small kitchenettes, but no phones. The staff is helpful in arranging car rentals, snorkeling, deep-sea fishing and also provide free Sunflower sailboats.

Palmetto Point. ☎ **888-688-4752** *in the U.S., or 242-332-1305. Fax: 242-332-1305. Internet:* www.ivacation.com/p6835.htm. *Rack rates: $100–$180 1-, 2-, and 3-bedroom villas. Extra person $30 winter. MC, V.*

Rainbow Inn
$$ Hatchet Bay

Two miles south of Alice Town and near a sandy beach, the Rainbow Inn is a venerable survivor in an area where many competitors have failed. Quirky and appealing to guests who return for quiet getaways again and again, it's an isolated collection of seven cedar-sided octagonal bunga-lows. The accommodations are simple but comfortable, spacious, and tidy; each has a kitchenette, lots of exposed wood, a ceiling fan, a small bathroom with a shower unit, a porch, and a TV but no phone. A sandy beach is a few steps away, the inn offers an on-site, mid-sized saltwater pool, along with a tennis court. You can rent cars, although bikes (and even snorkeling gear) are provided.

One of the most appealing things about the place is its bar and restaurant, a destination for residents far up and down the length of Eleuthera. It's an octagon with a high-beamed ceiling and a thick-topped woodsy-looking bar where guests down daiquiris and piña coladas amid nautical trappings. It has live Bahamian music twice a week and one of the most extensive menus on Eleuthera. The owners take pride that the menu hasn't changed much in 20 years, a fact that suits its loyal fans just fine. Local Bahamian food includes fish, conch chowder, fried conch, fresh fish, and Bahamian lobster. International dishes feature French onion soup, escargots, and steaks, followed by key lime pie for dessert. Table No. 2, crafted from a triangular teakwood prow of a motor yacht that was wrecked off the coast of Eleuthera in the 1970s, is a perpetual favorite.

Governor's Harbour. ☎ **800-688-0047** *in the U.S., or 242-335-0294. Fax: 242-335-0294. Internet:* www.rainbowinn.com. *Rack rates: $120–$150 studio, $200–$220 2- or 3-bedroom villas. MAP (breakfast and dinner) $40 per person extra. MC, V. Closed Sept 7–Nov 15.*

Unique Village
$$ Palmetto Point

Located on a steep rise above the Atlantic coast of Eleuthera, this 14-room hotel is the creative statement of a Palmetto Point businessman who also owns the local hardware store (Unique Hardware). Built in 1992, the hotel offers air-conditioned accommodations in several configurations (everything from conventional single or double rooms to a one-bedroom apartment with a kitchenette to two-bedroom villas with full kitchens). Each comes with a small bathroom with a shower-tub combination, but no phone. A flight of wooden steps brings you to the beach, where a reef breaks up the Atlantic surf and creates calm waters on this sandy cove. There's a bar and restaurant, also called Unique Village (see the entry later in this chapter), but few other luxuries. Although no sailing, scuba, or tennis is on-site, the staff can direct you to other facilities that lie within a reasonable drive. (You'll probably want a car here.)

N. Palmetto Point. ☎ **800-688-4752** *in the U.S., or 242-332-1830. Fax: 242-332-1838. Internet:* www.bahamasvg.com. *Rack rates: $120–$140 double, $160 1-bedroom apt for 2, $190 2-bedroom apt for up to 4. Extra person $25. MAP (breakfast and dinner) $35 per person per day. MC, V.*

Arriving in Eleuthera

Eleuthera has three main airports. **North Eleuthera Airport** (☎ 242-335-1242), obviously, serves the north along with the two major offshore cays, Harbour Island and Spanish Wells. **Governor's Harbour Airport** (☎ 242-332-2321) serves the center of the island, and **Rock Sound International Airport** (☎ 242-334-2171) handles traffic to South Eleuthera.

Make sure, when making your reservations, that your flight will arrive at the appropriate airport; one visitor flew into Rock Sound Airport, only to face a $100 taxi ride and a water-taxi trip before reaching his final destination of Harbour Island in the north.

Bahamasair (☎ 800-222-4262) offers daily flights between Nassau and the three airports in Eleuthera.

In addition, several commuter airlines, with regularly scheduled service, fly from the Florida mainland with either nonstop or one-stop service. Many private flights use the North Eleuthera Airport, with its 4,500-foot paved runway. It's an official Bahamian port of entry, and a Customs and Immigration official is on hand.

USAir Express operates what may be the most popular way of reaching two of Eleuthera's airports directly from the mainland of Florida. Flights depart once a day from Miami flying nonstop to North Eleuthera and then continue on, after briefly unloading passengers and baggage, to Governor's Harbour. **American Eagle** (☎ 800-433-7300) offers daily flights from Miami to Governor's Harbour. Usually, only one flight a day is scheduled, but if demand merits it, two flights can occur on Friday and three on Saturday and Sunday, because most visitors fly over for the weekend. Small carriers include **Twin Air** (☎ 954/359-8266), flying from Fort Lauderdale three times a week to Rock Sound and Governor's Harbour and four times a week to North Eleuthera.

A new interisland link, **Bahamas Fast Ferries** (☎ 242-323-2166), originates in Potter's Cay, beneath the Paradise Island Bridge, and fans out at regular intervals to Harbour Island, North Eleuthera, and Governor's Harbour. Round-trip fares are $100 for adults, $60 for children under 12.

Getting around Eleuthera

It's virtually impossible to get lost on Eleuthera — only one road meanders along the entire length of its snake-shaped form, and you'll stray from it only very rarely. Because it's so easy to tour the island, most visitors rent a car at least for one day. (Prices are usually around $80 a day.) If you prefer to take a taxi, you can arrange one by simply asking your hotel or any of the taxi drivers lined up either outside the North Eleuthera Airport or at the ferryboat docks heading to Harbour Island. Your other choices are walking or renting a bike.

  ✔ **Hoofing it.** At 100 miles from top to bottom, Eleuthera appears to be a daunting challenge. However, you can explore Eleuthera by rented car or taxi on a day trip. After that, most visitors confine themselves to the site of their resort such as Governor's Harbour. All the settlements — really, hamlets, in most cases — can easily be traversed on foot. With little traffic, walking is an enjoyable experience.

✔ **Wheeling around**. No American car-rental agency is located on the island. Usually, your hotel can arrange for a car rental. Often, we've ended up with someone's private car. The best bet for car rentals is the North Eleuthera-based **Fine Threads Taxi, Rental Cars & Tours** (☎ 242-359-7780). Here, owner Frederick Neely (nicknamed "Fine Threads" because of his well-tailored clothes) will either rent you a rental car or take you on a private island tour (available for up to six people). An 8-hour experience will cost $200. Tours usually begin at 8 a.m. and take in a series of bars, restaurants, and geological or historical attractions in Rock Sound, Lower Bogue, Palmetto Point, and Gregory Town. If you negotiate with your driver, you might also visit Preacher's Cave.

✔ **Taking a taxi**. Most visitors take a taxi only when they arrive at one of the local airports or when it's time to return to that airport for their flight back home. Taxis meet all incoming flights and are available at ferry docks. There is no central number to call, as cabbies are independent operators on Eleuthera, working out of their homes instead of offices. Should you need to call a taxi, your hotel staff can summon one for you, but it may take a while so plan ahead.

✔ **Sailing on a ferry**. For information about how to reach Harbour Island from Eleuthera, refer to Chapter 21. The other offshore island, Spanish Wells, is linked to North Eleuthera by convenient "on demand" ferry service. A boat runs between Gene's Bay in North Eleuthera to the main pier at Spanish Wells. The ferries depart whenever passengers show up, and the cost is $10 per person round-trip.

Dining in Eleuthera

Cambridge Villas
$ Gregory Town BAHAMIAN

This is one of the few choices in town, occupying a large cement-sided room on the ground floor of a battered hotel. (The accommodations aren't as appealing as the restaurant.) Harcourt and Sylvia Cambridge, the owners, serve conch burgers, conch chowder, and sandwiches, usually prepared by Sylvia herself. It's just a simple spot, where you might be entertained by the continually running soap operas broadcast from a TV over the bar.

Main St. No phone. Reservations not accepted. Sandwiches and platters: $4–$10. MC, V. Open: daily 7:30 a.m.–9 p.m.

The Cove Restaurant
$ Gregory Town BAHAMIAN/CONTINENTAL

Located at The Cove Eleuthera hotel 1½ miles north of Gregory Town, this spacious dining room is your best bet in the area. It's nothing fancy, but offers good homemade local fare. The restaurant is decorated in a light, tropical style. Lunch begins with the inevitable conch chowder; we recommend you follow it with a conch burger, a generous patty of ground conch blended with green pepper, onion, and spices. Conch also appears several times in the evening, including the best cracked conch in town, which has been tenderized and dipped in a special batter and fried to a golden perfection. The kitchen serves the best fried chicken in the area. People travel from miles around to attend the Saturday-night $28 buffet — the smoked dolphinfish dip is reason enough to stop in. They also offer a vegetarian buffet for $17.25.

At The Cove Eleuthera, Queen's Hwy. ☎ 242-335-5142. Reservations not necessary. Breakfast $5–$10; lunch $6–$12; main courses $10–$32. AE, MC, V. Open: daily 8 a.m.–10:30 a.m., noon–2:30 p.m. and 6:30 p.m.–8:30 p.m.

Cush's Place
$ Gregory Town   BAHAMIAN

Macushla Scavella (Cush, for short) is the owner of this big yellow stucco-sided building set about a half mile south of Gregory Town. Inside the somewhat sterile-looking interior, you'll find a jukebox, a pool table, and a bartender named Walter. Generous portions of Bahamian food are (slowly) served throughout the day and evening. Pork chops and chicken à la Cush (fried chicken) are ongoing staples, along with sandwiches, lobster tail, and steamed conch with black-eyed peas and corn on the cob. Come here to hang out with the locals, perhaps over drinks and a platter of food.

Queen's Hwy. ☎ 242-335-5301. Reservations: not necessary. Sandwiches: $2.75–$4; lunch and dinner main courses: $12–$18. No credit cards. Open: Daily 10 a.m.–midnight.

Pammy's
$ Governor's Harbour   BAHAMIAN

Tile-floored and Formica-clad, this is just a little cubbyhole with a few tables. Lunchtime brings sandwiches, and dinner features platters of cracked conch, pork chops, and either broiled or fried grouper. Don't expect anything fancy, 'cause this definitely ain't it. It's a true local joint serving up generous portions of flavor-filled food.

Queen's Hwy. at Gospel Chapel Rd. ☎ 242-332-2843. Reservations not accepted. Breakfast platters: $2–$6; lunch platters $3–$9; dinner main courses $11–$20. No credit cards. Open: Mon–Sat 8 a.m. –9 p.m.

Mate & Jenny's Piazza Restaurant & Bar
$ Palmetto Point   BAHAMIAN/AMERICAN

This popular restaurant, known for its conch pizza, has a jukebox and a pool table. It's the most frequented local joint, completely modest and unassuming. In addition to pizza, the Bethel family will prepare pan-fried grouper, cracked conch, or light meals, including snacks and sandwiches. Lots of folks come here just to drink. Try their Goombay Smash, Rumrunner, or piña colada, or just a Bahamian Kalik beer.

S. Palmetto Point, right off Queen's Hwy. ☎ **242-332-1504.** *Reservations: Not needed. Pizza $7–$24; main courses $12–$20. No credit cards. Open: Wed–Sat and Mon 11 a.m.–3 p.m. and 6 p.m.–10 p.m.*

Muriel's Home Made Bread and Restaurant
$ Palmetto Point   BAHAMIAN

Muriel Cooper's operation runs a bakery and a take-out food emporium. Her rich and moist pineapple and coconut cakes are some of the best you'll find in the Out Islands. A limited menu of true local cooking includes full dinners, such as chicken with chips, cracked conch, conch chowder, and conch fritters. If you want a more elaborate meal, you'll have to stop by in the morning to place your order. This arrangement is ideal if you're staying in a cottage or villa nearby.

N. Palmetto Point. ☎ **242-332-1583.** *Reservations: Not needed. Main courses: $7–$10. No credit cards. Open: Mon–Sat 10 a.m.–6 p.m.*

Sammy's Place
$ Rock Sound   BAHAMIAN

Hot gossip and cheap, juicy burgers make Sammy's the most popular hangout in Rock Sound — come here for a slice of local life. Sammy's is on the northeastern approach to the settlement, in a neighborhood that even the owner refers to as "the back side of town." Sammy Culmer (who's assisted by Margarita, his daughter) will serve you drinks (including Bahama Mamas and rum punches), conch fritters, Creole-style grouper, breaded scallops, pork chops, and lobster. If you drop in before 11 a.m., you may be tempted by a selection of egg dishes or omelets.

This is primarily a restaurant and bar, but Sammy does rent four rooms with air-conditioning and satellite TV, plus two efficiency cottages containing two bedrooms with a kitchen. These accommodations can be yours for $76 per night, double occupancy.

Albury's Lane. ☎ **242-334-2121.** *Reservations recommended only for special meal requests. Bahamian breakfasts: $7; lunch $3–$12; main courses $8–$15. No credit cards. Open: Daily 7:30 a.m.–10 p.m.*

Unique Village Restaurant & Lounge
$ Palmetto Point   BAHAMIAN/AMERICAN

This is the best place for food in the area, offering the widest selection. You can drop in for a Bahamian breakfast of boiled or stewed fish served with johnnycakes, or steamed corned beef and grits. ("Regular" breakfasts, including hearty omelets, are also available.) Lunch offerings include zesty conch chowder and an array of salads. Burgers are served, along with what the kitchen calls "Bahamian belly pleasers," including the steamed catch of the day. At night, the choices grow, and you'll find the best New York sirloin available in mid-Eleuthera, ranging in size from 8 to 16 ounces. Cracked conch fried in a light beer batter is one of the better renderings of this dish on the island.

In the Unique Village, N. Palmetto Point. ☎ **242-332-1830.** Reservations: Not needed. Main courses: $13.95–$32. MC, V. Open: daily 7:30 a.m.–11:30 a.m., noon–5 p.m., and 6 p.m.–9:30 p.m.

Having Fun on the Beach

The long "string" that is Eleuthera possesses some of the finest beaches in The Bahamas, though none is as fine as the three miles of pink sands at Harbour Island (see Chapter 21).

Now relatively deserted, **Cape Eleuthera** was once home to a chic resort and yacht club that drew some of the movers and shakers from America's East Coast. They're all gone now, but the splendid **white sandy beaches** — three of them — remain the same, and locals claim the deep-sea fishing is as fine as it ever was.

Directly north of the town of Tarpum Bay lies **Gaulding's Cay**, a lovely beach of golden sand with exceptional snorkeling.

None of the beaches of Eleuthera has facilities or lifeguards. Whatever you'll need on the beach, you should bring with you, including sunscreen and water.

Even without its posh hotel, **Windermere Island** is worth a day trip. **Savannah Sound,** with its sandy sheltered beaches and outstanding snorkeling, is particularly appealing (bring your own gear). There are also excellent beaches for shelling and picnicking, and bonefishing is good, with some catches weighing in at more than 10 pounds.

West Beach, a good place for sunning and swimming (great for children), is about a 10-minute walk from the shut-down Windermere Club. The beach is on Savannah Sound, and this body of calm, protected water separates Windermere from the main island of Eleuthera.

Visitors can enjoy a number of activities, from bonefishing to windsurfing. The dockmaster at West Beach is well-qualified to guide and advise about bonefishing, or perhaps you'd like to go deep-sea fishing for white marlin, dolphinfish, grouper, wahoo, Allison tuna, and amberjack. Because there is no permanent outfitter, you have to ask around locally about who can take you out.

At **Palmetto Point**, site of some villa rentals, you find **Ten Bay Beach**, one of the best beaches in The Bahamas, with its sparkling turquoise water and wide expanse of soft white sand. The beach lies a 10-minute drive south of Palmetto Point and just north of Savannah Sound. You won't find facilities, only idyllic isolation.

Near the center of **Governor's Harbour** are two sandy beaches known locally as the **Buccaneer Public Beaches;** they're adjacent to the Buccaneer Club, on the sheltered western edge of the island, facing Exuma Sound. Snorkeling is good here — it's best at the point where the pale turquoise waters near the coast deepen to a dark blue. Underwater rocks shelter lots of marine flora and fauna. The waves at these beaches are relatively calm.

On Eleuthera's Atlantic (eastern) side, about a half mile from Governor's Harbour, is a much longer stretch of mostly pale pink sand, similar to what you'll find in Harbour Island. Known locally as the **Club Med Public Beach,** it's good for bodysurfing and, on days when storms are surging in the Atlantic, even conventional surfing.

Don't expect any touristy kiosks selling drinks, snacks, or souvenirs at any of these beaches, because everything is very pristine and undeveloped.

Diving isn't a big sport on mainland Eleuthera where outfitters come and go quickly, few getting enough business to hold out until another winter. But diving is excellent off Harbour Island, with some of the best scuba-diving experts in The Bahamas (see Chapter 21).

Seeing Eleuthera on Dry Land

We like to drive the full 100-mile length of Eleuthera, stopping wherever something enchants us. There are no historical attractions, only those nature created. We begin our tour in the south and head north.

Located in South Eleuthera, **Rock Sound** is a small shady village, the island's main town and once its most exclusive enclave. The closing of two old-time landmark resorts, the Cotton Bay Club and the Windermere Club, has at least for now halted the flow of famous visitors, who once included everybody from the late Princess Diana to a parade of CEOs. No reopenings are yet in sight, but at least that means that you can have many of South Eleuthera's best beaches practically to yourself.

Rock Sound opens onto **Exuma Sound** and is located to the south of **Tarpum Bay.** The town is at least two centuries old, and it has many old-fashioned homes with picket fences out front. Once notorious for wreckers who lured ships ashore with false beacons, it used to be known as "Wreck Sound."

The **Ocean Hole,** which is about 1¼ miles east of the heart of Rock Sound, is said to be bottomless. This saltwater lake, which eventually meets the sea, is one of the most attractive spots on Eleuthera. You can walk right down to the edge of the water. Many tropical fish can be seen here; they seem to like to be photographed — but only if you feed them first.

The main reason to come to Rock Sound is to play the **Robert Trent Jones, Jr. Course** at the Cotton Bay Club (☎ 242-334-6156), a par-72, 18-hole, 7,068-yard course. Greens fees are $100 for 18 holes, but you must call ahead to reserve a tee time.

After leaving Rock Sound, head south, bypassing the abandoned Cotton Bay Club, and continue through the villages of **Green Castle** and **Deep Creek.** At this point, you take a sharp turn northwest along the only road leading to **Cape Eleuthera.** Locals call this Cape Eleuthera Road, though you won't find any markings other than a sign pointing the way. If you continue to follow this road northwest, you'll reach the end of the island chain, jutting out into Exuma Sound.

Back on the main road again, you can head north of Rock Sound for 9 miles until you come to the charming old waterfront village of Tarpum Bay, where a nostalgic decay hangs over the place. This tiny settlement, with its many pastel-washed, gingerbread-trimmed houses, is a favorite of artists, who have established a small colony here with galleries and studios.

Once the most exclusive vacation retreat in The Bahamas, **Windermere Island** is still here even if the exclusive Windermere Island Club is now closed. The island, reached by a small bridge, lies between the settlements of Rock Sound and Governor's Harbour.

It boasts a sandy beach running the length of its four-mile Atlantic shore where a pregnant Princess Diana was photographed in the 1980s, the picture gaining worldwide notoriety.

Many second homes of rich Americans are still here, and the island is patrolled by security guards.

You may have to do some sweet-talking to get past the security patrols. They generally will let you drive along the island if they think you're a sightseer and not a house burglar.

On the east side of Queen's Highway, south of Governor's Harbour, **North Palmetto Point** is a little village where visitors rarely venture (although you can get a meal there). This laid-back town will suit you if you want peace and quiet off the beaten track.

At some 300 years old, **Governor's Harbour** is the island's oldest settlement, reportedly the landing place of the Eleutherian Adventurers. The largest town on Eleuthera after Rock Sound, it lies midway along the 100-mile-long island; its airport is likely to be your gateway to the island.

The town today has a population of about 1,500, with some bloodlines going back to the original settlers, the Eleutherian Adventurers, and to the Loyalists who followed some 135 years later. Many old homes line the streets amid the bougainvillea and casuarina trees.

Leaving Queen's Highway, you can take a small bridge, thought to be about 150 years old, to Cupid's Cay. As you're exploring, you'll come upon one of the most interesting buildings in the area, an old Anglican church with its tombstone-studded graveyard.

Twenty-five miles north of Governor's Harbour, **Hatchet Bay** was once known for a sprawling British-owned plantation that had 500 head of dairy cattle and thousands of chickens. Today, that plantation is gone, and this is now one of the sleepiest villages on Eleuthera, as you can see if you veer off Queen's Highway onto one of the town's ghostly main streets, Lazy Shore Road or Ocean Drive.

Gregory Town stands in the center of Eleuthera against a backdrop of hills, which break the usual flat monotony of the landscape. A village of clapboard cottages, it was once famed for growing pineapples. Though the industry isn't as strong as it was in the past, the locals make a good pineapple rum out of the fruit, and you can visit the Gregory Town Plantation and Distillery where it's produced. You're allowed to sample it, and we can almost guarantee you'll want to take a bottle home with you.

Dedicated surfers have come here from as far away as California and Australia to test their skills at **Surfer's Beach,** a couple of miles south of Gregory Town on the Atlantic side. The waves are at their highest in winter and spring; even if you're not brave enough to venture out, the surfers are fun to watch.

South of town on the way to Hatchet Bay are several caverns worth visiting, the largest of which is called simply **the Cave.** It has a big fig tree out front, which the people of Gregory Town claim was planted long ago by area pirates who wanted to conceal the cave because they had hidden treasure in it. Local guides (you have to ask around in Gregory Town or Hatchet Bay) will take you into the interior of the cave, where the resident bats are harmless (even though they must resent the intrusion of tourists with flashlights). At one point, the drop is so steep — about 12 feet — that you have to use a ladder to climb down. Eventually you reach a cavern studded with stalactites and stalagmites. At this point, a maze of passageways leads off through the rocky underground recesses. The cave comes to an abrupt end at the edge of a cliff, where the thundering sea is some 90 feet below.

After leaving Gregory Town and driving north, you come to the famed **Glass Window,** Eleuthera's chief sight and narrowest point. Once a natural rock arch bridged the land, but it's gone now, replaced by an artificially constructed bridge. As you drive across it, you can see the contrast between the deep blue ocean and the emerald green shoal waters of the sound. The rocks rise to a height of 70 feet. Often, as ships in the Atlantic are being tossed about, the crew looks across the narrow point to see a ship resting quietly on the other side (hence the name Glass Window). Winslow Homer was so captivated by this spot that he once captured it on canvas.

The inhabitants of the **Current,** a settlement in North Eleuthera, are believed to have descended from a tribe of Native Americans. A narrow strait separates the village from Current Island, where most of the locals make their living from the sea or from plaiting straw goods. This small community often welcome visitors. There are no crowds and no artificial attractions. Everything focuses on the sea, a source of pleasure for visitors, but a way to sustain life for the local people.

From the Current, you can explore some interesting sights in North Eleuthera, including **Preacher's Cave,** where the Eleutherian Adventurers found shelter in the mid-17th century when they were shipwrecked with no provisions. (Note that your taxi driver may balk at being asked to drive there; the road is hard on his expensive tires.) If you do reach it, you'll find a cave that seems like an amphitheater. The very devout Eleutherian Adventurers held religious services inside the cave, which is pierced by holes in the roof, allowing light to intrude. The cave is not far from the airport, in a northeasterly direction.

Living It Up After the Sun Goes Down

Eleuthera is rather sleepy, but it does have a hot spot or two.

The place to be in Gregory Town, especially on a Saturday night, is **Elvina** on Main Street (☎ 242-335-5032). Owners Ed and Elvina Watkins make you feel right at home and practically greet you at the door with a cold beer. Although they won't be hired by the queen to decorate Buckingham Palace, they have given their place a funky charm, with local artwork, license plates, and surfboards. Surfers and locals alike flock here to chow down on burgers, Bahamian dishes, and Cajun grub, served daily from 10 a.m. to "whenever we close." Elvina's husband, "Chicken Ed," is from Louisiana, and does he ever know how to make a great jambalaya.

Also at Governor's Harbour, **Ronnie's Smoke Shop & Sports Bar,** Cupid's Cay (☎ 242-332-2307), is the most happening night spot in central Eleuthera, drawing folks from miles in either direction. It's adjacent to the cargo depot of Cupid's Cay, in a connected cluster of simple buildings painted in combinations of black with vivid Junkanoo colors. Most folks come here just to drink Kalik beer and talk at either of the two bars. But if you want to dance, it has an all-black room just for disco music on Friday and Saturday nights. There's also the only walk-in cigar humidor on Eleuthera. If you get hungry, order up a plate of barbecue, a pizza, chicken wings, or popcorn. The place is open daily from 10 a.m. 'til at least 2 a.m., and sometimes 5 a.m., depending on business.

Taking a Great Day Trip

Of course, the most enticing day trip is to **Harbour Island** (see Chapter 21). But **Spanish Wells** is intriguing as well as a journey back to a distant past.

Called a "quiet corner of The Bahamas," Spanish Wells is a colorful cluster of houses on St. George's Cay, half a mile off the coast of northwest Eleuthera. It is characterized by its sparkling bays and white beaches, sleepy lagoons, excellent diving, and fine fishing colony.

You can walk through the village, looking at the houses, some more than 200 years old, which have New England saltbox styling but bright tropical coloring. You can see handmade quilts in many colors, following patterns handed down from generations of English ancestors. Homeowners display these quilts on their front porches or out their windows, and they're for sale. No one locks their doors here or removes ignition keys from their cars.

Regardless of the time of day you arrive, a ferryboat will be either waiting for passengers or about to arrive with a load of them. See "Getting around Eleuthera," earlier in this chapter, for more details.

If you're on the island at lunch, head for **Jack's Outback,** along the Harbourfront (☎ 242-333-4219). Decent, unpretentious, and well-scrubbed, this little place stands along the waterfront in the heart of town. There's a hint of funkiness here, in its luncheonette-style combination of wood, plastic, and Formica, and its color scheme of pink and blue. Known for its home-cooking, it offers the usual array of sandwiches and cheeseburgers, as well as Bahamian foods like cracked conch, conch burgers, and conch chowder. It also offers steaks, barbecued ribs, and cheesy shrimp poppers. The interior is air-conditioned, with views of the sea. Sandwiches cost from $2.50 to $10, with main courses priced from $12 to $26. It is open daily from 8:30 a.m. to 1 a.m., and MasterCard and Visa are accepted.

Fast Facts: Eleuthera

Babysitting

Hotel staff can help you find a babysitter.

Banks

Governor's Harbour has a branch of Barclays Bank International on Queen's Highway (☎ 242-332-2300).

Information

The Eleuthera Tourist Office is on Queens Highway (☎ 242-332-2142); it's generally open Monday to Friday 9 a.m. to 5 p.m.

Medical Care

On Queen's Highway is the **Governor Harbour's Medical Clinic** (☎ 242-332-2001), open Monday through Friday from 9 a.m. to 5:30 p.m. The clinic is also the site of a dentist's office. The dentist is here from 9:30 a.m. until 3 p.m., Monday through Wednesday and Friday only. Call for an appointment before going here. A doctor and four resident nurses form the staff of the **Rock Sound Medical Clinic** (☎ 242-334-2226). Office hours are daily from 9 a.m. to 1 p.m.; after that, the doctor is always available to handle emergency cases.

Police

If you need the police, call ☎ 242-332-2111.

Post Office

At Governor's Harbour there's a post office on Haynes Avenue (☎ 242-332-2060).

Safety

Eleuthera is one of the safest Bahamian islands. Of course, take all the same precautions you would here that you would when traveling anywhere. Keep valuables in a safe place and don't wander into deserted, unfamiliar areas at night.

Taxis

Cabs meet incoming flights at all three airports. During your stay, your hotel staff can call a taxi for you should the need arise.

Chapter 23

Exuma

●●

In This Chapter

▶ Finding the best accommodations

▶ Staying on single-resort islands

▶ Enjoying spectacular sailing and kayaking

▶ Exploring George Town, the charming harborside capital

●●

Exuma — or the Exumas — is a string of some 365 cays, the islets Bahamians call "keys," one for each day of the year. (See the map Great Exuma/Little Exuma for details.) Most cays are either barely populated or completely uninhabited. The little archipelago is prime sailing, kayaking, fishing, scuba diving, and snorkeling territory.

The Lowdown on Exuma's Hotel Scene

Most hotels lie in and around **George Town,** the capital of the Exumas. Of the handful of hotels, most have fewer than 16 rooms. For escapists, two of Exuma's best accommodations are offshore *one-to-ones:* one island, one resort.

Finding a location right for you

George Town, on **Great Exuma,** the main island, is the easiest to reach. At the edge of **Elizabeth Harbour,** this postcard-pretty village isn't known for its beaches. However, just across the harbor from town, **Stocking Island** boasts some of the country's best sandy shores. A ferry links "mainland" hotels to this beach-rimmed island. If you want to stay here, your choice of Stocking Island hotels is limited to one — a great little find. Although a few George Town hotels have their own beaches, the swimming is far better on Stocking Island. For guests of the one accommodation on **Rolle Cay,** ferry service is free between this sandy harbor islet and George Town.

Sailing is excellent from any home base. Rent a boat, and you can anchor off some of the nearby uninhabited islets, where snorkeling and fishing are top rate. No matter which hotel you select, you can easily arrange scuba diving and fishing.

When you're ready to explore dry land, George Town is the starting point for renting a car or taking a taxi tour. A bridge links Great Exuma to **Little Exuma.**

Accommodations in Exuma are as distinct as they are small. If you like being in the middle of island action, book a room at **Club Peace & Plenty** in town. Guests preferring a secluded, elegant eco-resort can choose solar-powered **Hotel Higgins Landing** on Stocking Island.

No one ever heard of "the rat race" in sleepy Exuma. Hotel rooms may not have phones, and the few TVs may get only a couple of centrally controlled channels (meaning that you watch whatever the bartender turns to). The liveliest entertainment "jumps up" on weekends, generally at Club Peace & Plenty, where the Saturday and sometimes Wednesday night dance parties are legendary. Hotels are close enough to each other so that you can dine among them and mingle in a variety of settings. Some good local restaurants outside the hotels are also conveniently located in and around George Town.

Checking out the best accommodations

Club Peace & Plenty
$$$ In the heart of George Town

This pink and white harborside hotel is the virtual social center of the Exumas. Once a private home, Club Peace & Plenty was built on the site of a slave market during Loyalist days when British supporters fled to The Bahamas from colonial America after the Revolutionary War. A former kitchen during slavery has been transformed into the indoor tavern, decorated with old anchors, rudders, lanterns, and other maritime artifacts. During the island's **Out Island Regatta** each April, visiting and local yachties flock to this hotel's cozy lounge.

The handsome two-story building faces the main road on one side and **Elizabeth Harbour** on the other. With balconies, satellite TV, and queen, double, or twin beds, the 35 bright guest rooms overlook the harbor, freshwater pool, or greenery. Although perfectly comfortable, the rooms have a somewhat dated feel. Despite being Exuma's oldest hotel, each accommodation is well maintained and comfortable, containing a small tiled bathroom with shower. Dine indoors or al fresco at Club Peace & Plenty's popular restaurant, where local seafood is the specialty. Snorkel gear and Windsurfers are available, and a shuttle runs several times a day between the Club and its closest sibling, **Peace & Plenty Beach Inn.**

Great Exuma/Little Exuma

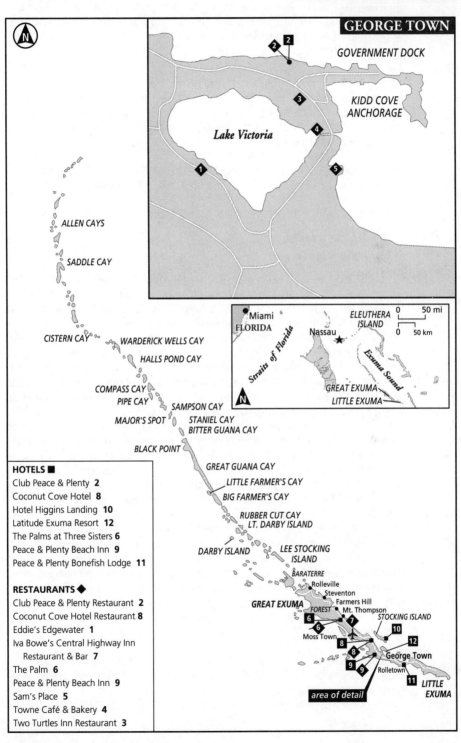

GEORGE TOWN

GOVERNMENT DOCK

KIDD COVE
ANCHORAGE

Lake Victoria

ALLEN CAYS

SADDLE CAY

CISTERN CAY
WARDERICK WELLS CAY
HALLS POND CAY

COMPASS CAY
PIPE CAY
SAMPSON CAY
MAJOR'S SPOT
STANIEL CAY
BITTER GUANA CAY
BLACK POINT

GREAT GUANA CAY
LITTLE FARMER'S CAY
BIG FARMER'S CAY

RUBBER CUT CAY
LT. DARBY ISLAND
DARBY ISLAND
LEE STOCKING
ISLAND
BARATERRE
Rolleville
Steventon
Farmers Hill
GREAT EXUMA
FOREST
Mt. Thompson
STOCKING ISLAND
Moss Town
George Town
Rolletown
LITTLE
EXUMA
area of detail

Miami
FLORIDA
Nassau
ELEUTHERA
ISLAND
Straits of Florida
Exuma Sound
GREAT EXUMA
LITTLE EXUMA
0   50 mi
0   50 km

HOTELS ■
Club Peace & Plenty **2**
Coconut Cove Hotel **8**
Hotel Higgins Landing **10**
Latitude Exuma Resort **12**
The Palms at Three Sisters **6**
Peace & Plenty Beach Inn **9**
Peace & Plenty Bonefish Lodge **11**

RESTAURANTS ◆
Club Peace & Plenty Restaurant **2**
Coconut Cove Hotel Restaurant **8**
Eddie's Edgewater **1**
Iva Bowe's Central Highway Inn
   Restaurant & Bar **7**
The Palm **6**
Peace & Plenty Beach Inn **9**
Sam's Place **5**
Towne Café & Bakery **4**
Two Turtles Inn Restaurant **3**

The ferry to Stocking Island beaches, just across the water, is complimentary to guests. For nonguests, it's $8 round-trip for adults and free for children age 10 and younger. Twice a week, the hotel features a poolside cocktail party for guests. The center of town is just steps away from the hotel's front door.

Peace & Plenty is Exuma's "chain" hotel. Peace & Plenty Beach Inn is about a mile up the road. Ten miles southeast of George Town lies **Peace & Plenty Bonefish Lodge,** an inn for anglers. Dinner is served at the lodge several nights a week, and free transportation is provided to guests of Club Peace & Plenty.

Queen's Hwy., George Town. ☎ *800-525-2210 or 242-336-2551. Fax: 242-336-2550. Internet:* www.peaceandplenty.com. *Rack rates: $150–$165 for a double room. AE, MC, V.*

Hotel Higgins Landing
$$$$$ Stocking Island

This intimate resort is on a tiny, virtually uninhabited, beach-rimmed island. Not only is it the only hotel on luscious Stocking Island, just a mile across Elizabeth Harbour from George Town, it is accessible only by ferry. No roads or cars are on the island, so feet and boats are the modes of transport. Frothy surf thrashes one side of the property, while the calm bay bathes the other. Sailing, kayaking, snorkeling, fishing, and hiking are popular pastimes, and you can make arrangements for scuba diving. This upscale resort is solar powered. Hilly twists and turns along rocky paths lead to the five cottages, which sport large decks. Strategically placed to ensure both privacy and proximity to the beach, each unit is beautifully furnished with antiques, such as four-poster, queen-sized beds and Oriental rugs. You're asked to conserve water, but running out of water isn't a problem. Ceiling fans cool the air, which floats in through glass-free screen windows. Cottages are equipped with enough voltage for fans and reading lights, but you have to go elsewhere at the resort to use standard 110-volt electricity. Instead of television, you can visit the hotel's little library. Bob Higgins, who runs the hotel with his wife, Carol, is in charge of breakfast, served on a deck overlooking **Silver Palms Beach.** One day, he may whip up coconut pancakes; the next, eggs Benedict. Carol takes over for lunch (lobster rolls or salad Niçoise, perhaps) and the candlelit, multicourse dinner may be black mushroom soup followed by grilled beef or seafood and espresso chocolate custard. Room rates may seem high, but they include a gourmet breakfast, lunch, dinner, and hors d'oeuvres daily, the boat trip to and from the island upon arrival and departure, and a variety of water sports.

Smoking is not allowed inside the buildings, but it is permitted on your deck or at the beach bar. Children under 18 are not allowed unless you rent the entire resort.

Across Elizabeth Harbour from George Town. ☎ *888-688-4752 or* ☎ *and fax 242-336-2460. Internet:* www.higginslanding.com. *Rack rates: $390 and up, including breakfast and dinner. MC, V.*

Latitude Exuma Resort

$$$ Rolle Cay

Views of Elizabeth Harbour, Stocking Island, and George Town are panoramic from private 40-acre **Rolle Cay,** which is home to only one resort. Latitude Exuma consists of appealing cottages just steps from a good beach. Spacious decks overlook the water. This resort is a good choice if you're traveling with children or a group of friends or relatives. Modern kitchens, sleeping lofts, full linens, rocking chairs, and other comfortable furnishings make you feel right at home — that is, if your home is on your own little island. A housekeeper cleans your cottage once a week, unless you pay the surcharge for daily tidying. Each unit comes with a small bathroom with shower. Rates include transportation to and from George Town, but you should consider renting a boat for more flexibility and for exploring the surrounding sea.

In Elizabeth Harbour, off George Town. ☎ *877-398-6222 or 242-336-2763; or* ☎ *and fax: 242-336-3033. Internet:* www.kayakbahamas.com. *Rack rates: 1-bedroom cottages begin at $1,500 per week for 2 people. Ask about money-saving weekly rates.*

The Palms at Three Sisters

$ 7 miles northwest of George Town

In 1994, this 14-room low-key resort opened on an isolated spot 7 miles from its nearest neighbor, on a 1,200-foot stretch of lovely white sand. Rooms lie within a two-story, motel-like building and have English colonial details and simple, summery furniture. It's a great place for privacy and seclusion. The resort, incidentally, is named after a trio of rocks (the Three Sisters) with a composition that differs radically from the coral formations throughout the rest of the Exumas. They jut about 15 feet above sea level just offshore from the beach. Bedrooms are comfortable, but basic, containing small bathrooms with shower units. Meals and drinks are served in a low-slung annex, with views stretching out over the Atlantic. Live music is presented every Saturday on a flowering patio.

Queen's Hwy., Bahama Sound Beach. ☎ *888-688-4752 or 242-358-4040. Fax: 242-358-4043. Email:* seaoats@batelnet.bs. *Rack rates: $110 double. MC, V.*

Peace & Plenty Beach Inn

$$$ A mile northwest of George Town

More subdued than its older sibling (**Club Peace & Plenty,** about a mile away in George Town; see its listing earlier in this section), this 16-room hotel sits on a small beach. Built in the early 1990s, it draws many snorkelers and bonefishermen. Everyone from newlyweds to families with children feel comfortable here. In the spacious, attractively decorated guest rooms, French doors open to large patios or balconies overlooking the swimming pool and ocean. Each accommodation comes with a small, tidily kept bathroom with shower unit. Steps from the saltwater pool lead down to the sand, with expansive views of Stocking Island, anchored across the water. The ferry to the beautiful beaches is complimentary for guests. A vaulted stained-pine ceiling hangs above the striking bar and dining room, where Bahamian favorites get a gourmet twist. Regular shuttles link Peace & Plenty Beach Inn with Club Peace & Plenty, the center of the George Town social scene.

Queen's Hwy., 1 mile northwest of George Town. ☎ *800-525-2210 or 242-336-2250. Fax: 242-336-2253. Internet:* www.peaceandplenty.com. *Rack rates: $140–$185 for a double room. Ask about bonefishing package rates. AE, MC, V.*

Arriving in Exuma

Nine miles from George Town, **Exuma International Airport** is the official port of entry for this 365-island archipelago. Flights come in from Nassau, as well as Florida (Miami, Fort Lauderdale, St. Petersburg, and Sarasota). At the small, well-kept airport, you have to clear customs unless you're coming from Nassau. Taxis waiting just outside, and the cab fare to George Town hotels is about $25 for two passengers.

If you're going on to **Stocking Island** or **Rolle Cay,** two islets in **Elizabeth Harbour,** you can make prior arrangements with your hotel for boat transfers.

Getting around Exuma

Exuma is very accessible, and you don't have to rent a car. Most visitors get around by walking, but you can rent bikes or motor scooters if you want to explore more of the island. Here are your options:

 ✔ **Hoofing it.** George Town is designed for strolling, but don't expect sights that scream tourist attraction. This is a handsome little waterfront village where browsing — and buying — at the tree-shaded straw market, sampling fresh conch salad at the dock, and mingling with residents and fellow vacationers over drinks and home-style meals are the big draws. The most idyllic walk is around **Lake Victoria.**

Shuttle service is provided to town from **Peace & Plenty Beach Inn,** or you may want to walk the scenic mile.

If you don't succumb to wheels, you can leisurely enjoy glimpses of the turquoise and neon blue water through the wispy casuarina pines and bushy coconut palms lining **Queen's Highway.** "Highway" is a serious overstatement, so walking here is fine as traffic is sparse. Silence accompanies you, except for the squawks of seagulls, the sudden rustling of lizards in the roadside bushes, the faraway cries of roosters, and that occasional car or bike.

✔ **Taking a taxi.** You have no problem finding a taxi to take you to and from the airport, far-flung restaurants, or on-land tours around Great and Little Exuma. Your hotel can assist you. Fares are regulated, but meters aren't used, so agree on a price before setting out.

Taxi driver **Kermit Rolle** (☎ 242-345-0002), who also farms and runs local restaurants, seems to know everything anyone could ever want to know about Exuma.

✔ **Going by boat.** For ferries between George Town and the beaches on Stocking Island, call Club Peace & Plenty at ☎ 242-336-2551. With departures two times a day, the ferries are complimentary to Club Peace & Plenty guests. If you're not staying at that hotel, the cost is $8 round-trip if you're over age 10; otherwise, the ride is free. For renting boats, see the section, "On Deck: Riding the Waves without Getting Wet," later in this chapter.

✔ **Pedaling by bike.** A bicycle is a pleasant way to get around. To rent one, contact **Starfish Activity Center** in Georgetown (☎ 242-336-3033). Mountain and cruiser bikes run $10 for 2 hours, $15 for a half-day, $25 for a full day, and $100 per week. Those rates include a helmet and a map. Starfish Activity Center also hosts guided bike tours. Rentals are also available at **N & D's Fruits & Vegetables** in George Town (about $10 a day).

✔ **Motoring around on motor scooters.** To zip around the island faster, contact **Exuma Dive Center** (☎ 800-874-7213 or 242-336-2390). You can rent scooters for $35 per day and up.

✔ **Choosing a car.** Vacationers based in and around George Town have no real need to rent a car. If you want to see the rest of Great Exuma and Little Exuma, you can find out more and have more fun by having a taxi take you around. But if you prefer to strike out on your own, try **Thompson's Car Rental** in George Town (☎ 242-336-2442 or 242-345-4189), where autos begin at about $65 per day, or **Don's Car Rental** (☎ 242-345-0112), conveniently located right at the airport, where daily rates start at $70.

You can find two gas stations in the George Town area, one near the airport and the other in Farmers Hill. They are generally open Monday through Saturday from 8 a.m. to 5 p.m., 8 a.m. until noon on Sundays, and 8 to 10 a.m. on holidays.

The speed limit is 30 to 45 miles per hour in some areas, slowing to 15 to 20 miles per hour through the settlements.

Dining in Exuma

Most of Exuma's restaurants are in George Town, but a rental car, taxi, or hotel shuttle can take you to some offbeat places in outlying areas. Visit hotel dining rooms for the most sophisticated and priciest dining. When local dishes are served in these upscale accommodations, they often have continental and American influences.

For the most authentic — and the least expensive — Bahamian cooking, such as turtle steak or cracked conch, try a local restaurant. The food stall near George Town's government dock makes a great fresh conch salad prepared to order. Hours are limited: It's open only on Monday, Wednesday, and Friday.

Most hotels fix reasonably priced picnic lunches for beach excursions and other ramblings. Dining rooms in and outside hotels close between meals, and the smaller spots don't accept credit cards. **Peace & Plenty Beach Inn,** the hotel about a mile from the center of George Town, provides shuttle service into town.

See Chapter 2 for details about Bahamian specialties and tipping and the Introduction for an explanation of the price categories used in the restaurant listings in this chapter.

Club Peace & Plenty Restaurant

$$$ In the heart of George Town
BAHAMIAN/CONTINENTAL/AMERICAN

Go here for the finest island dining, with plentiful and good home-cooked meals that leave most guests satisfied. Boiled fish and grits is a popular breakfast at this hotel dining room with harbor views. But, you can also order eggs, French toast, and other American favorites. The conch burgers are a treat for lunch. Appetizers include a savory conch chowder, pumpkin soup, or hearts of palm salad. Grouper — pan-fried or steamed with peppers and onions — makes frequent evening appearances, along with Bahamian lobster and T-bone steak. Pasta may be served with shrimp or a spicy tomato sauce.

Queen's Hwy., George Town. ☎ *242-336-2551. Reservations required for dinner. Main courses: $18–$26. AE, MC, V. Open: breakfast, lunch, and dinner.*

Eddie's Edgewater

$ George Town   BAHAMIAN

On Monday nights, this is the place to be for the weekly *rake and scrape,* when a band transforms rakes, saws, washboards, and other household items into instruments and turns the restaurant into a party — a wonderful, traditional Bahamian moment. At the edge of **Lake Victoria,** this casual hangout gets raves for its turtle steak and steamed chicken. If you have your heart set on either of those, call ahead to make sure that they're on the menu that day. Other well-prepared dishes for lunch and dinner include okra soup, conch chowder, and pan-fried grouper.

Charlotte St., by Victoria Lake. ☎ *242-336-2050. Main courses: $6–$14. MC, V. Open: Mon–Sat 7 a.m.–midnight*

Iva Bowe's Central Highway Inn Restaurant & Bar
$ About 7 miles northwest of George Town   BAHAMIAN

Islanders tell you that this is *the* place for that local favorite, cracked conch, and they're right. The chicken, fish, and lobster dishes are all excellent, too, as are the crawfish salad and the shrimp scampi. The dining room isn't fancy, but the home-style food makes a trip — or two — here well worth your time. When you're tooling around Great Exuma, this is a choice eatery to stop at for take-out.

Central Hwy., about ¼ mile from the International Airport. ☎ *242-345-7014. Main courses: $10–$20. Open: Mon–Sat noon–10 p.m.*

The Palm
$–$$ 7 miles northwest of George Town INTERNATIONAL

Set beside a sandy, isolated beach, 9 miles northwest of the Exuma capital, this airy, oceanfront restaurant is associated with one of the island's best resorts. Breakfasts are hearty steak-and-egg fare, although you can also get Bahamian coconut pancakes. Lunches include lobster salads, conch chowder, grouper fingers, burgers, and sandwiches. Dinners are more formal. Although the food is familiar, it's well prepared. Flame-broiled grouper is your best and freshest choice.

At the Palms at Three Sisters Hotel, Queen's Hwy., Bahama Sound Beach. ☎ *242-358-4040. Dinner reservations advised. Main courses: $16–$28; breakfast $5–$10; lunch platters and sandwiches $5.95–$12. MC, V. Open: Daily 7 a.m.–10 p.m.*

Peace & Plenty Beach Inn
$$–$$$ 1 mile from central George Town   BAHAMIAN

The well-chosen Bahamian menu changes nightly at this hotel restaurant. A stained pine cathedral ceiling makes a dramatic statement in the restaurant's attractive dining room. The chicken breast Alfredo is a good choice, along with the tender blackened mahi-mahi. New York-cut Angus steak is also well prepared.

Queen's Hwy., 1 mile northwest of George Town. ☎ *242-336-2552. Reservations required. Main courses: $15–$29. AE, MC, V. Open: Breakfast, lunch, and dinner.*

Sam's Place

$ George Town   BAHAMIAN/AMERICAN

Overlooking the marina in George Town, the broad veranda of this second-story restaurant provides a scenic setting for a morning, afternoon, or evening meal. The boating crowd comes here in droves to enjoy the ever-changing menu. Lunch could be conch chowder and a sandwich or maybe a succulent pasta dish. For dinner, you may choose local lobster tail, pan-fried wahoo (our favorite), tender roast lamb, or steamed chicken.

Main St., at the Marina. ☎ *242-336-2579. Main courses: $14–$21. MC, V. Open: Daily 7:30 a.m.–9:30 p.m.*

Towne Café & Bakery

$ George Town   BAHAMIAN/BAKED GOODS

For a good alternative to breakfast at your hotel, stop at this bakery-plus. Bahamians come for the filling pancakes and the *boil fish* cooked with onions and peppers and grits. The *chicken souse* is served with delicately sweet johnnycake (a mildly sweet bread). The best choices of the pastries are the coffeecake, fresh donuts, and bran muffins. Antique household items decorate the simple dining room. If the lunch menu includes grouper fingers, go for it.

Marshall Complex. ☎ *242-336-2194. Main courses: $5–$10. No credit cards. Open: Mon–Sat 7:30 a.m.–5 p.m.*

Two Turtles Inn Restaurant

$ George Town   BAHAMIAN/AMERICAN

A popular meeting place, this hotel dining spot within view of the marina has the feel of a sidewalk café. Laid-back, but often busy, it'is the only outdoor restaurant in town. Dishes prepared with fresh local seafood are excellent. For many years, the zesty Friday night barbecues have been drawing scores of residents and those visitors who make the discovery — now you know all about it, too!

Across from the village green and the straw market. ☎ *242-336-2545. Main courses: $12–$23. AE, MC, V. Open: Lunch daily 11 a.m.–3 p.m., dinner Tues–Sun beginning at 6 p.m.*

Fun On and Off the Beach in Exuma

Most of the excitement on Exuma is all wet. However, you can spend a day driving to and through some of the drowsy settlements scattered along Great Exuma and the adjoining Little Exuma. If you don't, you end up missing some low-key sights, such as historic gravesites, pink salt ponds, tiny brightly painted houses, a little museum-boutique, small farms, vestiges of plantation ruins, and plenty of greenery.

Walking around George Town gives you plenty of opportunities to meet and greet residents and other vacationers. Instead of spending a whole day touring the island on dry land, you may have more fun seeing the sights by water — in a sailboat, speedboat, or kayak. This way, you can explore some of the smaller offshore uninhabited cays.

With a finger in many different pots, the George Town-based **Starfish Activity Center** (☎ 242-336-3033) makes booking everything from kayaking and snorkeling to bicycle tours as simple as one phone call.

Hitting the beaches

George Town's best beaches aren't in George Town but across Elizabeth Harbour on a pencil-thin slip of land. Not even 5 miles long and barely half a mile wide, Stocking Island protects the harbor from the open ocean. Club Peace & Plenty provides ferry service to this beach-rimmed island (free for guests of Club Peace & Plenty, $8 for nonguests, free for all children — guests or not).

A regatta to remember

George Town may be known as a quiet, restful place, but in April the **Out Island Regatta** changes all that. If you visit at this time of year, book your hotel room many, many months in advance. Although the Regatta brings many a far-flung Bahamian back home for this weeklong event, the maritime competition seems almost incidental to the festivities on terra firma.

As the handcrafted sloops, owned and sailed by Bahamians, compete out in Elizabeth Harbour, vendors along the waterfront sell grilled chicken, fried fish, and conch in all its varieties. Reggae fills the air. Men huddle around card tables slapping dominos down with dramatic arcs of their arms. A Junkanoo parade — complete with loud drums and whistles, cowbells, and horns — pulses down the street. Spectators sit on the walls near the administration building as cars with blaring horns festooned with rainbow-hued streamers pass in a slow line.

When the police band takes center stage in **Regatta Park,** people surge onto nearby steps for the best views. Band members look distinguished in their white tunics, wide red belts, red-banded hats, and black trousers with red side stripes. But nothing is formal about the way their lively music stirs up the crowd. Feet tap, fingers snap, and hips swing, whether they belong to tiny tots or elderly grandmothers.

Stocking Island is traversed only by foot or boat. For the calmest swimming, your best bet is the soft, white sands of the harbor side. Take the path across the island to the Atlantic coast if you'd prefer rougher surf. Shelling is ideal on the Atlantic Ocean side of the island. If you didn't pack a picnic lunch, just visit the snack bar. Scuba divers and snorkelers are lured to Stocking Island by the *blue holes* (ocean pools of fresh water floating on heavier salt water), coral gardens, and undersea caves. **Mystery Cave,** for example, meanders for some 400 feet beneath this virtually uninhabited island.

Finding water fun for everyone

Exuma's best asset is, of course, its surrounding sea. Here's a guide to the best water sports that will help you get started on your ocean adventures.

Kayaking

Some of Exuma's most dramatic scenery is best appreciated from the peaceful perch of a sea kayak. In fact, many areas — including mangrove lakes, rivers, manta ray gathering spots, and bonefish flats — are too shallow for other boats to enter. Don't worry if you haven't hit the gym lately. Anyone in at least average physical condition — from children to seniors — can kayak with a smile. The **Starfish Activity Center** (☎ 242-336-3033) rents sit-on-top kayaks for singles and doubles. Singles are about $10 an hour, $20 per half-day, $30 a day, or $120 a week. Doubles run $15 an hour, $30 per half-day, $40 a day, or $150 a week.

For more adventure, book one of Starfish's guided kayak trips, which are offered daily. You don't have to spend the whole time paddling your kayak. During half- and full-day excursions, lunch and beverages are served, and the price covers all gear, including snorkeling equipment. You may find yourself watching a blizzard of fish swarm a shipwreck, searching for sand dollars on a deserted beach, snorkeling into a sea cave, or finding out about bush medicine while you hike along a nature trail. Guided trips begin at $35 for adults and $25 for children for an hour.

Scuba diving

Surrounding the Exumas, fields of massive coral heads, eerie blue holes, and exciting walls covered with marine life turn on scuba divers. Many excellent reefs are just 20 or 25 minutes away from the George Town area, so long boat rides don't cut into your underwater time. At the **Exuma Dive Center** (☎ 800-874-7213 or 242-336-2390), prices for dives begin at $60. If you've never gone diving before, consider a resort course ($100) or even becoming certified (about $405). Call your hotel to ask whether it offers a hotel/dive package. Another reliable outfit to try is **Exuma Scuba** (☎ 242-336-2893).

Snorkeling

Call **Cooper's Charter Services** (☎ **242-336-2711**) if you want to snorkel around some of Exuma's most well-preserved reefs. These three-hour-plus excursions cost $25 per person.

Another option is the half-day combination snorkel-sightseeing trips, which run $50 per person. You even get to visit some blue holes that Jacques Cousteau made famous.

This longer trip is BYOSG, meaning Bring Your Own Snorkel Gear. Because Captain Cooper doesn't take out vacationers unless he has at least five people, these half-day excursions do not run every day. Another good outfit to try for guided snorkeling trips is **Exuma Dive Center** (☎ **800-874-7213** or 242-336-2390).

On Deck: Riding the Waves without Getting Wet

If you like the water, but want to keep your feet dry, George Town makes a good home base for skimming the waves.

Sailing through the day

Through the **Starfish Activity Center** (☎ **242-336-3033**), you can rent *Hobie Waves,* high-performance sailboats that are easy to use. These stable, lightweight-yet-durable, 15-foot catamarans are great for families. You won't believe how simple they are to maneuver. With a minimum of two people, you can take a two-hour lesson for $30 per person. Renting one of these babies runs you $35 for two hours, $50 for a half-day, $75 for a full day, or — if it really looks good to you — $300 for a week.

If motor boats are more your speed, **Minns Water Sports** (☎ **242-336-3483** or 242-336-2604) rents these 17-, 18-, and 22-foot boats for $88, $120, and $170 per day, with daily rates dropping the longer you rent. **Exuma Dive Center** (☎ **800-874-7213** or 242-336-2390), where boat rentals start at $80 per day, also offers more economical rates when you keep a boat for a week or longer.

Fishing for a big one

For deep sea and bottom fishing, as well as sightseeing tours, try **Cooper's Charter Services** (☎ **242-336-2711**). You need two to four fellow anglers to hunt down the wahoo, dolphin, tuna, king fish, and bonita in Exuma's deepest waters. Plan to spend $400 for a half-day or $700 for a full day of fishing. If you're in the market for snapper or grouper, still fishing runs a group of two to five people $250 for a half-day or $500 for a full day. The full-day rate includes bait plus the use of fishing equipment, and you can even have your catch cleaned and filleted. Cooper's can also help you reel in sharks if you're that daring.

Exploring Exuma's Dry Land Options

George Town is one of the prettiest settlements in the Out Islands. Spend some time wandering around this small village bordering both a harbor and a serene lake.

An impressive flamingo-colored edifice with white columns, the **Government Administration Building** stands at the harbor's edge nearby. This location provides one-stop shopping for the post office, the police station, the courts, the jail, and the Ministry of Education.

Under the shady canopy of enormous trees out front of **N & D's Fruits and Vegetables,** women sit at their posts selling T-shirts, shell jewelry, various straw goods, and snacks, including inexpensive breakfast fare in the morning. Stop for some ice cream or other sweet treats.

Up the road a bit, **St. Andrew's Anglican Church** sits on a bluff. For a good view, go up the hill and around back to the gravesites. This resting place overlooks sparkling **Lake Victoria.** You may see small boats making their way toward the narrow opening that leads to the harbor. You pass small square houses with chickens running in front yards, a few mom-and-pop restaurants, and grand petite churches.

During your walk, you'll come to a table piled high with conch shells. This is a fish vendor whom you can watch hammer a shell, deftly cut out the dark mollusk, and then skin it, exposing the white flesh that tastes so delectable in so many Bahamian specialties, such as cracked conch or conch chowder. Spend some time sitting quietly on the pier at the water's edge, and you have a backside view of St. Andrew's church, on the rise across the lake.

Set aside part of a morning or afternoon for a taxi tour or a rental car drive down to Little Exuma, connected to Great Exuma by a bridge.

This is a faraway retreat, the southernmost of the Exuma Cays. It has a subtropical climate, despite being in the tropics, and lovely white-sand beaches. The waters are so crystal-clear in some places that you can spot the colorful tropical fish more than 60 feet down. The island, about 12 square miles in area, is connected to Great Exuma by a 200-yard-long bridge. It's about a 10-mile trip from the George Town airport. Less than a mile offshore is **Pigeon Cay,** which is uninhabited. Visitors often come here for the day and are later picked up by a boat that takes them back to Little Exuma. You can go snorkeling and visit the remains of a 200-year-old wreck, right offshore in about 6 feet of water. On one of the highest hills of Little Exuma are the remains of an old pirate fort. Several cannons are located nearby, but documentation is lacking as to when it was built or by whom. (Pirates didn't leave too much data lying around.)

Coming from Great Exuma, the first community you reach on Little Exuma is called **Ferry,** so named because the two islands were linked by a ferry service before the bridge was built. See whether you can visit the private chapel of an Irish family, the Fitzgeralds, erected generations ago. Along the way, you can take in **Pretty Molly Bay,** site of the now-shuttered Sand Dollar Beach Club. Pretty Molly was a slave who committed suicide by walking into the water one night. The natives claim that her ghost can still be seen stalking the beach every night.

Many visitors come to Little Exuma to visit the **Hermitage,** a plantation constructed by Loyalist settlers and the last surviving example of the many that once stood in the Exumas. It was originally built by the Kendall family, who came to Little Exuma in 1784. They established their plantation at **Williamstown** and, with their slaves, set about growing cotton. But they encountered so many difficulties having the cotton shipped to Nassau that in 1806 they advertised the plantation for sale. The ad promised "970 acres more or less," along with "160 hands" (referring to the slaves). Chances are you'll be approached by a local guide who, for a fee, will show you around. Also ask to be shown several old tombs in the area. Also at Williamstown (look for the marker on the seaside), you can visit the remains of the **Great Salt Pond.**

Fast Facts: Exuma

Banks

On Queen's Hwy., the **Bank of Nova Scotia** (☎ 242-336-2651) is open Monday through Thursday 9:30 a.m. to 3:00 p.m and Friday 9:30 a.m to 5:00 p.m.

Business Hours

Some restaurants and most shops, gas stations, and other businesses are closed or have limited hours on Sundays.

Doctors

For medical care, contact the government-run clinic (☎ 242-336-2088), located on Queen's Highway, about 15 minutes west of Club Peace & Plenty in George Town.

Information

The Exuma Tourist Office (☎ 242-336-2430) lies across the street from St. Andrew's Anglican Church, not far from Club Peace & Plenty.

Police

In an emergency, call ☎ 242-336-2666.

Taxis

Taxis are easy to find, and your hotel can assist you, but try Kermit Rolle (☎ 242-345-6038 or 242-345-0002).

Chapter 24

San Salvador

● ●

In This Chapter

▶ Reviewing San Salvador's hotels and restaurants

▶ Getting around the island

▶ Finding the best beaches, water sports, and historic land attractions

● ●

Drowsy San Salvador is so undeveloped that it has just two hotels and a handful of restaurants, most at the larger hotel. Fabulous scuba diving brings most visitors to these tranquil shores. Beautiful empty beaches and easygoing, friendly residents keep vacationers coming back. If bar hopping, night clubbing, and eating at a different restaurant every night of the week is what you have in mind, San Salvador isn't your island.

Getting the Lowdown on the Hotel Scene

Deciding where to stay on San Salvador is like choosing between pizza and filet mignon — the two beach hotels, Club Med-Columbus Isle and the Riding Rock Inn Resort & Marina, are both good, just different. The Riding Rock resembles a pleasant motel, while the larger resort is decked out in art and artifacts from around the globe.

The two beach hotels have one thing in common: They both offer excellent scuba-diving programs that allow you to take advantage of the island's main attraction, its underwater wonders.

Some 40 well-preserved dive sites are no more than 45 minutes away from both hotels by boat. Cockburn Town (pronounced "CO-burn"), the sleepy capital of the island, is a comfortable stroll or a quick bike or taxi ride away. However, calling the capital a town is like calling a caterpillar a snake. Cockburn Town features a restaurant, bar, and a bank that is open once a week, but the chance to mingle with friendly residents is the real reason for heading to town.

Checking Out the Best Accommodations

Club Med-Columbus Isle
$$$$$ **Bonefish Bay**

Until something better opens, this is the poshest resort in all of the Southern Bahamas, and far better than your typical Club Med vacation village. Set on the edge of one of the most pristine beaches in the archipelago, two miles of white sand, it lies 2 miles north of the settlement of Cockburn Town, employing some 30% of the island work force. This 270-room behemoth even operates on its own time clock, different from Eastern Standard Time. Clocks are set one hour earlier to give late-rising gates another hour of daylight. Built around a large free-form pool, the resort offers public rooms that are among the most lavish in the islands. Bedrooms each contain a private balcony or patio, furniture that was custom-made in Thailand or the Philippines, sliding glass doors, and feathered wall hangings crafted in the Brazilian rain forest by members of the Xingu tribe. Rooms are large (among the most spacious in the entire chain). Most have twin beds, but you may be able to snag one of the units with a double or a king-size bed if you're lucky. Each comes with a mid-sized bathroom with shower stall. Nightly entertainment is presented in a covered, open-air theater and dance floor behind one of the bars.

Most guests are couples without kids, with a few singles thrown in. Two single friends traveling together can each have a private room joined by a shared bath. These single rooms are much smaller than doubles, but still perfectly comfortable. This hotel isn't the best place for children, because you won't find any discount rates or special facilities for them.

Two miles north of Cockburn Town. ☎ *800-CLUB-MED or 242-331-2000. Fax: 242-331-2458. Internet:* www.clubmed.com. *Rack rates: $1,134 per person to $2,079 for seven nights in a double room (price depends on what time of year you go and where you are flying from); price includes all meals, most beverages, most activities, gratuities, round-trip airfare, and ground transportation to and from San Salvador's airport. AE, MC, V.*

Riding Rock Inn Resort & Marina
$$ **North of Cockburn**

In stark contrast to the lavish Club Med, with its perky staff, Riding Rock Inn offers a more tranquil atmosphere. The 42 rooms may be motel-like, but they're pleasantly decorated and outfitted with all the modern conveniences you need for a comfortable stay. The newer, two-story building houses the best digs, and each room features two double beds, a TV, a refrigerator, and a balcony or patio with an ocean view. The hotel's older, smaller rooms overlook the pool. No one ever seems to use the

San Salvador

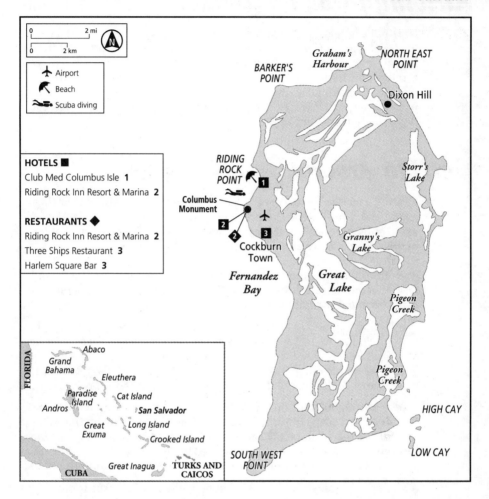

tennis court here, probably because most guests are avid divers who stay wet. Riding Rock offers excellent scuba packages, some including an island tour and a night dive as well as an underwater photography program. During the day while divers are away, this place seems downright empty. Night time is a different story, however. In fact, you can call Riding Rock Inn Resort & Marina San Salvador's social center. An oceanfront deck runs the length of the main building in front of the dining room, as well as in front of the adjacent **Driftwood Bar,** whose ceiling is paneled in driftwood. During the Wednesday night dance party, the joint is really jumpin', and Friday nights aren't so quiet either.

Just north of Cockburn Town. ☎ *800-272-1492 (in the U.S.), 954-359-8353 (in Florida), or 242-331-2631 (in The Bahamas). Fax: 242-331-2020. Internet:* www.ridingrock. com. *Rack rates: $137–$190. Ask about the all-inclusive packages. AE, MC, V.*

Arriving in San Salvador

Near both hotels, San Salvador's small airport is a cinch to access. If you're staying at Club Med, you'll arrive on a direct charter flight from Miami or New York. Club Med's all-inclusive rates cover airfare. You can arrange charter flights through the Riding Rock Inn Resort & Marina as well. Both hotels provide their guests with group transportation to and from the airport. If you're flying into New Providence, you can catch a flight on BahamasAir (☎ 800-222-4262).

Getting around San Salvador

Renting a car isn't necessary in San Salvador. If you want to tour the island, ask your hotel to help you with arrangements. The island is small enough to walk, but bicycles and motor scooters are available as well. Here's more about your transportation options:

- ✔ **Taking a taxi.** Your hotel can arrange taxi service for you. Island tours arranged through Club Med cost around $25 per person for the half-day ramble.

- ✔ **Going by car.** On San Salvador, you don't need to rent a car unless you'd like to explore far-flung places on your own. These include East Beach — see the section "Having Fun On and Off the Beach," later in this chapter. You can rent a car through Riding Rock Inn Resort & Marina (☎ 242-331-2631) for about $85 a day.

- ✔ **Motoring around on a scooter.** There's little traffic, so the island is a good place to ride a scooter. Remember to stay on the *left* side of the road. Contact **K's Scooter Rentals** (☎ 242-331-2125), where you can rent mopeds for about $40 to $50 a day. You can fuel up at the Riding Rock Marina gas station, which is close to both hotels.

- ✔ **Pedaling bicycles.** Club Med guests have use of bikes for cycling around the property and for guided tours around the island. If you're not staying at Club Med, you can rent two-wheelers at Riding Rock Inn Resort & Marina (☎ 242-331-2631) for about $10 a day.

Dining in San Salvador

If you're staying at Club Med, room rates include all your meals. However, you shouldn't leave the island without sneaking off campus for some local flavor.

Riding Rock Inn Resort & Marina
$$ Near Cockburn Town   BAHAMIAN/AMERICAN

Sit on the deck overlooking the water or eat inside; either way, you can dine on hearty portions of comfort food. Pancakes make a good choice for breakfast, and sandwiches are on the menu for lunch. The price-fixed dinners include soup, salad, main course, dessert, wine, and soft, chewy, just-baked Bahamian bread. Launch your meal with the well-seasoned conch chowder or okra soup and follow it up with steak, prime rib, veal, chicken, or fresh fish. Likewise, the Wednesday night barbecues, featuring reggae music, are popular social events.

Just north of Cockburn Town (within walking distance of Club Med). ☎ 242-331-2631. Internet: www.ridingrock.com. _Reservations recommended. Complete dinner: $28. AE, MC, V. Open: 6:30–9 p.m._

Three Ships Restaurant
$ Cockburn Town   BAHAMIAN

Since the early 1990s, Faith Jones, the owner, keeps visitors coming back for her cracked conch, steamed or fried grouper, and crab and rice, served with mounds of coleslaw, potato salad, or peas and rice. Spend some time here, and you're sure to strike up a conversation or two with Ms. Jones and the townspeople who stop in for food, drink, or just "to chew the fat" in more ways than one. Jones used to cater meals from her home next door before she opened this dining spot.

In the heart of Cockburn Town. ☎ 242-331-2787. Call ahead. Complete meal: $8. No credit cards. Open: 9 a.m.–6 p.m.

Having Fun On and Off the Beach

The focus of fun is diving, but plenty of other action awaits you, including snorkeling, fishing, windsurfing, kayaking, and water-skiing.

Exciting scuba diving is amidst incredible sea walls (wall diving) at sites where the coral reef drops off steeply. Riding Rock Inn Resort & Marina (☎ 242-331-2631), which specializes in scuba packages, offers a good underwater photography program, as well as night dives on Tuesday evenings.

Club Med-Columbus Isle should really be called an _almost_-all-inclusive resort, because scuba diving is not included in its rates. Resort courses run $100, and certification courses are $400. A one-tank dive costs $40 and a two-tank, $60.

Club Med-Columbus Isle offers ten tennis courts (three lit for night play), and Riding Rock Inn Resort & Marina has one (often empty) court. Fishermen test their skill against blue marlin, yellowfin tuna, and wahoo on a fishing trip, which you can arrange through Riding Rock Inn Resort & Marina (☎ **242-331-2631**). The trips run $400 for a half-day and $600 for a full day.

If you'd rather find a stretch of sand where the only footprints are your own, rent a car or a bike at Riding Rock Inn Resort & Marina or call a taxi. (See the section "Getting around San Salvador," earlier in this chapter.) Empty beaches are everywhere. Just remember to take plenty of water, and, of course, sunblock. You won't find much shade. Along the way, you can look for the island's various monuments to Christopher Columbus.

On the northeast coast, **East Beach** stretches for some six miles. Crushed coral and shells have turned the shore a rosy pink. Those deep turquoise patches in the clear waters are coral heads, but the beach isn't good for snorkeling. (Sharks have been spotted.) Tall sea wheat or sea grass sprouts up from the sand. Off mile marker number 24 on the main road, you can pick your way to the Chicago Herald Columbus Monument. (See the next section, "Seeing San Salvador on Dry Land," for details.)

Seeing San Salvador on Dry Land

For such a small island, San Salvador offers a great deal of history here, as well as some sights that merit a look.

Exploring Columbus monuments

Rent a bike, hire a taxi, or start walking, and see how many of the Columbus monuments you can hit. Just south of Cockburn Town, a small obelisk, the **Tappan Monument** stands on the beach at **Fernandez Bay** (mile marker number 5 on the main road). The monument was embedded here on February 25, 1951, by the Tappan gas company. At mile marker number 6, about 3 miles south of Cockburn Town, stands a tall cross at the edge of the water. (It has been there since 1956.) Along with a third monument that lies hidden on the ocean floor, these are all supposed to mark the spot where Columbus and his crew anchored the *Nina, Pinta,* and *Santa Maria* early that fateful morning in 1492. Nearby, another monument commemorates the 1968 Olympic Games in Mexico. A spiral walkway leads to the top of the structure, where the bowl of the dark metal sculpture held the Olympic flame that was brought from Greece. The flame burned here until being brought to the games in Mexico City.

The **Chicago Monument** is at mile marker number 24, on the east coast. To reach it, turn off the main road and drive a mile to **East Beach.** Unless you meet a resident who'll give you a ride in his or her four-wheel-drive, you have to get out and walk. Turn right and hike 2 miles parallel to the beach until the sandy road ends. You'll see a cave to the left, at the water's edge. Follow the path to the right. Cupped by vegetation, a stone structure lies on the slice of land between the ocean and the bay. Although many historians dispute the claim, the marble plaque boasts, "On this spot Christopher Columbus first set foot upon the soil of the New World, erected by the *Chicago Herald,* June 1891." The only problem with the monument's claim is that the treacherous reefs here make this a dangerous — and highly unlikely — landing spot.

Lighting the way

In the northeast of the island, the **Dixon Hill Lighthouse,** built in 1856, sends out an intense beam two times every 25 seconds. This signal can be seen for 19 miles. The oil-using lighthouse rises 160 feet into the sky and is still operated by hand. For permission to climb to the top, just knock on the door of the lighthouse keeper, who is almost always in the neighboring house.

After huffing and puffing your way up, seeing how tiny the source of light is will surprise you. The panorama from here takes in San Salvador's inland lakes, distant Crab Cay, and surrounding islets. Ask the lighthouse keeper to show you the inspector's log, with signatures dating back to Queen Victoria's reign. Be sure to leave at least a $1 donation when you sign the guest book on your way out. The lighthouse lies about a 30-minute taxi ride from Riding Rock Inn Resort & Marina or Club Med.

Living It Up after the Sun Goes Down: San Salvador's Nightlife

Club Med (☎ 242-331-2000) keeps its guests entertained every night, with musical revues and shows starring vacationers themselves. At **Riding Rock Inn Resort & Marina** (☎ 242-331-2631), the Wednesday-night barbecue features reggae music, and many locals come to party. If you're still game for some fun after the lodgings' festivities, head to the **Harlem Square Bar** (☎ 242-331-2777) across the road from Three Ships Restaurant in Cockburn Town. This friendly place is open daily from 9 a.m. to 7 p.m.

Fast Facts: San Salvador

Banks

The island's sole bank, **Bank of the Bahamas** in Cockburn Town, is open only on Friday from 11 a.m. to 2:30 p.m. You can always change travelers checks at your hotel.

Credit Cards

If you need credit-card assistance, contact MasterCard (☎ 800-307-7309) or call Visa collect (☎ 800-847-2911).

Medical Care

The San Salvador Community Clinic (☎ 242-331-2105), a five-minute drive north of Club Med, is open from Monday through Friday 9 a.m. to 5 p.m.

Police

In an emergency, call ☎ **242-331-2919.**

Safety

San Salvador is a safe island. However, you still need to take the same precautions that you should take anywhere you go: Keep valuables in a safe place and don't go into deserted, unfamiliar areas alone at night.

Taxis

Your hotel can arrange taxi service for you. Island tours arranged through Club Med costing around $25 per person for the half-day ramble.

Part VII
The Part of Tens

The 5th Wave   By Rich Tennant

Honestly — I thought it was an exotic sea urchin. It never occurred to me that someone would actually snorkel with a toupee on.

In this part . . .

*W*e give you the ten most common misconceptions about the Bahamas. For example, if you ever thought the Bahamas was a single, mountainous, casino-packed, Caribbean island, keep reading. We also share our top ten picks for quintessential island activities, from walking underwater in the Bahamas — without the benefit of scuba gear — to swimming with stingrays.

Chapter 25

Top Ten Myths about The Bahamas

● ●

In This Chapter

▶ Getting the geography straight

▶ Figuring out the weather

▶ Discovering that no two islands — or islanders — are alike

● ●

*T*his chapter explains some of the most common misconceptions about these sunny islands. So the next time someone starts talking about wanting to go mountain climbing in The Bahamas, you can set him or her straight.

The Columbus Landing Was at San Salvador

Historians aren't so certain that the Columbus's three strange-looking Spanish ships (at least strange to the Lucayans) actually landed at San Salvador, which used to be known as Watling's Island until the Bahamian legislature changed it in 1926. The Italian seafarer left no marker indicating his landfall. Some geographers have claimed the landfall occurred on one of the cays of Turks and Caicos; other site in the running is Cat Island. Artifacts of European origin, dating anywhere from 1490 to 1560, were found on San Salvador in 1983. In a meticulously researched article, *National Geographic* published evidence in 1986 that the landfall occurred at Samana Cay, some 65 miles to the southeast of San Salvador. The question will probably never be resolved. All we know is that at 2 a.m. on the moonlight night of October 12, 1492, Columbus and his men landed somewhere in the Southern Bahamas and woke up some sleepy Lucayans who called them "men from Heaven." In time, when these Indians were killed or sold into slavery, the seafarers may have been more aptly named "men from Hell."

The Bahamas Is One Island

The Bahamas is not one island — in fact, this archipelago is made up of more than 700 islands, from large land masses to sandbars. Only about 30 of the islands are inhabited and just a handful have hotels. You've probably heard the most about Nassau, which is not an island itself but the country's capital. Located on New Providence Island, Nassau is where you find the Cable Beach resort area and the adjoining Paradise Island. Grand Bahama, the second most developed island, is home to the Freeport and Lucaya resort areas. The rest of the country is known as the Out Islands, low-key outposts with the smallest, least developed, and least crowded vacation spots.

The Bahamas Is in the Caribbean

Sure, it begins with a *B,* just like Barbados and Bonaire, but The Bahamas (like Bermuda) is in the Atlantic — not the Caribbean. It's close enough — just north of Hispaniola, the island of Haiti and the Dominican Republic — that the weather most often feels like the West Indies. Scattered across some 100,000 square miles of ocean, the islands of the once-British Bahamas have their own special flavor. However, they do share a West Indian heritage with their Caribbean neighbors. Therefore, you do find some similarities in architecture, food, music, dance, and the accents of the people.

The Weather Is Always Hot Enough for the Beach

The weather is not always warm enough for the beach. The Bahamas does cool off around late December through March, to temperatures that are often spring-like. Those months are much better for golf and tennis than for swimming and sunbathing. The weather can change quickly during this time of year, moving in a flash from beach days to cool days, and then back again.

The Islands Are Mountainous

In the low-lying islands, mountains are more like molehills. The highest point in all The Bahamas — on sleepy Cat Island — is just 206 feet. Unlike the often majestic volcanic islands of the Caribbean, these Atlantic isles were created by coral reefs, which make for phenomenal scuba diving and snorkeling, starting in unusually shallow waters.

Palm Trees Are All Over the Place

Except around resorts and residential developments, where palms were planted, most of the trees you see are long-needled casuarina pines. Palms line some beaches, but the majority are bordered mainly with the wispy-looking evergreens, which lean in the direction of the prevailing wind.

For Casinos and Hot Nightlife, Pick Any Island

If you want to gamble into the wee hours or dance 'til the sun comes up, you need to choose the island(s) you visit carefully. In The Bahamas, head to Nassau, Cable Beach, or Paradise Island (all on or attached to the island of New Providence) or to Freeport or Lucaya (on Grand Bahama Island). There are no casinos on the rest of the islands, collectively known as the Out Islands, and what little nightlife there is gets liveliest on weekends.

All Bahamians Are of African Descent

On some islands, you find lots of locals with blue eyes, straight hair, and white skin. Almost everyone is of European ancestry in Spanish Wells, off Eleuthera, as well as on Man-O-War Cay and Guana Cay (both in the Abacos), for example. Most of these residents are direct descendants of some of The Bahamas' earliest settlers: the Eleutherian Adventurers. Arriving in Spanish Wells in the mid-1600s, they came from Britain in search of religious freedom. Fleeing to both Eleuthera and the Abacos, Loyalists were Euro-Americans who, siding with the British Crown, left New England and the Carolinas after the Revolutionary War.

Islanders Resent Tourists

Bahamians are some of the most personable folks around — that is, as long as visitors treat them with respect. For example, if you need to ask someone for directions, say "Hello" first and don't assume that every local you see works at the resort, store, or restaurant that you're visiting. Strike up a conversation with a resident, and you're sure to come away with a tip about a popular nightspot or a little-known beach. You may even end up with a new friend.

Reggae Music Is the Local Sound

Although you certainly hear reggae music in The Bahamas, it was born in Jamaica, not in these islands. You also hear plenty of calypso (originally from Trinidad), plus lots of American pop, R&B, and rock. But along with all those imports, The Bahamas has its own sound. Traditionally played with cowbells, goatskin drums, whistles, and trumpets, fast-paced *junkanoo* music is at the heart of the colorful carnival-like festival held on Boxing Day (December 26) and New Year's Day.

During the rest of the year, you can sometimes watch costumed dancers play this thumping, syncopated, African-inspired music at Nassau and Freeport hotels. You may get to hear the sounds of *Goombay* (a pared-down version of junkanoo generally played without the elaborate festival costumes). Particularly in the Out Islands, some nightspots still have old-fashioned *rake and scrapes,* where bands turn things like washboards, saws, and barrels into instruments.

Chapter 26

Top Ten Bahamas Moments

In This Chapter

▶ Walking on the ocean floor without scuba gear

▶ Hugging your honey in a horse-drawn carriage

▶ Diving with dolphins

Are you in the mood for a romantic stroll through manicured English-style gardens? Or is a ride in a horse-drawn carriage along the history-packed streets of Nassau more up your alley? Ever wondered if pink sand is as soft as the snow-white variety?

Along with scuba diving and snorkeling — phenomenal all over The Bahamas — here are other unforgettable adventures to consider putting at the top of your list.

Walking on the (Wet and) Wild Side

You can walk on the ocean floor without wearing scuba gear. You don't have to take lengthy classes, either — you just do it. While you're getting up close and personal with fish and coral, your face and hair stay dry. This fun activity is called *helmet diving*. To partake in this adventure, join one of Hartley's Undersea Walks on Nassau. In doing so, you don a lead and glass helmet as you descend a ladder into the ocean. Air is pumped into your aquatic bonnet through a long tube attached to a tank on the boat. For more information, see Chapter 12.

Taking a Surrey Ride through Nassau

Because Nassau, located on New Providence Island, is so full of the country's history, a good way to see this harborside city is from an old-fashioned horse-drawn carriage. You can take a leisurely ride along busy Bay Street, the main thoroughfare, past Parliament Square, with its eighteenth- and nineteenth-century Georgian-style government buildings (painted pink and white) and a statue of a young Queen Victoria, among other sights.

Wandering through Versailles Gardens

On Paradise Island, you can enjoy a setting that you think you'd fine only in the countryside of France. Studded with bright flowers, shady trees, a lily pond with turtles, and bronze and marble statues, **Versailles Gardens** (see Chapter 15 for details) is the site of a twelfth-century cloister. Dramatically perched on a rise, it was built by the Augustinian monks in France. In 1962, Huntington Hartford, the island's original developer, had it moved to the island and reassembled, stone by stone.

Making a Date with Dolphins

Dolphin skin feels like warm, buttery leather. Pet one, and you'll see what I mean. (Some marine studies, however, have suggested that petting is not politically correct in that the dolphins don't like this human contact. They are such friendly animals, though, you don't get that impression.) You can commune with dolphins on Grand Bahama or an island off New Providence. Some sessions allow you to wade in the water with these mammals while trainers tell you everything you ever wanted to know about them. In other programs, you can scuba dive with Flipper's cousins in the open ocean. For more information see Chapter 12 (New Providence) and Chapter 16 (Grand Bahama).

Feeding the Stingrays

If you find dolphins too tame, try feeding the stingrays that swim gracefully through the shallow waters around a tiny island off Green Turtle Cay (see Chapter 20) in the Abacos. If you don't know how to snorkel, your guide can teach you on the spot, or you can take to the water dressed in scuba gear. Either way, you're also treated to a beach picnic after your captain grills the fish or lobster that he just caught.

Digging Your Toes into a Pink Sand Beach

It may be only 3 miles long, but the soft, broad, pink sand beach along Harbour Island's eastern shore seems to go on forever. The unusual color comes from shells and coral that waves have pulverized over the years. This beach is pretty enough to make you roll out of bed in time to catch the sunrise. (Turn to Chapter 21 for more details.)

Watching the Sun Set on Dunmore Town

For some of the best sunsets in The Bahamas, head to Harbour Island's western coast. The spectacle is special here because of the glow that the sun casts on the eighteenth-century wooden cottages along the harbor front. Sip a Bahama Mama or a Goombay Smash at a waterside restaurant while you watch the show. (For more information, see Chapter 21.)

Visiting a Candy Cane–Striped Lighthouse

Sail through **Hope Town Harbor,** filled with small pleasure boats, or munch some conch fritters at the water's edge, and you can see the whimsical red-and-white striped lighthouse. For a sweeping view of narrow Elbow Cay, edged by fabulous beaches, climb to the top of the beacon, which has stood here since 1838. (See Chapter 18 for more information.)

Living It Up at Miss Emily's

In New Plymouth on Green Turtle Cay in the Abacos stands Miss Emily's Blue Bee Bar, the most famous watering hole in the Out Islands (see chapter 20 for more information). The rum-laced drink, The Goombay Smash, may as well have been invented here. It's called Abacos, answer to atomic fission. Miss Emily is gone now, but she left her secret recipe in the hands of her daughter.

Boating in the Abacos

No matter where you've boated before, nothing compares to sailing the Abacos in one of the vessels that you can rent at Marsh Harbour. (See Chapter 17 for details of how to do so.) Marsh Harbour is aptly known as "The Boating Capital of The Bahamas." In charge of your own vessel, you can visit uninhabited cays and seek out deserted beaches where you can go shelling, exploring, and picnicking in peace — and no one's around to witness if you want to go beachcombing in the buff.

Making Dollars and Sense of It

Expense	Daily cost	x	Number of days	=	Total
Airfare					
Local transportation					
Car rental					
Lodging (with tax)					
Parking					
Breakfast					
Lunch					
Dinner					
Snacks					
Entertainment					
Babysitting					
Attractions					
Gifts & souvenirs					
Tips					
Other					
Grand Total					

Fare Game: Choosing an Airline

When looking for the best airfare, you should cover all your bases — 1) consult a trusted travel agent; 2) contact the airline directly, via the airline's toll-free number and/or Web site; 3) check out one of the travel-planning Web sites, such as www.frommers.com.

Travel Agency_____ Phone_____
    Agent's Name_____ Quoted fare_____

Airline 1_____ Quoted fare_____
    Toll-free number/Internet_____

Airline 2_____ Quoted fare_____
    Toll-free number/Internet_____

Web site 1_____ Quoted fare_____

Web site 2_____ Quoted fare_____

Departure Schedule & Flight Information

Airline_____ Flight #_____ Confirmation #_____

Departs_____ Date_____ Time_____ a.m./p.m.

Arrives_____ Date_____ Time_____ a.m./p.m.

Connecting Flight (if any)

Amount of time between flights_____ hours/mins

Airline_____ Flight #_____ Confirmation #_____

Departs_____ Date_____ Time_____ a.m./p.m.

Arrives_____ Date_____ Time_____ a.m./p.m.

Return Trip Schedule & Flight Information

Airline_____ Flight #_____ Confirmation #_____

Departs_____ Date_____ Time_____ a.m./p.m.

Arrives_____ Date_____ Time_____ a.m./p.m.

Connecting Flight (if any)

Amount of time between flights_____ hours/mins

Airline_____ Flight #_____ Confirmation #_____

Departs_____ Date_____ Time_____ a.m./p.m.

Arrives_____ Date_____ Time_____ a.m./p.m.

Sweet Dreams: Choosing Your Hotel

Make a list of all the hotels where you'd like to stay and then check online and call the local and toll-free numbers to get the best price. You should also check with a travel agent, who may be able to get you a better rate.

Hotel & page	Location	Internet	Tel. (local)	Tel. (Toll-free)	Quoted rate

Hotel Checklist

Here's a checklist of things to inquire about when booking your room, depending on your needs and preferences.

- ❏ Smoking/smoke-free room
- ❏ Noise (if you prefer a quiet room, ask about proximity to elevator, bar/restaurant, pool, meeting facilities, renovations, and street)
- ❏ View
- ❏ Facilities for children (crib, roll-away cot, babysitting services)
- ❏ Facilities for travelers with disabilities
- ❏ Number and size of bed(s) (king, queen, double/full-size)
- ❏ Is breakfast included? (buffet, continental, or sit-down?)
- ❏ In-room amenities (hair dryer, iron/board, minibar, etc.)
- ❏ Other_____

Places to Go, People to See, Things to Do

Enter the attractions you would most like to see and decide how they'll fit into your schedule. Next, use the "Going My Way" worksheets that follow to sketch out your itinerary.

Attraction/activity	Page	Amount of time you expect to spend there	Best day and time to go

Index

See also Accommodations index, below.

• A •

Abaco Inn (Elbow Cay), 243–244, 248
Abacos Islands. *See also* Marsh
    Harbour, The Abacos
  description of, 11
  destinations of, 17–21
  fishing, 52
  map of, 18
  pros and cons of, 20–21
  Regatta Time, 54
  sailing, 343
  travel to, 89
accommodations. *See also*
    Accommodations Index
  all-inclusive, 61–62
  condos and timeshares, 63
  cost of, 96–98
  dining plans, 65
  great room, getting, 66–67
  guesthouses, 63–64
  hotels and resorts, 60–61
  kids' programs at, 70, 119, 128, 184
  package deal, 66, 84–86, 101
  renovations, 67
  service, expectations for, 41, 60
  symbols used to describe, 64–65
  types of, 57–60
  view from room, clarifying, 119
  villa rentals, 58, 62–63
air travel
  carriers and routes, 88–89
  with children, 70
  to Eleuthera Island, 299–300
  fare, finding best, 87–88
  to Grand Bahama Island, 187–188
  to New Providence Island, 131–132
airlines
  luggage, lost, 108
  package deals through, 85–86
Albert Lowe Museum (Green
    Turtle Cay), 20, 264

Albury's Ferry Service, 232, 241, 247
ancestry of island residents, 339
Angela's Starfish (Harbour Island), 286
Angler's Restaurant (Marsh Harbour),
    233
Anthony's Caribbean Grill (Paradise
    Island), 146
antiques, shopping for, 169
Arawak Cay, 46
Arawak Restaurant (Lucaya), 194
Ardastra Gardens & Zoo (Nassau),
    118, 159
art, shopping for, 169, 218, 221
Atholl Island, 156
Atlantis Aquarium (Paradise Island),
    160
Atlantis Paradise Island Resort &
    Casino
  accommodations, 119
  aquarium, 160
  casino, 160
  description of, 12, 117
  kids' program, 70
  nightlife, 174
  for romantic getaway, 72
ATM (automated teller machine),
    93, 94, 132, 135, 190
attractions
  cost of, 99–100
  Elbow Cay, 252–253
  Eleuthera Island, 305–308
  Freeport, 15, 212–213, 214
  Grand Bahama Island, 212–214
  Harbour Island, 290
  Marsh Harbour, 239–240
  New Providence Island, 159–166
  rating islands for, 35

• B •

baby sitter, hiring, 71, 135, 190
Bahama Breeze (drink), 248

Bahama Mama Booze Cruise, 211
Bahama Mama (drink), 47
Bahamas, The
  best experiences, 341–343
  climate, 10, 49–51, 338
  description and location of,
    1, 9–10, 338
  islands of, 31–39, 338
  mountains of, 338
  myths about, 337–340
  number of islands to visit per trip,
    30–31
Bahamas Coin and Stamp Ltd.
  (Freeport), 219
Bahamas Fast Ferry, 284, 300
Bahamas National Trust Rand Nature
  Centre (Freeport), 189, 212
Bahamas Post Office Philatelic Bureau
  (Nassau), 170
Bahamian dollar, 93
Bahamian Souvenir Outlet (Freeport),
  219
Bahamian Things (Freeport), 219
Balcony House (Nassau), 162–163
Balmain Antiques (Nassau), 172
banana boat, 208
Bandolera (Lucaya), 220–221
Barbary Beach, Grand Bahama Island,
  208, 215
bareboating, 238
Barefoot Sailing Cruises, 156, 157, 175
Barracuda's (Lucaya), 194
Barry's Limited (Nassau), 170
Basie, Count (musician), 222
Bay Street (Nassau), 162
beaches
  Elbow Cay, 251
  Eleuthera Island, 304–305
  George Town, 321
  Grand Bahama Island, 207–208
  Great Abaco Island, 237
  Green Turtle Cay, 263
  Harbour Island, 289
  New Providence Island, 124, 125,
    153–154
  Paradise Beach, 12, 132–133, 154
  rating islands for, 34
  Stocking Island, 321–322
  Treasure Cay, 267, 272

Beauty Spot, The (Nassau), 173
Becky's Restaurant & Lounge
  (Freeport), 44, 194–195
Beef Cellar (Cable Beach), 126
bicycle, touring by
  George Town, 317
  Grand Bahama Island, 189, 215
  Harbour Island, 285
  Marsh Harbour, 232
  Nassau, 135
  New Providence Island, 166–167
  San Salvador, 330
  Treasure Cay, 270
Bistro Mezzamare (Marsh Harbour),
  233–234
Black Angus Grill, The (Cable Beach),
  148
Blackwell, Chris (music mogul), 124,
  150, 283
Blue Bar (Harbour Island), 283
blue hole, 322
Blue Lagoon Island, 155, 175, 176
Bluff House (Green Turtle Cay),
  72, 256, 257, 260–261
boat, 211, 252, 264. *See also* cruises;
  sailing charters
Boat House Restaurant (Elbow Cay),
  248
bobo, 42
boil fish, 44, 51
Bonneville Bones (Nassau), 170
booking trip online, 88, 90–92
Boxing Day, 42, 51, 55
Brass and Leather Shop (Nassau),
  169, 171
Breezes (Nassau), 71–72, 75, 122, 125
British Colonial Hilton (Nassau),
  76, 122, 124
Buccaneer Public Beaches, Eleuthera
  Island, 305
bucket shop, 87
Buena Vista (Nassau), 138
bus travel, 98, 133–134, 188
Bustick Bay, Great Abaco Island, 231

• *C* •

Cabbage Beach, New Providence
  Island, 154

Cable Beach
  accommodations, 117–118, 122, 126,
    128–129
  beach, 153–154
  description of, 12
  map of, 123
  nightlife, 14
  restaurants, 148–151
  water sports, 154
Cable Beach Golf Course, 167
Café at the Great Hall of Waters
    (Paradise Island), 146–147
Café Johnny Canoe (Cable Beach),
    43, 126, 148, 150
Café Matisse (Nassau), 138
Café Skan's (Nassau), 139
calendar of events, 51–55
Cambridge Villas (Gregory Town), 301
Cape Eleuthera, 26, 304, 306
Cap'n Jacks (Hope Town), 249
Captain's Charthouse (Lucaya), 195
car, renting
  Eleuthera Island, 300–301
  Exuma Islands, 317
  Grand Bahama Island, 189
  Marsh Harbour, 232
  Nassau, 134
  Treasure Cay, 270
Caribbean Cargo (Freeport), 219
carry-on luggage, 108, 113
cash, carrying and using, 93–94
casinos
  Atlantis, 160
  budget and, 102
  Casino at Bahamia, 179, 221
  Crystal Palace, 174
  location of, 339
  Nassau, 118
  Paradise Island, 118, 119, 160
casuarina pines, 339
Casuarina Point, Great Abaco Island,
    230, 237, 240
Cave (Eleuthera Island), 307
cay, 268
Cherokee Sound, Great Abaco Island,
    239
Chicago Monument (San Salvador), 333
children
  attractions for, 212
  baby sitter for, 71, 135, 190

  beaches for, 304
  foods for, 43
  Out Islands accommodations for, 59
  rating islands for, 37
  reduced rates for, 58
  resort programs for, 70, 119, 128, 184
  sharing room with, 101
  traveling with, 69–71
China Temple (Freeport), 195
Churchill Beach, Grand Bahama Island,
    208
cigars, 169–170
Cleo's Boutique (Freeport), 219
climate, 10, 49–51, 338
Club Caribe (Taino Beach), 195–196
Club Med Public Beach, Eleuthera
    Island, 305
Club Med-Columbus Isle
  accommodations, 327, 328
  for couples, 72
  description of, 29–30, 61
  nightlife, 333
  for solo travelers, 74–75
Club Peace & Plenty Restaurant
    (George Town), 318
Club Soleil (Hope Town), 244, 249
Club Viva Fortuna (Grand Bahama
    Island), 72, 181
Club Waterloo (Nassau), 175
Cockburn Town, San Salvador,
    29, 30, 327
cocktails, 46–47
Coco Bay Beach, Green Turtle Cay,
    258, 263
Coconits by Androsia (Lucaya), 221
Coin of the Realm (Nassau), 170
Cole's of Nassau, 170
Colombian Emeralds International
    (Freeport), 219
Columbus, Christopher (explorer),
    28, 332, 337
Columbus monuments, San Salvador,
    332–333
Commander's Beach Bar & Restaurant
    (Harbour Island), 281, 286
Compass Point Beach Resort (New
    Providence Island), 72, 124–125
Compass Point (Cable Beach), 150
conch, 44

Conch Fritters Bar & Grill (Nassau), 139, 142
condos, renting, 63
consolidator, 87
copper, shopping for, 169
costs
  attractions, 99–100
  dining plans, 65
  dollar sign system for, 3
  lodging, 96–98
  low season, 50–51, 66, 67
  managing, 101–102
  meals, 98–99
  package deal, 85
  rating islands for, 32
  saving on airfare, 87–88
  solo traveler, 74
  taxes, 100–101, 104
  tipping, 43, 99, 132, 259
  transportation, 98
  travel agent, 83
  wedding, 73–74
Cotton Bay, South Eleuthera, 25
Count Basie Square (Lucaya), 180, 217, 222
courtesy, treating residents with, 339
Courtyard Terrace (Paradise Island), 147
Cove Restaurant, The (Gregory Town), 301–302
credit card, 94, 95
crowds, rating islands for, 33
Crown Room, The (Freeport), 196
cruises
  arrival in Freeport, 188
  arrival in Nassau, 132–133
  dinner, 157, 222
  sunset, 157, 289
crystal and china, shopping for, 218
cuisine, 43–46, 137, 193
currency, 93
Current Cut, between Eleuthera and Current Islands, 289
Current, North Eleuthera Island, 25, 308
Cush's Place (Gregory Town), 302
customs, clearing, 106, 132, 187
Cyber Café (Freeport and Lucaya), 196

• D •

day trip
  from Elbow Cay, 253–254
  from Eleuthera Island, 309
  from Grand Bahama Island, 222–223
  from Green Turtle Cay, 265–266
  from Marsh Harbour, 241
  from New Providence Island, 175–176
  from Treasure Cay, 273–274
Delaporte Beach, New Providence Island, 154
departure tax, 101, 104
Dickie Mo's (Cable Beach), 150–151
dining. See also cuisine; restaurants
  hotel breakfast buffets, 98
  meal plan rates, 65
  rating islands for, 33
dinner cruise, 157, 222
disability, traveler with, 77–78
Discovery Day, 54
diving
  Elbow Cay, 253–254
  Exumas, 322
  Great Abaco Island, 237
  Green Turtle Cay, 263, 265–266
  Harbour Island, 289
  New Providence area, 155–156
  rating islands for, 35
  resort course, 156, 210
  safety when, 111
  San Salvador, 29–30, 327, 331
  Sandy Cay Reef, 251
  Stocking Island, 322
  Treasure Cay, 272
  UNEXSO Underwater Explorer's Society and, 209–210
Dixon Hill Lighthouse, San Salvador, 29, 333
documents, travel, 103–106
Dolphin Encounter (Blue Lagoon Island), 155
Dolphin Experience (Grand Bahama Island), 209
dolphins, swimming with, 155, 209, 342
drift diving, 289
Driftwood Bar (Cockburn Town), 329

driving in The Bahamas, 134, 189, 317.
    See also car, renting
drugs, illegal, 110
Dundas Center for the Performing Arts
    (Nassau), 174
Dunmore Town (Harbour Island)
  accommodations, 282
  description of, 21, 280–281, 290
  restaurants, 286–287
  shopping, 290–291
  sunset, 343
duty-free allowance, 106–107, 168

● *E* ●

East Beach, San Salvador, 331
Easter Junkanoo Parade, 53
Eddie's Edgewater (George Town),
    318–319
Edison Key, 45
Elbow Cay. *See also* Hope Town,
    Elbow Cay
  accommodations, 243–246
  attractions, 252–253
  beaches, 251
  as day trip from Treasure Cay, 273
  day trips from, 253–254
  fast facts, 254
  getting around, 247
  lighthouse, 343
  map of, 245
  nightlife, 253
  overview of, 19–20, 243
  restaurants, 247–251
  transportation to, 232
  travel to, 246–247
Eleuthera Island. *See also* Governor's
    Harbour; Harbour Island
  accommodations, 293–299
  airports, 299–300
  beaches, 304–305
  day trip from, 309
  description of, 11
  destinations of, 23–26
  fast facts, 310
  getting around, 300

language of, 42
map of, 24, 295
nightlife, 308–309
restaurants, 301–304
touring, 305–308
travel to, 299–300
Elizabeth Harbour, Exuma, 311, 312
Elvina (Gregory Town), 308
Emerald Golf Course, Grand
    Bahama Island, 215
emergency, medical, 110
Endangered Species (Nassau), 75
E-savers, 90
event calendar, 51–55
Exuma Cays Land and Sea Park, 27
Exuma Islands
  accommodations, 311–316
  description of, 11
  destinations of, 26–28
  fast facts, 325
  George Town Cruising Regatta, 52
  getting around, 316–317
  map of, 28, 313
  restaurants, 318–320
  touring, 324–325
  travel to, 316
Exuma Sound, 305

● *F* ●

family. *See* children
Family Island Regatta. *See* Out
    Island Regatta
Far East Traders (Freeport), 219
Farmer's Cay Festival, 52
fashion, shopping for, 170, 219
Fatman's Nephew (Lucaya),
    44, 196–197
Fendi (Nassau), 170
Ferguson, Amos (painter), 164
Fernandez Bay, San Salvador, 332
Ferry, Little Exuma, 325
ferry, travel by
  cost of, 98
  to Elbow Cay, 247, 274
  to Eleuthera Island, 300

ferry, travel by *(continued)*
between George Town and Stocking
Island, 317
to Harbour Island, 284
to Man-O-War Cay, 274
from Marsh Harbour, 232
from Nassau to Paradise Island, 134
to Spanish Wells, 301
Ferry House Restaurant (Lucaya),
184, 197
festivals, 51–55
fire coral, 111
fishing
bonefishing, 230
Eleuthera Island, 304
Exumas, 312, 323–324
Grand Bahama Island, 211
Green Turtle Cay, 264
Harbour Island, 290
New Providence area, 158
overfishing and, 10
rating islands for, 36
tournaments, 52, 53, 54, 264, 267
Treasure Cay, 272
Five Twins (Paradise Island), 119, 147
flamingos, viewing, 159, 212
flight insurance, 109
Flippers Restaurant (Marsh Harbour),
234
Flovin Gallery (Freeport), 218
Flovin Gallery II (Lucaya), 221
Fort Charlotte (Nassau), 160–161
Fort Fincastle and Water Tower
(Nassau), 161, 162
Fortune Beach, Grand Bahama Island,
181, 208
Fortune Hills Golf & Country Club
(Grand Bahama Island), 216
Fowl Cay National Park, 254
Freeport
accommodations, 179, 180, 185–186
attractions, 15, 212–213, 214
cruising to, 188
International Bazaar, 179, 218–220
restaurants, 194–195, 196, 200–203
safety, 191
shopping, 11
travel to, 89
Freeport International Airport, 187
Froggies Out Island Adventures,
252, 253–254

• *G* •

Garbanzo Beach, Elbow Cay,
251, 252
Garden of the Groves Art Festival, 52
gardens
Eleuthera Island, 297
Freeport, 212, 213
Nassau, 118, 143–144, 159
New Plymouth, 20, 265
Paradise Island, 166, 342
Gaulding's Cay, 304
gay or lesbian traveler, 75–76
Gaylord's (Nassau), 142
Geneva's Place (Freeport), 197
George Town, Exuma. *See also* Out
Island Regatta
accommodations, 311, 312, 314
beaches, 321
Cruising Regatta, 52
description of, 27
touring, 324
travel to, 90
Glass Window, Eleuthera Island, 308
Gold Rock Beach, Grand Bahama
Island, 208, 209, 213
golf
cost of, 100
Eleuthera Island, 306
Grand Bahama Island, 184, 215–216
New Providence Island, 167
rating islands for, 34
tournaments, 53
Treasure Cay, 269–270, 272
golf cart, renting, 270
Goodman's Bay, New Providence
Island, 154
Goombay music, 42
Goombay Smash (drink), 47, 265
Gouldings Cay, 156
Government Administration Building
(George Town), 324
Government House (Nassau), 133, 162
Governor's Harbour, Eleuthera Island
accommodations, 296, 297, 298
beaches, 305
description of, 25, 307
hurricane and, 294
restaurant, 302

Grand Bahama Island. *See also*
    Freeport; Lucaya
  accommodations, 58, 179–186
  air travel to, 187–188
  attractions, 212–214
  beaches, 207–208
  cuisine, 193
  day trips from, 222–223
  destinations of, 15–17
  fast facts, 190–191
  festivals, 52
  getting around, 188–189
  map of, 16
  nightlife, 221–222
  overview of, 10
  pros and cons of, 17
  restaurants, 194–205
  shopping, 217–221
Graycliff (Nassau), 137, 142–143
Great Guana Cay, 229, 241
Great Inagua Island, 10
Green Turtle Cay. *See also* New
    Plymouth (Green Turtle Cay)
  accommodations, 255–259
  beaches, 263
  as day trip from Treasure
    Cay, 273
  day trips from, 265–266
  description of, 19, 20, 255
  fast facts, 266
  getting around, 260
  map of, 256
  nightlife, 265
  restaurants, 260–262
  transportation to, 232, 259
Green Turtle Club & Marina
  accommodations, 20, 58, 256, 258
  restaurant, 261
  for romantic getaway, 72
Gregory Town, Eleuthera Island,
    25, 294, 296–297, 301–302, 307
Guana Cay, 254
guava duff, 45–46, 137
Gucci (Nassau), 172
guesthouses, 63–64
Guiness Schoener Bay, Great Abaco
    Island, 237
Gusty's (Harbour Island), 291

• *H* •

Hairbraider's Centre (Nassau), 161
handcrafts, shopping for, 171
Harbour Island
  accommodations, 279–284
  attractions, 290
  beach, 289
  fast facts, 291
  getting around, 285
  map of, 22, 280
  nightlife, 291
  North Eleuthera and, 25
  overview of, 11, 21–23
  restaurants, 285–288
  shopping, 290–291
  travel to, 90, 284
Harbour Lounge (Dunmore Town),
    286–287
Harbour's Edge (Hope Town),
    249–250, 253
Harlem Square Bar (Cockburn Town),
    333
Harley-Davidson of Freeport, 221
Hartford, Huntington (grocery chain
    heir), 127, 166
Hartley's Undersea Walk (Nassau),
    155, 341
Hatchet Bay, Eleuthera Island, 294,
    298–299, 307
health insurance, 107
helmet diving, 155, 341
Heritage Trail (Grand Bahama Island),
    216
Hermitage, Little Exuma, 325
Hideaways International, 62
high season, 49–50, 66
hiking on Grand Bahama Island,
    189, 216
Hispaniola, 10
Hobie Wave, renting, 323
holidays, 54
honeymoon, planning, 71–72
honor bar, 59
Hope Town, Elbow Cay
  accommodations, 244–246
  Annual Art Exhibition, 52
  description of, 19–20, 243,
    252–253, 273
  restaurants, 247–251

Hope Town Harbour Lodge (Hope Town), 244–245, 250
horseback rides, 167, 216–217
horse-drawn carriage, 134, 162, 341
hotels, 60–61. *See also* accommodations; Accommodations Index
hurricane season, 50–51
Hydroflora Garden (Freeport), 213

• I •

identification, forms of, 103–104
Immigration Arrival/Departure card, 131
insect repellent, 110
insurance, travel, 107–109
Intercity Music (Freeport), 219
International Arcade (Freeport), 218
International Bazaar (Freeport), 179, 218–220
Island Bakery (Marsh Harbour), 232
Island, The (Cable Beach), 151
Island Galleria (Freeport), 218
Island Marine, 252
Island Things (Nassau), 171
island time, living on, 41
Islander's Roost (Freeport), 202
Iva Bowe's Central Highway Inn Restaurant & Bar (Exuma Islands), 319

• J •

Jack's Outback (Spanish Wells), 309
Jam Productions (Nassau), 173
jet skiing, 208
Jeweler's Warehouse (Lucaya), 221
jewelry, shopping for, 171, 219, 221
jitney, 132–134, 159
John Bull (Nassau), 171
Johnston, Pete (artist), 239, 240
Johnston, Randolph and Margot (artists), 239–240
Johnston's Foundry (Great Abaco Island), 239
Junkanoo Beach, Nassau, 125, 154
Junkanoo Expo, 43, 163

Junkanoo festival, 46
Junkanoo music, 42–43

• K •

Kalik (beer), 22, 46, 99
Kayak Nature Tours
  biking, 215
  hiking, 189, 216
  kayaking, 208–209
  to Peterson Cay, 222
  to Water Cay, 223
kayaking
  Exuma Islands, 322
  Grand Bahama Island, 208–209
  Green Turtle Cay, 263–264
  Harbour Island, 289
  to Peterson Cay, 222
Kennedy Gallery (Nassau), 169
King & Knights club (Cable Beach), 126, 174

• L •

Lake Victoria, Exuma, 324
Landing, The (Dunmore Town), 282, 287
language, learning, 42
Laura's Kitchen (New Plymouth), 261
Leather Masters (Nassau), 172
Leather Shop (Freeport), The, 220
Les Parisiennes (Freeport), 220
Lightbourn's, The (Nassau), 173
lighthouses, 29, 253, 333, 343
Linen Shop, The (Nassau), 172
Little Exuma, 324–325
lodging. *See* accommodations; Accommodations Index
Love Beach, New Providence Island, 124, 154, 156
low season, 50–51, 66, 67
Loyalist Cottage (Harbour Island), 290
Loyalists, 42, 339
Lucaya
  accommodations, 179–180, 181, 184–185
  beaches, 15, 207
  Port Lucaya Marketplace, 179, 217, 220–221

restaurants, 194, 195, 196–197, 200,
201, 204–205
safety, 191
Lucayan National Park, Grand Bahama
Island, 189, 208, 209, 213–214
Lucayan Park Golf & Country Club,
Grand Bahama Island, 216
Luciano's (Lucaya), 200
luggage, 108, 111–113
luxury
accommodations for, 60–61
rating islands for, 32

• *M* •

Ma Ruby's (Harbour Island), 284, 287
Mademoiselle, Ltd (Nassau), 170–171
Malone, Wyannie, Museum
(Hope Town), 253
Mama Loo's (Paradise Island), 119
Mama Lyddy's Place (Nassau), 44, 143
Mangoes Restaurant (Marsh Harbour),
234–235
Manjack Cay, 263
Man-O-War Cay
alcohol and, 273
as day trip from Elbow Cay, 254
description of, 19, 21, 241, 274
maps, shopping for, 172
Marborough Antiques (Nassau), 169
Marketplace (Paradise Island), 148
markets, 172–173, 291. *See also*
Straw Market
marriage, planning, 72–74
Marsh Harbour, The Abacos
accommodations, 228–231
attractions, 239–240
boating and, 343
day trips from, 241
fast facts, 242
getting around, 231–232
map of, 229
nightlife, 240
overview of, 19, 227
Regatta Week, 236
restaurants, 233–236
travel to, 89, 231
Mate & Jenny's Piazza Restaurant &
Bar (Palmetto Point), 302–303

McClean's Town Conch Cracking
Contest, 54
Medic Alert tag, 109
medical issues, 109–111
Memorial Sculpture Garden
(New Plymouth), 20, 265
Mermaid Reef, Marsh Harbour, 238
Ministry of Tourism Information Booth
(Nassau), 162
Miss Emily's Blue Bee Bar
(Green Turtle Cay), 265, 343
Miss Mae Tea Room and Fine Things
(Dunmore Town), 291
money for trip, 93–96
Montagu Gardens (Nassau), 143–144
Moorings, The, 238–239, 252
Mother Merle's Fishnet
(Dundas Town), 235
motor scooter, renting,
134, 189, 317, 330
Munchie's (Hope Town), 250
Muriel's Home Made Bread and
Restaurant (Palmetto Point), 303
music
Beat Retreat, 55
Count Basie Square, 222
George Town, 318
Goombay and Junkanoo, 42–43, 340
One Bahamas Music & Heritage
Festival, 54
rake and scrapes, 340
reggae, 340
shopping for, 173, 219
mutton, 45
Mystery Cave, Stocking Island, 322

• *N* •

N & D's Fruits & Vegetables
(Exuma Islands), 317, 324
Nassau
accommodations, 117–118, 122, 124,
125, 126–127
Ardastra Gardens & Zoo, 118, 159
Beat Retreat, 55
cruising to, 132–133
festivals, 54
Fort Charlotte, 160–161

Fort Fincastle and Water Tower,
161, 162
Government House, 133
Hairbraider's Centre, 161
historic area, 162–163
ice skating in, 125
map of, 120–121
overview of, 12, 338
Polar Bear Swim, 52
Queen's Staircase, 162, 165
restaurants, 138–146
safety, 14, 111
shopping, 11, 163, 168–169, 173
special events, 51
travel to, 89
Nassau Beach Hotel, 76, 126
Nassau General Post Office, 162
Nassau International Bazaar, 172
Nassau Public Library and Museum, 162
New Plymouth Club & Inn (Green
Turtle Cay), 256, 258–259, 261–262
New Plymouth (Green Turtle Cay)
accommodations, 258–259
Albert Lowe Museum, 20, 264
description of, 20, 241, 273
Memorial Sculpture Garden, 20, 265
restaurants, 261–262
New Providence Island. *See also* Cable
Beach; Nassau; Paradise Island
accommodations, 58, 117–119,
122–129
attractions, 159–166
beaches, 12, 132–133, 153–154
cuisine, 137
day trips from, 175–176
destinations on, 11–14
fast facts, 135–136
getting around, 133–135
golf, 167
map of, 13
nightlife, 174–175
overview of, 10
pros and cons of, 14
shopping, 168–174
travel to, 131–133
New Year's Day events, 51–52
night diving, 210
nightlife
Cable Beach, 126
Club Peace & Plenty, 312

cost of, 100
Elbow Cay, 253
Eleuthera Island, 308–309
Exuma Islands, 27
Freeport/Lucaya, 15
Grand Bahama Island, 221–222
Green Turtle Cay, 265
Harbour Island, 22, 291
Marsh Harbour, 240
music, 43
Nassau, 75
New Providence Island, 14, 174–175
rating islands for, 33
safety and, 43
San Salvador, 30, 329, 333
Nipper's Beach Bar & Grill
(Great Guana Cay), 241–242
North Palmetto Point, Eleuthera
Island, 306
nyam, 42

• O •

Ocean Club Golf & Tennis Resort
(New Providence Island), 72, 100
Ocean Hole, Eleuthera Island, 306
off-season. *See* low season
online, booking trip, 88, 90–92
Our Lucaya resort (Grand Bahama
Island), 70, 72, 181, 184, 217
Out Island Regatta, 27, 46, 53, 312, 321
Out Islands, 11, 31, 58–59, 64. *See also*
Abacos Islands; Eleuthera Island;
Exuma Islands; Harbour Island

• P •

package deal, 66, 84–86, 101
packing luggage, 111–113
Palm, The (Exuma Islands), 319
Palmetto Point, Eleuthera Island, 294,
298, 299, 302–304, 305
Pammy's (Governor's Harbour), 302
Paradise Beach, Paradise Island,
12, 132–133, 154
Paradise Island
accommodations, 58, 117–119, 124,
127, 129
Atlantis Aquarium, 160

bridges to, 133
casinos, 118, 119, 160
map of, 13, 120–121
nightlife, 14
overview of, 10
restaurants, 119, 140–141, 146–148
safety, 14
Versailles Gardens and Cloister,
    166, 342
water sports, 154
parasailing, 156, 210–211
Paris in The Bahamas (Freeport), 220
Parliament Square (Nassau), 162
Parrot Jungle's Garden of the Groves
    (Freeport), 212
passport, obtaining, 104–106
patois, 42
Peace & Plenty Beach Inn
    (Exuma Islands), 315–316, 319
peace and quiet, rating islands for, 37
Pelican Cays, 251
Pelican Cays Land and Sea Park, 237, 251
Pepper Pot, The (Freeport), 200
perfume and cosmetics, shopping for,
    173, 214, 220
Perfume Bar, The (Nassau), 173
Perfume Factory Fragrance of
    The Bahamas, The (Freeport),
    214, 220
Perfume Shop, The (Nassau), 173
Peterson Cay, 222–223
Pete's Pub (Great Abaco Island), 240
phone call, 102
Pier 1 (Freeport), 200–201
Pigeon Cay, 324–325
Pindling, Lynden (prime minister), 293
Pink Pearl Café , The (Nassau), 44, 144
Pink Sands Beach, Harbour Island,
    281, 289, 342
Pink Sands (Harbour Island),
    58, 72, 282, 288
Pirates of Nassau Museum, 163
Pisces (Lucaya), 201
planning trip
  airfare, finding best, 87–88
  booking online, 88, 90–92
  calculating costs, 96–101
  deciding number of islands to visit,
    30–31
  last-minute details, 114

managing costs, 101–102
narrowing choices between islands,
    31–39
package tour, 66, 84–86, 101
travel agent and, 81–84
Plymouth Rock Liquors and Café
    (New Plymouth), 262
Polar Bear Swim (Nassau), 52
Pompey Museum (Nassau), 163, 164
Poop Deck, The (Nassau), 144–145
Port Lucaya Marketplace, 179, 217,
    220–221
Poseidon (Harbour Island), 281, 286
Potter's Cay (Nassau), 46, 164–165
powerboat, renting, 252, 264
Preacher's Cave, North Eleuthera
    Island, 308
Pretty Molly Bay, Exuma Island, 325
Prince George Plaza (Nassau), 172–173
Prince George Wharf (Nassau), 162
Prince of Wales Lounge (Freeport), 202
Pub at Port Lucaya, The, 201
Pub on the Mall, The (Freeport), 202
Pyfroms (Nassau), 174

• *Q* •

Queen's Staircase (Nassau), 162, 165

• *R* •

rack rate, 66, 96–97, 118
Radisson Cable Beach
    (New Providence Island), 70, 128
rainfall, average monthly, 50
"Rate the Islands" scorecard, 31–39
Rawson Square (Nassau), 134, 162
Red Dog Sports Bar (Freeport), 202
Reef Course, The (Grand Bahama
    Island), 184, 216
reef running, 289
regattas, 52, 54, 236. *See also* Out
    Island Regatta
resorts. *See also* accommodations;
    Accommodations Index
  all-inclusive, 61–62
  kids' programs at, 70, 119, 128, 184
  pros and cons of, 60–61
  shuttle bus, free, 98

Resorts at Bahamia (Freeport), 179, 185–186, 215, 217
resources
    airfare, low, 87–88
    family trip planning, 71
    gay or lesbian traveler, 75–76
    island Web sites, 92
    marriage in Bahamas, 73
    medical, 109
    package deal, 85–86
    passport, 105
    senior traveler, 76
    travel agent, 83
    travel insurance, 109
    travel Web sites, 91–92
    traveler with disability, 77–78
respect, treating residents with, 339
restaurants
    Cable Beach, 126, 148–151
    cost of, 98–99
    cuisine, 43–46, 137, 193
    dress requirements, 112
    Elbow Cay, 247–251
    Eleuthera Island, 301–304
    Exuma Islands, 318–320
    Grand Bahama Island, 194–205
    Green Turtle Cay, 260–262
    happy hour, 138
    Harbour Island, 285–288
    Marsh Harbour, 233–236
    Nassau, 138–146
    Paradise Island, 119, 140–141,
        146–148
    rating islands for, 33
    San Salvador, 330–331
    Treasure Cay, 271
Retreat, The (Nassau), 165–166
Rib Room, The (Freeport), 202
Riding Rock Inn Resort & Marina
    (San Salvador), 30, 327, 328–329,
    331, 333
Roberts, Billy (sea captain), 259
Rock Sound, Eleuthera Island,
    294, 303, 305–306
Rolle, Kermit (taxi driver), 317
Rolle Cay, 311, 315
romantic trip, planning, 71–74
Ronnie's Smoke Shop & Sports Bar
    (Cupid's Cay), 308–309

Rooster's Rest Pub and Restaurant
    (New Plymouth), 262, 265
Rose Island, 157, 175
Ruby Golf Course
    (Grand Bahama Island), 215
Rudy's Place (Hope Town), 250–251
Runaway Hill Club (Harbour Island),
    72, 283–284, 288

• S •

Safari Restaurant (Freeport), 202–203
safety
    credit cards and cash, carrying, 95
    Freeport and Lucaya, 191
    Marsh Harbour, 242
    Nassau, 14, 111
    New Providence Island, 135, 136
    nightlife and, 43
    overview of, 2
Sail Shop (Man-O-War Cay), 274
sailing charters, 158, 238, 264, 312, 343
Samana Cay, 28, 337
Sammy's Place (Rock Sound), 303
Sam's Place (George Town), 320
San Jacinto wreck, diving, 263
San Salvador Island. *See also* Club
        Med-Columbus Isle
    accommodations, 327–329
    beaches, 331
    Columbus and, 337
    fast facts, 334
    getting around, 330
    map of, 29, 329
    nightlife, 329, 333
    restaurants, 330–331
    touring, 28–30, 332–333
    travel to, 90, 330
Sand Bar (Marsh Harbour), 240
Sandals Royal Bahamian Hotel
        (Cable Beach), 61, 71–72, 128–129
Sandy Cay Reef, Elbow Cay, 251
Sapodilly's Bar & Grill
        (Marsh Harbour), 235, 240
Saunders Beach, New Providence
        Island, 154
Savannah Sound, Eleuthera Island, 304
Sea Gardens Marine Park (Nassau), 158
Sea Grape Boutique (Nassau), 171

Sea Spray Resort (Hope Town), 246, 252, 253
Seagrapes (Harbour Island), 291
seasickness, 158
seasons, 49–51
Seaworld Explorer, 158
senior traveler, 76
service, expectations for, 41, 60
shark diving, 209–210
shelling, 322
Shenannigan's Irish Pub (Lucaya), 204
Shoal Restaurant and Lounge (Nassau), 44, 145
shopping
  duty-free allowance, 106–107, 168
  estimating cost of, 100
  Grand Bahama Island, 17, 179, 217–221
  Harbour Island, 21, 290–291
  hype about bargains, 11
  New Providence Island, 14, 168–174
shuttle bus, free, 98
sightseeing, rating islands for, 35.
    See also attractions
Silvano's (Freeport), 202, 203
Silver Palms Beach, Exuma Islands, 314
Smith's Point beach, Grand Bahama Island, 208
snorkeling
  Elbow Cay, 253–254
  Eleuthera Island, 304, 305
  Exumas, 312, 323, 325
  Grand Bahama Island, 208, 210–211
  Great Abaco Island, 238
  Green Turtle Cay, 263, 265–266
  Harbour Island, 289
  Little Exuma, 325
  Love Beach, 124, 154, 156
  New Providence area, 156–157
  Peterson Cay, 222–223
  rating islands for, 35
  Stocking Island, 322
Sole Mare (Cable Beach), 151
solo traveler, 74–75
South Ocean Golf Club (New Providence Island), 167
Southwest Reef (New Providence Island), 156
souvenir, cost of, 100, 102

Spanish Wells
  accommodations, 294
  day trip to, 309
  description of, 25
  language of, 42
  travel to, 301
spas on New Providence Island, 167
speedboat. *See* powerboat, renting
spice, rating islands for, 34
spilligatin', 42
Spinnaker Restaurant (Treasure Cay), 270, 271
sportfishing. *See* fishing
spring break, 50, 75
Spruce Cay, 156
St. Andrew's Anglican Church (George Town), 324
St. John's (Harbour Island), 290
stamps, shopping for, 170
Star Club, The (West End), 203–204, 222
steel drums, shopping for, 174
stingray, swimming with, 265, 342
Stocking Island, 27, 311, 312, 314–315, 321–322
Stoned Crab, The (Lucaya), 204
Straw Market
  Freeport, 218
  Nassau, 163, 168–169, 173
submarine platform, 9
submarine ride, 158
Sun And.... (Nassau), 137, 145–146
sun exposure, 110
sunset, best, 343
sunset cruise, 157, 289
Superior Watersports, 211, 222
Surfer's Beach, Eleuthera Island, 307
surfing, 252, 305, 307

• *T* •

Tahiti Beach, Elbow Cay, 20, 251
Taino Beach, Grand Bahama Island, 195–196, 207
Tappan Monument (San Salvador), 332
Tarpum Bay, Eleuthera Island, 294, 296, 297, 305, 306
taxes, 100–101, 104

taxi
  from airport to hotel, 132, 188, 232
  cost of, 98
  Eleuthera Island, 301
  Exuma Islands, 317, 325
  Grand Bahama Island, 188, 191
  Harbour Island, 285
  Marsh Harbour, 242
  New Providence Island, 134, 136
  San Salvador, 330
  Treasure Cay, 270, 275
temperature, average monthly, 50
Ten Bay Beach, Eleuthera Island, 305
tennis, 167, 217, 272
"things," 60
Thompson, Billy (ice cream vendor),
    232
Three Ships Restaurant
    (Cockburn Town), 331
Tilloo Cay, 251
timeshare, renting, 63
tipping, 43, 99, 132, 259
Touch of Class (Treasure Cay), 271
tour. *See also* bicycle, touring by;
    Kayak Nature Tours; walking tours
  cost of, 100
  horse-drawn carriage, 134, 162, 341
  package, 66, 84–86, 101
Towne Café & Bakery (George Town),
    320
Trade Winds Café (Lucaya), 185
transportation. *See also* air travel;
    car, renting; taxi
  from airport to hotel, 132, 188
  boat, 211, 252, 264
  bus, 98, 133–134, 188
  cost of, 98
  golf cart, 270
  on Grand Bahama Island, 188–189
  to Harbour Island, 23
  jitney, 132–134, 159
  motor scooter, 134, 189, 317, 330
  on New Providence Island, 133–135
  to other island, 31
  to Out Islands, 11, 21
  rating islands for, 36, 38
travel agent, 66, 81–84
travel insurance, 107–109
traveler's check, 94–96

traveling
  with children, 69–71
  solo, 74–75
Treasure Cay
  accommodations, 267–270
  beach, 267, 272
  day trips from, 273–274
  description of, 19, 20
  fast facts, 274
  getting around, 270
  map of, 269
  restaurants, 271
  travel to, 270
Treasure Cay Golf Club, 272
Tropique International Smoke Shop
    (Nassau), 169
Two Turtles Inn Restaurant
    (George Town), 320

• *U* •

UNEXSO Dive Shop (Lucaya), 221
UNEXSO Underwater Explorer's
    Society, 209–210
Unique Village Restaurant
    & Lounge (Palmetto Point),
    303–304
Unusual Centre (Freeport), 220
U.S. Customs and Immigration, 106

• *V* •

Valentines Dive Center, 289, 290
Vendue House (Nassau), 164
Versailles Gardens and Cloister
    (Paradise Island), 166, 342
VHR Worldwide, 62
Vic-Hum Club (Harbour Island), 291
Villa d'Este (Paradise Island), 119
villa rentals, 58, 62–63
Voyagers Disco (Paradise Island), 174

• *W* •

walking tours
  Dunmore Town, 290
  George Town, 316–317, 321, 324

Grand Bahama Island, 189
Nassau, 135, 162–163, 166
wallet, lost or stolen, 95
Wally's (Marsh Harbour), 236, 240
Water Cay, 223
water, drinking, 110
water sport. *See also* diving; snorkeling
banana boat, 208
Cable Beach and Paradise Island,
119, 154
cost of, 100
Elbow Cay, 252
Exuma Islands, 322
Grand Bahama Island, 207, 208–211
Great Abaco Island, 237–238
Green Turtle Cay, 263
Harbour Island, 289
jet and water-skiing, 208
parasailing, 156, 210–211
surfing, 252, 305, 307
Treasure Cay, 272
waters, description of, 1
water-skiing, 208
weather, 49–51, 338
Web sites, travel, 90–92
wedding in Bahamas, 72–74
Wesley Methodist Church
(Harbour Island), 290
West Beach, Eleuthera Island, 304
West End, Grand Bahama Island,
193, 203, 214, 222
Western Esplanade, 154
wheelchair, traveler in, 59, 77–78
William's Town beach, Grand
Bahama Island, 207
Williamstown, Little Exuma, 325
Windermere Island, 304, 306
winter season. *See* high season
Woodes Rodgers Walk (Nassau), 163
Wrecking Tree, The
(New Plymouth), 262

• *X* •

Xanadu beach, Freeport, 207

• *Y* •

Yellowbird (drink), 47
Yellowbird Showroom, 221

• *Z* •

Zoo Nightclub (Nassau), 174–175
Zorba's Greek Cuisine (Lucaya),
204–205

• *Accommodations Index* •

Abaco Beach Resort & Boat
Harbour, 228
Abaco Inn, 243–244, 248
Adventurer's Resort, The, 294
Atlantis Paradise Island Resort &
Casino, 12, 70, 72, 117, 119,
160, 174
Banyan Beach Club, 268
Bluff House Beach Hotel, 72, 256, 257,
260–261
Breezes, 71–72, 75, 122, 125
British Colonial Hilton, 76, 122, 124
Buccaneer Club, 296
Cartwright's Ocean Front Cottages, 296
Castaways Resort & Suites, 180
Club Med-Columbus Isle, 29–30, 61, 72,
74–75, 327, 328, 333
Club Peace & Plenty, 312, 314
Club Soleil Resort, 244, 249
Club Viva Fortuna, 72, 181
Coco Bay Cottages, 257–258
Comfort Suites Paradise Island, 124
Compass Point Beach Resort, 72,
124–125
Conch Inn Resort & Marina, 228
Coral Sands, 281
Cove Eleuthera, The, 296–297
Dillet's Guest House, 125
Dolphin Beach Resort, 229
Duck Inn and Orchid Gardens, 297
Dunmore Beach Club, The, 281–282
Green Turtle Club & Marina,
20, 58, 72, 256, 258, 261

Hilton's Haven Motel and
Restaurant, 297
Holiday Inn Junkanoo Beach
Nassau, 125–126
Hope Town Harbour Lodge,
244–245, 250
Hope Town Hideaways, 246
Hotel Higgins Landing, 312, 314–315
Landing, The, 282, 287
Latitude Exuma Resort, 315
Laughing Bird Apartments, 298
Lofty Fig Villas, 230
Nassau Beach Hotel, 76, 126
Nassau Marriott Resort & Crystal
Palace Casino, 126–127
Nettie's Different of Abaco, 230–231
New Plymouth Club & Inn, 256,
258–259, 261–262
Ocean Club Golf & Tennis Resort,
72, 100, 127
Our Lucaya, 70, 72, 181, 184, 217
Palmetto Shores Vacation Villas, 298

Palms at Three Sisters, The, 315
Peace & Plenty Beach Inn, 315–316, 319
Pelican Bay at Lucaya, 184–185
Pink Sands, 58, 72, 282, 288
Port Lucaya Resort and
Yacht Club, 185
Radisson Cable Beach, 70, 128
Rainbow Inn, 298–299
Resorts at Bahamia, The, 185–186
Riding Rock Inn Resort & Marina,
30, 327, 328–329, 331, 333
Runaway Hill Club, 72, 283–284
Sandals Royal Bahamian Hotel,
61, 71–72, 128–129
Sea Spray Resort Villas & Marina,
246, 252, 253
Sunrise Beach Club and Villas, 129
Sunset Point Resort, 231
Tingum Village, 284
Treasure Cay Hotel Resort & Marina,
269–270
Unique Village, 299

FOR DUMMIES®

A world of resources to help you grow

TRAVEL

0-7645-5453-0

0-7645-5438-7

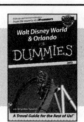

0-7645-5444-1

Also available:

America's National Parks
For Dummies
(0-7645-6204-5)

Caribbean For Dummies
(0-7645-5445-X)

Cruise Vacations For
Dummies 2003
(0-7645-5459-X)

Europe For Dummies
(0-7645-5456-5)

Ireland For Dummies
(0-7645-6199-5)

France For Dummies
(0-7645-6292-4)

Las Vegas For Dummies
(0-7645-5448-4)

London For Dummies
(0-7645-5416-6)

Mexico's Beach Resorts
For Dummies
(0-7645-6262-2)

Paris For Dummies
(0-7645-5494-8)

RV Vacations For
Dummies
(0-7645-5443-3)

EDUCATION & TEST PREPARATION

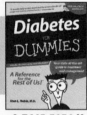

0-7645-5194-9

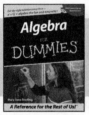

0-7645-5325-9

0-7645-5249-X

Also available:

The ACT For Dummies
(0-7645-5210-4)

Chemistry For Dummies
(0-7645-5430-1)

English Grammar For
Dummies
(0-7645-5322-4)

French For Dummies
(0-7645-5193-0)

GMAT For Dummies
(0-7645-5251-1)

Inglés Para Dummies
(0-7645-5427-1)

Italian For Dummies
(0-7645-5196-5)

Research Papers For
Dummies
(0-7645-5426-3)

SAT I For Dummies
(0-7645-5472-7)

U.S. History For Dummies
(0-7645-5249-X)

World History For
Dummies
(0-7645-5242-2)

HEALTH, SELF-HELP & SPIRITUALITY

0-7645-5154-X

0-7645-5302-X

0-7645-5418-2

Also available:

The Bible For Dummies
(0-7645-5296-1)

Controlling Cholesterol
For Dummies
(0-7645-5440-9)

Dating For Dummies
(0-7645-5072-1)

Dieting For Dummies
(0-7645-5126-4)

High Blood Pressure For
Dummies
(0-7645-5424-7)

Judaism For Dummies
(0-7645-5299-6)

Menopause For Dummies
(0-7645-5458-1)

Nutrition For Dummies
(0-7645-5180-9)

Potty Training For
Dummies
(0-7645-5417-4)

Pregnancy For Dummies
(0-7645-5074-8)

Rekindling Romance For
Dummies
(0-7645-5303-8)

Religion For Dummies
(0-7645-5264-3)

Available wherever books are sold. Go to www.dummies.com or call 1-877-762-2974 to order direct

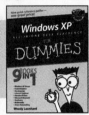

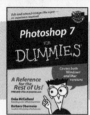